OLD TESTAMENT IN ITS CULTURAL, HISTORICAL AND RELIGIOUS CONTEXT

Dane R. Gordon
Rochester Institute of Technology

VERSITY
ESS OF
ERICA

Lanham • New York • London

University Press of America®, Inc.
4720 Boston Way
Lanham, Maryland 20706

3 Henrietta Street
London WC2E 8LU England

©1985 by Prentice-Hall, Inc., Englewood Cliffs, New Jersey 07632

Library of Congress Cataloging-in-Publication Data
Gordon, Dane R.
[Old Testament]
Old Testament in its cultural, historical, and religious context / Dane R. Gordon.
p.   cm.
Originally published: The Old Testament. Englewood Cliffs, N.J. : Prentice-Hall, © 1985.
Includes bibliographical references and index.
1. Bible. O.T.—History of Biblical events. 2. Bible. O.T.—Introductions. I. Title.
[BS1197.G67   1994]   221.9'5—dc20   94–4728 CIP

ISBN 0–8191–9500–6 (pbk. : alk. paper)

 The paper used in this publication meets the minimum requirements of American National Standard for Information Sciences—Permanence of Paper for Printed Library Materials, ANSI Z39.48–1984.

To my wife
Elizabeth

CONTENTS

Contents

PREFACE

This book is intended for use in a one-semester or one-quarter college course. The students are not expected to have any prior knowledge of the Old Testament, nor are they expected to have any religious commitment. They are, however, expected to study the documents, that is, the Old Testament itself, and value them as a remarkable primary text.

Students are frequently astonished to discover that there is a religious and historical development throughout the Old Testament, that it is not simply a collection of pious fragments. Equally astonishing to students is the discovery that ancient Israel existed in an historical and cultural context, that is, it was not an isolated phenomenon in a mythical past.

This book attempts to deal with those astonishments by tracing the historical development of Israel and by giving attention to the societies among which that development took place.

Not all the Old Testament is discussed here, only as much as might reasonably be covered in ten or fifteen weeks. Hopefully, what has happened many times before will happen again; that those who begin a serious study of the Old Testament will not want to stop.

Among those who read and commented upon my manuscript I wish to mention with particular appreciation Dr. Richard Henshaw, Professor of Old Testament at Colgate Rochester Divinity School, Bexley Hall, Crozier Theological Seminary in Rochester, New York. I also wish to acknowledge the assistance of Professor Denis Baly, Professor Emeritus at Kenyon College, Gambier, Ohio, in preparing the maps.

CASPIAN SEA

HATTI

URARTU

MEDIA

Lake Van

Lake Urmia

ECBATANA

H U R R I A N S

MITANNI

ELAM

CARCHEMISH

HARAN

NINEVEH

ASSYRIA

NUZI

PERSIAN GULF

HAMATH

R. Euphrates

R. Tigris

ESHNUNNA

AKKAD

DAMASCUS

MARI

BABYLONIA

BABYLON

SUMER

JERICHO

UR

KITTIM
(CYPRUS)

JERUSALEM

GAZA

BEERSHEBA

KEDAR

ARABIA

MEDITERRANEAN SEA

AVARIS

MIDIAN

RED SEA

EGYPT

AKHETATON

THEBES

River Nile

...indication of the area of the Fertile Crescent which follows the course of the rivers

CHAPTER ONE
ABRAHAM
AND THE
PATRIARCHAL PERIOD

MESOPOTAMIA

The early chapters of Genesis are outside the realm of history. They present the Hebrew version of stories shared by societies throughout the world, stories that attempt to answer questions which everyone asks: Where did the world come from? Who made men and women? Why do people speak different languages? What is God like?

But with the reference to Abraham and to the cities of Ur[1] and Haran the concerns of the narrative change from prehistory to a period of ancient history about which we know a great deal. The work of archeologists and philologists has given us a greater knowledge of those remote Old Testament times than the chroniclers had who wrote the biblical text we read. The book of Genesis is compiled from materials written long after the events it describes, and the writers, themselves a part of ancient history, were not able to verify the accuracy of what they wrote or edited as a student of the Old Testament can today.

[1]The reliability of the reference to Ur has been questioned as it is not found in the third century B.C. Greek translation of the Old Testament known as the Septuagint. William F. Albright suggests that there was textual corruption in the texts on which this translation was based in *The Biblical Period from Abraham to Ezra* (New York: Harper, 1963), pp. 2 and 97, and so would favor accepting the reference to Ur. John Bright discusses the issue in his History and seems to be cautiously against accepting the references. John Bright, *History of Israel* (Philadelphia: Westminster Press, 1981), p. 90.

1

The knowledge that we now have about Mesopotamia is relatively new. Akkadian, the language of Mesopotamia, did not begin to be deciphered until the 1840s.[2] The site of Ur was not known until J. E. Taylor discovered its ruins in 1854. A map of the ancient Near East, in the possession of this writer, published in 1709, shows Ur north of Babylon about 200 miles from its actual site.

We now have extensive information about the cities, the rulers, the wars, the trade, and many intimate and trivial details of the life of Mesopotamian society. Perhaps, because the story of Abraham follows closely the stories of creation and the flood, it seems as if Abraham himself were from the remotest times. But the city of Ur had been in existence for more than a thousand years before Abraham was born. He belonged to an already ancient civilization, the civilization of Sumer, located at the head of what is now the Persian Gulf, whose origins go back to four millennia before Christ.

We have evidence of the level of civilization of this era from the royal tombs of Ur, excavated by Sir Leonard Wooley from 1922 to 1934. The tombs are from the great Third Dynasty of Ur (ca. 2120–1800). Wooley writes, for example, about a gold dagger found in the early days of the expedition. Its blade was gold; its hilt, blue lapis lazuli decorated with gold studs; its gold sheath, decorated to resemble plaited grass.[3] Nearby was discovered a gold toilet case containing a set of little gold toilet instruments. These were so unlikely in the context of what was known at the time about Mesopotamian culture that a recognized expert decided, incorrectly, that they were Arabian from the thirteenth century A.D. rather than 4000 years old.

The magnificent treasures of Ur were evidence not only of wealth and artistic achievement but of extensive trade, because, although Mesopotamia was rich in craftsmanship, it was poor in raw materials. The gold and silver in the tombs had to be imported, and so did copper, lead, various kinds of wood, olive oil, hides, wool, and lapis lazuli. Abraham may have seen donkey caravans with as many as two hundred animals going to or coming from distant parts of the Mediterranean world.

The basis of Mesopotamian society was agriculture, which depended totally upon a complex system of irrigation. The Egyptians could count on the Nile to deposit a layer of rich dirt on the land which it flooded every year. But in Mesopotamia the river water had to be altogether guided by irrigation canals. This required a carefully managed corporate effort with detailed regulations to protect the individual from those who were careless or selfish in their use of water. It was due partly to the necessity for such regulations that Mesopotamia was characteristically a society that respected law. Systems of law have been discovered in Mesopotamia as early as the end of the third millennium before Christ. It is probable that every city state had its own system of laws adapted to local conditions. The earliest known, that of Ur-Nammu

[2] James B. Pritchard, *Archaeology and the Old Testament* (Princeton, N.J.: Princeton University Press, 1958), pp. 127–34.

[3] Magnus Magnusson, *BC The Archaeology of the Bible,* Anson E. Rainey trans. (London: The Bodley Head, 1977), p. 32.

A Bedouin encampment. Photo by Elizabeth Gordon.

founder of the third dynasty of Ur (2113–2096) is approximately eight hundred years earlier than the law of Moses.

As far as we know, Abraham was not a city dweller; he was a herdsman who lived outside the city in the environs of Haran, moving every so often from place to place to find pasture and water for his animals.[4] But he was a part of a society that included artists, weavers, butchers, jewellers, hairdressers, scribes, musicians, traders, farmers and slaves, a society in many ways as varied and as gifted as cosmopolitan societies in our own day. We catch very brief glimpses in the Old Testament, but the only personalities described are those of Abraham and his family.

WHAT WAS THE TIME OF ABRAHAM?

If Abraham lived in an already ancient civilization, do we have any way of knowing more precisely when that was? Did he live in the third millennium B.C., or the second, or the first? The matter is not decided, although a great deal has been written about it. A number of scholars are of the opinion, however, that the second millennium best fits the available evidence.

Part of the data frequently cited in connection with this question are the clay tablets excavated from the northern Mesopotamian city of Nuzi. These records and

[4]Norman K. Gottwald, *The Tribes of Yahweh* (Maryknoll, N.Y.: Orbis Books, 1979), pp. 451–53.

others from other cities, such as Mari on the middle Euphrates, and Alalakh on the Orontes, have provided an immense amount of information about second millennium society in Mesopotamia. Where incidents in the patriarchal narratives, that is, narratives about Abraham, Isaac, Jacob, and Joseph, appear to reflect laws and customs of Mesopotamian society at a certain period, we have, it is claimed, a way of dating the biblical stories.[5]

According to Nuzi documents of the mid-second millennium, a childless couple could adopt a son who would take care of them in their old age and give them a proper burial. In return he would inherit their property. If a son were born, however, it was the son who inherited the property. In Genesis 15:3–5, there is a similar situation where Abraham complains to God, "Behold, thou hast given me no offspring; and a slave born in my house will be my heir." Then the word of the Lord came to him, "This man shall not be your heir; your own son shall be your heir."

According to Nuzi law a person could sell his inheritance. There is a record of a brother selling a grove he had inherited for three sheep. This is comparable to what Essau did when he was hungry. He sold his birthright to Jacob (Genesis 25:29–34).

In Genesis 31 we read that Jacob, who had been living with his father-in-law in Paddan-aram in upper Mesopotamia, decided to leave. "Laban had gone to shear his sheep, and Rachel (Laban's daughter and Jacob's wife) stole her father's household gods. And Jacob outwitted Laban the Aramaen, in that he did not tell him that he intended to flee. He fled with all that he had . . ." Laban, however, caught up with him although it took him a week, and complained that this was not a proper way to behave. "Why did you flee secretly, and cheat me, and did not tell me, so that I might have sent you away with mirth and songs, with tambourine and lyre?" Then he makes a curious comment, "but why did you steal my gods?" (Genesis 31:19–30). These gods, or more correctly "household gods," were small figurines called teraphim in the Old Testament. In Nuzi law their importance was not only religious but legal. Whoever held these gods had the right to the family inheritance. No wonder that Laban was anxious.

The alleged agreement between these documents and the biblical records in-

[5]There is a diversity of opinion about this matter. See John Marshall Holt, *The Patriarchs of Israel* (Nashville, Tenn.: Vanderbilt University Press, 1964). "In part, so many actions, practices, and customs shown in the patriarchal legends are now to be seen through archeological study as reflecting those of people with whom the Hebrews had close cultural contact that we can feel entirely safe in accounting the picture of family life in the legends largely true, not only in the general, human sense, but in the specific period and place of the patriarchal age," p. 91.

Gaalyah Cornfeld, in *Archeology of the Bible: Book by Book* (New York: Harper and Row, 1976), p. 24, is more cautious about the relevance of Nuzi parallels to Genesis. See also *The Cambridge Ancient History:*

"The nature of the evidence, with its emphasis on the future of Israel rather than on personal details concerning the patriarchs, does not allow us to draw conclusions about the history of individuals, or about the period in which they lived."

The Cambridge Ancient History, 3d edition, Vol. II, part 2, p. 314.

dicates that Abraham and his immediate successors came from northern Mesopotamia at a time when Nuzi customs were influential.[6]

But that conclusion is much debated. A recent survey of scholarly opinion describes the relevance of the Nuzi texts to the dating of the patriarchal era as a "minority view."[7] One writer argues that the patriarchal period falls in the first millennium, considerably *later* than the time we have been discussing.[8] Recently it

[6]Albright, *The Biblical Period,* p. 2.

[7]Perhaps the most striking example of how opinions can change with regard to the relevance of Mesopotamian texts to the patriarchal stories is in connection with Genesis 12:10–17. In this passage Abraham and Sarah travel to Egypt because of a famine. On their way Abraham tells Sarah to say that she is his sister. He is afraid that her beauty will attract attention and he will be killed. Sarah does indeed attract the Pharaoh's attention. The result is a series of plagues inflicted upon Egypt by God. Only then does the Pharaoh discover Abraham's deception.

On the face of it, the incident is strange. Abraham compromised his host, he compromised his wife, and he acted like a coward. Many commentators have attempted to explain this passage.

Several years ago an explanation was provided by E. A. Speiser based upon a reading of three texts from Nuzi and upon what was known about Hurrian society. The Hurrians (in the Old Testament, Horites) appeared in northern Mesopotamia during the third millennium and gradually became the dominant cultural element in an area which included the cities of Nuzi and Haran. If the patriarchal period were during the second millennium Abraham would presumably have been familiar with Hurrian customs.

According to Speiser it was a mark of high esteem in Hurrian society for a woman to be both a wife and to be adopted by her husband as a sister. Because the custom was associated with upper class women, it implied status. The likelihood is that Abraham did indeed tell the Pharaoh that Sarah was his sister, not to deceive him but to impress him. The fact that a variant of the story was included at two other places in Genesis (20:1–18 and 26:6–11), and the motivation was changed indicates that by the time the incident was included in the text there were different versions of it, and the underlying Hurrian customs had been forgotten.

But a subsequent examination of the Nuzi texts by Samuel Greengus has shown that they do not support Speiser's claim that a woman could be wife and adopted sister to the same man. That conclusion was an interpretation made by Speiser but is not found unambiguously in the texts themselves. There were indeed several degrees of sisterhood at Nuzi, but these typically were not among upper class women, as Speiser claimed, but among women who were socially inferior. Greengus writes that there appears to be "no reason to maintain the theory of sister-wife at Nuzi; and that there is therefore no Nuzian basis for assuming the presence of a sister-wife tradition in the patriarchal narratives."

See Ephraim A. Speiser, *The Anchor Bible,* 2d ed. (Garden City, N.Y.: Doubleday, 1964) pp. 91–94.

Samuel Greengus, "Sisterhood Adoption at Nuzi and the 'Wife-Sister' in Genesis," Hebrew Union College Annual, Vol. XLVI (1975), p. 5.

John H. Hayes and J. Maxwell Miller, *Israelite and Judaean History* (Philadelphia: The Westminster Press, 1977), p. 96.

William G. Dever, "The Peoples of Palestine in the Middle Bronze I Period," *Harvard Theological Review* 64 (April–July 1971), p. 226.

[8]John Van Seters, "Jacob's Marriages and Ancient Near East Cusotms: A Reexamination," *Harvard Theological Review* 62 (October 1969), p. 377.

John Van Seters, *Abraham in History and Tradition* (New Haven: Yale University Press, 1975), pp. 310–12.

Cornfeld, *Archeology of the Bible,* pp. 28–29, expresses similar views regarding the anachronisms of Genesis.

See also Yohanan Aharoni, "Nothing Early and Nothing Late: Rewriting Israel's Conquest," *The Biblical Archeologist,* Vol. 39.2 (May 1976), p. 71.

"Since the digging of the well (at Beer-sheba) did not antedate the settlement period it seems certain that neither can the patriarchal narratives associated with Beer-sheba refer to an earlier period."

seemed that evidence had been found for an *earlier* date for Abraham and the patriarchs,[9] although that claim was withdrawn.[10]

The point for a student to bear in mind is not simply that scholars are in disagreement about the time of Abraham and the patriarchal period, or about other matters, but that biblical studies is a continuing endeavor, that there is not yet an unchallengeable account of biblical origins. But whereas a hundred or even fifty years ago, differing views were necessarily based upon limited evidence, there is now considerable evidence, and year by year fresh evidence is discovered, so that we may reasonably hope to be able to decide between different historical theories on the basis of empirical data.

WAS THERE SUCH A PERSON AS ABRAHAM?

So far we have referred to Abraham without questioning whether he actually lived. But it is a question that is asked. Was there such a person? Do we have any evidence for his existence? Was he a fictitious folk hero, part of a "myth of origin," a "true history" but not historical, as we ordinarily understand that term?[11]

A number of scholars take the view that, while there is no specific evidence outside the biblical record, there is no reason to doubt the "general accuracy" of the patriarchal stories.[12] It is argued that some real individuals led the ancient Israelite clans, so it is "captious" to deny the possibility that Abraham, Isaac, and Jacob were clan chiefs who actually lived,[13] and that if the figure of Abraham had not been included in the biblical record it would have to be conjectured.[14]

A more cautious view points to the long process of editorial revision which would surely have taken place before the narratives reached their present form in Genesis.[15]

With regard to new discoveries see *The Biblical Archeologist,* Vol. 39.2, for an account of remarkable finds in the third millennium ruins of Ebla in North Syria, Giovanni Pettinato, "The Royal Archives of Tell Mardikh-Ebla." See also Paolo Matthiae, *Elba: An Empire Rediscovered,* (New York: Doubleday, 1981). For more recent discussions about the excavations at Ebla, see Lorenzo Vigano and Dennis Pardee, "Literary Sources for the History of Palestine and Syria: The Ebla Tablets," *The Biblical Archeologist,* Vol. 47.1 (March 1984), p. 6.

[9]David Noel Freedman, ed., "Letter to the readers," *The Biblical Archeologist,* Vol. 40.1 (March 1977), p.4.

[10]Robert Biggs, "The Ebla Tablets: An Interim Perspective," *The Biblical Archeologist* Vol., 43.2 (Spring 1980, p. 76.

[11]Robert Michaud, *Les Patriarches: Histoire et Theologie,* (Paris: Les Editions Du Cerf, 1975), p. 23.

[12]Ibid., p. 5. This view was expressed early in this century by John Skinner, *Genesis, The International Critical Commentary* (Edinburgh: T and T Clark, 1930), p. xxvi.

[13]John Bright, *A History of Israel* (Philadelphia: The Westminster Press, 1981), p. 93. Compare the discussion in Magnusson, *BC The Archaeology of the Bible,* pp. 34–42.

[14]Ephraim A. Speiser, "Genesis" in *Anchor Bible* (New York: Doubleday, 1964), p. xlv. For a comment on Speiser's views, see Brevard S. Childs, *Introduction to the Old Testament as Scripture* (Philadelphia: Fortress Press, 1979), p. 142.

[15]See the discussion in Hayes and Miller, *Israelite and Judaean History,* pp. 96–102.
See also Gerhard Von Rad, *Genesis, Revised Edition* (Philadelphia: The Westminster Press, 1972), p. 165.

A street in Hebron, one of the oldest continuously occupied cities in Israel. It is associated in the patriarchal narratives with Abraham (*Genesis 23:2*). Photo by Elizabeth Gordon.

Other writers describe them as pious fiction,[16] which should be placed in the same category as Christian, Islamic, or even Buddhist lives of the saints.[17] The question of Abraham's real identity is far from settled, yet it would seem to be of relevance when we examine what is the most important aspect of his role in the scriptures. The promise of God would still be primary in the history of Israel if the story of Abraham's call were fiction rather than fact. The many biblical references to Abraham, and to the promise which God made to him, acquire additional force when understood as God's initiation of a great event through a real individual. It is also consistent with how God has made his purposes known throughout biblical history. Yet if Abraham were an historical personality we are confronted with a mystery of divine will. A great number of people lived in Mesopotamia, why Abraham? What could have led to his becoming the first recorded follower of the Israelite God?

[16]Gottwald, *The Tribes of Yahweh*, p. 42.

[17]George E. Mendenhall, " 'Change and Decay in All Around I See: Conquest, Covenant, and *The Tenth Generation,*" *The Biblical Archeologist,* Vol. 39.4 (December 1976), pp. 152–57. See also Roland le Vaux, *The Early History of Israel,* translated by David Smith (Philadelphia: The Westminster Press, 978), pp. 186–92.

WHAT DID ABRAHAM BELIEVE BEFORE HE WAS CALLED BY GOD?

When God appeared to Moses in the wilderness he announced himself with these words, "I am the God of your father, the God of Abraham, the God of Isaac, and the God of Jacob" (Exodus 3:6). The phrase, "the God of Abraham," is repeated throughout the Old Testament. Abraham was the one to whom God spoke, who obeyed God's call to leave his homeland and travel in unknown places. His faith in God's promise became a normative example of how one should trust God. To have faith like Abraham was to have great faith.

Yet according to the scriptural record Abraham was an old man when he received his call. If the experience referred to in Genesis 12:1-3 was his first encounter with God, he lived and grew old with religious beliefs very different from those for which he is remembered.

The Mesopotamian religious beliefs of the earliest Israelites during patriarchal times are referred to in the book of Joshua. At a gathering in Shechem, shortly after much of the promised land had been conquered by the Israelites, Joshua called upon the people to affirm or reaffirm where they stood with God. "Now therefore fear the Lord, and serve him in sincerity and faithfulness; put away the gods which your fathers served beyond the River, and in Egypt, and serve the Lord." (Joshua 24:14).

The reference to the gods of Egypt makes clear that by the time of the Exodus the Israelites were losing touch with their patriarchal traditions. The reference to the gods of the Euphrates reminds us of the origins of the people in Mesopotamia, of the family of Terah from whom they all came, and of all the other families in Mesopotamia whose descendants joined the Israelites. They worshipped the gods of their homeland and it is possible that among those who worshipped these gods was Abraham.

MESOPOTAMIAN RELIGION

As we have seen, we could not have described Mesopotamian religion at the beginning of the nineteenth century. Now we have a great deal of evidence: the excavated remains of ancient cities, large collections of clay tablets inscribed with prayers, incantations, and the details of temple business, religious sagas comparable to those in our own Bible, reflections upon the nature of life, accounts of dreams, the names of gods and goddesses. There is, it would seem, more information than we can use. Yet a scholar who has devoted his professional life to a study of ancient Mesopotamia begins his discussion of its religion with the heading, "Why a 'Mesopotamian Religion' should not be written." He asks how much would a distant and alien generation or visitor from outer space know about Western Christianity from the remains of church buildings.[18] Even surviving texts might tell us very little. There is the physica

---

[18]A. Leo Oppenheim, *Ancient Mesopotamia* (Chicago: University of Chicago Press, 1977), pp. 171-73.

and conceptual structure of a faith, and there is the way in which members of the faith experience what they believe. That is extremely difficult to capture.[19]

Yet, providing we recognize the difficulties and the possibility of distortion and misunderstanding, we can surely make an effort to understand. Otherwise we remain as cut off as if the materials we now have from ancient Mesopotamia had never been discovered. So, perhaps we can make a cautious attempt to glimpse behind the biblical account and try to find out something about the religious life out of which Abraham came.

As a member of Mesopotamian society Abraham would possibly have believed that he lived in a world whose natural forces and objects were alive. The distinction between animate and inanimate was not drawn closely as it is in our own day. The universe was a cosmos in which every part was likely to have a character and will of its own, and one of the necessities of life was to be alert to the consequences of that. Fire was not as we now understand it; it had a mysterious divine quality, as did the river. A sand storm was a raging demon; in fact Abraham was surrounded by innumerable supernatural forces, almost all of them waiting for an opportunity to do him harm. To protect himself he probably wore an amulet. It would bear a picture of the demon or devil against which protection was sought, and a magical incantation.[20]

Demons were especially attracted to people who were sick and weak and at a disadvantage. Had Sarah borne Isaac before she left Haran she might have worn an amulet against the female demon Lamashtu, who tried to steal newborn babies from their mother.[21] Details of life that we would not now associate with the supernatural were closely associated then. For example, when a tooth was extracted there was an incantation against the worm that lay at the bottom of the affected tooth,[22] and in a land of fiercely hot west winds there was an incantation against the evil wind-demons.[23]

Yet at such a great distance, we need to be cautious about stating what people believed. As one writer has expressed it, "The Mesopotamian was consciously aware that the phenomenon [the wind, fire, river] was not the actual divine being." But there was a strong sense of numinous, or spiritual power in the natural world.[24] No doubt this affected some more than others, as it still does.[25]

[19]Ibid., p. 183.

[20]H.W.F. Saggs, *The Greatness That Was Babylon* (New York: Hawthorne Books Inc., 1962), p. 303.

[21]H.W.F. Saggs, *Everyday Life in Babylonia and Assyria* (New York: G. P. Putnam, 1965), p. 185.

[22]Saggs, *The Greatness that was Babylon,* p. 306.

[23]Ibid., pp. 302–24, plate 57a.

[24]H.W.F. Saggs, *The Encounter with the Divine in Mesopotamia and Israel* (London: Athlone Press, 1978), pp. 89 and 157.

[25]A recent example of belief in demons comes from a newspaper. A young convert to the Unification Church told a reporter that she was so convinced of the presence of evil spirits "that I thought I could actually see them flying around me." Another member of the church refused to get up at a commune early one morning because she was exhausted. The team leader then warned her that evil spirits were hovering over her bed. The girl reported "when I opened my eyes I saw them there. I was terrified. I got up immediately." Article 3 in the series, "New Messiahs," Peter Arnett, *Rochester Times Union,* December 24, 1975, p. 2b.

Abraham came from the environs of Haran, whose principal diety was the moon god Nanna. Other cities worshipped other gods. Mari, about 200 miles southeast of Haran on the middle Euphrates, especially venerated Dagon. There is an account preserved of how Dagon appeared to a man in a dream with a warning message for his King, Zimri-Lin, who reigned from 1779 to 1766. Dreams were widely respected in the ancient world, as we see from the Old Testament story of Joseph (Genesis 41). Many years after Abraham, Dagon is referred to as the Philistine god humiliated by the presence of the captured Ark (1 Samuel 5:1–5). Another god, Addad, associated with Syria, appears in the name Ben-Hadad King of Syria, an enemy of Israel during Ahab's reign (1 Kings 20:1).

There were thousands of gods in Mesopotamia, but at their head stood the great gods: Anu, the creator, King of the gods; Enlil, the storm god, violent and unpredictable; and Ea-Enki, who was peace loving, the god of wisdom and magic, the friend of man. It was Enlil who attempted the destruction of mankind by flood, and Ea who, out of pity, preserved it. There were goddesses, Ereshkigal, Queen of the Underworld, and Ishtar who could be seen as the planet Venus, the morning and evening star which Abraham would have looked at, no doubt with awe, many times.

In Jewish and Christian religions a collection of books tells the story of God. In Mesopotamia there were epic accounts of the birth of the gods and the creation of the heavens and earth and of man, which, if not known to Abraham as we know them from surviving tablets, would have been known in earlier forms. He may have heard them read at a New Year's Festival, or he may have discussed them or recited them himself, and he may have wondered at how remote these stories and the gods and goddesses themselves were from the day-to-day life of men and women.[26]

Yet while in general the Mesopotamian gods were remote and not concerned with the individual, we know from surviving texts that in the second millennium there were worshippers who conceived of their gods in a personal way and addressed one or the other as father, for example:

To the god, my father, speak!
    thus says Apil-adad thy servant
Why have you neglected me (so)?
Who is going to give you one?
Who can take my place?[27]

The personal nature of the gods appeared, however, to be more of a wish than an assurance. A sufferer who had appealed to his gods without getting a response laments

[26]Openheim, *Ancient Mesopotamia,* p. 176.

[27]Thorkild Jacobsen, *The Treasures of Darkness, A History of Mesopotamian Religion* (New Haven: Yale University Press, 1976), p. 160. See Chapter 5, "Second Millennium Metaphors, The Gods as Parents: Rise of Personal Religion."

Tomb of the Patriarchs Mosque, Hebron: tomb of Abraham and Sarah, Isaac and Rebekah, Jacob and Leah. Photo by Elizabeth Gordon.

No god came to my aid or grasped my hand,
  my goddess did not pity me,
  walked not at my side.

Nevertheless, it was believed, at least to a limited extent, that despite their remoteness and failure to take action, the gods were concerned with individual men and women and could be moved by supplication to act on their behalf. It was this belief, however limited, held by at least some of the people of his time, that may help to explain Abraham's encounter with God. Because he was aware of the spiritual experiences of others, he may have seen that his own spiritual relationshps were open to reflection and possibility.

How much of the revelation Abraham understood we cannot know. Perhaps his understanding, such as it was, was intuitive, understandable to himself but not explainable. He could hardly have grasped the meaning of the promise. He may have believed it because he could not disbelive it; it was too extraordinary to comprehend. His faith may be notable, not because he believed in a promise which could not be fulfilled while he lived, or that he believed that he and Sarah could still have a child, or that he left familiar places for unfamiliar, but that he had faith in the spiritual experience itself, strange and different as it was, and permitted it to change the emphasis of his life.

CHAPTER TWO
THE LAND
OF CANAAN

THE FERTILE CRESCENT

If we take a map of the ancient Near East and find Ur, the city from which Abraham's family came, and follow the main concentration of cities and towns from Ur to Haran, and then from Haran to southern Palestine, we will have traced a right angle whose two arms enclose the great Arabian desert.

North of the route from Ur to Haran are mountains; west of the route from Haran to the Negeb is the Mediterranean Sea.

Abraham journeyed to Canaan but continued on to Egypt because of famine. Joseph's brothers went to Egypt for the same reason. It was, we now know, a long-established custom of the Egyptians to allow foreigners to enter Egypt and buy food if they otherwise might starve.

Continuing to follow the cities and towns, this time in Egypt, we trace a route south to Thebes. We have now completed an arc: Ur to Haran, Haran to the Negeb and northern Egypt, northern Egypt (which is known as Lower Egypt) to Thebes.

The final arm of the arc has the Red Sea and the Arabian desert to the east, the North African desert to the west, and the Mediterranean to the north.

Since James H. Breasted coined the term (although as he understood it the arc stopped at the Negeb), this arc is commonly described as the Fertile Crescent,

There are extremes of climate in Israel. The nearest car is below sea level and going down to the Dead Sea. The Hebrew is literally "face of the sea." Photo by Elizabeth Gordon.

a corridor of more or less fertile land which bordered the Tigris and Euphrates rivers from Syria to southern Palestine, and the river Nile through Egypt.

The great civilizations of Egypt and Mesopotamia were possible only because of the rivers. In the case of Egypt a yearly inundation of land bordering the Nile left a deposit of fertile soil which enabled the Egyptians to grow crops for another year. The Nile flood, however, was not predictable. It could be too small so people would starve, or too great and destroy fields and dikes and houses. Dikes and canals and catch basins had to be built and constantly maintained. In the case of Mesopotamia the river waters, as we have already noted, had to be guided by a system of irrigation canals without the help of an inundation. Both civilizations were largely the result of the cooperative effort required to make effective use of the rivers. Where there was no water there was desert, and the desert was always a threat. The line between cultivated land and desert still is, in places, very sharp.

Between these two great lands, Egypt and Mesopotamia, lay Canaan, the land which God promised to give to the descendants of Abraham. When Abraham set out, his back to Haran, the country of his origins stretching southeast to his left, Canaan lay before him to the south.

A later writer praising Abraham's faith said that he ''went out, now knowing where he was to go'' (Hebrews 11:8). This was undoubtedly correct in that he had

One of the sources of the Jordan near Dan. Photo by Elizabeth Gordon.

no clear destination. But his journey was not like that of Columbus who had hardly any idea of what lay beyond the horizon. There was a great flow of traffic between Egypt and Mesopotamia, and the way from one to the other was through Canaan by ancient routes along the coast and to the east of the Jordan which joined routes to other parts of the Near East. When David and Solomon, and later Jeroboam II and Uzziah, controlled this area they made considerable profit from the merchandise passing through it.

These routes were used also by armies, and because Canaan was a bridge the empires at either end considered it very important that they control it for trade, for maneuvering, and for protection. Canaan was therefore not often left to take care of its own affairs. Until the twelfth century it was controlled mainly by Egypt. After a long respite from the twelfth to the ninth century, when no outside power was strong enough to dominate the country, and Israel established itself as a nation, the land came under the control first of Assyria, then Babylonia, then Persia. In the fourth century it was conquered by Alexander and, after his death, it was ruled by his successors. In the first century B.C., following a brief period of independence, it came under the control of Rome. The point is that the geographical location of this small territory has made an enormous difference to its history and its culture, from direct military and political interference to the influence of art and ideas.

Abraham should therefore have been familiar with the country promised to his descendents even though he had never been there, because during his long life in Haran he must have met many people who had.

CANAAN

Egypt and Mesopotamia were dependent upon their rivers, but the farmer in Palestine could get a good harvest from the dew and the rain. He was far less dependent upon his own efforts, and far more dependent upon conditions which were out of his control. The difference is brought out in the Old Testament.

> For the land which you are entering to take possession of it is not like the land of Egypt, from which you have come, where you sowed your seed and watered it with your feet, like a garden of vegetables; but the land which you are going over to possess is a land of hills and valleys, which drinks water by the rain from heaven. (Deuteronomy 11:10–11)

The agricultural products of the land are described in another passage from Deuteronomy.

> For the Lord your God is bringing you into a good land, a land of brooks of water, and of fountains and springs, flowing forth in valleys and hills, a land of wheat and barley, of vines and fig trees and pomegranates, a land of olive trees and honey. (Deuteronomy 8:7–9)

Grain was grown on the coastal plain. Grapes and figs were grown on the slopes of the mountain range, which ran the length of the country between the plain and the river. Pomegranates and olives were grown in many parts of Palestine. Dates were grown in the Jordan Valley.

Innumerable references to these crops throughout the scriptures indicate the extent to which they were a part of Israelite life. When Isaiah wanted to describe God's disappointment with Israel he wrote about a vineyard on which its owner had lavished every care, and then produced sour fruit (Isaiah 5). The standard biblical description of peace and prosperity was that every man should be under his own vine and fig tree (1 Kings 4:25). Pomegranates of blue, purple, and gold decorated the robe of the High Priest (Exodus 28:33). Jeremiah, warning his people of God's judgement, wrote, "The Lord once called you 'A green olive tree, fair with goodly fruit'; but with the roar of a great tempest he will set fire to it, and its branches will be consumed." (Jeremiah 11:16).

To supplement the biblical record we have a letter from an Egyptian named Sinuhe who fled his country for political reasons and settled in Palestine. What makes this letter interesting is that it was written about 1900 B.C., roughly the time of Abraham according to one view, so it would be in a sense a contemporary account from another person who had come to Palestine from outside, in Sinuhe's case from Egypt, the other end of the great arc. He writes:

Hills with terraced olive trees. Photo by Elizabeth Gordon.

It was a good land. . . . Figs were in it, and grapes. It had more wine than water. Plentiful was its honey, abundant its olives. Every (kind of) fruit was on its trees. Barley was there, and emmer [an early type of wheat]. There was no limit to any (kind of) cattle. . . [1]

Abraham kept mainly to the central highlands, and he and his son Isaac and his grandson Jacob lived somewhat apart from the native population. On the other hand, according to Genesis, Isaac and Jacob kept in touch with their original homeland, Mesopotamia, and this was important in a way that had considerable influence upon the traditions of the Hebrew people.

[1]James B. Pritchard, ed., *Ancient and Near Eastern Texts Relating to the Old Testament* (Princeton, N.J.: Princeton University Press, 1969), p. 19.

For more information about the land of Canaan, the following works will be found useful:

G. Ernest Wright and Floyd V. Filson, *The Westminster Historical Atlas to the Bible* (Philadelphia: The Westminster Press, 1956).

Denis Baly and A. D. Tushingham, *Atlas of the Biblical World* (New York: World Publishing Co., 1968).

Yohanan Aharoni and Michael Avi-Yonah, *The Macmillan Bible Atlas* (New York: Macmillan, 1974).

Denis Baly, *The Geography of the Bible,* new and revised edition (New York: Harper and Row, 1974).

Yohanan Aharoni, *The Land of the Bible, A Historical Geography,* 2d ed., A. F. Rainey ed. and trans. (Philadelphia: The Westminster Press, 1980).

Azaria Alon, *The Natural History of the Land of the Bible* (New York: Paul Hamlyn, 1969).

Fauna and Flora of the Bible, 2d ed. (New York: United Bible Societies, 1980). Prepared in cooperation with the Committee on Translations of the United Bible Societies.

CHAPTER THREE
THE INFLUENCE
OF MESOPOTAMIA

Abraham left Mesopotamia, but he still regarded it as his own country. Years later he sent his servant there to find a wife for Isaac (Genesis 24:1–4). Rebecca left willingly to live with Isaac, but she also remained closely attached to her homeland. When her own sons were grown, she spoke to the younger son, Jacob. "You shall not marry one of the Canaanite women. Arise, go to Paddan-aram to the house of Bethuel, your mother's father; and take as wife from there one of the daughters of Laban your mother's brother." (Genesis 28:1–2). Jacob subsequently spent twenty years in Mesopotamia with his uncle's family.

Mesopotamian influence is reflected in an almost casual way throughout Genesis. For example: Two of the rivers that flow from the Garden of Eden, the Tigris and the Euphrates (Genesis 2:14), are the rivers referred to in the name Mesopotamia, which means "between the rivers."

In the Table of Nations (Genesis 10:1–32), the Kingdom of Nimrod, the mighty hunter, includes the southern cities of Babylon, Erech, and Accad in the land of Shinar (Sumer and Babylonia) and the northern cities of Nineveh and Calah in the land of Ashur or Assyria.

According to one view, the mighty hunter Nimrod (Genesis 10:8–12) was Tukulti-Ninurta I,[1] the first Mesopotamian ruler to control both Babylon and Assyria in the thirteenth century about the time of Moses and the Exodus.

[1]Ephraim A. Speiser, "Genesis," *The Anchor Bible,* 2d ed. (Garden City, N.Y.: Doubleday, 1964), pp. 72–73.

What brought the Mesopotamian origins of the early Genesis stories most strikingly to public attention was a discovery made by a young man named George Smith in a room in the British Museum in 1872. Smith had received no formal training in Assyrian studies. He intended to be an engraver, but he was so enthusiastic about Assyria that he spent his spare time reading books about it, and during his lunch hours visited the British Museum to look at Assyrian artifacts. The keeper of Oriental Antiquities at the Museum noticed him and offered him a job repairing the tablets from Nineveh. About ten years later, in 1872, having learned Assyrian, he was copying cuneiform signs from the tablets when he discovered first a reference to a ship grounded on Mount Nisir, and then an account of a dove and a swallow and a raven being sent across the water to find a place to land. The similarity between this and the Biblical story of the flood appeared to him to be so apparent that he began to look for more parallels, and he gradually pieced together what no one had imagined could exist, an account of a flood that came from another source than the Bible and was very similar to it. There was already a widespread controversy about Charles Darwin's *Origin of the Species,* published thirteen years earlier in 1859, so when Smith read the results of his work to a meeting of the Society for Biblical Archeology he created a public sensation. *The London Daily Telegraph* gave Smith a grant of a thousand guineas to go to Nineveh himself to find more tablets, which he did on that and a subsequent expedition.[2]

A BABYLONIAN FLOOD

The name of the Babylonian Noah was Utnapishtim. Like Noah he was warned by a god, Ea, the benevolent god of the earth, to build a ship and take on board "the seed of all living things." Everyone helped to built it.

> The little ones carried bitumen
> While the grown ones brought all else that was needful.
> On the fifth day I laid her framework
> One whole acre was her floor space
> Ten dozen cubits the height of each of her walls.
> Ten dozen cubits each edge of the square deck. . .
> On the seventh day the ship was completed.
> The launching was very difficult,
> So that they had to shift the floor planks above and below,
> Until two thirds of the structure had gone into the water.

[2]James B. Pritchard, *Archeology and the Old Testament* (Princeton, N.J.: Princeton University Press, 1958), p. 160.

See also H. Darrell Lance, *The Old Testament and the Archeologist* (Philadelphia: Fortress Press, 1981), pp. 5–6.

W. G. Lambert and A. R. Millard, *Atra-Hasis, The Babylonian Story of the Flood* (Oxford at the Clarendon Press, 1969), pp. 2–4.

A. R. Millard, "A New Babylonian 'Genesis' Story," *Tyndale Bulletin* 18 (1967), 1–18.

Fragment of clay tablet with Babylonian account of the flood, written in cuneiform script (*Courtesy of British Library*).

The vessel was loaded and there followed a wild storm which blew for six days and nights. When it subsided Utnapishtim opened a hatch and looked out upon the water. All mankind had returned to clay. He sat down and wept. But the level of the waters fell and the ship grounded.

On Mount Nisir the ship came to a halt.
Mount Nisir held the ship fast,
     allowing no motion...

When the seventh day arrived.
I sent forth and set free a dove.
The dove went forth, but came back;
Since no resting-place for it was visible,
    she turned around.
Then I sent forth and set free a raven.
The raven went forth and, seeing that the
    waters had diminished,
He eats, circles, caws and turns not around.[3]

Utnapishtim then left the ship and offered a sacrifice. The gods crowded around like flies. Finally Enlil, god of storm and destruction, who had brought about the flood, told Utnapishtim and his wife that they would be immortal like the gods.

THE BABYLONIAN CREATION STORY

George Smith's discovery was especially important because it made clear as nothing else had done before how deeply the Bible is indebted to the broader context from which it came, and how rich is that context. Until then it was generally thought that the biblical stories were unique. It became evident with Smith's discovery that they were expressions of traditions far more ancient than the Israelites themselves. As if to emphasize this, only three years later, in 1875, Smith published a translation of fragments from a Babylonian account of creation called Enuma Elish after the opening words of the poem.

This myth describes the birth of the gods, a great battle between Tiamat, goddess of primordial waters, and Marduk, the young champion of the gods, the creation of heaven and earth, setting constellations, making man for the service of the gods, and a divine banquet. The details of the myth do not compare with the biblical accounts of creation as they do in the story of the flood, and one scholar argues that we should not look for similarities;[4] there are many creation myths from many parts of the world which are surprisingly similar without their being dependent upon one another.[5] Yet it is claimed that there are similarities between the Babylonian and Old Testament accounts. A tabulation given by A. Heidel in *The Babylonian Genesis* illustrates this.[6]

---

[3]James B. Pritchard, *Ancient and Near Eastern Texts Relating to the Old Testament* (Princeton, N.J.: Princeton University Press, 1969), pp. 93–95.

[4]D. Winton Thomas, *Documents from Old Testament Times* (New York: Harper and Row, 1961), p. 14.

[5]See for example Geoffrey Parrinder, *Religion in Africa*, Chapter 2, "Philosophy and Cosmology" (London: Penguin Books, 1969), p. 29.

[6]Alexander Heidel, *The Babylonian Genesis*, 2d ed. (Chicago: University of Chicago Press, 1951), p. 129.

ENUMA ELISH	GENESIS
Divine spirit and cosmic matter are co-existent and co-eternal	Divine spirit creates cosmic matter and exists independently of it
Primeval chaos; Tiamat enveloped in darkness	The earth a desolate waste, with darkness covering the deep (tehom)
Light emanating from the gods	Light created
The creation of the firmament	The creation of the firmament
The creation of dry land	The creation of dry land
The creation of luminaries	The creation of luminaries
The creation of man	The creation of man
The gods rest and celebrate	God rests and sanctifies the seventh day

THE GILGAMESH EPIC

Whatever view one takes, the creation myth and others are remarkable for the abiding human concern which they preserve about personal existence and immortality. This is very clear from the context in which the flood story is found. The myth of the flood is part of a larger work known as the Gilgamesh Epic, named after the hero who tries to discover the secret of immortality.[7] His friend has died and he is afraid of death.

> He who with me underwent all hardships—
> Enkidu, whom I loved dearly,
> Who with me underwent all hardships—
> Has now gone to the fate of mankind!
>
> Day and night I have wept over him.
> I would not give him up for burial—
> In case my friend should rise at my plaint—
> Seven days and seven nights,
> Until a worm fell out of his nose.
> Since his passing I have not found life,
> I have roamed like a hunter in the midst of the steppe.
> O ale-wife, now that I have seen thy face,
> Let me not see the death which I ever dread.[8]

There is intense poignancy in Gilgamesh's vain hope that grief will return his friend to life. The story of Gilgamesh is an epic, but it surely expressed the experience

[7]Gilgamesh knew that Utnapishtim, a mortal, had become immortal, so he searched for him and found him, hoping to discover the secret. It was then that Utnapishtim told Gilgamesh the story of the flood and of how, after the flood, the god Enlil had rewarded him with everlasting life. Gilgamesh learned that immortaility was for Utnapishtim only. But Utnapishtim pitied him and gave him a plant which could renew life; this was stolen from him, so all his efforts failed.

[8]Pritchard, *Ancient and Near Eastern Texts,* pp. 89–90.

of many people for whom the epic was, in some sense, their theology. To that extent it could not have failed to influence the thought of the earliest Hebrews.

Since the time of George Smith many more texts have been discovered and translated, and much more is known about literary developments in Mesopotamia itself. Within the past few years another version of the flood story has been reconstructed.[9] The hero of this version is Atrahasis rather than Utnapishtim. It was written about 1600 or 1700 B.C.[10]

The story is similar to the story which George Smith discovered, but some of the details are different; Atrahasis builds a reed boat of a kind common then, reeds fastened to a wooden framework. Also, at the point where the text might refer to the birds being sent out to find dry land, several lines are missing.[11]

The reconstruction of the Atrahasis text, portions had been known to George Smith, makes clear that, while the Old Testament writings have gone through a process of development, so have the nonbiblical texts. The account of the flood is influenced by the Utnapishtim story, but that is "largely derived" from the Atrahasis account.[12] There was, in fact, a considerable amount of literary activity during these very ancient times and the evolution of the Old Testament was a part of it.

THE DISTINCTIVENESS OF THE GENESIS ACCOUNTS

Much of the value for biblical studies of these Mesopotamian traditions is how the Old Testament authors interpreted them. It is a false alarm to be concerned for the uniqueness and trustworthiness of the Genesis stories because of similarity in detail and their apparent dependence upon older, nonbiblical material. What is more striking in the Old Testament versions is their difference in theological emphasis.

According to the Old Testament, the one God decides to destroy mankind because of its wickedness. The Noah account is immediately preceded by the story of the Nephilim, the sons of the gods who had intercourse with the daughters of men (Genesis 6:1-8). But righteous Noah and his family are to be saved. God warns him and instructs him to build an ark with the intent that through him and his descendants there will be a new world order. There would seem to be a strong moral emphasis in the Old Testament absent in those Babylonian versions where the flood is either

---

[9]Lambert and Millard, *Atra-Hasis,* p. 11. The story of Atra-Hasis begins at the time when only the gods lived. It describes the revolt of the junior gods who had been assigned menial work, the creation of human beings to do that work, the complaint of Enlil about their noisy behavior, and then, after unsuccessful attempts to quieten them, the "final solution" of the flood.

[10]Lambert and Millard, Atra-Hasis, p. 24.

Tikva Frymer-Kensky, "The Atrahasis Epic and Its Significance for Our Understanding of Genesis 1–9," *Biblical Archeologist,* Vol. 40.4 (December 1977), p. 148.

[11]Lambert and Millard, *Atra-Hasis,* pp. 12 and 97–99.

[12]Frymer-Kensky, "The Atrahasis Epic," p. 148.

[13]Lambert and Millard, Atra-Hasis, p. 11.

an arbitrary decision, or an attempt to control the noise created by an overpopulated world which deprived the gods of their sleep.[14]

Similarly, the story of the Tower of Babel gives an explanation of why there are so many languages. But the main point is not philological, it is theological, to show what happens when men and women become overly proud.

With regard to the creation stories there are similarities as we have seen, but they are on the level of detail and order. The differences are more significant. Instead of an assembly of gods arguing and fighting among themselves there is one God who knows what he intends to do, and does it. Dramatic confrontations and savage punishment are absent from the biblical account. God creates the heavens and the earth not from a dismembered goddess but from his own creative power. Despite its cosmic grandeur it is done simply, and when he has finished, God's restrained comment is that it is "good." In the Babylonian epics, mankind is created to serve the gods; in Genesis, Adam is created for his own sake, and Eve to be his companion. They are created in the divine image, and until the Fall are on familiar terms with God. They have work to do, but it is in the context of a blessing, they are not slaves. Only when they have sinned does their condition change, and even then they never lose their status as created beings endowed with the qualities of their Creator.

The biblical story has a decisively different character from the Babylonian in its concept of God and man and their relationship, and the moral requirements that man must live up to. For this reason it is unfortunate that the Genesis narrative should have become associated with unthinking biblicism because it represents an important development of critical thought in intellectual history. From its earliest times to the destruction of Mesopotamian civilization there was little change in Mesopotamian religion other than in the relative importance of the gods; for example, Enlil was the hero of earlier versions of the Creation stories rather than Marduk.[15] But in the much briefer period from Abraham to the time when the Genesis accounts were written there was a notable advance in the Hebrew concept of God, and it continued, as we will see, in the reflections of the prophets.

Yet, in attempting to make a fair comparison between Israelite religion and the religion of Mesopotamia, we should consider certain factors. Most writers on the subject are drawn to it because of their predisposition to Judaism or Christianity. How much might that affect their understanding of ancient non-Israelite religion?

To what extent are the presently known religious documents from Mesopotamia representative of the full range of Mesopotamian religious beliefs? Much of what Christians and Jews understand from the Old Testament is what they bring to it from their general knowledge of the Judaeo-Christian tradition. Almost three thousand years later than the writing of the Atrahasis Epic, St. Thomas Aquinas wrote:

[14]Frymer-Kensky, "The Atrahasis Epic."
Robert Davidson, Genesis 1–11 (Cambridge: Cambridge University Press, 1973), pp. 66–67.
John Skinner, Genesis, The International Critical Commentary, 2d ed. (Edinburgh: T and T Clark, 1939), pp. 178–79.
[15] H.W.F. Saggs, The Greatness That Was Babylon (New York: Hawthorne Books, 1962), p. 331.

"The thing Known is in the Knower according to the mode of the Knower."[16] Perhaps we should ask how much the Mesopotamian worshipper may have brought to his religious writings when he read them or heard them read.

It is, perhaps, tempting from a Judaeo-Christian perspective to dismiss the Mesopotamians as "heathen," and applaud such mocking descriptions as Isaiah's account of how a heathen image is made out of a log of wood (Isaiah 44:12-20). Yet, as we tried to show, there was a personal, spiritual element in the Mesopotamian religious experience. If we accept that as genuine, as indeed the Apostle Paul did (Romans 1:19-20), what does it mean? Could it be, as Oppenheim suggested, that there is a great deal we do not know about Mesopotamian religion, far too much for us to make a confident judgment? Israelite religion was strongly ethical and spiritually profound. But for a great number of Israelites it was an ideal never attained. Mesopotamian religion appears by comparison to have had a restricted concept of the nature of divinity. But could some of its adherents have gone beyond that?

The student of the Bible is faced with a difficult task if he/she wishes to understand the character and development of Israelite religion while remaining sympathetic to the other religions, which are usually compared unfavorably to it.[17] The task, however, may be unexpectedly relevant to broader issues. We live in a world in which Western philosophy and religion are no longer dominant. The Judaeo-Christian tradition must be understood within a world context of many other views. It is not enough to assert or assume its distinctiveness and superiority.[18] If we so believe, and there are many reasons for regarding the Old Testament and the faith it teaches as both remarkable and unique, we must give reasons which go beyond the reasons usually given. That, in the contemporary situation and in the historical situation of Mesopotamia, requires continued inquiry.

GENESIS 1-11

To be even slightly familiar with the Mesopotamian background of the stories in Genesis 1-11 helps us to deal with them as an expression of their time. It helps us to shift our attention from what may be thought strange or unbelievable about them to their reasonableness. For example, the enormous life spans of the ancient patriarchs are seen to be even modest by comparison with the life spans of the Babylonian Kings,

[16]Thomas Aquinas, *Summa Theologica* II/II Q.I. Art.2. This quotation is used by John Hick in *Philosophy of Religion,* 3d ed. (Englewood Cliffs, N.J.: Prentice-Hall, 1983). See Chapter 8, "The Conflicting Truth Claims of Different Religions," p. 120.

[17]For example, what is the theological value, as compared with the historical value, of the non-biblical Mesopotamian stories of creation and the flood? One writer argues that the Atrahasis epic is of great importance in this respect to our understanding of Genesis 1-9.
Frymer-Kensky, "The Atrahasis Epic."

[18]H.W.F. Saggs, *The Encounter with the Divine in Mesopotamia and Israel,* (London: University of London, Athlone Press, 1978), pp. 4 and 15.
Hans Küng, *On Being a Christian,* (Garden City, N.Y.: Doubleday, 1976), p. 98.

one of whom reigned for almost 65,000 years.[19] Similarly the issue of whether or not the two Old Testament creation stories are scientifically reliable can be seen in another light if one thinks of the ancient writers as having made use of the best scientific knowledge available to them. It is conceivable that in another era with other data the details of what they wrote would have been different.

It is also helpful, when trying to understand why there should be two accounts of creation or two sets of instructions in the story of the flood, in each case with apparent contradictions, to be acquainted with the view (to be discussed in Chapter 6) that the first eleven chapters of Genesis as well as other parts of the first five books of the Old Testament are a compilation of several documents. These, it is proposed, were written by different authors at different times who brought to the same story different viewpoints.

But knowledge of the background and of the history of the text are only part, and by no means the most important part, of what we need to know about these stories in order to understand them. We must deal with the question of what was their purpose. If they were borrowed from Babylonian traditions why were *they* borrowed and not others? If different texts were used why were apparent contradictions allowed to remain and not smoothed away? The ancient editors surely did not overlook them. These stories appear at the beginning of the Old Testament; what is their relationship to what follows?

Much attention has been given to how true the stories are: was the world really created in six days, was there actually an ark, are different languages really the consequence of human ambition? The first question is currently the subject of a widespread public debate, meanwhile a group of religiously motivated explorers is trying to find physical evidence of Noah's Ark.

Yet even were it possible to substantiate the empirical truth of these stories, what is important about them is not the facts but what the facts represent. Whether or not God created the world in six days, both creation stories assert that God exists and is the creator of all things. That is a premise basic to the Old Testament and so is rightly placed at its beginning. Whether or not Eve was tempted by a serpent and ate the fruit and encouraged her husband to eat it against God's orders, the story tells us something fundamental about human nature, about the process of developing the independence which God gave to men and women when he created them, "in his image." It provides a description of a motif that pervades the Old Testament.

Those who reject the stories as fact often refer to them as myth. A myth is a story in symbolic form which conveys a truth about God. The literary mechanism is the same as that of a New Testament parable. We do not ask what was the name of the Prodigal Son, or whether he was a real person. That is not the point. The point is the lesson or the message; similarly with the early Genesis stories. On the level of fact they provide information which we may or may not accept as true, but

[19]Speiser, "Genesis."

their importance lies in what they mean. The factual level invites us to accept or reject a description of events. The symbolic level invites us to a never-to-be-ended process of spiritual reflection.[20]

In Chapter 6 we will refer to an approach to the interpretation of scripture known as canonical criticism. While not neglecting historical origins, this approach proposes that when we study a passage of scripture we should attempt to discover its function for the community of faith which produced it. Taking that approach to the first eleven chapters of Genesis one can see them not as prehistorical tales but as the beginning of history, [21] the cosmic beginning of the story of God's covenant relationship with his people Israel. The call of Abraham is not an unexpected change of character in the biblical record but that moment when cosmic history first interacts with events in recorded time. The first eleven chapters are therefore pointing implicitly to what follows them. They are, as one writer put it, a priestly doctrine,[22] not simply fabulous tales adapted to some extent from contemporary Mesopotamian tradition. These chapters therefore repay study for themselves certainly, but also for what they can lead us to understand about the Old Testament as a whole.

[20]See Paul Ricoeur's discussion of the ''Adamic'' myth in *The Symbolism of Evil*, translated from the French by Emerson Buchanan (Boston: Beacon Press, 1967), pp. 235–243.

Also Foster R. McCurley, *Ancient Myths and Biblical Faith* (Philadelphia: Fortress Press, 1983.) Francois Jacob, *The Possible and the Actual* (Seattle: University of Washington Press, 1982). See particularly the chapter ''Myth and Science.''

[21]Gerhard Von Rad, *Genesis,* revised edition, John H. Marks trans. (Philadelphia: Westminster Press, 1961), p. 45.

[22]Ibid., pp. 46, 63.

QUESTIONS FOR DISCUSSION

The following questions refer to Chapters 1–3.

1. If historical reliability is not the only or even the most important consideration in understanding a biblical text, how important is historical reliability? If Adam and Eve, Noah, and Abraham were not historical persons, how does that affect the religious value of the Old Testament narratives in which they appear?

2. How might the biblical story have been different had God promised Mesopotamia or Egypt to Abraham? Do you think that it was part of a long-range divine plan to promise the land of Canaan rather than another territory? Is there anything fundamentally important about the geography of the promise?

3. A growing number of scholars argue that the difference between the religion of the early Israelites and the religion of their contemporaries was not as great as has often been claimed. For example, the personal qualities of God are now said not to be unique to Israel. If this is so, and the matter is by no means settled, why did the religion of Israel survive and become a major force in world culture and the other religions disappear?

4. The first eleven chapters of Genesis are a very small part of the Old Testament and are distinctly different. What would have been lost from the Old Testament as a whole had these chapters been lost?

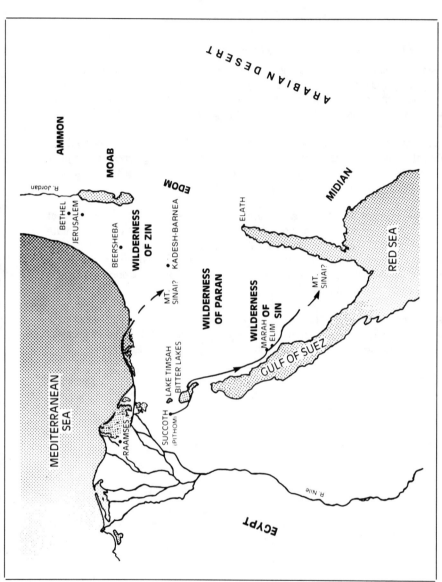

The Exodus. Possible routes of the Exodus, such as those indicated, must be very tentative, first, because the Old Testament does not give sufficient details to establish just where the Israelites travelled, second, because there is considerable controversy [...] historical event actually amounted to.

CHAPTER FOUR
ISRAEL IN EGYPT

The central figures in Genesis are Abraham, Jacob, and Joseph. Isaac was essential for the continuation of Abraham's family, and so for the eventual fulfillment of the promise, but little attention is given to him as an individual. The text dwells upon the often unlikeable but religiously more important life of Jacob. Jacob had twelve sons who are the traditional progenitors of the tribes of Israel. One of these sons was Joseph. His life, with its difficult beginning and triumphant end, is the subject of Genesis 37–50.

The story of Israel can be seen as a series of large-scale movements. The first begins with Abraham's call and his journey south to Canaan. The only part of the promised land which he and his family obtain is the cave of Machpelah and the land surrounding it, purchased by Abraham as a burial site (Genesis 23). The next movement is Joseph's involuntary journey to Egypt, where he is either sold or captured and becomes a slave. Eventually Joseph's father and brothers follow him, and the Israelites settle in Egypt.

The third movement begins with Moses, the Passover, and the Exodus and concludes with the Israelites under Solomon in possession of the land which had been promised to them through Abraham.

With the adventures of Joseph, therefore, the locus of the story of Israel shifts from Mesopotamia, at the northern end of the Fertile Crescent, to the equally ancient civilization of Egypt to the south. Just as we find evidence of Mesopotamian influence in the early chapters of Genesis, so we find evidence of Egyptian influence in the later chapters of Genesis and the early chapters of Exodus.

It was, for example, a custom for Egyptians to allow desert people or Bedouin to enter Egypt during periods of drought and famine and live in the delta area. An inscription from about 1350 B.C. states that a group of such persons "who knew not how they should live, have come begging a home in the domain of Pharaoh. . ., after the manner of your [the Pharaoh's] father's father since the beginning. . . ."[1] (Compare Genesis 41:53–57.) There is even a picture of a Bedouin family dressed in brightly colored robes and accompanied by cattle and donkeys which had come to Egypt about 1900 B.C. to trade a black eye cosmetic, stibium, a favorite with the Egyptians.[2] There must have been many such groups over the years.

The titles "chief butler" and "chief baker" (Genesis 40:2) are found in Egyptian inscriptions. Joseph's official position (Genesis 41:40–45), is now known to correspond to the position of Prime Minister or Vizier of Egypt, second to Pharaoh.[3] The Pharaoh's birthday was a time of celebration and possibly release of prisoners (Genesis 40:20). The giving of a signet ring to Joseph, and arraying him in fine linen and a gold chain were in accord with Egyptian custom (Genesis 41:41–42). When Sinuhe returned to Egypt, he was "clad in fine linen and anointed with oil."[4]

The story of Joseph and Potiphar's wife is similar to an Egyptian folk tale of two brothers, in which the hardworking and conscientious younger brother, Bata, refuses the advances of his older brother's wife, and is then accused by her of assault.[5] But Joseph's predicament is likely enough for it to be an independent, actual experience.

An important detail of the Joseph narrative is the Pharoah's dream about seven lean cows and seven fat cows (Genesis 41). An Egyptian text from the second century B.C. records a tradition 2500 years earlier of seven lean years because of the low level of the Nile.

"The Nile had not come in my time for a space of seven years. Grain was scant, fruit were dried up, and everything which they eat was short." Then in a dream the Pharaoh is told by the god that there will be a time of plenty. "The starvation year will have gone, and (peoples) borrowing from their granaries will have departed. Egypt will come into the fields, the banks will sparkle. . .and contentment will be in their hearts more than that which was formerly."[6]

[1]G. Ernest Wright, *Biblical Archeology,* new and revised edition (Philadelphia: Westminster Press 1962), pp. 53–57.

[2]James B. Pritchard, ed., *Ancient and Near Eastern Texts Relating to the Old Testament* (Princeton N.J.: Princeton University Press, 1969), p. 229.

[3]Wright, *Biblical Archeology,* p. 531.

[4]Pritchard, *Ancient and Near Eastern Texts,* p. 22.

[5]Ibid., p. 23.

[6]Ibid., pp. 31–32.

Moses is an Egyptian name (compare Amosis, Tutmose, Rameses). Hophni and Phinehas, the sons of Eli (1 Samuel 2:34), are Egyptian names, as is Merari (Genesis 46:11), a son of Levi.

References to Egyptian life and customs occur almost casually.[7] For example, in Genesis 50:26 Joseph dies, full of honor, at age 110. In the ancient and well-known Egyptian wisdom book of Ptah Hotep, the author reaches the age of 110 at the end of a long and successful career. A coincidence, possibly, but perhaps a subtle comparison intended to show that Joseph compares favorably with one of the greatest of Egyptian sages.[8]

THE HYKSOS

The tradition of Israel in Egypt is supported in numerous ways, but it may still seem surprising that Joseph, a foreigner, should have become so powerful. This, however, was not unusual; in the new empire or kingdom, which began in the sixteenth century, slaves rose to positions of prominence, perhaps because, being foreign, the Pharaohs trusted them more than their own countrymen. But there is another possible explanation in the case of Joseph.

During the eighteenth century the power of Egypt had begun to decline. This led to infiltration and eventual control by a mixed group of West Semitic Hurrian and other peoples known as the Hyksos.[9] The name means "foreign chiefs" or "rulers of foreign lands," and they ruled from about 1720 to 1570, approximately one hundred and fifty years.[10] They established their Egyptian capital in Avaris, in the delta region in the north, near Goshen where Joseph's family settled. Before the time of the Hyksos the capital was at Thebes in the south. After 1100 B.C. Avaris was given the name Tanis. A monument found in the ruins of the city was erected by Rameses II (1290–1224) to commemorate the founding of the city, possibly by a Hyksos ruler 400 years before, about 1700.[11] There is a reference in Numbers 13:22: "Hebron

[7]John Marshall Holt, *The Patriarchs of Israel* (Nashville, Tenn.: Vanderbilt University Press, 1964), p. 197.

[8]Ibid., p. 202.

[9]*The Cambridge Ancient History II,* Part 1, 3d ed. I.E.S. Edwards, E. J. Gadd, N.G.L. Hammond, E. Sollberger, eds. (Cambridge: Cambridge University Press, 1973), pp. 54–58.

[10]Roland de Vaux, *The Early History of Israel,* David Smith trans. (Philadelphia: Westminster Presss, 1978), pp. 75–81.

John A. Wilson, *The Culture of Ancient Egypt* (Chicago: The University of Chicago Press, 1951), pp. 154–65.

John Bright, *A History of Israel,* 3d ed. (Philadelphia: The Westminster Press, 1981), pp. 59–61.

Yohanan Aharoni and Michael Avi-Yaweh, *The Macmillan Bible Atlas* (New York: Macmillan, 1968). Maps 28 and 29 indicate the extent of Hyksos rule and how Amosis expelled them.

Wilson discusses the ambiguity of Egyptian chronology, *The Culture of Ancient Egypt,* p. 319.

[11]Roland de Vaux, *The Early History of Israel,* p. 303.

Cornfeld believes that the stele was erected earlier than Rameses II. Gaalyah Cornfeld, *Archaeology the Bible: Book by Book* (New York: Harper and Row, 1976), p. 13.

was built seven years before Zoan in Egypt'' (Zoan refers to the same city as Tanis). The question is why the Israelite chronicler would be interested in the founding of an Egyptian city (Avaris, Rameses, Tanis, Zoan). The most probable answer is that the Israelites were closely associated with the city when they were in Egypt, that they possibly came there during Hyksos rule. It is arguable that Joseph and his father and brothers and their families would have been welcomed by the Hyksos rulers, who were to some extent related to them.

The third century B.C. Egyptian historian Manetho writes about

> men of ignoble birth out of the eastern parts, who had boldness enough to make an expedition into the country and easily subdued it by force without a battle. And when they got our rulers under their power, they afterwards savagely burnt down our cities and demolished the temples of the gods, and used all the inhabitants in a most hostile manner, for they slew some and led the children and wives of others into slavery.[12]

The Hyksos controlled not only Egypt, but Canaan and Syria, and their influence extended as far as Crete. They are memorable for introducing a new weapon of war, the horse-drawn chariot, and they built enclosures for their chariotry which were protected by huge beaten earth embankments.

About 1600 B.C. the Egyptians began a war of liberation, and under Amosis (ca. 1552–1527) drove the Hyksos out and fought them through Palestine into Syria.[13] This is significant for biblical history because Exodus 1:8 records that a king ascended the throne of Egypt ''who did not know Joseph.'' It is possible, though not probable, that this king was Amosis. At least one can postulate that after the expulsion of the Hyksos, conditions became less pleasant for the Israelites.

The events of Exodus 1:8–11, if they refer to Amosis, can be dated during his reign which ended around 1527. The building of Pithom and Rameses on which the Israelites were employed (Exodus 1:11) took place about 240 years later. This we know because the city of Rameses did not exist by that name until the reign of Seti I (1305–1290) or his son Rameses II (1290–1224). A city in that vicinity had been built centuries before by the Hyksos. Rameses II, as mentioned, set up a monument commemorating the 400th anniversary of the founding of the city, about 1700 B.C. The Israelites may, therefore, have been in a condition of increasing servitude for 300 years before the Exodus, from the expulsion of the Hyksos, about 1600, to the reign of Rameses II and the building of the city of Rameses, about 1290.[14]

THE CITY OF RAMESES

Rameses became the foremost city in Egypt. It had a huge temple, numerous great buildings, and colossal statues of the Pharaoh. A poetical work of the time celebrates the splendor of the city:

[12]George Ernest Wright, Floyd Vivian Filson, *Westminster Atlas* (Philadelphia: Westminster Press, Revised edition 1956), pp. 27–28).

His majesty has built himself a castle, the name of which is "the Great of Victories"... and is full of food and provisions. The sun rises in its horizon and sets within it. All men have left their towns and settled in its territory. Its west is the Temple of Amon, its south is the Temple of Seth.... Its ships come out and go back to mooring, so that supplies and food are within it every day. One rejoices to dwell within it, and there is no one who expresses a lack to it.... The young men of "the Great of Victories" are dressed up every day, with sweet oil upon their heads and newly dressed hair. They stand beside their doors, with their hands bowed down with flowers...when (Rameses II) enters in.... The ale of "the Great of Victories" is sweet...beer of Cilicia from the harbor and wine of the vineyards.... The singers of "the Great of Victories" are sweet, having been instructed in Memphis. So dwell content of heart and free, without stirring from it. O (Rameses II), thou god![15]

Rameses must have been a place of continuous activity, where troops were marshalled and sent out to win wars, where all kinds of commercial activities were organized for the whole Mediterranean world and Asia, where enormous building projects were carried on. It was the royal city with a constant coming and going of envoys and foreign dignitaries speaking many languages. Rameses was to the ancient world as London or New York is to our own, a great cosmopolitan center, an exciting place to be.

At the heart of its hustling activity lived Moses. At least this seems likely, for he was a member of the court, brought up as an Egyptian nobleman, no doubt enjoying the pleasures and privileges of his position. But despite his preoccupation with Egyptian affairs he became curious about his own people. If we accept the story that his mother was his nurse, he undoubtedly learned a great deal from her, for there was another side to the grandeur of the city of Rameses, the hardships of the Israelites employed by Egyptians who "made the people of Israel serve with rigor, and made their lives bitter with hard service" (Exodus 1:13–14). This must have stirred Moses very deeply. At some point he "went out to his people" and saw an Egyptian beating[16] an Israelite. In sudden anger he killed him (Exodus 2:11–15). He attempted to hide the murder by burying the body, but the word got out, the Pharaoh tried to arrest him, and so Moses escaped to Midian, to the desert where he remained until he was an old man.

EGYPTIAN RELIGION

In our discussion about Abraham we tried to find reasons in the religious background of his time for his concept of God, and his subsequent journey south to Palestine. Moses, although he had been in the desert for forty years before his vision of the burning bush, grew up in Egypt so that, initially, Egyptian religious traditions would be most familiar to him.

---

[15]Ibid., pp. 251–52.

[16]Martin Noth, *Exodus: A Commentary,* J. S. Bowden trans. (Philadelphia: Westminster Press, 1962). Noth translates this as the Egyptian "killing" an Israelite, which would make Moses' extreme reaction more understandable (pp. 35–36).

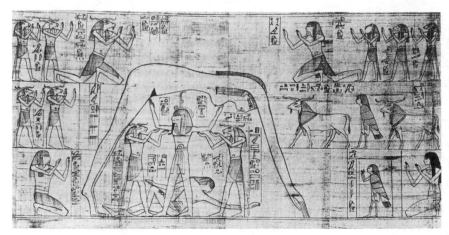

Egyptian gods: Sky-goddess Nut, supported by air-god Shu with earth-god Geb on the ground (*Courtesy of British Library*).

Egyptian religion, like Mesopotamian, was polytheistic. In a picture of Egyptian cosmology in the Book of the Dead [17] Nut, the sky goddess, is shown supported by Shu, the air god, who stands on Geb, the earth god. Many gods were represented as animals (Horus as a falcon, Thoth as a baboon, Hathor as a cow), and often as composite creatures, partly human, partly animal. [18]

Different gods were associated with different parts of Egypt. Amon, the "Hidden One," the god of wind and breath of life, was associated with Thebes; Ptah, the power of the earth, was associated with Memphis. Frankfort refers to about eighty gods but how many there were he admits we do not know. [19]

In the fourteenth century the Pharaoh Amenhotep IV attempted to reform Egyptian religion by substituting one god for the multiplicity of gods. He changed his name to Akh-en-Aten and declared that the one God to be worshipped would be Aten, the sun disc, and he devoted his energies to suppressing traditional Egyptian polytheism. His enthusiasm for the new religion was fanatical. For example, he sent agents to erase the name Amon, [20] the creator of gods, from all inscriptions throughout the country, an enormous task which was never completed. Imagine trying to erase the name "God" from all public monuments and inscriptions in any modern Judaeo-Christian country.

[17]James B. Pritchard, *The Ancient Near East in Pictures Relating to the Old Testament* (Princeton, N.J.: Princeton University Press, 1969), figures 542 and 573.

Henri Frankfort, *Ancient Egyptian Religion*, (New York: Harper, 1961), pp. 8–14.

[18]Pritchard, *The Ancient Near East in Pictures*, figures 567, 572.

[19]Frankfort, *Ancient Egyptian Religion*, p. 4.

[20]Wilson, *The Culture of Ancient Egypt*, p. 221.

RELIGIOUS INFLUENCES AT THE TIME OF MOSES

Atenism has been regarded as the earliest expression of monotheism. This, however, is unlikely. Not all other gods were repressed, and while Akh-en-Aten himself worshipped the sun disc, his subjects worshipped him as a god.[21] Nevertheless the Hymn to Aten, discovered in Tell-el-Amarna, Akh-en-Aten's new capital, is very much like Psalm 104, which extols the creative power of God. To take one passage for comparison, The Psalmist writes:

> O Lord, how manifold are thy works!
> In wisdom hast thou made them all;
> the earth is full of thy creatures. (Psalms 104:24)

In the Hymn to Aten we read:

> How manifold it is, what thou has made!
> They are hidden from the face (of man).
> O sole god, like whom there is no other!
> Thou didst create the world according to thy desire,
> Whilst thou went alone:
> All men, cattle, and wild beasts,
> Whatever is on earth, going upon (its) feet,
> And what is on high, flying with its wings.

The new religion failed largely because of the hostility of the priests, but very much more because it had no popular support. Within a few years after Akh-en-Aten's death it had been expunged from Egyptian life as relentlessly as Akh-en-Aten had tried to expunge Amon. So that by the time of Moses, approximately eighty years later, Egypt had returned to its ancient traditional beliefs. But it seems unlikely that the attempted reformation with its many serious political and military repercussions would have been forgotten, especially not in the Egyptian court where Moses grew up. Yet long before the religious revolution of Ahk-en-Aten there were elements in Egyptian religion which seem to suggest an early monotheism. An example of this is the Hymn to Amon as sole god:

> The first to come into being in the earliest times, Amon, who came into being at the beginning, so that his mysterious nature is unknown. No god came into being before him; there was no other god with him, so that he might tell his form. He had no mother, after whom his name might have been made. He had no father who had begotten him. . . . All (other) gods came into being after he began himself.[22]

---

[21]Ibid., p. 223.
[22]Pritchard, *Ancient and Near Eastern Texts,* p. 368.

From a contemporary perspective, this seems to be at least monotheistic "in spirit." But just as a student examining twentieth century Christianity four thousand years from now might point to prayers addressed to the Virgin Mary, to saints, to separate members of the Trinity as evidence of polytheism and be wide of the mark, so we must be careful to distinguish between genuine expressions of monotheism in ancient Egypt, if there are any, and expressions which concentrate upon one god *as if* there were no other.[23]

The extent to which Israelite beliefs were affected by Egyptian beliefs is debatable. Moses himself may have reflected upon the traditions of his once adopted country, but the mass of Israelites who followed him were probably interested only in becoming free and surviving.

Besides Egyptian culture another important influence upon Moses would be the traditions of his earliest ancestors, Joseph, Jacob, Isaac, and Abraham. We do not *know* that he learned about them from his mother and his fellow Israelites in Egypt, but when God confronted him in the wilderness it was as the God of Abraham, Isaac, and Jacob (Exodus 3:6).

How much was contributed by the Kenites, the tribe with whom Moses lived, we also cannot be certain. According to one view the Kenites were worshippers of Yahweh "from time "immemorial""[24] and not only Moses but all the Israelites in Egypt received their knowledge of God, Yahweh, from them. The Kenites would therefore be the major religious influence upon Moses and his people.

Whatever the mixture was of these elements, and perhaps others, it led Moses to a concept of God which we now know as the God of the Old Testament.

THE CONFLICT BETWEEN MOSES AND THE PHARAOH

The nature of the conflict between Moses and the Pharaoh is misunderstood if one reads only the biblical account. Moses is presented as the champion of his people, courageously challenging a despotic king who regards the Israelites as expendable slaves and stubbornly refuses to listen to the word of God. A full account, if we could find one, would be less one-sided, for the biblical version is written from a point of view, and that is a characteristic of the Bible which we must accept and try to understand when we study it. But while accepting it we must correct for it.[25] For

[23] John A. Wilson, "The Function of the State" in *The Intellectual Adventure of Ancient Man* (Chicago: The University of Chicago Press, 1977), p. 225.

Henri Frankfort, *Kingship and the Gods* (Chicago: University of Chicago Press, 1977), p. 225.

de Vaux, *The Early History of Israel*, p. 462.

[24] Harold H. Rowley, *From Joseph to Joshua* (London: Oxford University Press, 1950), pp. 149–60.

Roland de Vaux, *Ancient Israel*, Vol. 2, Darton trans. (New York: McGraw Hill, 1965), pp. 293–94.

See also Wiliam F. Albright, "Moses in Historical and Theological Pespective," Frank Moore Cross ed., in *The Mighty Acts of God* (New York: Doubleday, 1976), p. 124.

[25] In this connection see Eric Weil, "What Is a Breakthrough in History?" *Daedelus* (Spring 1975), p. 22.

example, the Egyptologist accepts but must correct for the glowing interpretation that Rameses II gave of his nearly disastrous campaign against the Hittites in 1286. Similarly, we can accept but must correct for the Old Testament chronicler's interpretations. Put another way, we should try to see biblical events from the other side as well as from the one given. With regard to the struggle between Moses and the Pharaoh this is difficult. There is an intellectual and spiritual link between us and Moses; we are separated from the Egyptians by an immense span of time through which there is little continuity of belief or thought. To us, in the Judaeo-Christian tradition, it is quite reasonable, if not obvious, that Moses would proclaim the authority of his one God. But eighty years after what was regarded by the Egyptians as an infamous heresy, which had disturbed and weakened the Empire, the proclamation of one God could not fail to arouse distaste and anger. Moreover, the claim that there was one God, different from the gods of Egypt, was a personal affront to the Pharaoh, and the god, Horus, and the great god, Amon. The Pharaoh was god. He represented the divinity of Amon, the creator, mediated through Horus, on earth. Such a concept is most foreign to the twentieth century, and if we think in biblical terms it is preposterous and blasphemous. But it was a normal way of thinking for the ancient Egyptian. For example,

> There can be no doubt about this. The practical organization of the Egyptian commonwealth implies it; the texts and monuments proclaim it; and it is confirmed by the absence of any trace of revolution in three thousand years of recorded history. Pharaoh was no mere despot holding an unwilling people in slavery. He ruled in the strictest sense by divine right; and any attempt to describe the Egyptian state irrespective of the doctrine of Pharaoh's divinity would be fatuous. We might as well discuss a modern democracy without reference to the doctrine of the freedom and equality of men. We know how thoroughly this last doctrine has molded our mores and institutions; we shall see that the belief in the divinity of their king similarly affected the everyday life of the Egyptians.[26]

THE EGYPTIAN POINT OF VIEW

To the Hebrews Moses was a prophet of God. To the Egyptians he was an escaped fugitive, a murderer, a violator of Maat, and he was violating that principle even more by his presumptuous return. Maat was a principle of cosmic order in which all things within the universe moved with eternal regularity.[27] It was therefore a principle of harmony and justice. Even the gods lived by Maat. The Pharaoh, as the

[26]Frankfort, *Ancient Egyptian Religion*, p. 31.
    See also Frankfort, *Kingship and the Gods*, p. 47. "Said the Vizier Rekhmire in the Eighteenth Dynasty, 'What is the King of Upper and Lower Egypt? He is a god by whose dealings one lives, the father and mother of all men, alone by himself, without an equal' "
    [27]Frankfort, *Kingship and the Gods*, pp. 51 and 277–78.
    John A. Wilson, "The Values of Life," in *The Intellectual Adventure of Ancient Man*, pp. 108–9.
    William McKane, *Proverbs* (Philadelphia: The Westminster Press, 1975), p. 7. There is a useful discussion of Maat in the section on Egyptian Wisdom literature.

divine leader, was responsible for justice and order in all aspects of the nation's life. The criminal or rebel, the man or woman who broke the law or defied the Pharaoh, was challenging the justice and order of the universe. The ancient Egyptians were a cheerful and tolerant people, but at some things they drew the line, and this was true of the Pharaoh. It is not really explanatory to say that his heart was "hardened." He had an altogether different way of interpreting life. According to the biblical writers the Pharaoh is acting correctly when he relents and incorrectly when he breaks his promise, that is, when God hardens his heart. But from the Egyptian point of view relenting is to admit that the violator of Maat deserves sympathy, which is wrong. Hardening the heart is to remember the correct view, according to the Egyptians, that no one must be allowed to violate Maat the principle of order and justice. The conflict between Moses and the Pharaoh was therefore fundamental and irreconcilable. The Egyptians were not likely to change a world view which at that time was over a thousand years old. Moses and his people were not likely to develop their new tradition, new by Egyptian chronology even if traced back to Abraham, in that environment. Even if the Pharaoh had allowed the Israelites their personal and religious freedom within Egypt they could hardly have developed as they did, *there*. It would be requiring from the Egyptians as impossible level of tolerance to expect that they could have allowed the Israelites within Egypt to create their own set of religious laws. Yet for the Israelites the law was basic to their belief; without it there could have been no Judaism as we know it. The conclusion is that there had to be an Exodus. There was no other way for the Israelites to become a separate identifiable people, and it was Moses, the man who understood both cultures, who led them from the one to the other.

CHAPTER FIVE
STAGES
TOWARD FREEDOM

GOD'S REVELATION TO MOSES

The history of Israel began with a promise. It was an impossible promise because Abraham and Sarah were too old, but despite that and their own doubts, they had a son and the family grew.

By the time of Rameses II, possibly as much as six hundred years later, the Israelites were still not a people of any distinction. Their great future was as unlikely as it had been when God first made the promise, yet a tradition had survived so that when God called to Moses from the burning bush he identified himself as the "God of your father, the God of Abraham."

Abraham's encounter with God had been prosaic; God spoke, Abraham responded. No explanation was given or requested. But when God called to Moses he explained carefully why he had decided to reveal himself:

> I have seen the affliction of my people who are in Egypt, and have heard their cry because of their taskmasters; I know their sufferings, and I have come down to deliver them out of the hand of the Egyptians, and to bring them up out of that land to a good and broad land...(Exodus 3:7-8)

When God announced himself to Moses as the God of his forefathers he spoke as if Moses would understand, and indeed we might assume that, for it was by attempting to learn about the traditions of his people that Moses murdered the Egyptian and had to escape to the desert. In forty years he must have reflected upon those traditions many times. Nevertheless, he felt it necessary to ask for God's name. God's reply is still indefinable.

> "I AM WHO I AM." And he said, "Say this to the people of Israel, 'I AM has sent me to you.' " (Exodus 3:14)

It is a statement both of what he is and what he does, self-sustaining, unchanging in himself and in his attitude to his creation. In that respect he was like the Egyptian gods who were also unchanging, but I AM was taking the initiative to talk directly to a man about a human problem, and that set him apart from all other gods of the time.[1]

Moses' question about God's name may not have been simply because he did not know who God was. It was a common belief in the ancient world that names are an actual part of the person who bore them, and to know a person's name is to be in possession of the person. When, for example, Jacob was confronted by a mysterious adversary (Genesis 32:22–32), he asked for his name. He didn't get a straight answer. Similarly, when Manoah, Samson's father, entertained an angel of the Lord he asked, "What is your name, so that, when your words come true, we may honor you?" (Judges 13:17). The angel's reply was an evasive, "Why do you ask my name, seeing it is wonderful?"

Moses may have thought that if he were to be his people's leader he should be able to tell them that he knew the name, and so had a special kind of relationship with the God who bore it.

A SLAVE MENTALITY

We would be on more secure historical ground regarding the Exodus if there were any known Egyptian records of the event. Even if we accept the biblical account without question the information it provides is meager.

If, for example, the subjection of the Israelites began when the Hyksos were overthrown by Amosis (about 1552–1527), and if Moses lived during the reign of Rameses II (1290–1225), the Israelites would have been in a condition of servitude for almost 300 years, from the time of Amosis in 1552 to the time of Rameses II in 1290. However, if the Pharaoh who "did not know Joseph" (Exodus 1:8), was

[1]Von Rad cautions against trying to find a philosophical statement about God's being in the enigmatic "I AM, that is who I am . . ." Gerhard Von Rad, *Old Testament Theology,* D.M.G. Stalker trans. (New York: Harper and Row, 1962), p. 180.

Martin Buber, however, believes that the innermost nucleus of the name captured a quality of God's being that exerted a continuous vital influence upon "the souls of generations." Martin Buber *Moses* (Harper and Row, New York: 1958), p. 54.

Rameses II and not Amosis, the severe hardships suffered by the Israelites would have begun during the first eighty years or so of the life of Moses.

Both views assume that a single group of Israelites was involved. It is quite likely that, as well as those Israelites whose descendents entered Egypt with Joseph, many others subsequently emigrated from the desert because of famine, or were captured by Egyptian soldiers.[2]

The indications are that, in whatever way the Israelites entered Egypt, and during whatever period, they had suffered harsh treatment for more than a lifetime by the beginning of the Exodus. It was certainly apparent in their response to Moses.

At first when they heard from Moses and Aaron what God had done "they bowed their heads and worshipped." (Exodus 4:31) But their enthusiasm did not last long. Moses and Aaron asked the Pharaoh to let the Israelites go on a three-day journey into the wilderness to sacrifice to the Lord. The Pharaoh refused, and spitefully ordered them to find their own straw for making bricks. Straw was used in bricks as metal rods are used in poured concrete. The consequence was that the Israelites quickly turned on their would-be champions.

"The Lord look upon you and judge, because you have made us offensive in the sight of Pharaoh and his servants, and have put a sword in their hand to kill us." (Exodus 5:21).

The message was: We have a bad situation, don't make it worse by trying to help when you don't understand. Moses' last attempt to help had resulted in murder.

The interest in the events from this point to the actual Exodus is in how the people's attitudes changed about themselves.

> Slaves are not necessarily rebellious and ready to follow any leader who promises them liberty; they may be utterly demoralized and fully resigned to their bondage. Their situation seems hopeless, and they dare not make the slightest protest, lest the oppressor bear down upon them harder than ever. Such was the case of the Hebrews in Egypt, so that what they needed to overcome their despair was the assurance that they had a God who could make things happen, who could bring to pass the promises He had made to them through Moses.[3]

But the assurance by itself may not have been sufficient. In recent times we have learned what should have been obvious, that when people are treated in a derogatory manner they develop a poor estimate of themselves. This is not corrected

[2]William Albright, "Moses in Historical and Theological Perspective" in *The Mighty Acts of God,* Frank M. Cross, Werner E. Lemke, Patrick D. Miller, Jr., eds. (Garden City, New York: Doubleday, 1976), p. 126.

H. Caselles, "The History of Israel in the Pre-Exilic Period" in *Tradition and Interpretation,* G. W. Anderson ed. (Oxford: University Press, 1979), p. 283.

[3]William H. Brownlee, "The Ineffable Name of God," *Bulletin of the American Schools of Oriental Research,* No. 226 (April 1977), p. 45. See also Brownlee's reference in the same article to Albright's interpretation, "He causes to be, creates," p. 39.

simply by providing opportunities for them to change; there has to be some kind of socially dynamic interaction which will destroy existing attitudes and develop new ones. In the United States of America the dynamics were at first sit-ins and then riots. These were destructive and bloody, they put American society into a turmoil, but they brought about important changes in attitude. The position of black people in the United States, how they are now regarded and how they regard themselves, has become significantly different. In thirteenth century Egypt comparable changes were achieved by the plagues. Whatever they were in actual fact, just as described in Exodus or a series of natural disasters, they brought about a profound change of attitude on the part of the Egyptians towards the Israelites and on the part of the Israelites towards themselves. At the beginning of the story it is clear that the Pharaoh and his people had a harsh and contemptuous attitude toward the Israelites. Shortly before they left we read that ''The Lord gave the people favor in the sight of the Egyptians. Moreover, the man Moses was very great in the land of Egypt, in the sight of Pharoah's servants and in the sight of the people.'' (Exodus 11:3)

THE PASSOVER

The Passover was the last and the most fearsome of the ten plagues. The Israelites were told to kill a lamb, smear some of the blood on the doorposts and lintels of their houses and to remain inside. ''For the Lord will pass through to slay the Egyptians; and when he sees the blood on the lintel and on the two door-posts, the Lord will pass over the door, and will not allow the destroyer to enter your houses to slay you.'' Then at midnight the Lord destroyed all the first-born in the land of Egypt, ''from the first-born of Pharaoh who sat on his throne to the first-born of the captive who was in the dungeon, and all the first-born of the cattle.'' And all through Egypt there was a 'great cry' (Exodus 12: 23.29–30).

How much the Israelites appreciated the significance of the Passover at the time we cannot know, but to the Old Testament chronicler it was of the greatest significance, so much so that it was to be remembered every year forever. The point is made three times in the one chapter.

> This day shall be for you a memorial day, and you shall keep it as a feast to the Lord; throughout your generations, you shall observe it as an ordinance for ever. (Exodus 12:14)
> You shall observe the feast of unleavened bread, for on this very day I brought your hosts out of the land of Egypt; therefore you shall observe this day, throughout your generations, as an ordinance for ever.'' (Exodus 12:17)
> You shall observe this rite as an ordinace for you and for your sons for ever. (Exodus 12:24)

The biblical writer introduces the Passover as if it were new, but the sacrifice of a lamb in the spring, the eating of unleavened bread, and the dedication of the firstborn can be explained on the basis of existing customs. Communal sacrifice was not new among the Israelites. The initial conflict with the Pharaoh was over the Israelites' request that he permit them to offer sacrifice in the wilderness (Exodus 5:1-5). The practice of sacrifice was widespread and ancient.

Similarly, among people whose lives depended upon the harvest, the spring and autumn were times of celebration and solemnity. Even in our contemporary technological society the tradition continues. Anglican churches have a Sunday morning service of Harvest Thanksgiving held once a year at the end of the harvest. This writer remembers that going to a country church in England on that Sunday is an especially pleasant occasion. Around the altar and in the aisles are sheaves of wheat and barley, baskets of apples, and freshly baked loaves, all of which are especially trying to a young and hungry worshipper. There was a Canaanite feast of the barley harvest when unleavened cakes were eaten. It appears that this feast and the lambing feast, the sacrifice of a lamb, were combined in what became the Passover, "a telling example," as one writer put it, "of the victory of the religion of Moses over the religion of Canaan."[4]

The third element was the consecration of the firstborn. The Lord said to Moses, "Consecrate to me all the firstborn; whatever is the first to open the womb among the people of Israel, both of man and of beast, is mine." (Exodus 13:1-2). The firstborn was sacred, and the sacrifice of a firstborn was a potent offering. The willingness of Abraham to sacrifice his firstborn, Isaac, was therefore the supreme test of his faith (Genesis 22:1-18). When Mesha, King of Moab, found himself in a desperate situation while fighting the Israelites, he sacrificed "his eldest son, who was to reign in his stead." The Israelites were so dismayed at this sight that they fled (2 Kings 3:26-27).

These three elements, the sacrifice of a lamb, eating unleavened bread and the dedication of the firstborn, were no doubt associated only gradually.

THE CONTINUING SIGNIFICANCE OF THE PASSOVER

Apart from how the Passover developed, and when the accounts of it were written, it became a festival of great symbolic importance. The blood on the doorposts and lintels, which protected those inside the house from the destroying angel, symbolized to all succeeding generations of Jews that God protects his people.

In the New Testament the blood of the lamb became a symbol of the blood of Christ bearing mankind's punishment for sin. When John the Baptist saw Christ his response was "Behold the Lamb of God, who takes away the sin of the world!" (John 1:29) The Apostle Paul in his letter to the Corinthians wrote, "For Christ, our paschal lamb, has been sacrificed." (1 Corinthians 5:7) Whatever the historicity of the event it has immense religious value for Jews and Christians. It represents the moment of breaking free from bondage, not only from the Pharaoh but from

[4]Eric W. Heaton, *Everyday Life in Old Testament Times*, (London: Batsford Ltd., 1956), pp. 228-29.

all oppressors at all times, and not only external bonds but those which the scriptures describe by the theological word "sin."

The thrice repeated admonition to the Israelites in Exodus 12 that they should keep the Passover "as an ordinance for ever" has been faithfully observed and it is a well-known and widely celebrated event of the Jewish year. Its significance has not changed. The final benediction of the Passover meal, the seder, which innumerable Jewish families share, embodies a hope that is common to people of all religious faiths:

> The Passover service is now completed. With songs of praise we have lifted up the cup, symbolizing the divine promises of salvation, and we have called upon the name of God. Let us again lift our soul to God in faith and hope. May He who broke Pharaoh's yoke, forever shatter all fetters of oppression and hasten the day when swords shall at last be broken and wars ended. Soon may He cause the glad tidings of redemption to be heard in all lands so that mankind—freed from violence and from wrong and united in an eternal confidence of brotherhood—may celebrate the universal Passover in the name of our God of Freedom...

CROSSING THE RED SEA

The next major religious event in Exodus after the Passover was the Covenant, but before the Israelites reached Sinai they were faced with an overwhelming crisis. The Pharaoh had told the Israelites to leave; he then changed his mind and sent his troops after them. The Israelites found themselves caught between the Egyptian army and the Red Sea. As they cried in despair and railed against Moses God performed a miracle. He parted the waters, allowing the Israelites to cross, and drove the waters back, thereby drowning the Egyptians. The Israelites sang a song of victory to the Lord with the triumphant refrain,

> I will sing to the Lord, for he has triumphed gloriously; the horse and his rider he has thrown into the sea. (Exodus 15:1–18)

Many attempts have been made to explain the event in terms of natural phenomena, including even the suggestion that a violent eruption of an underground volcano in the Aegean temporarily drained the rivers that ran into the Mediterranean. But the phenomenon of waters dividing or being driven back is not improbable, allowing for some elaboration over the years.[5] The major objection to the story is the unlikelihood that the Israelites would have traveled so far south. It made sense to avoid the most direct route to Palestine, along the coast, which was guarded by Egyptian troops, but to travel a route that placed the Red Sea between them and their destination would have been folly. In fact they neither went near the Red Sea

[5]Theodore H. Gaster, *Myth, Legend and Custom in the Old Testament,* Vol. 1 (New York: Harper and Row, 1969), pp. 237–40.

Martin Noth, *Exodus,* J. S. Bowden trans. (Philadelphia: Westminster Press, 1962), p. 119.

nor does the Hebrew text say that they did. The Red Sea of the story is more correctly Reed Sea, or Marsh Sea, probably a marshy lagoon between a strip of land and the mainland about sixty miles northwest of the Bitter Lakes.[6] There, most likely, is the locale of some event of a remarkable nature which enabled the Israelites to escape at the last moment when it seemed that they were doomed.

Their rejoicing was unbounded:

> The Lord is a man of war;
>   the Lord is his name.
> Pharaoh's chariots and his host
>   he cast into the sea;
> and his picked officers are sunk
>   in the Red Sea.
> The floods cover them;
>   they went down into the depths like a stone.
> Thy right hand, O Lord, glorious in power,
>   thy right hand, O Lord, shatters the enemy. (Exodus 15:3-6)

Not unexpectedly one finds no compassion for the Egyptian soldiers in the biblical account, any more than for the ordinary Egyptians whom the Israelites plundered (Exodus 12:36) of their silver and gold and clothing. The Bible gives no clue that the ancient Egyptians were a cheerful and good-natured people, but they were not cheerful and good-natured to the Israelites, except when, because of the plagues, their attitude began to change (Exodus 12:36).

The thanksgiving concludes with a song of Miriam, ''Sing to the Lord, for he has triumphed gloriously; the horse and the rider he has thrown into the sea'' (Exodus 15:21b), which is generally regarded as very ancient, possibly ''the oldest formulation preserved to us in the Old Testament of the account of the divine miracle at the sea.''[7]

MANNA, QUAILS AND WATER

The miraculous provision of food and water in the desert could have been providential natural phenomena. A mannalike substance is produced by insects that suck the sap of tamarisk trees to obtain nitrogen. What fluid the insects do not need, they give off as drops which fall to the ground and evaporate into a honeylike sticky substance (Exodus 16:14-18). Quails migrate across the Mediterranean from Europe in September and October. They land exhausted in northern Sinai, so are easy to catch (Exodus 16:13).

---

[6]See *The Macmillan Bible Atlas* (New York: Macmillan, 1968), map 48. See also Gaalyah Cornfeld, *Archeology of the Bible: Book by Book* (New York: Harper and Row, 1976), pp. 38-41.

[7]Noth, *Exodus*, p. 121.

Moses found water by striking a rock (Exodus 17:6). An incident similar to this took place in recent years when some British troops in the Sinai Desert, who had stopped and were looking for water near a limestone rock, accidentally struck the rock. Immediately there was a gush of clear water.[8]

Before its trees and vegetation were cut down for fuel and overgrazed by goats and camels, the Sinai peninsula was not the desert it is now. There was much more subsurface water, wild game, more vegetation, and more stands of tamarisk trees whose manna could support a "considerable number" of people.[9]

Moses himself spent forty years in these areas, and must have been familiar with survival techniques. He must surely have known about manna, and quail, and where to find water. It is possible that he may have known how to pick his way through a swamp. Moses grew up as an Egyptian, so he would have known about Egyptian soldiers and their equipment. He was a spiritual leader who was competent in many practical ways, and these may be examples. Nevertheless, from the point of view of the Old Testament writers, these events are presented as miracles wrought by God and should be so considered by the reader who wishes to appreciate the force of the biblical narrative.

OLD TESTAMENT LAW

The central event in Exodus after the Passover is the Covenant ceremony, the making of an agreement between God and the people, and the giving of the law.

The Old Testament is divided into three major parts: the Law, the Prophets, and the Writings. The first of these is the shortest, but so highly is it regarded that the whole Old Testament has been described as law. In John 10:34 and 15:25, for example, passages from the Psalms are cited as from "the Law," as is a passage from Isaiah referred to in 1 Corinthians 14:21 as "in the Law." Martin Luther writes in his *Preface to the Old Testament*, "Know, then, that the Old Testament is a book of laws and again, the peculiar and chief teaching of the Old Testament is the teaching of laws, the showing of sin, and the furtherance of the good." This identification of the Old Testament with Law remains current to the present day.[10]

The most well-known laws in the Old Testament are those found in Exodus 20:2–17, the Decalogue, which Luther described as the "significant kernel," and the "essential content" of the Old Testament. Yet the Decalogue is only one of many collections of Old Testament law to be found in the Pentateuch.

Chapters 4–30 of Deuteronomy consist of laws, which include the Book of the Law (Chapters 12–26), discovered during the reign of Josiah, in 621 B.C. Almost

[8]G. Ernest Wright, *Biblical Archeology*, revised and expanded edition (Philadelphia: Westminster Press, 1962), p. 65.

[9]Albright, "Moses," pp. 125–26.

[10]Martin Noth, *The Laws in the Pentateuch and Other Essays*, R. Ap-Thomas trans. (London: Oliver and Boyd, 1966), pp. 3–4.

the entire book of Leviticus consists of laws, divided into smaller collections, such as the Holiness code (Leviticus 17–26) and laws concerning purity (Leviticus 11–15). Laws dealing with the Passover and unleavened bread are to be found in Exodus 12:1–20, and 43–49. In Numbers there are directions for sacrifice (Chapters 28–29:15, also Chapters 5, 6, and 19). Various prohibitions are found in Exodus 34:11–26, and a set of curses in Deuteronomy 27:14–26.

Exodus 20:23–23:19 is the Covenant Code, given to the people at Mount Sinai, immediately following the Ten Commandments (Exodus 20:2–17), whose counterpart is Deuteronomy 5:6–21).

These laws were written at different times and include a wide variety of content. What gives them an appearance of unity is that at various times they have been traced back to Moses.[11] But more than appearance and despite all its inner divisions, the law in the Old Testament "can and must be treated as one,"[12] and this has been supported by canonical tradition, which regards the law as a distinct and cohesive entity.

THE HISTORICAL CONTEXT OF MOSAIC LAW

It is long since zealous critics of the Old Testament argued that Moses could not have received the tablets of the law because writing was not yet known. By Moses' time translatable writing had existed for perhaps 1400 years. In pictographic form, it had existed for 500 years before that. According to recent claims, it may have developed much earlier.[13] Both Mesopotamia and Egypt were literate societies, as the survival of great quantities of written material can testify.

It is also not the case, as zealous supporters of the Old Testament once argued, that the Mosaic laws were the first of their kind, although until recently this was difficult to disprove. In 1901–02 the French archeologist Jacques de Morgan discovered parts of a monument in Susa on which were inscribed the laws of Hammurapi, King of Babylon from 1728–1686 B.C., some five hundred years before the time of Moses. Very recently, since the end of World War II, law codes have been discovered from as early as 2000 B.C. Now it seems likely that many of the ancient city-states in Mesopotamia had their own codes adapted to local needs. There are quantities of legal documents which record details such as real estate transactions, the purchase and sale of slaves, loans, marriage contracts, divorces, and lawsuits.

[11]Ibid., p. 9.

[12]Ibid., p. 10.

[13]"The Book of Writing," *Time*, August 1, 1977, p. 76, discusses a theory about the origins of writing proposed by Professor Schmandt-Besserat, an archeologist at the University of Texas. According to her theory, writing developed from the prior use of clay tokens used for trade as early as 8000 B.C. There is a critical discussion of this in *Biblical Archeologist*, Vol. 41.2 (June 1978), p. 45.

Ignace J. Gelb, *A Study of Writing*, revised edition (Chicago: University of Chicago Press, 1963) Chapter VI, "The Evolution of Writing," p. 190.

Cuneiform script from the reverse of the stela of Hammurapi Paragraph 196. "If a seignior has destroyed the eye of a member of the aristocracy, they shall destroy his eye" (*Courtesy The Louvre, Paris*).

Of interest to the student of the Old Testament is the relation of these ancient documents to the biblical record, because Old Testament law was not separate from the ancient Near Eastern legal context. It was part of it.

One of the most well-known Old Testament prescriptions is the Lex Talionis, "an eye for an eye and a tooth for a tooth." We find similar laws in other ancient Mesopotamian codes.

The biblical text reads, in the case of bodily injury: ". . . you shall give life for life, eye for eye, tooth for tooth, hand for hand, foot for foot, burn for burn, wound for wound, stripe for stripe." (Exodus 21:23–25), and in Leviticus 24:19, "when a man causes a disfigurement in his neighbor, as he has done it shall be done to him."

In the code of Hammurapi we read:

> If a seignior has destroyed the eye of a member
>   of the aristocracy, they shall destroy his eye.
> If he has broken another seignior's bone, they
>   shall break his bone . . .
> If a seignior has knocked out a tooth of a seignior
>   of his own rank, they shall knock out his tooth.[14]

[14]James B. Pritchard, *Archeology and the Old Testament* (Princeton, N.J.: Princeton University Press, 1958), p. 222.

The Lex Talionis, long identified as a uniquely Old Testament law, was in existence several hunderd years before the time of Moses. What is now evident is that when an Old Testament law can be paralleled in other codes, the Old Testament is not always more humane. In the case of bodily injury, which is the concern of the Lex Talionis, the codes of Ur-Nammu and Eshnunna, dated about 2100–2000, approximately eight hundred years before the time of Moses, prescribe money payments for bodily injury rather than a retaliatory wound.

Rape was a problem in ancient times as it is today, and it was given considerable attention in ancient law, including that of the Old Testament where a practical distinction is made.

> If there is a betrothed virgin, and a man meets her in the city and lies with her, then you shall bring them both out to the gate of that city, and you shall stone them to death with stones, the young woman because she did not cry for help though she was in the city, and the man because he violated his neighbor's wife; so you shall purge the evil from the midst of you. But if in the open country a man meets a young woman who is betrothed, and the man seizes her and lies with her, then only the man who lay with her shall die. But to the young woman you shall do nothing; in the young woman there is no offense punishable by death, for this case is like that of a man attacking and murdering his neighbor; because he came upon her in the open country, and though the betrothed young woman cried for help there was no one to rescue her. (Deuteronomy 22:23–27)

Everything but a very small area of the land was country then, and largely deserted. The towns by contrast were extremely crowded. One can get some idea by visiting the Old City in Jerusalem or the ancient sections of Hebron where streets resemble passageways. A woman calling for help would certainly be heard by someone. If she were not, the presumption was that she did not want to be.

The earlier codes of Hammurapi and Eshnunna, however, do not make a practical distinction between rape in town and country. Perhaps they recognized that a man could stifle a woman, or she might be too shocked to call out. In any case, if a woman is raped in town or country, whether or not she cries out, and the man is caught, he alone is put to death. The earlier nonbiblical codes appear to be more sensitive to women in this respect than the Old Testament.[15]

These comparisons show that ancient Mesopotamia had a well-developed tradition of law from which the Law of Moses emerged as a particular expression.

THE DECALOGUE: ORIGIN AND DISTINCTIVENESS

The most well known of the Mosaic laws are the Ten Commandments or the Decalogue, literally the Greek for "ten words." Because they are prominent in Judaism and, indirectly, in Christianity, questions about their origin and uniqueness are regarded as especially important. Was Moses himself the author of the Ten Com-

[15]Ibid., p. 225.

mandments? Whether or not he was, is there anything distinct about them which sets them apart form the tradition of law of their time?

Origin

The question of the origin of the Decalogue is related to the larger question of the origin of the Pentateuch. On both issues opinion is divided. One scholar, for example, argues that the origins of the individual commandments of the Decalogue "probably go back to Mosaic times and even before that."[16]

Another points out that that is a view which is widely assumed but scarcely demonstrated.[17] More recently the canonical importance of the Decalogue has been stressed as an alternative to preoccupation with the history of the text, namely, the importance attached to the Decalogue by those editors who gave the final form to the Old Testament books. From that perspective the *position* of the Decalogue is significant. Its prologue (Exodus 20:2) "summarizes the previous narratives of the first eighteen chapters" and the fifteen verses which follow serve as "an interpretive guide to all succeeding material."[18]

Given the wide range of varied and sometimes conflicting opinions it seems that the question of authorship is not resolvable except by faith (there are many who choose that option), in which case the date of the Decalogue may be less critical than its nature and significance. God, as one writer points out, has always been regarded as its author, so the question of its human origin is not of fundamental importance.[19]

Distinctiveness

Although Old Testament law is indebted to the context of ancient Near Eastern law in which it developed, it was not simply an adaptation. How distinctive then is the content of the laws of the Decalogue?

It has become a widely accepted view that the command to worship one God, the prohibition against images, and the sense of personal concern between God and his people are unlike anything to be found in the ancient Near East. Only in Israel do we find so clearly that concept of God, and of men and women's relationship to him, which was expressed by the writing prophets of later centuries.

According to biblical tradition the beginning of this process is to be found in Mesopotamia with Abraham, proceding slowly through the experiences of the Patriarchs, the long stay in Egypt and then the Exodus. Yet although Moses had a sense of the tradition, it seems unlikely that many other Israelites did. The Covenant

[16]Johannes Jakob Stamm and Maurice Edward Andrew, *The Ten Commandments in Recent Research*, studies in biblical theology, second series-2 (London: SCM Press Ltd., 1967), p. 69.

[17]Ronald E. Clements, "Pentateuchal Problems," in *Tradition and Interpretation*, George W. Anderson ed. (Oxford: Clarendon Press, 1979), p. 114.

[18]Brevard Childs, *Introduction to the Old Testament as Scripture* (Philadelphia: Fortress Press, 1979), p. 174.

[19]Noth, *Exodus*, p. 168.

was therefore a real beginning, and the Decalogue may be taken to represent a primary understanding of God, filled with possibility for the future but not yet realized.

With regard to individual commandments, even though images in the Old Testament were not necessarily worshipped as gods, and the scathing comments of Isaiah (Isaiah 44:9-20) possibly represent a misunderstanding of the role of idols in non-Israelite worship, the prohibition against images was a difficult and unusual demand for the ancient world. Yet it appears to have been followed by the Israelites. Many images or figurines of gods have been found in Canaanite towns, but no figure of Yahweh has been found in an Israelite town.[20] In practice, however, the function of the image may have been taken over by the Tabernacle, whose construction is described starting at Exodus 25, and the Temple, which were the physical location of the presence of God. Also, during the Exodus itself, God was identified by a pillar of fire by night and a cloud of smoke during the day (Exodus 13.21).

The fourth commandment, calling for observance of the Sabbath, became an important characteristic of Israel. The Babylonians had a day called Shapattu, the fifteenth day or mid-point of the lunar month,[21] which was thought to be the origin of the biblical Sabbath. It is now recognized that we really do not know this.[22] Reversing the earlier view, it is argued that rather than having been derived from the Babylonian shapattu, the Sabbath was ''an innovation of biblical religion.''[23] Apart from the origin of this commandment, it represents a belief in Jewish religion that every man and woman should rest, not only for pleasure, although Hebrew holy days were enjoyable (see Deuteronomy 16:13-15), nor to observe a festival, as was common, or a position of the moon (the Sabbath did not coincide with a phase of the moon), but to honor God and reflect upon his creative work.

Commandments five to nine can be paralleled in other codes. Proscriptions against murder, theft, sexual license, and deceit are essential to the existence of a society. As is often pointed out these laws are extremly general, for example, the Israelites did kill, in war, and plundering people of their goods was not regarded as theft when the people plundered were non-Israelites (Exodus 12:35-36). The laws do not indicate in what circumstances they apply. It is also pointed out that there is no command against lying, although this possibly is included in the ninth commandment, which is against perjury.

The tenth commandment, however, is of particular interest because of the word ''covet,'' which implies not an action but an attitude. One is reminded of the Sermon

---

[20]Wright, *Biblical Archeology,* pp. 112-18.
Norman K. Gottwald, *The Tribes of Yahweh* (Maryknoll, N.Y.: Orbis Books, 1979), p. 684.
[21]Stamm and Andrew, *The Ten Commandments,* p. 90.
[22]Noth, *Exodus,* p. 164.
B. Z. Wacholder, ''Sabbath,'' in *Interpreters Dictionary of the Bible,* supplementary volume, Keith Crim et al. eds. (Nashville, Tenn.: Abingdon, 1976).
[23]Mayer Gruber, ''The Source of the Biblical Sabbath,'' *Journal of the Ancient Near East Society of Columbia University,* 1969, p. 172.
Alan R. Millard, ''A New Babylonian 'Genesis' Story,'' *Tyndale Bulletin,* 18, 1967, p. 16.

on the Mount (Matthew 5:27–28), where Christ exhorted his listeners not only to refrain from committing certain acts but not even to think of committing them. From that point of view we encounter an extremely sophisticated ethic at a very early date, about eight hundred years before Aristotle's Ethics.

Yet this would be a hasty conclusion. The Hebrew word used in this commandment shows that it does not aim only at the will "but simultaneously at the violent intrigues which a person uses in order to attain to the property of his neighbor."[24] We must therefore be careful not to credit the early Israelites with a more advanced concept of morality than they had.

Nevertheless, in Deuteronomy 5:21, where the same commandment is found, another Hebrew word is used for covet that does stress "covet" in the sense of impulse of the will.[25] Deuteronomy can be dated to the eighth and seventh centuries B.C., a time of political and moral decay. Hence the interpretation of the tenth commandment, familiar to us, was begun some hundreds of years after Moses in the Old Testament itself.[26]

MOSES

The personality of Moses dominates the story of the Exodus. It was his courage, his intelligence, his persistence, above all his faith in God which led the people, almost against their will, from slavery to freedom. He was a giant in the Old Testament yet it is almost impossible to classify him. He was not a king, not a priest, not a seer or a medicine man, not a military commander.[27]

Michelangelo represented him as an intense, physically powerful man with long hair and beard, and horns sprouting from his head.[28] He alone could speak to God face to face as one man speaks to another (Exodus 33:11). His anger at the apostasy of his people was gigantic, smashing the tablets of the law and ordering the tribe of Levi to kill the offenders, (Exodus 32:15–29). With the same angry impatience he struck the rock (Numbers 20:1–13) and so provoked God's anger that at the very last Moses was not allowed to enter the promised land.

Yet the scriptures describe him as the meekest man in all the earth

[24]Stamm and Andrew, *The Ten Commandments*, p. 103.

[25]Ibid., p. 104.

[26]Ibid., p. 105. The meaning of the tenth commandment, in particular the word translated "covet," is discussed by Walter Harrelson in *The Ten Commandments and Human Rights* (Philadelphia: The Fortress Press, 1980), p. 148.

[27]Walther Eichrodt, *Theology of the Old Testament*, Vol. 1, J. A. Baker trans. (Philadelphia: The Westminster Press, 1967), p. 289.

[28]According to the tradition that after he left the presence of God horns shone from his head (Exodus 34:29). This was based upon Jerome's translation of the Hebrew word in this passage, which can mean either "to have horns" or "to emit a ray of light." Martin Noth comments, "The word used here for 'becoming shining' has a root similar in sound to the word 'horn.' For this reason old translations, among them the Latin Vulgate, speak here of a 'horned' Moses." Noth, *Exodus*, p. 267.

(Numbers 12:3). He was given the opportunity by God to have the people of Israel refounded through him. That is, the promise would be taken from the descendents of Abraham and transferred to his descendents. But Moses refused the offer and pleaded with God for the erring people (Exodus 32:9–14). Like that other great Old Testament prophet, Elijah, he could be overwhelmed by his responsibilities. There is immense poignancy in his cry, when he was surrounded by people wanting him to do things for them, "Am I their mother?" (Numbers 11:12, The New English Bible. In the Revised Standard Version "Did I conceive all these people?")

What is Moses' role in the development of Israelite religion? Can he be credited with the beginning of the concept of one God? Was it through him that a higher religious life and moral culture emerged in Western civilization,[29] comparable to the influence of the sixth century Greek thinker Thales in conceptual thinking? Pythagoras, who lived somewhat later than Thales, is credited with the discovery of numerical proportion in the musical scale. That discovery made possible advances in music which otherwise could not have been made. Can we argue that the work of Moses advanced religious thought in a similar fashion?

We probably can never know for certain what role Moses played, or whether he had any historical connection with the event which took place on Sinai.[30] Opinions on this matter vary considerably.[31] But the question of historicity is only one factor in the study of the work of Moses. One could argue that, whether or not we have a defensible basis to prove or disprove the historical identity of Moses, the force of his personality is so strong in the Bible that we have to use our historical imagination *not* to recognize at the root of the Moses tradition a real individual.

THE COVENANT

In the account of the Covenant given in Exodus 24, Moses relates to the people "all the words of the Lord and all the ordinances." In response the people declare, "All the words which the Lord has spoken we will do." Moses then sets up twelve pillars and oversees a sacrifice. He reads the book of the Covenant to the people and once again they say "All that the Lord has spoken we will do." Moses throws half the blood on the altar and half over the people, saying "Behold the blood of the covenant which the Lord has made with you in accordance with all these words."

The concept of the Covenant is of great significance in the Old Testament, but there are different opinions about how that significance is to be understood depending on when the Covenant ceremony is thought to have taken place. Did the Covenant

---

[29]Albright, "Moses in Historical and Theological Perspective," p. 131.

[30]Martin Noth, *The History of Israel,* Stanley Godman trans. (New York: Harper and Brothers, 1958), p. 135.

[31]Albright, "Moses in Historical and Theological Perspective," p. 120.
Compare Gottwald, *The Tribes of Yahweh,* pp. 37 and 42.

ceremony take place at the beginning of the Exodus, and so provide a unifying force which enabled a polyglot collection of fugitives to become a people under the leadership of Moses and Joshua? Or was the Covenant a culminating event, which marked the conclusion of the Israelites' Holy War against the Canaanite inhabitants of the Promised Land?

A proponent of the first view writes, "The safest starting-point for the critical examination of Israel's relationship with God is still the plain impression given by the Old Testament itself that Moses, taking over a concept of long standing in secular life, based the worship of Yahweh on a Covenant agreement."[32] According to this it was in the Covenant agreement that the tribes found their unifying bond.[33]

The longstanding concept taken from secular life was the custom, widespread throughout the ancient world, of treaty making. When two people, or two groups of people, usually nations, wished to enter into formal relationship with one another, they would make a treaty or a covenant indicating what that relationship would be. The important factor was the extent of obligation which the parties owed to one another. In recent years attention has been drawn to these differences, in particular to the difference between what are called suzerainty covenants or treaties, in which the parties are unequal, and parity covenants, in which the parties are equal.[34] In the case of a large nation and a small, in which the relative strengths are unequal, the small nation would be obligated to the large one, such as paying an annual tribute. But the large nation would also have an obligation, or else there would be no point in a treaty. For example, it would be obligated to protect the smaller nation in case of attack. This would be a suzerainty treaty. Sometimes the two nations would be equally strong, such as Egypt and the Hittite empire in the latter part of the thirteenth century. In such a case there would be equal obligation, or a parity treaty.

According to one view the suzerainty covenants used by the Hittite empire provided the pattern for the Mosaic covenant.[35] The Hittite empire was destroyed in the latter part of the thirteenth century. It would therefore follow that if the Mosaic covenant was modelled upon it, it could not have occurred very much later than then.

But not everyone agrees with this view. One scholar proposes from his own investigations that suzerainty treaties were used before the rise of the Hittite empire and continued to be used after it was destroyed.[36] If that is correct, Hittite treaties do not help establish a date for the Mosaic covenant.

A quite different explanation of the covenanted unity of Israel is that of the

---

[32]Eichrodt, *Theology of the Old Testament*, p. 37.

[33]Ibid., p. 39.

[34]George Mendenhall, *Law and Covenant in Israel and the Ancient Near East* (reprinted from *The Biblical Archeologist*) (Pittsburgh Pa.: 1955).
George Mendenhall, "Covenant," in *Interpreters Dictionary of the Bible,* George A. Buttrick ed. (Nashville, Tenn.: Abingdon Press, 1962), p. 719.

[35]Mendenhall, "Covenant," p. 719.

[36]Dennis J. McCarthy, *Old Testament Covenant* (Richmond, Va.: John Knox Press, 1972), pp. 15–19. Stamm and Andrew, *The Ten Commandments in Recent Research,* pp. 42–43.

"holy war," the series of battles which the Israelites fought with the Canaanites, then with various enemies such as Ammon and Midian, and finally the Philistines. The need to band together to survive brought about first an operational unity and then an ideological unity represented by the Covenant.[37]

Other commentators place the origin of the Covenant in the Deuteronomic period (the seventh century) particularly in connection with the reforms of Josiah.[38] The Covenant then becomes a retrospective explanation of the origins of Israel, representing many generations of reflection upon the relationship between God and his people.

It seems to this writer, however, that the Covenant concept is too powerful and pervasive an influence in the historical record of Israel for the Covenant event to have occurred at such a late date. If, indeed, treaties were common in the ancient Near East, that is, if people commonly sought some type of formal association among themselves, the earliest Israelites would have done so as well. People ordinarily turn to those modes of expression with which they are familiar. In the case of the Israelites the desire for cooperation and equality within the context of their religious belief would quite normally seek expression in a covenant. If that is so, one would expect it to play a vital role in the *development* of Israel as a people and what they believed, and not to be the culmination of development already achieved.

[37]McCarthy, *The Old Testament Covenant,* pp. 8–9.
[38]Walther Zimmerli, "The History of Israelite Religion," in *Tradition and Interpretation,* p. 379.

CHAPTER SIX
THE COMPOSITION
OF THE PENTATEUCH
The Old Testament
Canon and Text

The traditional view is that Moses wrote the Pentateuch. We see this in the New Testament. For example, Christ is reported as asking "have you not read in the book of Moses, in the passage about the bush, how God said to him. . .? (Mark 12:26) Also "Moses has had in every city those who preach him, for he is read every sabbath in the synagogues." (Acts 15:21)

Until the mid-nineteenth century most students of the Bible believed that Moses wrote the Pentateuch, and a number still do. Yet at an early date there were questions. A twelfth century rabbi, Abraham Ibn Ezra, noted that the reference to Canaanites in Genesis 12:6, "Abram passed through the land to the place at Schechem, to the oak of Moreh. At that time the Canaanites were in the land" must have been written when the Canaanites were no longer in the land, which was long after the death of Moses.[1] Later scholars raised further questions, most notably the English philosopher Thomas Hobbes (1588–1679) and the Dutch philosopher Benedict Spinoza (1632–1677).

It is not difficult to find several instances in Genesis which are perplexing if one supposes that the work was written by a single author. For example, Chapter 1 tells us that man and woman were God's final creation. Chapter 2, a second account

---

[1]Otto Eissfeldt, *The Old Testament*, P. R. Ackroyd trans. (New York: Harper and Row, 1965) p. 159.

of creation, tells us that God created trees and plants and animals after he created man and woman. In the story of the flood one set of instructions from God orders Noah to take two of every kind of animal into the Ark (Genesis 6:19-20). Another set of instructions orders him to take seven pairs of all ritually clean animals and one pair of unclean (Genesis 7:2-3).

In Exodus 6:2 we read "I am the Lord. I appeared to Abraham, to Isaac, and to Jacob, as God Almighty, but by my name the Lord I did not make myself known to them." But Genesis 4:26 informs us that the name began to be used by the earliest descendents of Adam and Eve. "To Seth also a son was born, and he called his name Enosh. At that time men began to call upon the name of the Lord."[2]

One can try to reconcile these repetitions and discrepancies, or one can accept a view which many hold that the biblical records have developed like other records spanning a great length of time, from many sources. The contradictory accounts of creation in Genesis 1 and 2 are not contradictory when understood as two traditions from different times brought together by an editor or editors who respected and wished to preserve both. This view, which is known as the documentary hypothesis, explains the development of Genesis to Deuteronomy as a compilation of at least four identifiable traditions that were drawn together at certain times from the tenth to the fifth centuries.

The origin of this hypothesis is generally credited to Jean Astruc, physician to Louis XV, who published a book anonymously in 1753 on the compilation of the book of Genesis.[3] He did not doubt that Moses was the compiler, but he argued that Moses used a number of sources by authors other than himself. Chief among these was one that referred to God as Elohim, and another that referred to God as Jehovah.

During the following one hundred and thirty years the documentary hypothesis was examined and elaborated in great detail. It received what was considered to be its definitive expression in Julius Wellhausen's book *Prolegomena to the History of Israel*, published in 1883. Wellhausen's position in Old Testament criticism has been likened to that of Darwin in the intellectual history of modern times. He took an idea which

---

[2]Two words are used to refer to God in the Old Testament: Yahweh, which is the name, and Elohim, which is the generic term. Another word, Adoni, is translated as Lord. To understand how these words are used it is helpful to know a little about the Hebrew alphabet. The Hebrew alphabet consists of 22 consonants to which were added later a system of vowel indicators. The vowel indicators are a combination of dots, dashes, and vertical strokes which are placed above, below, and within the consonants.

The Masoretes considered the name Yahweh too sacred to be pronounced, so the *consonants* of Yahweh were written in the text, but the *vowels* of Adoni were added to those consonants. The combination of the consonants of Yahweh and the vowels of Adoni produced a word which, when pronounced, sounds like Yehowah or Jehovah, the word familiar to English readers of the Bible (see for example Exodus 6:4), which was introduced into the English language by William Tyndale.

[3]H. B. Witter was actually the first to attempt an analysis of Genesis with reference to parallel narratives and different names of God. But his commentary, published in 1711, did not go beyond Genesis 7:27. Eissfeldt, *The Old Testament,* p. 160.

had been "broached by others before him, but he gave the theory its classic formulation."[4]

According to Wellhausen, four major sources could be identified in the Pentateuch. They were known as J, E, D, and P, in chronological order. J, the oldest, was dated about 850, E about 750. The two documents were combined about 650. The Deuteronomic code of Josiah's reformation, which took place in Jerusalem in 621 (2 Kings 22:1–23:25) was added to J and E about 550. Finally, with the addition of the Priestly Code, about 400, the Pentateuch reached, substantially, its present form.

The four sources are referred to so frequently in works on the Old Testament that it would be useful to give a brief description. More detailed accounts can be found elsewhere.[5]

THE FOUR SOURCES J, E, D, P

J is regarded as the earliest of the four sources. His interest is in people, their personalities, and their idiosyncracies. It is J who writes about Noah's drunkenness (Genesis 9:18–27), the deceitful manner in which Jacob obtained his father's blessing (Genesis 27:1–45), and the miniature short story about Judah and Tamar (Genesis 38).

J's concept of God is anthropomorphic, that is, has human qualities: God walks in the garden, Adam and Eve hide from him, and there is a brief conversation between God and the first man (Genesis 3:8–13). Abraham barters with God to try save Sodom (Genesis 18:30–33). Moses persuades God to change his mind and not destroy all the Israelites (Exodus 32:9–14).

J has been described as a literary genius, one of the most creative writers in Israelite literature.[6] Another biblical scholar calls J "not only the most gifted biblical writer, but one of the greatest figures in world literature."[7] He considers that his finest piece of writing is in the Joseph story. When Judah offers himself as a substitute hostage for Benjamin, Joseph knows that his brothers have reformed

[4]Herbert F. Hahn *The Old Testament in Modern Resarch* with a survey of recent literature by Horace D. Hummel (Philadelphia: Fortress Press, 1966), p. 11.

[5]With regard to the occurrence of J, Eissfeldt makes the following comment, "The material to be assigned to J is roughly as follows (here as elsewhere no distinction is made between its original compass and any later but relatively insignificant amplifications)." He makes a similar comment in connection with E. *The Old Testament*, pp. 199–200.

Robert H. Pfeiffer, *Introduction to the Old Testament* (New York: Harper and Row, 1948), p. 129
Norman K. Gottwald, *A Light to the Nations* (New York: Harper and Row, 1959). The different sources are discussed in different parts of the book.

Descriptions of documentary sources may be found in other introductions and biblical reference works.

[6]J. Philip Hyatt, "The Compiling of Israel's Story" in *The Interpreters One Volume Commentary on the Bible,* Charles M. Laymon ed. (Nashville, Tenn.: Abingdon Press, 1971), p. 1082.

[7]Ephraim A. Speiser, "Genesis," *Anchor Bible* (New York: Doubleday, 1964), p. xxvii.

(Genesis 44:18–34). Judah's appeal is very moving, "For how can I go back to my father if the lad is not with me? I fear to see the evil that would come upon my father."

Since the time of Wellhausen there has been much discussion about the date of the four documents. J would appear to be not earlier than the tenth century, possibly the ninth. Internal evidence suggests this. The conquest of Edom (Esau is the ancestor of Edom) (Genesis 27:40), and the importance of Judah (Genesis 49:8–12) appear to be assumed, but neither was realized until the time of David in the tenth century. It was probably not until then that a history of the nation was written, because it was only then that the Israelites achieved nationhood with the opportunity for reflective pursuits.

E, the second of the four sources, is closely related to J. It is dated in the eighth or ninth century. Some scholars think that it was written at the same time as J. The initial letter stands for Elohim, the Hebrew name for God used by this writer as contrasted with Yahweh, the Hebrew name for God, used by J. E gives an emphasis to northern traditions associated with Bethel and Schechem (Genesis 31:13, 33:15–20). Coincidentally, E stands for Ephraim, a name used for the northern kingdom. There are other obvious differences between the two writers. E uses the term Amorites; J calls them Canaanites. Isaac's son is Jacob in the E narrative, Israel in J. The Holy Mountain is Horeb in E, Sinai in J. E calls Moses' father-in-law Jethro; J calls him Hobab or Reuel.

God deals less directly with people in E than in J. He makes his wishes known far more through angels and dreams. When Abraham is about to sacrifice Isaac an angel appears and stops him (Genesis 22:1–14). At Bethel Jacob dreams about angels of God going up and down a ladder (Genesis 28:11–12). A dream precipitates the whole Joseph story and the role of Egypt in the history of Israel (Genesis 37:1–11). The dreams of the butler and baker (Genesis 40:1–23) lead to Joseph interpreting the Pharaoh's dream (Genesis 41:1–36).

E has a particular interest in ritual, for example, the sacrifice of Isaac (Genesis 22:1–14), Jacob pouring oil on the stone pillar at Bethel (Genesis 28:17–18), and Moses' consecration of the people at Horeb (Exodus 19:14–16).

E's material is more fragmentary than J's and this had led to questions about the existence of E as a separate document. E does not appear in Genesis until Chapter 15,[8] so it is more difficult to estimate his literary ability. He seems to have made use of older Mesopotamian traditions, as did J. The story of Moses in the bullrushes (Exodus 1:15–2:10) may have been inspired by the Legend of Sargon, the Akkadian monarch of approximately 2400 B.C. who was reportedly cast adrift

[8]With regard to the occurrence of E, Eissfeldt makes the following comment, "To E is to be assigned roughly the following material, again with specification of the secondary additions preserved in the basic material." *The Old Testament,* p. 200.

With regard to the existence of E see:

Ronald E. Clements, "Pentateuchal Problems" in *Tradition and Interpretation,* G. W. Anderson ed. (Oxford: Clarendon Press, 1979). p. 96.

Brevard S. Childs, *Introduction to the Old Testament as Scripture* (Philadelphia: Fortress Press, 1979), pp. 122–23.

like Moses, found and cared for by a gardener, and became a great king. One of the most powerfully presented incidents in the Old Testament, the sacrifice of Isaac, is attributed to E. The two sources J and E are often similar and there is disagreement about what precisely is to be attributed to the one and the other, for example, Genesis 37:21 is attributed to J by one scholar[9] and to E by another.[10]

The third source, D, is contained in one book, Deuteronomy. Deuteronomy is a composite work, the first eleven chapters of which review Israel's wilderness journey and the requirements laid upon the people by the Covenant. The final eight chapters, 27–34, include Moses' blessings and cursings, his final charge to the nation, the appointment of Joshua as leader of Israel, and Moses' death. The original form of both these sections has been debated, but there is a wide agreement that chapters 12–26 can be identified as the Book of the Law discovered in the Temple in 621 during the reign of Josiah.

Deuteronomy is a liturgical work. In it is the Shema, the Jewish prayer "Hear, O Israel: The Lord our God is one Lord; and you shall love the Lord your God with all your heart, and with all your soul, and with all your might." (Deuteronomy 6:4) Another passage is included in Deuteronomy specifically for liturgical use: "And you shall make response before the Lord your God, 'A wandering Aramean was my father; and he went down into Egypt and sojourned there, few in number; and there he became a nation, great, mighty, and populous!'" (Deut. 26:5–10)

Although the Book of the Law was "discovered" in 621, it most likely had a long history. It is thought that it came originally from the Northern Kingdom and was brought to Jerusalem after the fall of Samaria in 721. It was then quietly developed during the reign of Manasseh. Its purpose seems clearly to remind people of their ancient traditions and religious obligations, and, in that, it initially succeeded, for under Josiah it stimulated a brief but thorough religious reform.

The fourth strand of the Pentateuch, P (for the Priestly Code), could be described as a work of genealogies and covenants. It begins with creation in the opening chapter of the Bible, and focuses with increasing sharpness upon the place and the people chosen by God to fulfill his purpose.[11]

The race of mankind, the family of Adam, is first separated from all else that has been created. To Adam is given what may be described as the covenant of the Sabbath (Genesis 2:1–3), and his descendents are traced to Noah (Genesis 5). God makes a covenant with Noah (Genesis 9:1–17), which he ratifies by the sign of a rainbow. Of Noah's three sons, Shem is the one through whom the purposes of God are carried foward, and his descendents are traced to Terah (Genesis 11:10–27). Of Terah's descendents God gives his promise to Abraham, with whom he makes the covenant of circumcision (Genesis 17:1–27). The focus narrows to Abraham's grand-

---

[9]Norman K. Gottwald, *A Light to the Nations* (New York: Harper and Row, 1959), p. 216.
[10]Speiser, "Genesis," pp. 290–91.
[11]Eissfeldt, *Old Testament,* pp. 204–5.

son Jacob and his descendents. Genesis 37 begins, ''Jacob dwelt in the land of his father's sojournings, in the land of Canaan. This is the history of the family of Jacob.'' It is from Jacob's son Levi that Moses and Aaron are descended (Numbers 3.1), and God makes the final covenant of the Law with Moses.

P provides a framework of history divided into major sections identified by covenants and linked by genealogies from the creation to the point at which the Israelites are about to enter the promised land. In this framework are included detailed instructions for the building of the Tabernacle, an equally detailed description of the priests' vestments, instructions about sacrifices and purifications, and a great emphasis upon the importance of holiness before God. All Leviticus and almost all of Numbers are ascribed to P. Leviticus 17-26, however, is regarded separately as the Holiness Code and was originally an independent law code included at some point in the P material.

P is generally dated after the exile, that is, after the Edict of Cyrus in 538 which allowed the Jews to return to Jerusalem. But there has been much discussion about this and now it is believed that P contains both postexilic and preexilic material although its final form was achieved after the exile.[12] Certainly, the elaborate requirements for worship described in Leviticus do not seem to reflect the relatively simple arrangements which appear to have sufficed for Israel before the time of David.

Wellhausen's hypothesis was widely accepted. The division, J, E, D, and P with some emendations, ''had triumphed and it seemed that little or nothing remained to be done.''[13] Yet even at the time of the publication of Wellhausen's book there were doubts expressed about the literary independence of the four sources. J was divided into J[1] and J[2]. One scholar identified an ancient source S,[14] another proposed that underlying J and E was an earlier document, a Grundlage, that is, a foundation or groundwork known as G.[15] The independent existence of E was challenged,[16] and there were other emendations. The purpose of this was to get as close as possible to the original sources, yet increasingly refined divisions of the text raised doubts about the appropriateness of a purely documentary approach. There was a danger that literary analysis could become an end in itself.[17]

Much discussion concerned itself with the dates of the five sources, in particular, as we noted with the date of P.[18] There were different opinions about how many books should be included in the Pentateuch: four, excluding Deuteronomy, so that

[12]Clements, *Tradition and Interpretation,* pp. 105-6.
Childs, *Introduction,* pp. 122-24.
[13]Christopher R. North, "Pentateuchal Criticism" in *The Old Testament and Modern Study,* H. H. Rowley ed. (Oxford: Oxford University Press, 1951), p. 48.
[14]Pfeiffer, *Introduction to the Old Testament,* p. 140.
[15]Clements, *Tradition and Interpretation,* p. 100.
[16]Ibid.
[17]Hahn, *The Old Testament in Modern Research,* p. 22.
[18]Clements, *Tradition and Interpretation,* pp. 105-6.

is was a Tetrateuch; or six, so that it was a Hexateuch, including Joshua. Some scholars wanted to include the historical books through Kings.[19]

These qualifications of the documentary theory seemed to add weight to the criticisms of those who rejected it on various grounds. One scholar concluded his criticism of the theory with the sweeping statement that it "has in reality nothing to support it and is founded on air."[20] Another scholar noted that while Hebrew literature has many affinities with other ancient Near Eastern literature, among which it grew up, "nowhere in the Ancient Orient is there anything which is definitely known to parallel the elaborate history of fragmentary composition and compilation of Hebrew literature (or marked by just such criteria) as the documentary hypothesis would postulate."[21]

It became apparent that concern with documents was only one stage in the examination of the origin and meaning of the Pentateuch, that attention should be given to the social, political, and cultic settings of the documents and the role of oral tradition in shaping them.[22] Pentateuchal criticism thereupon moved from an exclusive study of literary sources to what is known as Form Criticism and Tradition Criticism. The term "criticism" as it is used here does not mean finding fault with, which is a common use of the term. It means rather a careful examination of the biblical text in order to understand it as fully and as accurately as possible. Form Criticism and Tradition Criticism refer to particular kinds of careful examination. They can be treated separately, but they are so interrelated that their distinctiveness from one another is not always clear.[23]

FORM CRITICISM AND TRADITION CRITICISM

A major figure in the development of Form Criticism and Tradition Criticism was Hermann Gunkel. Gunkel's concern was "to find a way of studying the material which would enable the scholar to go beyond literary dissection and to enter esthetically into the interior experience of the people, into their real history."[24] Similarly, "to understand properly the structure and content of the Pentateuch as a whole and in its details, one must attempt to penetrate into the early stages of the history of its traditions."[25] To do that it was necessary to see Israel as part of the broader culture

---

[19]Childs, *Introduction to the Old Testament*, p. 119.

[20]Umberto Cassuto, *The Documentary Hypothesis and Composition of the Pentateuch*, eight lectures, translated from the Hebrew by Israel Abrahams (Jerusalem: The Nagnes Press, 1961).

[21]Kenneth A. Kitchen, *Ancient Orient and Old Testament* (Chicago: InterVarsity Press, 1966).

[22]Samuel H. Hooke, "Introduction to the Pentateuch" in *Peakes Commentary on the Bible,* H. H. Rowley ed (London: Nelson, 1962), p. 170.

[23]Clements, *Tradition and Interpretation*, p. 99, note 7.

[24]Bernhard W. Anderson, "Introduction" and translation, Martin Noth, *A History of Pentateuchal Traditions* (Englewood Cliffs, N.J.: Prentice-Hall, 1972, p. xviii.

[25]Noth, *Pentateuchal Traditions*, p. 2

in which her traditions grew, to see the situation in which she lived. This is the characteristic endeavor of Form Criticism.[26]

The Tradition critical method emphasizes the important role of oral tradition in the development of the Pentateuch. This is not really new. Wellhausen believed that a long period of oral tradition preceded the first written sources. But in the years following the Second World War it was argued that the literary critical method was a modern, anachronistic "book view," based upon a "complete misunderstanding" of the Semitic way of thinking. According to this the alternation of the divine names is not due to different documents but to the different intentions of the writers who used the two names to convey different ideological overtones. In fact the alternation to a large degree "is due to a later attempt at unification," in other words, it is not original. According to this the major sources of the Pentateuch are two oral traditions, and we should "do away" with the documents.[27]

The opposition between written and oral traditions may, however, be a false one. Both methods of transmission existed together during the development of the Pentateuch. The existence of written documents appears certain, so that literary critical methods of analysis "remain indispensable to the study of the Pentateuch."[28] As one writer puts it, "if we bury the 'documents,' we shall have to resurrect them—or something very like them."[29]

REDACTION CRITICISM

Redaction Criticism, a more recent development in Pentateuchal criticism,[30] is so called because of its concern with the redactor, or the editor, of the books which make up the Pentateuch. Clearly, the person who edited them into their final form played a very important role, as significant, perhaps, as the authors of the original documents.[31] Such editorial work was so important that one should ask whether the final edited version had not become "greater than merely the sum of its parts."[32]

The view of Redaction Criticism is that to understand the composition of the Pentateuch, one must study not only the underlying sources but also, if possible, how and why they were put into their final form. This will involve not only a study of the *final* redactor because the Pentateuch consists of many documents, each edited

[26]Albrecht Alt, "The Origins of Israelite Law" in *Essays on Old Testament History and Religion,* R.A. Wilson trans. (New York: Doubleday Anchor, 1958), p. 160.

[27]Ivan Engnell, *Critical Essays on the Old Testament,* translated from the Swedish by John T. Willis with Helmer Ringgren (London: S.P.C.K., 1970), pp. 53–55.
See also North, "Pentateuchal Criticism," pp. 65 and 76.

[28]Clements, *Tradition and Interpretation,* p. 97.

[29]North, "Pentateuchal Criticism," p. 77.

[30]Clements, *Tradition and Interpretation,* p. 119.

[31]Ibid., p. 122.

[32]Noth, *Pentateuchal Traditions,* p. 25.

and combined, reedited and recombined many times. The primary importance of the authors of J, E, D, and P then yields to the influence of the *redactors* who edited them, although the distinction between an author and a redactor may be a difficult one to draw.[33]

A POST-CRITICAL ALTERNATIVE

Concern with the final form of the biblical text is similar in certain respects to what is described as a "post-critical alternative." From the publication of Astruc's book in 1753 to the present, there has been an enormous amount of scholarship devoted to the composition of the Pentateuch. Any attempt "to offer a different approach to the study of the Pentateuch which does not take into account the achievements of historical critical scholarship over the last two hundred years is both naive and arrogant."[34] Nevertheless, an alternative has been proposed which is a significantly different approach from those critical methods which we have considered. It rests upon the belief that while we should be familiar with historical origins we should also look closely at the biblical text to "discern its function for a community of faith."[35] The Bible is ultimately and primarily a religious document, whose value to members of that community is in how it functions for them as believers.

This is illustrated in connection with the question of Mosaic authorship. As we have seen, there are many reasons against the claim that Moses wrote the Pentateuch. Yet the Old Testament declares specifically that Moses wrote down all the words of the law (Exodus 24:4), and that he wrote down the laws in a book "to the very end" (Deuteronomy 31:24–25). To regard this as a historical issue, it is argued, is to misunderstand it.[36] The claim of Mosaic authorship is not a historical judgment. The biblical redactors did not intend it to be. It is a theological judgment, intended to support the authority of the law with which Moses was associated.

The claim therefore "functioned theologically within the community to establish the continuity of the faith of successive generations with that which had once been delivered to Moses at Sinai."[37]

The modern reader who understands this may recognize that a historically invalid claim is theologically valid in terms of the meaning it is intended to convey to members of their community. It is then no longer an unintentional historical contradiction but an intentional theological assertion.

[33]Clements, *Tradition and Interpretation,* p. 120.

[34]Childs, *Introduction to the Old Testament,* p. 127.

[35]Ibid., p. 83.

[36]Ibid., p. 133.

[37]Ibid., p. 135. For a critical review of Brevard Child's position see Sean E. McEvenue, "The Old Testament, Scripture or Theology," *Interpretation* Vol. XXXVI.3 (July 1981), p. 229. He writes that "for the most part, the canon is no more than an anthology of inspirational books, linked for the most part without altering the meaning of the individual books."

Caves at Qumran, the northeast corner of the Dead Sea, where numerous ancient copies and fragments of Old Testament texts were discovered in 1947. Photo by Elizabeth Gordon.

THE OLD TESTAMENT CANON AND TEXT

The Old Testament was written in Hebrew[38] over a period of about a thousand years. One of the earliest Old Testament passages is the Song of Deborah (Judges 5:1–31), which may be contemporary with the events it describes (ca. 1200). The latest Old Testament book is Daniel, written during the persecution of Antiochus Epiphanes just before the Maccabean revolt in 167 B.C. About a hundred years earlier, during the third century B.C., a Greek translation of the Old Testament was made for the Greek-speaking Jews who lived in Egypt. This translation was called the Septuagint or LXX (the Roman numerals for 70) because of the tradition that seventy-two translators, six from each of the twelve tribes of Israel, were employed in making the translation.

The Septuagint was the scripture of the New Testament world, and quotations in the New Testament from the Old Testament are taken, in most instances, from the Septuagint. At that time, the time of Christ and his first followers, there was no closed Hebrew canon, no definitive list of authoritative Hebrew books regarded as divinely inspired. Such books, in the language of the day, "defiled the hands," they were so holy that they infected the hands which touched them with their holiness.

The process of closing the Hebrew canon was accelerated by the fall and destruction of Jerusalem in A.D. 70. The loss of Jerusalem, the ancient center of Jewish worship, made it essential that the Jewish people know which of their religious books had unquestioned authority and which were simply edifying. It is possible that the spread of the new religion, Christianity, whose original converts were all Jews, also provided an impetus to make clear which books were an authoritative account of Jewish faith.

The canonical process began almost two hundred years before the Christian era and most of the books which were finally included in the Hebrew canon were recognized as canonical by the middle of the first century A.D. But the process was not complete until the end of the second century.

On the frontispiece of a Hebrew Bible, which is found in what is ordinarily the back of the book because Hebrew is written from right to left, is the title "Book of Law, Prophets and Writings."

The Protestant canon is the same as the Hebrew canon except that the books are numbered differently; Samuel, Kings, Chronicles, and Ezra-Nehemiah are each one book in the Hebrew canon. They are each two books in the Protestant canon. The Book of the Twelve is one book in the Hebrew canon, twelve books in the Protestant canon. This division creates 15 additional books, which increase the 24 books of the Hebrew canon to 39 books of the Protestant canon.

The Roman Catholic canon includes several books not included in the other two canons. These books, which are found in the Apocrypha in Protestant Bibles, are as follows:

[38]Some parts of the Old Testament were written in Aramaic, notably Ezra 4:8–6:18, 7:12–26, and Daniel 2:46–7:28.

Tobit
Judith
The Wisdom of Solomon
Ecclesiasticus (or the Wisdom of Ben Sirach)
Baruch, which includes the Epistle of Jeremiah
I Maccabees
II Maccabees

The Roman Catholic canon also includes additional material in Esther and Daniel. Esther is 107 verses longer, Daniel includes the Prayer of Azariah, the Song of the Three Young Men, the Story of Susanna, and the Story of Bel and the Dragon.

Modern translations of the Old Testament are based on the Massoretic text, so called after the Massoretes, Jewish scholars who worked in Palestine and Babylonia from the sixth to the tenth centuries A.D. The name massora is the Hebrew word for tradition. The Massoretes devoted themselves to ensuring that the Hebrew text was copied exactly and that traditional interpretations and corrections of the text were carefully preserved. The oldest Massoretic text is from the eleventh century A.D., a long time removed from the events of the Old Testament. Yet the discovery at Qumran, a few miles south of Jericho, of Hebrew texts which are almost 1300 years earlier, 150–170 B.C., has shown that the Massoretes were extremely accurate. We may therefore be confident that what we read in our English Bible is very close to what was originally written.,

For many centuries the Bible of Western Europe was the Vulgate, a Latin translation made by Jerome between A.D. 382 and 405. An English translation of the Vulgate was made, or initiated, by John Wycliffe, an Oxford theologian, in the latter part of the fourteenth century, a thousand years later.

The first English translation of the Hebrew and Greek texts was the work of William Tyndale. His New Testament appeared in 1525 and the Pentateuch and other parts of the Old Testament in 1534. Vigorous efforts made to suppress the books failed because, with the invention of printing, copies could be produced faster than they could be destroyed. Unhappily Tyndale was martyred for his courageous scholarship but not long after his death the use of the Bible in English was officially sanctioned in England.

By the end of the sixteenth century there were so many translations and so many editions that a conference of church leaders proposed that a new translation be made ''as consonant as can be to the original Hebrew and Greek.'' The result was the publication in 1611 of what we know as the Authorized or King James Version, which for 300 years was the preeminent Bible of the English-speaking world.

The publication of the Revised Version of the New Testament on May 17, 1881, was a major event on both sides of the Atlantic. The Chicago Tribune and the Chicago Times each published the entire contents in their paper five days later. Three million copies of the Revised New Testament were sold in England and the United States in the first year of publication. The Old Testament appeared May 19, 1885.

Working with the English revisers were Old Testament and New Testament American committees which prepared the American Standard Edition of the Revised Version (American Standard Version), published in 1901.

In the half century following the publication of the English Revised Version, many older biblical manuscripts were discovered, which led to a greater understanding of the biblical text. It was found that the New Testament was written in Koine Greek, that is, in the common language of the first century Mediterranean world. The Apostle Paul, for example, was not writing in a special ''biblical'' language as some had thought, but in the everyday language of the ordinary people he lived with.

In light of the advances in knowledge of the biblical languages, the International Council of Religious Education authorized a committee, in 1937, to prepare a revision of the 1901 American Standard Version. The resulting New Testament was published in 1946 and the complete Bible in 1952. This version, the Revised Standard Version, has been widely adopted. It is the version used for quotations in this text.

Other notable translations of the Bible are those of James Moffat, 1926, and Ronald Knox, 1949, both of which are excellent but are not now well known. The Jerusalem Bible was published in 1966, the New English Bible in 1970, and Good News for Modern Man in 1976.

The translators of the Revised Standard Version concluded their Preface with this conviction, that the Word of God ''must not be disguised in phrases that are no longer clear, or hidden under words that have changed or lost their meaning. It must stand forth in language that is direct and plain and meaningful to people today. It is our hope and our earnest prayer that this Revised Standard Version of the Bible may be used by God to speak to men in these momentous times, and to help them to understand and believe and obey his Word.''[39]

It is a hope which has been fulfilled. There has never been a time when those who wish to read and study the scriptures without a knowledge of Hebrew or Greek can do so with such accuracy.

[39] *The Holy Bible,* Revised Standard Version containing the Old and New Testaments (New York: Thomas Nelson and Sons, 1952), p. x.

QUESTIONS FOR DISCUSSION

The following questions refer to Chapters 4–6.

1. If historical concerns must be set in perspective when studying the biblical text (see Chapter 6), is that not also true with regard to cultural considerations? For example, what value is there for the student of the Old Testament in knowing details of the religion of Mesopotamia, or what is the purpose of attempting to understand the Exodus from the Egyptian point of view?

2. If the Pentateuch is a compilation of many documents written at different times, how are we to understand the claim that it is divinely inspired? Wouldn't the inspiration be the human achievement of the final editors rather than the work of God?

3. The title of Chapter 4 is "Israel in Egypt," but can we really speak of "Israel" before the Covenant? What connection is there between the family of Abraham and his immediate descendents and the people who gathered at Sinai and at Shechem?

4. The giving of the Covenant has been regarded as the central event of the Old Testament. Yet the Covenant was largely neglected after the time of Joshua. How important do you think the Covenant was in the development of the religious life of Israel?

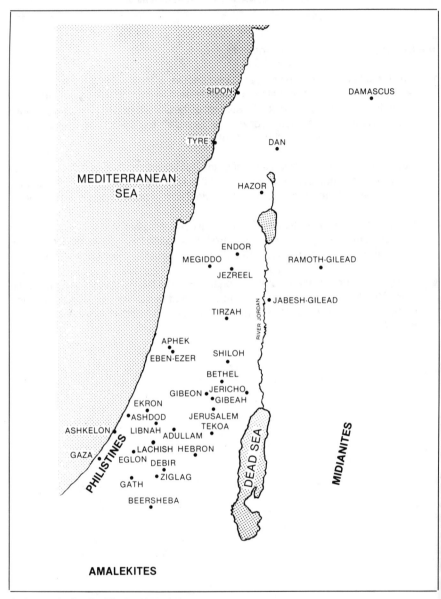

Joshua to the Death of Saul c 1250–1000 B.C.

CHAPTER SEVEN
THE CONQUEST

According to Exodus 16:35, the Israelites were in the wilderness for forty years. Much of that time was spent at the oasis of Kadesh Barnea, which they either occupied or conquered; at any rate it became their semi-permanent home. They had attempted to advance into Palestine from the south but were defeated (Numbers 13-14), and it was a long time before they entered the Promised Land. When they did so it was from the east, from what is known as Transjordan.

We read in Numbers 20:14-17 that Moses sent messengers from Kadesh to the king of Edom "Now let us pass through your land. We will not pass through field or vineyard, neither will we drink water from a well; we will go along the King's Highway, we will not turn aside to the right hand or to the left, until we have passed through your territory." The Edomites, however, did not trust them and refused permission to enter. This is not surprising. Although the reported number of Israelites who left Egypt, 600,000 men, not counting dependents and "a mixed multitude who went up with them", was certainly inflated (Exodus 12:37-38), by the time they reached Edom they were probably a considerable number. We are not told how many, but after skirting both Edom and Moab they fought and defeated the kingdom of Sihon and Bashan (Numbers 21:27-35). There were therefore enough men to be dangerous. Without a mutual agreement any country could be attacked by any other, so it was practical wisdom to be suspicious of strangers, especially armed strangers in large numbers.

Part of the evidence frequently used to support a thirteenth century data for the Exodus is the claim, based on archeological investigations, that the Transjordan states were themselves only recently established. Had the Israelites passed through this territory any earlier than they did, it is claimed, they would have encountered no opposition because the states would not have been there.[1] This would appear to preclude a date before the thirteenth century. But it does not preclude a later date. Subsequent explorations in the area of ancient Edom suggest that it is "most unlikely that there was any national unity in Edom, of a kind implied by the biblical narrative, before the mid-ninth century B.C."[2]

By the time the Israelites crossed the Jordan they had gained considerable territory on the east side. Moses was dead, Joshua was the new leader. The book of Joshua represents them as fighters with high morale, so it seems plausible that they could have swept through Palestine, as the text describes, scoring victory after victory until the land was theirs.

The crossing of the Jordan was an occasion of great solemnity. In a manner reminiscent of the crossing of the Red Sea (Exodus 14), when the priests carrying the Ark stepped into the river, the waters parted. Twelve stones were set up on the river bed, one for each of the tribes of Israel, and as they completed their crossing the waters returned back. Joshua then spoke to the people.

> When your children ask their fathers in time to come, "What do these stones mean?" then you shall let your children know, "Israel passed over this Jordan on dry ground." For the Lord your God dried up the waters of the Jordan for you until you passed over as the Lord your God did to the Red Sea, which he dried up for us until we passed over, so that all the peoples of the earth may know that the hand of the Lord is mighty that you may fear the Lord your God for ever. (Joshua 4:21–24)

JOSHUA'S THREE CAMPAIGNS

The chapters following (Joshua 5–11) tell the story of Joshua's victorious campaign Joshua 5–8 describe the first campaign, the capture of Jericho and Ai in the centr part of the country. It was a victory of great strategic importance. With their alread captured territory to the east of the Jordan, not all of which they continued to occup these two cities provided the Israelites with a powerful bridgehead from which to atta the other parts of Canaan.

It was then that a number of Canaanite rulers decided they must band togeth to fight the new enemy. Canaan was nominally under the control of Egypt, but

---

[1] Nelson Glueck, *The Other Side of the Jordan* (Cambridge, Mass.: American Schools of Orier Research, 1970), p. 153.

[2] John H. Hayes and J. Maxwell Miller, *Israelite and Judaean History* (Philadelphia: The Westmins Press, 1977), pp. 90, 153, 258.

View from ruins of ancient city of Jericho looking toward the Jordan (*Joshua 5:12–6:31*). Photo by Elizabeth Gordon.

was ineffective control, which would partly explain the success of the Israelites against superior Canaanite forces and their well-defended cities. The Gibeonites, for example, did not trust their allies and made a separate treaty with Israel, even though they lied about who they were (Joshua 9:3–15). The initial coalition (Joshua 9:1–2) apparently did not do anything, but another coalition was formed hastily against Gibeon (Joshua 10:1–5). The Israelites, by contrast, are represented as having a unified command and a clear objective. When Gibeon appealed to them for help against the five kings of the southern cities: Jerusalem, Hebron, Jarmuth, Lachish, and Eglon, the Israelites responded with élan. They set out during the night from their encampment in Gilgal, attacked the coalition, drove the Canaanite forces through the mountainous country west toward the sea as far as Beth Horon, trapped the five Kings, and killed them (Joshua 10:7–27).

The Israelites pressed their initiative, destroying one city after another between the highlands and the sea: Makkedah, Libnah, Lachish, Eglon, Hebron, and Debir (Joshua 10:28–43). That was the second campaign.

The third campaign culminated in the capture of the northern city of Hazor.[3]

---

[3]There is an instructive drawing of what the city may have looked like in G. Ernest Wright, Robert Johnston, and James B. Pritchard, "Great People of the Bible and How They Lived," *Reader's Digest,* '4, p. 107.

By ancient standards it was huge, with 40,000 inhabitants, finely constructed buildings, and great double walls. Jabin, the King of Hazor, became alarmed at the success of the Israelites and gathered a coalition of city-states to attack them at the waters of Merom. Joshua acted as promptly as he had done before. He made a surprise attack, routed the enemy forces, hamstrung their horses, and burned their chariots. He then turned to Hazor, which without its troops was defenseless, captured it, destroyed everything there that breathed, and set it on fire (Joshua 11:6–14). The reader is left to imagine the sudden horror which fell upon the unprotected population as the Israelites stormed in to kill and smash and burn.

The account of Joshua's campaigns concludes, "So Joshua took the whole land, according to all that the Lord had spoken to Moses: and Joshua gave it for an inheritance to Israel according to their tribal allotments. And the land had rest from war." (Joshua 11:23)

QUESTIONS ABOUT THE BIBLICAL ACCOUNT

But this relatively straightforward narrative has been challenged as providing neither a complete nor an accurate account of what actually happened. At the beginning of the book of Judges the people's first concern after Joshua's death was: Who will fight the Canaanites? (Judges 1:1) Hebron, reputedly captured by Joshua (Joshua 10:36–37), had to be captured again, similarly Debir (Judges 1:11; see also Joshua 10:38–39). In other words, the whole country had not been taken, it was not at peace.

A number of years ago it appeared that Jericho's great wall had collapsed violently at about the time it was believed the Israelites attacked it, but more recently it has been shown that in the thirteenth century, the time of the conquest, Jericho was little more than a fort. The walls had been destroyed long before.[4]

The word Ai means "ruin," which is explained in Joshua 8:28 as the result of the ruinous condition to which it was reduced by Joshua. But by Joshua's time the city had been a ruin for almost a thousand years.[5] These discrepancies and contradictions are part of the material of a considerable scholarly debate about how the Israelites settled in Canaan. This debate is concerned not only with the historical value of the Joshua narrative itself, but with entirely different alternatives, or "models" as one writer calls them.[6] The biblical account is only one of these models, presenting the settlement as a conquest. The other models reject, almost entirely, the idea of conquest in favor of an immigration of peoples into Canaan, or a revolt of the native Canaanite inhabitants.

[4]Kathleen Kenyon, *Digging Up Jericho* (New York: Praeger, 1957), Chapter xi.
See also "Interpretation and Excavation" in John R. Bartlett, *Jericho* (Grand Rapids, Mich.: William B. Eerdmans, 1983), p. 27.
[5]Kathleen Kenyon, *Archeology and the Holy Land* (London: Ernest Benn Limited, 1960), p. 15
[6]Norman K. Gottwald, *The Tribes of Yahweh* (Maryknoll, N.Y.: Orbis Books, 1979), pp. 191–9

SOME RESPONSES TO THE QUESTIONS
ABOUT THE BIBLICAL ACCOUNT

In general the biblical account of the conquest is not regarded as historical. One writer describes it as "a fictional construction."[7] Yet before we accept such a judgment we should consider what responses there are to the critical questions. Is the matter settled, or is something still to be said for the biblical account?

If, for example, Joshua 1–12 and Judges 1 are understood as parallel histories of the same events, they are not contradictory. This view is widely held, with Judges 1 believed to be the earlier account.

Moreover, before we criticize such a passage as Joshua 11:23, "So Joshua took the whole land, according to all that the Lord had spoked to Moses. . ." which was not correct because much of the land still remained to be conquered, we should consider what the book had *not* claimed that Israel conquered. Joshua 11:16 reports "So Joshua took all that land, the hill country and all the Negeb and all the land of Goshen and the lowland and the Arabah and the hill country of Israel and its lowland. . . ." Not claimed were the coastal plain and the Plain of Jezreel, which were along the line of an important trade route between Egypt and Syria, Gezer and Jerusalem. Moreover, in the case of cities reported captured in Judges 1, which were already captured in Joshua 1–11, there is archeological proof of cities being captured, recaptured, and captured again in those tumultuous times.[8]

The questions about Ai and Jericho must, it is argued, be set in a larger context. The work of archeologists has shown that some of the claims in Joshua 1–11 are inaccurate. But it has also shown, according to some scholars, that in general the account given in Joshua is reliable.

If, for example, Joshua were to lead a campaign against the territory occupied by Judah, "then we must admit that Joshua 10 described precisely the way he should have done it."[9]

The cities of Libnah, Lachish, and Eglon, between the sea and the highlands, had to be taken to control the area of southern Palestine, which was the strategy used by both the Assyrian King Sennacherib and the Babylonian King Nebuchadnezzar hundreds of years later.

Excavations in Lachish indicate a tremendous destruction during the thirteenth century, that is, the time of the Conquest. A bowl found in the debris in the place where it was smashed suggests that it was broken during the destruction of the city. Pottery such as bowls and pieces of pottery were frequently used for writing notes. On this bowl was written a memorandum of wheat deliveries from local harvests dated the fourth year of the reigning Pharaoh. The Pharaoh is not identified for sure, but he writing indicates the reign of Mereneptah or his immediate successors, which

[7] J. Alberto Soggin, *Joshua* (Philadelphia: The Westminster Press, 1972), p. 17.
[8] John Bright, "Joshua," *The Interpreters Bible*, Vol. 2 (Nashville, Tenn.: Abingdon Press, 1953).
[9] G. Ernest Wright, *Biblical Archeology* (Philadelphia: The Westminster Press, 1972), p. 4.

Archeological dig: Lachish (*2 Chronicles 32:9*). Photo by Elizabeth Gordon.

would place the fall of the city in the last twenty years of the thirteenth century, the time which other evidence indicates for the conquest. If the surmise is correct, Lachish and the neighboring cities were destroyed about 1220–1200 B.C., a view supported by excavations at Eglon and Debir, both of which were destroyed completely between 1250–1200.

With regard to Joshua's campaign in the North, excavations have shown that Hazor was occupied up to the time it was destroyed.[10] Homes have been uncovered with furnishings still there. The end came suddenly and violently in the thirteenth century. In the cases of Hazor, Debir, Lachish, and Bethel, the next level of building consisted of poor settlements with limited occupation without city walls.[11] Not until the time of Solomon, 200 years later, did Israelite cities achieve the sophistication of the Canaanite cities which Joshua and his army destroyed.

[10]William F. Albright, *The Biblical Period from Abraham to Ezra* (New York: Harper and Row, 1963). Albright's discussion in Chapter III, "The Conquest of Palestine," essentially accepts the biblical account in terms of his extensive knowledge of the period.

Yigdal Yadin, "Further Light on Biblical Hazor," *Biblical Archeologist,* Vol. 20.2 (May 1957), p. 34.

[11]Roland de Vaux, *The Early History of Israel,* David Smith trans. (Philadelphia: Westminster Press, 1978), p. 660.

What about Jericho and Ai? An explanation for the story of Ai is that it has been confused with Bethel, only a mile away. There is no account of the destruction of Bethel in Joshua, although it is referred to in Judges 1:22–25. It is known that the city was destroyed with great violence in the thirteenth century, the same time as the other cities referred to. The tradition of Ai could then refer to the capture and destruction to Bethel.

There is no such useful explanation for the Jericho story, but as the first city in Palestine to be conquered by the Israelites, the memory of its former greatness may have given the event an importance it did not merit.

We therefore have evidence that those cities which the Bible claims were captured and destroyed by Joshua were destroyed at about the time that the Israelite forces would have been entering Palestine. We do not know that the destruction was caused by the Israelites, but it seems to be a reasonable assumption.

FURTHER QUESTIONS ABOUT THE BIBLICAL ACCOUNT

Nevertheless, these explanations themselves call for explanation. Granting that the biblical account does not mention territory which had not been conquered, it was still a considerable part of the land, and it remained non-Israelite for a long period. In the light of that, how do we understand the "settlement"? Jerusalem, for example, was not conquered until it was defeated by David and Joab. There is no record of Schechem having been taken, and it is likely that it was acquired by the Israelites in some way other than by conquest.

There are also further uncertainties in the biblical account. Many cities were destroyed in the thirteenth century at about the time that the Israelites established themselves in Canaan. We do not know for sure that the Israelites were the ones who caused the destruction, even though it has seemed reasonable to suppose that they were responsible. We know, however, that at least some military activity in Canaan was initiated by the Egyptians. The often quoted stele or monumental tablet, erected by Pharaoh Mereneptah (1224–1211) to celebrate his victories in Canaan, lists a number of cities which he destroyed.

> Canaan is plundered with every evil;
> Ashkelon is taken; Gezer is captured;
> Yanoam is made nonexistent;
> Israel lies desolate; its seed is no more[12]

The reference to Israel, the earliest reference outside the Bible, indicates a people rather than country permanently settled.

But to conclude that the Israel of the stele are the Israelites of the Bible is,

[12]D. Winton Thomas ed., *Documents from Old Testament Times* (New York: Harper, 1958), p. 139.

according to one scholar, "neither a necessary interpretation nor one that . . .can easily be harmonized with the biblical narratives of the conquest."[13] Yet, insofar as the stele commemorates Egyptian conquests it shows that not all destruction in Canaan at that time can be attributed to the Israelites. It is possible, as we shall see, that many Canaanite cities were destroyed by the Canaanites themselves in a protracted revolution against their Canaanite overlords. According to one view nothing in the archeological evidence shows that the cities were destroyed in a coordinated campaign rather than a period of twenty-five to fifty years during the late thirteenth and early twelfth centuries. "Any combination of Israelite, Egyptians, Canaanite, or other attackers could have destroyed many more than the score or so cities so far identified."[14]

The biblical account of Joshua's conquests is therefore not without difficulties for those concerned with historical exactness.[15]

IMMIGRATION AND ASSIMILATION

A far-reaching alternative to the biblical account is to regard the conquest as a lengthy process of immigration and assimilation. It has been proposed that Israelite occupation did not ensue from a warlike encounter, but that the occupation of the land took place "fairly quietly and peacefully on the whole and without seriously disturbing the great mass of the previous inhabitants."[16] This would have been a long process in which different tribes settled the land at different times. They resorted to force on occasion and were victorious, but those were minor military conquests which did not bring the Israelites into conflict with the "main mass of the Canaanites."[17] For the most part the newcomers and the resident population lived together and were assimilated to one another.

This explanation of the Israelite settlement has been criticized as itself a selective interpretation of the biblical text. It is as difficult to establish that force was rarely if ever used by the Israelites as it is to establish that it was used in all the instances of Canaanite cities destroyed in the thirteenth century.[18] Yet the immigration model offers an explanation which seems to be consistent with what we know about those

[13]Hayes and Miller, *Israelite and Judaean History,* p. 152.

[14]Gottwald, *Tribes of Yahweh,* p. 202.

[15]Brevard S. Childs, *Introduction to the Old Testament as Scripture* (Philadelphia: Fortress Press, 1979 p. 243.

See Rivka Gonen, "Urban Canaan in the Late Bronze Period," *Bulletin of the American Schoo of Oriental Research* No. 253 (Winter 1984), pp. 69–70.

"Only a handful of settlements were surrounded by a wall during the entire period (14th an 13th centuries) or even during part of it . . .The historic implications of this picture, especially in conne tion with the later Israelite conquest and settlement, may be far reaching . . ."

[16]Martin Noth, *The History of Israel,* Stanley Godman trans. (New York: Harper and Bros., 1958 p. 69.

[17]Ibid., p. 68.

[18]Gottwald, *Tribes of Yahweh,* p. 205.

shifting patterns of settlement among ancient peoples who did not live in towns or villages.

THE REVOLT MODEL

What is described as the "revolt model" derives considerably from a thesis that every 250 or 300 years, namely, every tenth generation, there was widespread disruption throughout the ancient Near Eastern world.[19] By the end of the late Bronze Age, a period which lasted from approximately the middle of the thirteenth century to the end of the twelfth, the empires and city-states of the area had reached a "critical mass" stage and they broke down entirely.[20] "Society everywhere, then, became fragmented, poor, and crude in comparison with the preceding epoch."[21]

Conditions had been badly disturbed in Canaan for a long period. Traditionally the country was subject to Egypt, but in the fourteenth century we know that Egyptian control was lax and ineffective. Letters written then by rulers and officials in Canaan, appealing to the Pharaoh for help which never came, and filled with mutual accusations of disloyalty, also blamed a group of people known as Habiru for much of the disruption. The Habiru were gypsylike nomads, Semites and non-Semites who infiltrated Canaan from the north, who often hired themselves out as mercenaries and for a time controlled areas of the country, in particular around Shechem under the leadership of an individual, Labayu. The name Hebrew may be derived from Habiru. It is possible that the Habiru formed a group which was at least partially related to the Israelites, and so were ready to welcome the Israelites when they arrived in Canaan from Egypt.[22]

The rise and fall of Egyptian control affected the rulers of city-states in Canaan, but not the lower class of people at the bottom of the social hierarchy. Conditions did not change for them no matter who ruled. Many of these people would appear to have joined with the Habiru to overthrow their Canaanite feudal masters. According to this view social and political disruption became so widespread and severe that existing political structures were not able to cope. It was then that the Israelites of the Exodus arrived at Canaan, which had already suffered extensive destruction independently of the "so-called Israelite conquest."[23] The movement of the Israelites was therefore more an occupation than a conquest, and such fighting as there was consisted of mainly "guerilla type attacks upon very small professional units."[24]

[19]George E. Mendenhall, *The Tenth Generation,* (Baltimore: The Johns Hopkins University Press, 1973).

[20]George E. Mendenhall, "Change and Decay in All Around I See: Conquest, Covenant, and the Tenth Generation,* printed in *Biblical Archeologist* Vol. 39.4 (December 1972), p. 152.

[21]Ibid.

[22]Mendenhall, *The Tenth Generation,* p. 122.

[23]Mendenhall, "Change and Decay," p. 154.

[24]Ibid.

The objections which have been raised against this model are that it has no foundation in the biblical text, and that it imposes modern notions of revolt upon an ancient situation.[25] If, however, we consider modern examples of revolt, we might also have to modify the ideological character of the revolt model. Not all Russian peasants who joined the revolution in 1917 did so because they were converted to Communism; for many it must have been because it was the thing to do, for others because it promised an advantage. We may assume that the inhabitants of Canaan were no less eclectic in their reasons for joining the Yahwehist revolution. We need to be as much on guard against the almost seductive attractions of sociological explanation, which seem to explain so much, as we must be against a critical desire to reject the biblical account, which seems to explain so little. One suspects that the truth of the matter will include all three models: conquest, assimilation, and revolt and, in fact, one is seldom advanced independently of the other two.[26]

THE PURPOSE OF JOSHUA

Joshua was written or edited in its final form for a purpose, only part of which was that of recording history. Much more, it was a record of God at work in fulfillment of his promise. The "fictional construction" of the book could therefore be described as deliberate and no more deceptive than the parables of the New Testament. The Deuteronomic history as a whole, of which Joshua is a part, "sets out to show to a community which was ready to listen, the actions which God had carried out through the history of mankind," in particular through the history of his chosen people.[27] It is history written with a theological purpose, but it is not fiction. The discipline of historiography was not unknown in Israel by the seventh century B.C., and one would suppose that scribes responsible for such work, who were members of an ancient intellectual profession, would have had certain inhibitions about how they handled traditional material. The exception to this would be if the editor produced a book which, like Jonah or Esther, was manifestly not intended to be historical. But it is not unequivocally clear that that is so. In fact, as we have noted, the first twelve chapters of Joshua may be regarded, with reservations, as a plausible account of what happened

It would seem then, that in assessing the historicity of the book of Joshua and the validity of various models we should not assume that the case for any of the model is closed.[28]

[25]Gottwald, *Tribes of Yahweh*, p. 885

[26]Ibid., p. 191

[27]Soggin, *Joshua*, p. 4.

[28]de Vaux, *The Early History of Israel*, p. 673.

CHAPTER EIGHT
JUDGES

The picture given in the book of Judges seems to be one of a fairly easygoing relationship between the Israelites and the Canaanites. We read that "The people in Israel dwelt among the Canaanites, the Hittites, the Amorites, the Perizzites, the Hivites and the Jebusites; and they took their daughters to themselves for wives, and their own daughters they gave to their sons; and they served their gods." (Judges 3:5-6)

The worship of Baal was so normal among the Israelites that Gideon's father worshipped at a Baal altar, and when Gideon destroyed it his parent's neighbors were outraged and tried to kill him (Judges 6:25-30).

To the editor of the book of Joshua, this was just another example of the degenerate condition into which the Israelites could fall when they allowed themselves to be seduced by the religion of the country they had conquered. Yet, if we accept the views, discussed in the preceding chapter, that the Israelites were predominantly Canaanite, or that large numbers of disaffected Canaanites willingly embraced the new religion in the course of revolution, the prevalence of Baal worship is understandable. In the christianizing of Europe heathen practices were often incorporated into the new faith with little more than a change of name. There would seem to be similarities between this and what happened in the early stages of the Israelite settlement. While the later editors of the book of Judges regarded this as gross paganism, it could well have seemed to Israelites, such as Gideon's family, religiously sensible behavior.

Excavation at Dan: note small size of rooms (*Judges 20:1*). Photo by Elizabeth Gordon.

Even if we do not argue for assimilation or revolt the victorious conquerors could have acted upon what seemed to them a logical train of thought. In the ancient world survival depended upon adequate harvests, which were under the control of the gods. It may have seemed to the newly settled followers of Joshua that while Yahweh was Israel's God and had brought them victory, when it came to growing crops in Palestine the gods in the Canaanite pantheon knew best.

Perhaps, too, the poor and uncultured Israelites squatting on the ruins of Canaanite cities discovered that Canaanite religion was emotionally and aesthetically more appealing than the religion they brought with them.[1] What we should bear in mind, however, when discussing this matter, is that ultimately it was not the Baalim who became the gods of Israel but Yahweh, the God of Abraham. That tremendous fact is somewhat obscured in the biblical account because it so clearly is what is going to happen. If, however, the other interpretations are considered, the victory of Yahweh over Baal was an event of immense importance which was by no means a foregone conclusion. Even so, we find at the beginning of the corporate life of Israel a commitment to God more profound than the general appearance given by scripture might indicate; Gideon's father was ready to excuse his son's destruction of the Baal altar

[1]William F. Albright, *The Biblical Period from Abraham to Ezra* (New York: Harper, 1963), p. 3.

and the angry neighbors were willing to be persuaded (Judges 6:28–32). After the horrible episode of Gibeah (Judges 19), which incidentally shows that the Old Testament writers did not try to give an idealized picture of the growth of their nation, the Levite appealed to the scattered tribes by proclaiming, "Such a thing has never happened or been seen from the day that the people of Israel came up out of the land of Egypt until this day; consider it, take counsel, and speak." (Judges 19:30)

It was an appeal that worked. We read that "all the people of Israel came out from Dan to Beersheba" (Judges 20:1). Despite the Israelites' ugly selfishness and their apostasy, there was respect for the tradition of God who brought them out of Egypt. Their reply, and the strong action they took against the Benjaminites who refused to punish the crime committed in their territory, implied that the moral commands of God, though held loosely much of the time, could not be disregarded. That was the often muted but essentially dynamic factor which held the tribes together.[2]

During this period, though near the end of it, we find the simple faithfulness of Hannah, the mother of Samuel (1 Samuel 1). Clearly then, the way of life that God required was not forgotten, even if widely ignored.[3]

ISRAELITE STUBBORNNESS AND GOD'S RESPONSE

While the Israelites faced religious and cultural dangers they faced a more obvious danger from various peoples who wished to destroy them. The chance of that happening was real because of the geographical separateness of the Israelite tribes. The tribes in the north were separated from those in the south by the Jezreel Valley, where the Canaanites were still powerful, and the tribes in the east were separated from all the other tribes by the Jordan river and the central highlands.

As well as these physical barriers there were personal antagonisms between the tribes; for example, Ephraim's jealous behavior with both Gideon and Jephtha (Judges 8:1–3, 12:1–6) and Benjamin's haughty and defensive attitude toward their fellow Israelites (Judges 20:12–15). Rather like the Canaanite kings the tribes united only in moments of gravest danger. Even in such moments not all the tribes took part in the various battles; for example, in the battle against the Canaanites there were divided loyalties in the tribe of Reuben, and competing interests in Dan and Asher (Judges 5:15–17).

[2]George E. Mendenhall, "Social Organization in Early Israel," *Magnalia Dei: The Mighty Acts of God,* essays on the Bible and Archeology in memory of G. Ernest Wright, edited by Frank Moore Cross, Werner E. Lemke, and Patrick D. Miller, Jr. (Garden City, N.Y.: Doubleday, 1976), p. 138.

George E. Mendenhall, *The Tenth Generation* (Baltimore: The Johns Hopkins University Press, 1973), Chapter vii.

John L. McKenzie S. J., *The World of the Judges* (Englewood Cliffs, N.J.: Prentice-Hall, 1966), p. 100.

George E. Mendenhall, "Change and Decay in All Around I See," *Biblical Archeologist,* Vol. 39.4 December 1976), p. 152.

Albrecht Alt, "The Settlement of the Israelites in Palestine," *Essays on Old Testament History and Religion,* R. A. Wilson trans. (Garden City, N.Y.: Doubleday, 1968), p. 173.

[3]Edward F. Campbell, Jr., *Ruth* (Garden City, N.Y.: Doubleday, 1975), pp. 10, 23.

Market in Beersheba. "From Dan to Beersheba" is a term used frequently in the Old Testament to deno **the full extent of the land of Israel.** (*Judges 19:30*). Photo by Elizabeth Gordon.

It is around such moments of danger that the book of Judges revolves. Th periods of Israelite oppression are seen by the later historians who brought the trad tions together as occasions when God chastised his people for neglect of his law

A formula is introduced in Judges 3:7–12 which reveals the strongly theologic purpose of the book:

And the people of Israel did what was evil in the sight of the Lord, forgetting the LORD their God, and serving the Baals and the Asheroth. Therefore the anger of the LORD was kindled against Israel, and he sold them into the hand of Cushan-rishathaim, King of Mesopotamia; and the people of Israel served Cushan-rishathaim eight years. But when the people of Israel cried to the LORD, the LORD raised up a deliverer for the people of Israel, who delivered them, Othniel the son of Kenaz, Caleb's younger brother. The Spirit of the LORD came upon him, and he judged Israel; he went out to war, and the LORD gave Cushan-rishathaim King of Mesopotamia into his hand; and his hand prevailed over Cushan-rishathaim. So the land had rest for forty years. The Othniel the son of Kenaz died. And the people of Israel again did what was evil in the sight of the LORD; and the LORD strengthened Eglon the King of Moab against Israel . . .

In simplest terms the formula is as follows:

The people sin.
God punishes them through an oppressor.
The people cry to God and repent.
God hears their cry.
He raises a deliverer to save them.
When the deliverer dies the people sin once more.
God punishes them through another oppressor.

The formula emphasizes a cardinal aspect of Jewish religion: that God is the Lord of history. No matter what happens he is in control, whether it is a petty king in the time of Judges, whom God raises as an instrument of his displeasure, mighty Assyria, whom the prophet described as the rod of God's anger (Isaiah 10:5), or the even mightier Cyrus, as God's messenger of reconciliation (Ezra 1:1–4).

Yet the fact that the formula was used shows that there was often a wide gap between what was expected of the Israelites as children of God, and how they behaved. The period of the Judges was, as one writer put it, a fluctuating movement between "tearing-asunder multiplicity and a completion-desiring unity."[4]

THE JUDGES

The book of Judges as we now have it is the product of a long development. It includes some of the earliest materials in the Old Testament, such as the Song of Deborah (Judges 5). Tracing the several stages of that development "is beset with difficulties."[5] As we have seen, Judges and Joshua are closely associated and may have used the

[4]Martin Buber, *Kingship of God,* "In those days, there was no King in Israel." Quoted in Robert G. Roling, *A Light Unto My Path: Old Testament Studies in Honor of Jacob M. Myers,* Howard N. Bream, Ralph D. Heim, Carey A. Moore eds. (Philadelphia: Temple University Press, 1974), p. 33.

[5]Jacob M. Myers, "Introduction to Judges," *Interpreters Bible,* Vol. 2, George A. Buttrick ed. Nashville, Tenn.: Abingdon Press, 1952). p. 678.

same account of the conquest. Compare Judges 1:10–15, 20, 21, and 27–28 with Joshua 15:3–19, 63, and 17:11–13.

The period of the Judges extended from the death of Joshua to the accession of Saul, that is, from about 1200 to 1020, or 180 years. The text makes it appear much longer because the thirteen Judges are referred to as if they lived one after the other. Adding their years in that way gives a total of 410. It is obvious then that a number of the Judges must have been contemporary.

Othniel	Judges 3:7–11
Ehud	3:12–30
Shamgar	3:31
Deborah	4:4–5:31
Barak	4:6–5:31
Gideon	6:1–8:32
Abimelech	9:1–57
Tola	10:1–2
Jair	10:3–5
Jephtha	10:6–12:7
Ibzan	12:8–10
Elon	12:11
Abdon	12:12–15
Samson	13–16

Some of these Judges are among the most well-known personalities of the Bible, for instance Samson and Gideon. Others are mentioned with only the barest detail. It is possible that there were others who took the initiative at critical moments in various parts of Israel.

The Judges were not judges in the contemporary sense, officials who make judicial decisions. Deborah comes the closest to that (Judges 4:4–5). They were, rather, charismatic leaders, brave and resourceful, recognized by the people as spirit-filled.[6]

The first Judge to be clearly described is Ehud, who destroyed a coalition of Moabites, Ammonites, and Amalekites (Judges 3:12–30). Moab and Ammon were two small Kingdoms which were undoubtedly anxious to prevent the growth of any new power. The Amalekites were inveterate enemies of Israel since the early days of the Exodus (Exodus 17:8–16, Psalm 83:7). The account of how Israel was delivered after eighteen years illustrates the highly individualistic way in which the Judge worked. Ehud avenged his people by a stealthy and exceedingly cool assassination. The details are so complete that they may go back to a first-hand account. At any rate, Ehud's action, like Jael's (Judges 4:20–24), shows that the ancient Israelites were no different from their neighbors in employing deceit and murder to achieve their ends.

[6]Abraham Malamat, "Charismatic Leadership in the Book of Judges," *Magnalia Dei*, p. 152

THE ONE BATTLE AGAINST THE CANAANITES

The story of Deborah and Barak is important for several reasons. The Song of Deborah (Judges 5), is, as we said, one of the oldest and one of the best pieces of writing in the Old Testament. There is a fine irony in how the writer describes Sisera's mother waiting for her son to return, peering through the lattice window hoping to see him and not knowing that he is dead.

"Are they not finding and dividing the spoil?" asks one of her attendant princesses. "A maiden or two for every man . . ." (Judges 5:30). Literally it is a "womb" for each man, which refers to the fate of captured women who would henceforth be kept as concubines. Sisera was murdered by Jael; she drove a tent peg through his head while he was asleep in her tent taking refuge as both kinsman and guest.[7] It was the woman's task to set up the tents. Jael would therefore be used to

[7]Harold H. Rowley, *The Growth of the Old Testament*, 3d ed. (London: Hutchinson's University Library, 1967), p. 61. Rowley argues that in the poem Jael kills Sisera while he is bending over the bowl drinking milk, that is *before* he went to sleep and while she is facing him. There was, therefore, according to this, no deceit.

Ancient jars in the museum at Hazor (*Joshua 11:1–15*). Photo by Elizabeth Gordon.

handling a tent peg and mallet, and if, as seems possible, her family were smiths the peg could have been made of metal and so was a lethal weapon.

Of particular interest is that this is the only battle referred to in Judges which was fought against the Canaanites. Israel's enemies at the time included Ammonites, Moabites, Amalekites, Midianites, and Philistines, all of whom lived on the perimeter of Israelite territory. Only once was the enemy the Canaanites, which has led to the perhaps extreme comment that in all other instances the Judges "defended Canaanites and Israelites against intruders," and "the book of Judges makes it clear that it was not by defeating the Canaanites, but by defending them that Israel attained a dominant position in Palestine."[8]

THE ROLE OF ARCHEOLOGY
IN SOLVING A TEXTUAL PROBLEM

The battle with the Canaanites provides an instructive example of how archeology can help resolve a textual problem. Two accounts have been preserved, a prose version in Judges 4, and a poem, known as the Song of Deborah, in Judges 5. The coalition of kings described in these accounts assembled a powerful chariot force which, in terms of military hardware, gave the Canaanites an overwhelming advantage. But Deborah launched a surprise attack and caught the Canaanites unprepared. At the same time there was a rainstorm; the river Kishon became a torrent which overflowed, and the Canaanites bogged down. The result was total victory for the Israelites and the murder of the Canaanite commander Sisera as he lay asleep in Jael's tent.

In most details the prose version and the poem agree, but there is an important difference. The prose version identifies the leader of the Canaanite forces as Jabin, the Canaanite king who ruled in Hazor (Judges 4:2). Jabin, however, had been killed by Joshua generations before (Joshua 11:10–11) and his city completely destroyed. Were there two Jabins and two Hazors? Was the one Jabin a descendent of the other? Had he retaken the city and rebuilt it? Was only a part of Hazor captured by Joshua? We know that there was an upper city and a lower city. Did Deborah and Barak then recapture the remaining part, probably the upper city? Has the biblical historian confused two events? Yigdal Yadin in his book on the excavations at Hazor discusses various theories and then describes how his team of archeologists resolved the long-standing problem.[9]

If, after Joshua's victory, the city of Hazor remained even in part under Canaanite control there should be some evidence in the strata above the level of Joshua. What Yadin discovered was that the city was entirely destroyed at the time of Joshua; beyond that there was evidence only of Israelite occupancy. Yadin concludes that the

[8]Norman K. Gottwald, *A Light to the Nations* (New York: Harper and Row, 1959), p. 166. Rowley, *Growth*, p. 60.

[9]Yohanan Aharoni, *The Land of the Bible,* 2d ed., Anson F. Rainey trans. (Philadelphia: The Westminster Press, 1980), p. 206.

reference to Jabin in Judges 4 is an interpolation.[10] There will undoubtedly be further discussions but not about when the Canaanites ceased to inhabit Hazor.[11]

JEPHTHA

The Ammonites (who have given their name to the modern Jordanian city of Amman) had refrained from attacking Israel since the time of Ehud (Judges 3:12–30). In fact the Israelites began to worship, or continued to worship the Ammonite gods and forsook the Lord. According to the text,

> The anger of the Lord was kindled against Israel, and he sold them into the hand of the Philistines and into the hand of the Ammonites, and they crushed and oppressed the children of Israel that year. For eighteen years they oppressed all the people of Israel that were beyond the Jordan in the land of the Amorites, which is in Gilead. And the Ammonites crossed the Jordan to fight also against Judah and against Benjamin and against the house of Ephraim; so that Israel was sorely distressed. Judges 10:7–9

The Judge whom God called upon this time to deliver his people was Jephtha, an unlikely person, an illegitimate son by a prostitute; he was turned out by his brothers and he made his living as the leader of a band of "worthless fellows" on the edge of the Arabian desert at Tob, north of Ammon. The Bible does not explain why the men who acted cruelly and contemptuously toward him when he was young later turned to him for help, but he is described as a "mighty warrior," and he had manifest abilities as a leader and fighter. Understandably, Jephtha demanded a firm guarantee from the Israelites that if he were successful they would continue to recognize him as their leader. This guarantee was given, and so he set about his task.

The student of scripture should reflect upon the account of how he did it. He did not immediately summon his people to arms and attack the enemy. He first sent a mission to the king of Ammon to ask "What have you against me, that you have come to me to fight against my land?" (Judges 11:12) The debate which followed is impressive even if it was reconstructed after the Exile. The King of Ammon's careful statement of grievances against Israel and Jephtha's equally measured reply are reminiscent of the debate between Sparta and Athens just prior to the outbreak of the Peloponnesian war;[12] but the Greek debate was in the fifth century and the debate

[10]Yagael Yadin, *Hazor* (Jerusalem: Weidenfield and Nicholson, 1975) pp. 249–255, "The Enigma of Joshua and Deborah!"

[11]The work of archeology as it relates to the Old Testament is discussed in H. Darrell Lance, *The Old Testament and the Archeologist* (Philadelphia: The Fortress Press, 1981).

The evolution and development of biblical archeology is discussed in William G. Dever, 'Archeological Method in Israel: A Continuing Revolution," *Biblical Archeologist,* Vol. 43.1 (Winter 1980) and Eric M. Meyers, "The Bible and Archeology," *Biblical Archeologist,* Vol. 47.1 (March 1984). Also Roger Moorey, *Excavation in Palestine* (Grand Rapids, Mich.: William B. Eerdmans, 1983), particularly Chapter 7, "After Excavation: The use and abuse of archeology in biblical studies," p. 110.

[12]Thucidydes, *The Peloponnesian War,* Book I, Chapter 6. There are many editions of this work.

between Jephtha and the King of Ammon probably in the twelfth. In both cases there were deeply felt wrongs on both sides, and in both cases a willingness and an ability to give reasons before proceeding to further action. In the disturbed conditions described by the book of Judges we must remember the debate between Jephtha and Ammon as well as the violent self-interest of Abimelech (Judges 9) and the even more violent and outrageous behavior of the Danites and the Benjamites (Judges 17–19).

Jephtha defeated the Ammonites but his victory became a personal tragedy. He had vowed that if he were successful he would sacrifice "whoever comes forth from the doors of my house to meet me" (Judges 11:30). It was a strange vow, and he obviously did not expect what happened, for when he returned to his house he was met by his daughter with tambourines and dances, obviously delighted as a daughter would be to see her father again. Jephtha's response was an anguished cry. The New English Bible translation especially brings out its poignancy. "Alas, my daughter, you have broken my heart, such trouble you have brought upon me. I have made a vow to the Lord and I cannot go back."[13] (Judges 11:35)

The characterization of Jephtha indicates clearly, though subtly, that the Judges were not simply local men of courage, but were men and women whose lives were informed by wisdom. Some already possess it when we meet them in the Old Testament, such as Deborah. Others develop it through their experience and suffering, such as Jephtha. This quality in the book distinguishes it altogether from what it may appear to be at a first reading. Behind its many stories there is the presence of religious obligation required of all at all times, understood and accepted, although imperfectly, by a few. It was the almost invisible operating power of the Covenant.

GIDEON AND THE MIDIANITES:
THE PROBLEM OF LEADERSHIP

A most serious threat to Israel came from the Midianites. These were Arab raiders who introduced a new element of warfare, the camel. Camels were not unknown in the Near East, but their use in Palestine by the Midianites was a novelty. Rather like the Nazi Panzer divisions early in the Second World War, they could attack with unprecedented speed and ferocity and then ride away. The Israelites were especially vulnerable because, with the relatively new development of lined cisterns, it was possible to establish communities in remote areas away from natural sources of water. The Midianites attacked when crops were ready, took what they wanted and destroyed the rest, leaving nothing, neither crops nor cattle. (Judges 6:4) The effect was disastrous, and the Israelites were forced to find hollow places in mountains, caves, and strongholds. This went on for seven years.

The story of how Gideon tested God to assure himself that his call was genuine,

---

[13]Alberto R. W. Green, *The Role of Human Sacrifice in the Ancient Near East* (Missoula, Mont.: Scholars Press, University of Montana, 1976).

how he then chose three hundred men from twenty-two thousand, and how he surprised the Midianites and stampeded them to their defeat with a clever use of smashed pots, shouts, and flaming torches is one of the classics of biblical literature.[14]

Without that victory the Israelites might have been destroyed before they had properly settled into the Promised Land. In their gratitude they offered to make Gideon their king, but he refused: "I will not rule over you, and my son will not rule over you; the Lord will rule over you." (Judges 8:23) His fine devotion to Yahweh was somewhat spoiled, however, when he made a golden ephod for the Israelites to worship. Thus he reverted to the custom of his father who combined the worship of God with the worship of idols.

Gideon wanted God only as ruler of Israel, but one of his sons, Abimelech, whose mother was a concubine from Shechem (Judges 8:31), murdered his half brothers and had himself appointed king. His reign was short and unpleasant; it is significant, however, as the first attempt at monarchy in the theocratic Israelite state. Although Gideon had turned down the kingship, Abimelech was able to appeal to his kinsmen in Shechem by contrasting his rule with that of his seventy brothers, which suggests that the idea of monarchy was active and may have developed in some way after Gideon's death apart from Abimelech.

The fact was that the people needed a national leader. The book of Judges closes with the comment that there was no king in Israel and every man did what was right in this own eyes (Judges 21:25). But the situation was aggravated because of the emergence of a new enemy, more powerful than any of the others. These were the Sea People, displaced from the Aegean, whom we know in the Old Testament as the Philistines (see Chapter 9).

THE CANAANITES

God promised the Israelites the land of Canaan. But to secure it they had to destroy, or subjugate, or come to terms with the inhabitants, the Canaanites. Who were these people? If we accept the Old Testament account, which is understandably biased, they were a heathen people, whose licentious forms of worship were totally abhorrent to the God of Israel. Only occasionally do we see the Canaanites as more real people, such as Rahab, the harlot of Jericho (Joshua 2), and the inhabitants of Gibeon, who tricked the Israelites into a covenant. These two incidents may indicate that there were divided opinions about the invaders in various Canaanite cities, and that the Israelites were willing to negotiate whenever they could. Such an explanation might

[14]There is an instructive article in the *Biblical Archeologist* which discusses the acoustics of various incidents in the Bible. It helps to explain how the shouting and smashing of pots of Gideon's forces on the hill of Moreh could be so startling to the Midianites camped in the valley below. B. Cobbey Crisler, "The Acoustics and Crowd Capacity of Natural Theaters in Palestine," *Biblical Archeologist,* Vol. 39.4 (December 1976), p. 128.

lie behind the Gibeon incident, which otherwise shows up the Israelites as surprisingly inept.

THE DISCOVERY OF UGARIT

Until a few years ago not much more was known about the Canaanites than is found in the Old Testament. In 1928 a farmer accidently discovered the remains of the city of ancient Ugarit (modern Ras Shamra) in Syria while he was ploughing a field. As a result, our knowledge of the life and religion of Canaan has increased enormously. We now know how they lived, what they believed, how they were governed, and what they wore. We can to some extent compare the ways of life of Canaan and Israel, and we can better understand the influence which the worship of Baal had upon the worship of God.

The Canaanites and the Israelites were part of the great complex of Western Semitic peoples also called Amorites, Eastern Canaanites, and Proto-Aramaeans (originally from the Syrian desert) who infiltrated and finally conquered the settled areas of the Fertile Crescent from about 2300 to 2000.[15] The population of Ugarit was part of this complex.[16] From these large-scale disruptions came both the people we know as Canaanites and possibly the family of Terah, Abraham's family.[17] In other words, the Israelites and the Canaanites were closely related.

CANAANITE SOCIETY

At the time of Joshua the Israelites were a rudimentary people compared with the Canaanites, who were a settled, sophisticated people with complex political and religious traditions. Canaanite city-states were independent. They did not unite unless there was a great emergency. Even then they were slow in joining forces, as we have seen. Their society was feudal, with a king and aristocracy at the top, an artisan and mercantile class next below, and at the bottom peasants and slaves.

From tomb remains at Jericho it has been possible to reconstruct the style of life of a prosperous Canaanite household. The houses were small, but could have several rooms with well-made and elegant furniture and household wares. Clothes were simple, fastened together with bronze toggle pins and, by the time of Joshua, even safety pins. The women wore their hair long, held with a band around the

---

[15]*Cambridge Ancient History,* 3d ed., Vol. II, part 1, pp. 25 and 86–87; Vol. II, part 2, p. 312.
[16]*Cambridge Ancient History,* Vol. II, part 1, p. 21.
Cyrus H. Gordon, *The Ancient Near East* (New York: Norton, 1965), p. 93.
[17]Kathleen Kenyon, *Amorites and Canaanites* (London: Oxford University Press, 1966), p. 76.
John Bright, *A History of Israel,* 3d ed. (Philadelphia: The Westminster Press, 1981), pp. 77 and 115–16.
John Gray, *The Canaanites* (London: Thomas and Husdon, 1964).
Magnus Magnusson, *BC The Archaeology of the Bible Lands* (London: The Bodley Head, 1977), p. 81.

**Baal, holding what may
be lightning in his hands.**
Photo by James B. Pritchard.
Reprinted by permission
of Princeton University Press.

forehead. They used anklets, bracelets, earrings, and small decorated pots for cosmetics, and mirrors made of polished bronze. Hundreds of years later the prophet Isaiah objected to similar "vanities" among the women of Judah (Isaiah 3:18–23).

The Canaanites were predominantly traders. That branch known as Phoenicians traded widely, from the east coast of Africa to all parts of the Mediterranean. The Canaanite city of Hazor was a large commercial center, and Ugarit, on the coast, received special privileges from the Hittites and the Egyptians because it was important to them both to have a trading center in the northwest Mediterranean area.

THE ALPHABET

Because the Canaanites dealt extensively with many countries they became familiar with languages, and it is common to assign to them the origin or the invention of the alphabet. More precisely the west Semites, of whom the Canaanites were a part, developed a prototype alphabet known as Proto-Semitic. This was in the second quarter of the second millennium, during the Hyksos period, a time of great political and social disturbance. One writer proposes that these conditions favored the creation of a "revolutionary" writing "a script which we can perhaps term democratic (or rather a 'people's script') as compared with the 'theocratic' scripts of Egypt and Mesopotamia."[18] The Proto-Semitic script then became the mother of all the alphabets: Hebrew, Greek, Latin, and ultimately our own.[19]

CANAANITE RELIGION

Canaanite religion was polytheistic with a pantheon whose chief deities were El, a remote figure living in the "deep" (the underworld), and his wife Asherah. Her symbol was a tree or pole, which must have been very familiar to people of Israel because of the numerous commands that they be cut down (Deuteronomy 7:5, 12:3; Micah 5:14).[20]

El and Asherah had many children, but the most important was Baal, Lord, the god of thunder and of vegetation. He is called "Lord of Heaven," and "Rider of the Clouds," and his voice is the thunder. A relief discovered at Ras Shamra shows him striding the mountains with a bolt of lightning in his hand.

---

[18]David Diringer, *The Alphabet,* a Key to the History of Mankind, 3d ed., completely revised with the assistance of Reingold Regensburger, Vol. I (New York: Funk and Wagnalls, 1968), p. 161.

[19]Ignace J. Gelb, *A Study of Writing,* revised edition (Chicago: The University of Chicago Press, 1963), p. 204.

[20]*Cambridge Ancient History,* Vol. II, part 2, p. 148.

G. Ernest Wright, "Canaanite Religion and Literature," *Biblical Archeology* (Philadelphia: The Westminster Press, 1962), p. 108.

Baal's wife (or sister) was Anath or Astarte. She is depicted as a bloodthirsty goddess. An Egyptian tablet pictures her with shield and lance in her one hand and an axe in the other.[21] A poem describes how she locked a number of men in her house and proceeded to batter them to death until she waded in their blood and laughed the laugh of victory, although it is possible that what is described is intended as a ritual or sham combat.[22] Anath was also the goddess of fertility.

Baal's enemy was Mot, the god of summer drought. In a great battle Mot killed Baal and the earth began to wither, and the crops and vines to die. It was not until Anath descended to the underworld, killed Mot, and rescued her husband that the earth came to life again.

The struggle between Baal and Mot and Baal's resurrection took place every year. It was the mythological explanation of the rotation of the seasons at a time when society relied absolutely upon the productivity of the land. A familiar explanation of this is that the Canaanites believed that the fertility of the earth depended upon the sexual fertility of Baal and Anath; it was therefore important for the two gods to engage in the sexual act as frequently as possible. This could be ensured by acting out on earth the union of the gods in heaven, that is, by men and women performing the sexual act, which was the reason for what the Israelites regarded as the widespread practice among the Canaanites of cultic prostitution. Both men and women prostitutes were associated with the Canaanite temples, and to make use of them was to perform a necessary religious act.[23]

Objections to the practice are sometimes overdone by biblical commentators. What we know of Canaanite life as a whole makes it clear, if such a truism needs to be made clear, that sex was not their only interest, that there were normal relationships within families and a full quota of daily business.[24] The fact, however, may be that there was no such practice as cultic prostitution among the Canaanites during the period referred to by the Old Testament writers. What was thought to be proof of the existence of the practice may be a misunderstanding of a term referred to in Ugaritic records.[25] The stern prohibition of Deuteronomy 23:17–18 could then be an example of a writer putting the worst interpretation upon the behavior of the enemy.

It is also possible that the relation between the Baal myth and changes in the seasons was both more complex and less erotic than has been supposed. A study of the Ugaritic Myth of Ba ͨlu has shown that there was a detailed correlation between

[21]Pritchard, *Ancient Near East in Pictures*, figure 473 and notes on p. 304.

[22]Pritchard, *Ancient and Near Eastern Texts*, p. 136a (cf. Psalms 2:4).

Johannes C. De Moor, *The Seasonal Pattern in the Ugaritic Myth of the Ba ͨlu:* According to the version of Ilimilku. Alter Orient and Altes Testament (Neukirchen-Vluyn: Verlag Butyon und Bercker Kevelaer, 1971), p. 95.

[23]Gerhard Von Rad, *Old Testament Theology*, Vol. I, Dorg Stalker trans. (New York: Harper and Row, 1962), p. 22.

Gray, *The Canaanites*, p. 136.

[24]Gray, *The Canaanites*, p. 53

[25]*Cambridge Ancient History*, Vol. II, part 2, p. 150.

De Moor, *The Seasonal Pattern*, p. 95.

the acts of the gods and the seasons of the year, and that the recitation and perhaps the representation of these acts throughout the year were part of the Ugaritic cult. It is suggested that the nature-myth "also deserves a place in the history of science since it embodies an early attempt of man to give a comprehensive explanation of the mechanisms of the climate in his surroundings."[26]

Canaanite religions would seem to have been primarily functional but the discovery of small incense altars and figurines, and the prevalence of trees and poles or Asherath and some expressions in their religious poems make it seem unlikely that Canaanite religion was devoid of all personal, emotional content that could have an effect upon a worshipper's life. Nevertheless, the role of the personal and moral element, prominent in Israelite religion, is not apparent among the Canaanites. The richness of a personal association with one God, undisputed Lord of all things in heaven and earth, through a Covenant which God as well as the believer is bound to honor, was a significant advance in religious understanding.

[26]De Moor, *The Seasonal Pattern*, p. 249.

CHAPTER NINE
THE PHILISTINES
AND THE BEGINNING
OF THE MONARCHY

THE PHILISTINES

The story of Samson (Judges 13–16) is one of the notable tales of the Old Testament. It is improbable, its hero is foolish, but it is a stirring bit of propaganda with right triumphant at the end and the hero and his God vindicated.

The story is important, not only because of its drama or its message but because of what it tells us about the people whom Samson fought, the Philistines. These were the Sea People who in the late thirteenth century and early twelfth century B.C. came from the Aegean area, in particular Crete, or Caphtor (see Amos 9:7) as part of a huge migratory wave. They moved into the countries that bordered the eastern Mediterranean and destroyed the Mycenean civilization and the Hittite Empire, which only a hundred years before had been too powerful for the Egyptians to conquer, and attacked Egypt itself.

These migrations have been generally regarded as the cause of the social, economic, and political disruption in the eastern Mediterranean at this time. But a recent study has proposed that they were the result of these disruptions. According to this theory, prolonged and widespread drought in the Aegean and Anatolia led to famine, which was so severe that throngs of starving people ransacked their own towns and cities and then moved en masse from land to land in search of food. It was this, rather than attacks from the outside, which destroyed the Mycenean civilization and the Hittite Empire. When the Sea People invaded Egypt it was not primarily for territory or plunder. They were trying to find a place where they could survive.

This could explain why, in the Egyptian reliefs of the invasion, the attacking Sea People were accompanied by their wives and children in ox-drawn carts. Some parts of Palestine also would have experienced drought which, it is suggested, could have contributed "to the creation of stateless brigands and groups of semi-nomads who joined with a band of escaped slaves from Egypt to form the Israelite Tribes."[1]

A contemporary text from Rameses III Temple at Thebes laments the devastation which the invaders caused, and their menacing self-confidence. "They laid their hands upon the countries as far as the circuit of the earth, their hearts confident and trusting: 'Our plan will succeed.' "[2] They were defeated, however, by Rameses. Wall reliefs at Thebes show a naval battle in the Nile Delta, during which the Philistines, wearing tall feathered headdresses, are overwhelmed by the Egyptians who fought them from their ships with bows and arrows and spears.[3]

Rameses took many prisoners, "as numerous as hundred-thousands," but after his reign the Egyptians withdrew to their own country and the Philistines settled in the land which was eventually to be called by their name, Palestine. They settled primarily in five cities: Gaza, Ashkelon, Ashdod, Ekron, and Gath, each under a Lord or Tyrant, who were usually independent but would work together as the need arose.

Both they and the Israelites were newcomers to Palestine. The Israelites by this time were relatively settled, but were still in conflict with neighboring states and unconquered Canaanites. The Philistines had established themselves in a limited area, but were trying to extend their control. It is not surprising that there was animosity between the two peoples. Yet there was intermarriage, as in the case of Samson, and the Israelites worshipped the Philistine gods, (Judges 10:6).

The danger to the Israelites in Canaan was therefore twofold: religious and cultural assimilation, and military domination. It was the second which is the theme of the first book of Samuel.

The Philistines possessed great advantages. They were well-disciplined warriors, as compared with the informal levies of the Israelites during the period of the Judges, and they knew the secret of iron and so had superior weapons and armor.

The importance of iron was such that it gave its name to a new age, the Iron Age, which replaced the late Bronze Age about 1200 B.C. The Israelites had already discovered iron's superior value in war. "The Lord was with Judah and he took possession of the hill-country, but he could not drive out the inhabitants of the plain, because they had chariots of iron" (Judges 1:19, Joshua 17:16).

---

[1]William H. Stiebing, "The End of the Mycenean Age," *Biblical Archeologist,* Vol. 43.1, (Winter 1980), p. 7.

[2]James B. Pritchard, ed., *Ancient and Near Eastern Texts Relating to the Old Testament,* 3d ed. with supplement (Princeton, N.J.: Princeton University Press, 1969), p. 262.

[3]G. Ernest Wright, *Biblical Archeology,* new and revised edition (Philadelphia: Westminster Press, 1962), p. 87.
James Pritchard, ed., *The Ancient Near East in Pictures* (Princeton, N.J.: Princeton University Press, 1969), p. 114

The processes of iron making had been known and used by Hittites for centuries, but they kept it secret. A wrought iron dagger given by the Hittite King to Tutankhamen in the mid-fourteenth century has been described as a "rare and novel gift."[4] The Philistines apparently discovered the secret from the Hittites and were determined not to share it.

"Now there was no smith to be found throughout all the land of Israel; for the Philistines said, 'Lest the Hebrews make themselves swords or spears'; but every one of the Israelites went down to the Philistines to sharpen his plowshare, his mattock, his axe, or his sickle; and the charge was a pim for the plowshares and for the mattocks, and a third of a shekel for sharpening the axes and for setting the goads" (1 Samuel 13:19–21). One would describe it in contemporary terms as like an ancient oil embargo. The effects are similar, whatever the age, when a vital commodity is denied to a country that needs it.

This was the background at the beginning of the period covered by the two books of Samuel.

THE TEXT OF SAMUEL

Like Joshua and Judges, 1 and 2 Samuel were compiled from a variety of sources. For example, Goliath is killed by David in 1 Samuel 17, but by Elhanan in 2 Samuel 21:19. The contradiction is best explained as the result of two documents by different authors, although the author of Chronicles (1 Chronicles 20:5), writing much later, after the Exile, explains that it was Lahmi, Goliath's brother, whom Elhanan killed. Saul is twice proclaimed king before the people (1 Samuel 10:24–25, 11:4–15). The different sources are particularly evident with regard to the nature of the monarchy. In 1 Samuel 9, God takes the initiative through Samuel to have Saul chosen as king to deliver the people of Israel. In 1 Samuel 8 it is the people who insist upon a king much to the displeasure of God and Samuel.

Attempts have been made to explain these differences by positing a pro-monarchical source (1 Samuel 9:1–10:16; 11:1–15) and an anti-monarchical source (1 Samuel 8:1–22, 10:17–27, 12:1–25), but the issue is not settled and there are revisions and alternative explanations. One writer comments that options between rival theories are almost endless with little prospect of adjudicating between one and the other.[5]

---

[4]Wright, *Biblical Archeology,* p. 92b.
   A portion of an iron blade found in the twelfth-century stratum XII of the Tell Qasile excavations, 1973–74, is one of the earliest iron artifacts to be discovered in Israel. Amihai Mazar, "Additional Philistine Temples at Tell Qasile" *Biblical Archeologist,* Vol. 40.2 (May 1977), p. 83.

[5]Brevard Childs, *Introduction to the Old Testament as Scripture* (Philadelphia: Fortress Press, 1979), p. 271.
   Otto Eissfeldt, *The Old Testament,* an introduction translated by Peter R. Ackroyd (New York: Harper and Row, 1965), p. 271.
   See also the introduction and relevant sections in Hans Wilhelm Hertzberg, *I and II Samuel,* John S. Bowden trans. (Philadelphia: The Westminster Press, 1964).

But this debate scarcely affects the value of the two books of Sameul, which are recognized as containing some of the best historical writing in the Old Testament. 1 Chronicles 29:29 credits the authorship to Samuel, Nathan, and Gad, contemporaries of the events which they described. Much of the writing has an immediacy and an objectivity unrivalled until the work of the Greek historian, Thucydides, who lived in the fifth century B.C.

The division of the two books was made for convenience. Originally, in the Hebrew scriptures, 1 and 2 Samuel were one book, but in the Septuagint, the Greek translation of the Hebrew scriptures made in the third century B.C., Samuel and Kings were divided into four sections under the title, The Books of the Kingdoms. The division of Samuel into two parts has been adopted by the Hebrew Bible at least since the fifteenth century A.D. and possibly as early as the development of the Massoretic Text.

HANNAH AND SAMUEL

The final editor of the first book of Samuel might have begun his work with an account of the general situation of Israel, barely settled in its new country, surrounded by enemies, chief of which were the Philistines. But he chose to begin with the personal story of a woman who wanted a child and whose faith in God was blessed by being given one.

In the opening chapter of 1 Samuel we encounter Hannah and her husband, Elkanah, who had gone to Shiloh to worship. Shiloh was the principal religious sanctuary of Israel, the site of the Tabernacle or Tent of Presence, and of the Ark, a wooden chest built to contain the tablets of the law, and symbolizing the presence of God (Exodus 25:10–22). The portrait of Hannah is sympathetic. We see her, grief stricken because she is childless, baited by her co-wife, comforted in a cruel way by her husband, and unjustly charged with drunkenness by Eli, the Priest. There are few passages in the Old Testament where this is so obviously a man's world.[6] A son is born and he is named Samuel. Hannah's prayer for a child has been answered; she is glad to lend him to the Lord for his whole life (1 Samuel 1:28). We read about the little cloak that she made for her son when she visited him once a year (1 Samuel 2:19), and how God called him at night and used him to convey a message of judgment upon Eli and his family for the misconduct of his sons (1 Samuel 3). Samuel grew and his word had authority in "all Israel" (1 Samuel 4:1).

STRUGGLE WITH THE PHILISTINES

It was at this point, about 1050, that the Philistines decided to attack. Perhaps there were more incidents, like those in the story of Samson, which finally provoked the Philistines to deal with the Israelites by force. The Philistines had been in Canaan

---

[6]Carol Meyers, "The Roots of Restriction: Women in Early Israel," *Biblical Archeologist*, Vol. 41.3 (September 1978), p. 91.

for about 100 years, during which time they slowly increased their territory. The tribe of Dan, which settled west of what is now Jerusalem, was obliged to move north, beyond Hazor, because of the Philistines. At the beginning of the book of 1 Samuel, they occupied a considerable part of the coastal plain.

The battle was fought between Aphek and Ebenezer. The Israelites were routed. They did not have a properly trained army, and they used inferior weapons. In a military sense they stood little chance. But they decided to try again. That time they took the Ark of the Covenant of the Lord into the battle with them, which was, in effect, the Israelites' ultimate weapon, for the Ark represented the presence of their God, of whom the Philistines were also in awe. The scripture records that the Philistines heard a great shout in the Israelite camp. "When they learned that the ark of the Lord had come to the camp, the Philistines were afraid; for they said, 'A god has come into the camp...Woe to us!...Woe to us!' " (1 Samuel 4:6–8)

It is a reflection upon the honesty of the Israelite writer that the Philistines are shown to be brave men. They were also experienced fighters. The text records how they steadied themselves. "Take courage, and acquit yourselves like men, O Philistines, lest you become slaves to the Hebrews as they have been to you; acquit yourselves like men and fight." The result was a second victory for the Philistines. The Israelites were defeated with considerable loss of life; Eli's sons Hophni and Phineas were killed, and the Ark was captured (1 Samuel 4:1–11).

The scene in which the aged and sightless Eli is told the news of the battle is a powerful vignette: his sons dead, the Ark which was his duty to protect captured by the enemy. It was a message that underlined his life's failure. "When he mentioned the ark of God, Eli fell over backward from his seat by the side of the gate; and his neck was broken and he died, for he was an old man, and heavy. He had judged Israel forty years." (1 Samuel 4:18)

The Philistines now had almost absolute control over the whole country. The Ark was returned, but it was housed ignominiously, probably under Philistine supervision in Kirjath-jearim.[7] Shiloh, the central sanctuary was presumably destroyed (Jeremiah 7:12) and Philistine garrisons established throughout the country (1 Samuel 10:5, 13:3). Philistine pottery with its distinctive patterns has been excavated in many parts of Israel. Yet the Philistines did not attempt to exterminate the population or enslave them as, for example, David did to the inhabitants of Moab and Edom (2 Samuel 8:2, 13; 1 Kings 11:15–16). The Philistines were a military aristocracy which appeared to be more interested in control of territory than in the defeat or extermination of the people they controlled. In certain respects their occupation was similar to that of the Egyptians before them. They were powerful, ready to assert authority, but not obtrusive.

Perhaps because of this, as well as the character of their faith, the Israelites did not lose their identity, although in some respects they were a conquered people. Samuel, the priest and prophet (1 Samuel 3:20), retained his authority and travelled in a circuit dispensing justice among Bethel, Gilgal, Mizpah and Ramah where he

---

[7] Roland de Vaux, *The Early History of Israel* (Philadelphia: Westminster Press, 1978), pp. 798–99.

lived and, significantly, "governed Israel" and built an altar to the Lord (1 Samuel 7:15–17).

Just as Eli's sons proved unworthy to succeed to the priesthood (1 Samuel 2:22–26), so did Samuel's. The comment that Samuel's sons walked not in his ways (1 Samuel 8:5) could refer simply to their moral and spiritual behavior, but could also refer to their lack of ability to be leaders at a time when effective leadership was crucial. They were enough of a disappointment that the elders of Israel approached Samuel and asked him to appoint a king "to govern us, like other nations" (1 Samuel 8:5–6).

THE ISRAELITES DEMAND A KING

There are conflicting accounts of how Saul became King. In the one he is a young man looking for his father's lost asses. He does not find them but meets Samuel who is expecting him, entertains him at a banquet and anoints him King (1 Samuel 9:1–18). In 1 Samuel 8 it is the people who demand a king against the strong objections of Samuel. In 1 Samuel 10:17–27 Saul is picked by lot as if he had not yet been chosen. There are also ambiguities in age. Saul is a "young man," (1 Samuel 9:2), and this is supported by his unusual modesty in 1 Samuel 10:21–23, where he hides among the baggage. In 1 Samuel 11:4–11 he acts with the experienced self-assurance of a much older man, which he must have been because the text gives the impression that at the very beginning of his reign he had a grown son (1 Samuel 13:1–2). Jeremiah, for example, is a diffident young man when he is called by God (Jeremiah 1), and a clearly older person when he denounces the people of Judah in the Temple (Jeremiah 26). There is no question of his being the same age in the two incidents, but the difference in assurance is not more distinct than in the case of Saul.

In general, however, the issue of Saul becoming king is clear. Israel was a theocracy governed, like none of the surrounding people, by God alone acting through a priest or judge. These men (and women, as in the case of Deborah) were chosen by God who sent his spirit upon them.

The people of Israel, therefore, had considerable independence of any human leader. An example of this can be found in the story of Abimelech, one of Gideon's sons, who assumed the monarchy at Shechem but lost it when his own people disagreed with him (Judges 9:23–56). There was no further attempt to establish a monarchy, and it is possible that the failure of that experiment had convinced many it should not be tried again.

According to one view the prophet's uncomplimentary description of monarchy (1 Samuel 8:11–18) was not a complaint written after the fact, a rewriting of history as some have supposed, but "an authentic description of the semi-feudal Canaanite society as it existed prior to and during the time of Samuel himself,"[8] which would appear to support the validity of the antimonarchical view.

[8]Isaac Mendelsohn, "Samuel's denunciation of kingship in the light of the Akkadian documents from Ugarit," *Bulletin of the American Schools of Oriental Research*, No. 143 (October 1956), pp. 17–22.

More recently this has been disputed. "Samuel's effort to divert the people from its desire for a King, by enumerating the many calls and services a King would impose, does not represent a historical record of facts but a tendentious distortion of the truth."[9] Accordingly, all that the Israelite tribes did was to surrender their right to call out a military levy to their new king, which would suport the promonarchical view.

It is not impossible that the text preserves a real debate between Samuel, committed to a theocratic view of Israelite polity, and the people, who, after the defeat at Aphek, were convinced that the system of priests and judges did not work. It was an urgent matter. Perhaps a king would be harsh, but he would be their own king. The alternative appeared to be loss of their independence and subjugation by another king.

There may have been a personal factor in Samuel's objections. When he was a child and delivered his message from God he could not have appreciated Eli's humiliating disappointment. Even less would he have imagined that the same humiliation would come to him: his own leadership discounted, his sons obviously venal and incompetent (1 Samuel 8:3). Moreover, Samuel had led the Israelites to victory against the Philistines (1 Samuel 7:2–14). Why could he not continue to do so? He complained to God but got no sympathy. The brief conversation is unusual: "Hearken to the voice of the people," says the Lord in reply to Samuel, "in all that they say to you; for they have not rejected you, but they have rejected me from being King over them." (1 Samuel 8:7).

There is an almost petulant tone, yet it makes clear that Israel was different, not like other nations, and although by taking a king she would preserve herself in certain ways, she would diminish herself in others.

But the people insisted; perhaps Samuel's victory was not as complete as the text suggests. From their perspective, living under the threat of a powerful enemy, they needed a strong leader, and that, in those days, meant a king. Finally Samuel, or God, yielded, and a king was chosen, the hitherto unknown Saul, from the tribe of Benjamin. It was, in effect, another experiment and it proved to be a tragic one.

SAUL

Saul's reign began with an act that was long remembered. Nahash, the king of Ammon, besieged the city of Jabesh-gilead in the territory of Manasseh on the Jordan, about twenty miles south of the Sea of Galilee. The men of the city offered to surrender and be subject to Ammon, but Nahash, taking advantage of their plight, declared that "On this condition I will make a treaty with you, that I gouge out all your right eyes, and thus put disgrace upon all Israel." (1 Samuel 11:2).

This message was brought to the new King Saul as he was driving his oxen back from the field. He was immediately seized with a great anger. He killed a pair

[9]*Cambridge Ancient History,* Vol. II, part 2, p. 574.

of oxen, cut the animals into pieces, and sent the pieces to the twelve tribes proclaiming that the same would be done to any man's oxen who did not follow Saul and Samuel into battle. Then the fear of the Lord fell on the people; there was a muster of three thousand men from Israel and thirty thousand from Judah. The Ammonites were defeated and Jabesh-gilead was saved.

There had earlier been complaints about Saul (1 Samuel 10:27) from those who doubted his ability. Now it was clear that, like the Judges, he had genuine charisma. It is noteworthy that in the account of Saul's anointing he is not referred to as king (melek) but as a leader or commander (nagid).[10] Nevertheless, after Jabesh-gilead he was recognized by the people as a king and increasingly acted like one.

CONFLICT BETWEEN SAMUEL AND SAUL

One of Saul's first acts was to select from the tribes a fighting force of three thousand men, two thousand to be with him in Micmash and the hill country of Bethel, and a thousand to be with Jonathan in Gibeah of Benjamin. Rather like Gideon (Judges 7:7) he then sent the rest of the people home (1 Samuel 13:2).

Saul had taken the initiative in challenging the Philistines, but if one accepts the numbers of their troops and chariots he was fighting against tremendous odds. Not surprisingly the Israelites found themselves in caves and holes. Some crossed the river to be even further removed.

The Philistines were incensed because Jonathan had killed the Philistine governor in Gebah, which was close to Saul's city, Gibeah, a few miles north of Jerusalem. They mounted a large force, no doubt to crush a potential rebellion. It was therefore necessary for Saul to act promptly before he was both outnumbered and outmaneuvered, and before his army lost its courage. Samuel had told Saul to wait for him so that he could offer a sacrifice. Not until then could the Israelites fight, but Samuel did not come and the army began to drift away. In modern times weather conditions, availability of supplies, and enemy movements are the kinds of factors that determine when an army will fight. But in ancient times religious considerations were paramount. There is an incident in Thucydides history of the Peloponnesian War (431–404) in which the Athenian forces, having been badly defeated by the Syracusans on the Island of Sicily, decided to retreat while they still could and return with what was left of their forces to Athens. But just as they were about to sail there was an eclipse of the moon, and the soldiers themselves urged their general to wait. So they waited for the "thrice nine days" recommended by the soothsayers.[11] By then the chance for retreat was gone, and the entire Athenian army was eventually destroyed.

---

[10] John Bright, *A History of Israel,* 3d ed. (Philadelphia: Westminster Press, 1981), p. 190.

[11] Thucydides, *The Peloponnesian War,* Book 7, Chapter 5. There are many editions of this work. See also André Lemaire, "The Ban in the Old Testament and at Mari," *Biblical Archeologist,* Vol. 47.2 (June 1984), p. 103.

Thucydides, the writer, himself a general, was obviously not in sympathy with the soothsayers. Had he been in command it seems likely that he would have ignored the eclipse and saved his army. That was Saul's attitude. While Samuel delayed, the military situation became more serious than could wait upon the niceties of a religious code. So Saul offered the sacrifice himself and at that moment Samuel appeared filled with wrath and denunciation (1 Samuel 13:11–14). Perhaps, if Saul had waited and his army had been defeated, he would be remembered by the chronicler as a valiant and God-fearing king. When the Jews refused to defend themselves on the Sabbath, in the early days of the Maccabean revolt and were slaughtered (168 B.C.), they decided to change the rules (1 Maccabees 2:29–41), but the Sabbath requirements were adhered to until they were proven impractical. Saul made a decision ahead of time to prevent that kind of defeat.

The consequence was a serious breach between Saul and Samuel. Samuel was unrelenting. "You have done foolishly; you have not kept the commandment of the Lord your God, which he commanded you; for now the Lord would have established your kindgom over Israel for ever. But now your kingdom shall not continue; the Lord has sought out a man after his own heart; the Lord has appointed him to be prince over his people, because you have not kept what the Lord commanded you." (1 Samuel 13:13–14).

Despite this, but largely due to Jonathan's initiative, the Israelites won an important victory. It was decisive enough that those Hebrews who had been fighting with the Philistines changed sides (1 Samuel 14:21). Curiously, Saul exhibited the same religious intransigence during this battle as had Samuel about the sacrifice. Samuel had been prepared to disinherit a king because of a ritual error which was, by ordinary standards, not excusable. Saul was willing to put his son Jonathan to death because of a ritual error committed by Jonathan in ignorance.

Before the battle, Saul had spoken to the people, saying, "Cursed be the man who eats food until it is evening and I am avenged on my enemies." (1 Samuel 14:24) Like Jephtha whose "rash vow" led to the death of his daughter (Judges 11:29–40), Saul's equally rash vow could have led to the death of his son, because Jonathan, who had not heard of the vow, ate some honey from a honeycomb he found in the forest. Saul was prepared to carry out the sentence, but the people would not allow it (1 Samuel 14:45–46). Fortunately the Israelite monarchy was still informal enough that the good sense of the people could temper the excesses of their king.

Yet in obvious ways Saul was not excessive. Compared with the kings of Israel who succeeded him his manner of life was simple. The incident of Saul's being told about Jabesh-gilead as he was coming from the field driving in the oxen (1 Samuel 11:4–5) is reminiscent of an incident in the life of Cincinnatus, the unpretentious hero of the old Roman republic who, in a time of emergency (458 B.C.) was called from ploughing his farm to be dictator. Saul's "palace" or fortress at Gibeah has been excavated. It was a two-story building with double walls and defensive towers at the corners. It was large, about 169 feet long by 114 feet wide, but from all the evidence it was a modest residence for a king. There are no remains of ivory inlays or fine pottery, as for example were found in the ruins of buildings in Samaria. In Saul's fortress were found the ordinary pots and cooking utensils used in any Israelite home of the period. It was primarily a strong fortress with a broad view of the surrounding country and, like many English medieval castles, was probably cold and uncomfortable. It was destroyed once during Saul's life, possibly before the battle of Micmash. It was almost immediately rebuilt.[12]

Saul's retinue was also simple. He seems not to have had a standing army or bodyguard, despite his choosing three thousand men before the battle of Micmash (1 Samuel 13:2). However, Abner, his nephew (1 Samuel 14:50), was commander in chief until Saul's death.

Saul proved to be a capable leader. "He fought against all his enemies on every side, against Moab, against the Ammonites, against Edom, against the kings of Zobah, and against the Philistines; wherever he turned he put them to the worse. And he did valiantly, and smote the Amalekites, and delivered Israel out of the hands of those who plundered them" (1 Samuel 14:47-48). It was in connection with the Amalekites that the final break came between Samuel and Saul.

The Amalekites were ancient enemies ever since they attacked the Israelites on their way from Egypt (Exodus 17:8-16). Samuel now told Saul that Israel was to be avenged. He, Saul, was to attack the Amalekites and exterminate them. God had placed them under the ban. The word used was *herem,* total extermination. Saul could spare no one. "Kill both man and woman, infant and suckling, ox and sheep, camel and ass" (1 Samuel 15:3). Generations of lessons from the pulpit have blunted the reality of such phrases. In contemporary terms it would be like the Mai Lai massacre during the Viet Nam war, but not as the result of one man's savagery subsequently hidden as long as it could be, but as an open policy for every soldier to kill everything alive. In the ancient world this was not regarded as an inhuman command. A city or a people placed under the ban was devoted to God. It was a sacrifice, and it became an act of sacrilege to save anything from its destruction. This was Achan's sin during the siege of Ai (Joshua 7), and the same reasoning underlies the sin of Ananias and Sapphira (Acts 4:32-5:11). Saul certainly knew about *herem* and how serious it was to disregard it. Had he not been prepared to kill his son? But for some reason he chose to flaunt custom, cruel though it was, without even such extenuating circumstances as there were when he sacrificed at Micmash. He even argued with Samuel in an attempt to justify what he had done.

The prophet was outraged, and in terms of those days he was right, even though years later David spared some of the Amalekite flocks as his own spoil (1 Samuel 30:20). But David was not instructed to put the tribe under the ban. He was, in fact, acting in self-defense. Saul clearly disobeyed a prophetic order and so came under severe punishment. Samuel's classic words were blunt.

---

[12]Wright, *Biblical Archeology,* pp. 122-24. Curiously, a contemporary monarch has built on the same site. King Hussein of Jordan began the construction of a residence on the ancient ruins but it was not completed. It is now in Israeli-held territory, a short distance behind the suburban house of a friend of the author.

Has the Lord as great delight in burnt offerings and sacrifices,
    as in obeying the voice of the Lord?
Behold, to obey is better than sacrifice,
    and to hearken than the fat of rams. (1 Samuel 15:22)

Then he pronounced the punishment. Earlier, Saul's family had been rejected. Now it was Saul himself. "Because you have rejected the word of the Lord, he has also rejected you from being king." (1 Samuel 15:23) It was a public humiliation in which Saul was formally stripped of his authority to make place for "a better man." Samuel never saw Saul again to the day he died.

The Amalekite incident suggests that Samuel became unmitigatingly hostile towards Saul. Yet this may be a mistaken impression. The text continues (1 Samuel 15:35), "but Samuel grieved over Saul." Apparently his grief was deep and long-lasting. God had to speak sharply to Samuel, "How long will you grieve over Saul, seeing I have rejected him from being king over Israel?" (1 Samuel 16:1) Even then Samuel could not rid himself of the thought of his former protégé. When the prophet was attempting to choose Saul's successor from among the sons of Jesse he assumed it was Eliab because he was handsome and tall (1 Samuel 16:7), a characteristic that distinguished the well-favored Saul when he was chosen king (1 Samuel 9:2, 10:23).

THE INDIVIDUAL IN THE OLD TESTAMENT

If one is cautious about it there is much to be discovered in the Bible by examining how personal relationships are handled. The two books of Samuel are to a great extent character studies, and the history of the nation is presented through them. In the personalities of Samuel, Saul, David, and Solomon we see the development of Israel from a loose confederation to a nation-state. Similarly, the earlier years are presented through Abraham, Jacob, Joseph, Moses, and Joshua. The book of Judges is consistent with this emphasis upon individuals, and so are the later books. Elijah, Ahab, Jezebel, Jehu, and the great prophets of the eighth century and later carry the story of the nation and its faith toward its Old Testament conclusion.

A great deal of biblical material is not focused upon individuals: yet the role of personality is so important that individuals are clearly as much the efficient cause of what happens as is God, and this, intentionally or not, is consistent with Judaic tradition. Throughout the Old Testament the formal Covenant relationship is set within the context of a personal relationship. God sees his pepole, he cares for them, he dwells among them, he chastises them, he rescues them, he overwhelms them with his majesty; he loves them and relates to them like another person. Part of the uniqueness of Judaism is that, although God is the creator and ultimate arbiter, he appears in the Old Testament just as often as a participant moved in one direction or another by the other participants.

DAVID

The "better man" referred to in 1 Samuel 15:28 was David, and it is with his career that the narrative becomes increasingly concerned. We saw that there was more than one account of how Saul became king. David's introduction to Saul is also described in more than one way. He is presented first as the youngest of several brothers, "he was ruddy, and had beautiful eyes" and is anointed by the prophet (1 Samuel 16:1–13). He is next hired by the king's servant to play music to the king, who has lost the spirit of the Lord and, on occasions, is seized by an evil spirit from the Lord. David is apparently well known as a brave man and a good fighter, which indicates that he was not a youngster but an experienced professional soldier (1 Samuel 16:14–23). Saul takes a liking to him, and "he found favor" with him (1 Samuel 16:22). But when he is visiting his brothers at the battlefield with food, David is presumably too young to be in the army; he declares that he will fight Goliath and is introduced to Saul, who has never seen him and asks Abner who he is (1 Samuel 17:55–58). These differing accounts indicate more clearly than in other instances that the biblical text was drawn from numerous sources.

THE SLING AS AN ANCIENT WEAPON

The story of the combat between David and Goliath illustrates the point that, although the historicity of various incidents may be in question, the details of the narrative are sometimes unexpectedly accurate. The story also provides us with information about ancient warfare.

According to the text, David killed the giant almost easily by using a sling. The chronicler was assuming knowledge about the lethal power of a sling which, in the course of almost thirty centuries, has been largely forgotten. The sling is now regarded more as a toy than as a serious weapon, yet Assyrian wall carvings show slingers firing from behind archers, which may indicate that the sling could outdistance the arrow. In a modern experiment in Turkey, for example, some young men, who had neither special skill nor specially shaped missiles, cast the pebbles over 230 meters. Given training and carefully made stone, clay, or lead missiles, "it seems probable that a slinger casting lead missiles could obtain a range in excess of 400 meters." The ancient slinger could use the sling with great accuracy. Livy, a Roman historian, reports that Achaean slingers could sling their missiles through a ring of "moderate circumference set up at a distance" and so they "would wound not merely the heads of their enemies but any part of the face at which they might have aimed."[13] In the book of Judges we read that "there were seven hundred picked men from Gibeah," where later Saul had his fort, "left handed men, who could sling a stone and not miss by a hair's breadth" (Judges 20:16).

[13]The information on slings in this chapter is taken from Manfred Korfmann, 'The Sling as a Weapon," *The Scientific American,* October 1973, pp. 34–42.

A shepherd, such as David, had to be able to protect his flock from lions and other predatory animals which were common in Israel during biblical times (1 Samuel 17:31–37). The large and slow-moving Philistine would have made an excellent target compared with a marauding animal. The battle, therefore, between David and Goliath was certainly unequal, but not in Goliath's favor. It was as if the giant had confronted a teenage marksman who was armed with a rifle while the giant was armed only with a spear. The speed of a missile from a sling can exceed sixty miles an hour. Providing that he kept his nerve, David couldn't miss, and he had four shots in reserve. The whimsical but perhaps not unsupportable conclusion is that it is Goliath who deserves our sympathy, not David.

ANTAGONISM BETWEEN SAUL AND DAVID

In the early days there was a warm friendship between Saul and David, and a particularly close one between Saul's son Jonathan and David. Saul gave his daughter Michal to be David's wife, and David proved himself worthy of the marriage by a great act of valor (1 Samuel 18:17–29). But this changed abruptly, according to the text, when the king heard some women sing

Saul has slain his thousands,
and David his ten thousands. (1 Samuel 18:7)

One can hardly credit that song alone with the power to corrupt Saul's affections and distort his life, but it may have been the catalyst of private suspicions which proved, or appeared to prove, the truth of what he thought.

Saul was an ecstatic. There was an expression among the people of Israel: "Is Saul also among the prophets?", that is, among that group of men who would on occasion dance and shout and throw off their clothes in an ecstasy of prophetic rapture (1 Samuel 10:10–12, 19:23–24). Such men were more than usually capable of emotional expression and of intense determination to achieve a goal. With Saul, in the case of Jabesh-gilead, this led to the defeat of the Ammonites. In the case of David it led to an obsession that nearly destroyed the nation. Saul's massacre of the priests and their families at Nob, because they had given shelter to David, not knowing that he was a fugitive (1 Samuel 22), was indefensible. His own men would not obey their king's command to kill the priests. He hurled a spear point-blank at David when David was playing the harp for him (1 Samuel 19:9–10). On another occasion he threw his spear at Jonathan (1 Samuel 20:33). His behavior was often demented.

Yet given a highly strung nature and a superstitious respect for the power of religion characteristic of the times, Saul's behavior can be understood. We don't know what effect Samuel's terrible curse had upon him, but we can assume it was considerable. Both David (2 Samuel 12:1–25) and Ahab (1 Kings 21:27) were overwhelmed when confronted by the word of God through the prophets Nathan and Elijah. Ahab seems to have become incoherent for a time. Samuel's words to Saul must have had an equally powerful effect. But it was not only his own interests at stake. Saul was well aware of the political implication for his son of David's growing prominence, and it infuriated him that Jonathan refused to recognize it and was even a close friend of the man whom Saul knew intended to supplant him. When Jonathan attempted to argue the point, it was then that Saul threw a spear at him (1 Samuel 20:33).

Saul was obsessed with his hatred of David. Yet as Samuel mourned for Saul, although he had condemned him, Saul loved David, although he tried to kill him, and that love was returned. Twice David could have killed the king (1 Samuel 24 and 26), but a mixture of affection for his former father-in-law and genuine respect for the Lord's anointed held him back. In fact, he revealed his presence to the king in the cave, and later in the wilderness of Ziph. Both meetings were extraordinary.

> And David said to Saul, "Why do you say listen to the words of men who say, 'Behold, David seeks your hurt'? Lo, this day your eyes have seen how the Lord gave you today into my hand in the cave; and some bade me kill you, but I spared you. I said, 'I will not put forth my hand against my lord; for he is the Lord's anointed.' See, my father, see the skirt of your robe in my hand; for by the fact that I cut off the skirt of your robe, and did not kill you, you may know and see that there is no wrong or treason in my hands. I have not sinned against you, though you hunt my life to take it." (1 Samuel 24:9–11)

Saul's response was a sorrowful and affectionate admission that David had right on his side. Perhaps the chronicler makes that more evident than it was. But it is clear from this incident and the incident in Ziph that Saul's emotions were not all going in the same direction.

Despite these brief reconciliations, and the fact that if David could have killed the king, the king, once he knew where David was, and having his army with him, could have captured and killed David, David had no doubt that he was in real danger. After the meeting in Ziph where Saul actually blessed David, the younger man's calculated thought was "One of these days I shall be killed by Saul." (1 Samuel 27:1, New English Bible translation). Many people admired David but he could not count on their support. They were still loyal to the king. He rescued the city of Keilah from the Philistines, but had to leave when Saul discovered he was there because the Lord told him that despite what he had done for them, if he stayed there the citizens of the town would surrender him (1 Samuel 23:1–13). The incident with Nabal (1 Samuel 25) may indicate less that Nabal was a fool than that David was not as well known as he expected to be. What Nabal did "know" about him was that he was a runaway slave trying to set himself up as chief (1 Samuel 25:10). The mixed company of debtors and malcontents who followed David (1 Samuel 22:1–2) would not impress a prosperous sheep farmer whose loyalty was to his king.

On one occasion David fled to Achish, king of Gath, but Achish had heard the song that angered Saul about thousands and tens of thousands, so David pretended to be mad to get away, because a madman was untouchable (1 Samuel 21:10–15). Later he returned to Gath and engaged in the extremely risky business of pretending t fight his own people. Perhaps the Philistines did not know that the Amalekites and the Geshurites and the Gizrites were not Israelites (1 Samuel 27). At any rate it was in Philistine interests to have the Israelites divided. David's deceptions worked, and Achish trusted him: "He has made himself utterly abhorred by his people Israel; therefore he shall be my servant always." (1 Samuel 27:12)

Saul's preoccupation with David may have been one reason why the Philistines decided to attack. A country with a king who did not rule, whose mind was affected, whose people were, at least from the outside, divided, was clearly vulnerable. We don't know how damaging to morale Saul's obsession was, but when all his efforts were directed to capturing David, and twice he could have done so and twice he did nothing, the people involved would wonder what was the point. On another occasion the Philistines attacked, unwittingly saving David and so insuring their own defeat (1 Samuel 23:26–28), but that seems to have been a raid. This time they assembled in strength at Aphek, where they had defeated Israel before (1 Samuel 29:1), in units of a hundred and a thousand. David was among them with his troops, presumably not enjoying the prospect but having to give an appearance of willingness to fight his own people. He was saved from a difficult decision by the objection of the Philistine commanders who argued with King Achish that the Hebrews could turn against them at a critical moment in the battle. David protested but Achish sent him and his men back to their city, freeing him to fight the Amalekites and to distribute spoils to the elders of Judah and his friends (1 Samuel 29 and 30).

THE DEATH OF SAUL AND DEFEAT OF THE ISRAELITES

Saul's final days were tragic (1 Samuel 28). He panicked at the sight of the Philistines, yet decided to fight. He tried to get help from God through dreams and prophets and by the Urim and Thummin, the sacred lot, but there was silence. Even an Egyptian king was allowed an interpretation of his dreams. In desperation, Saul resorted to the one means that he himself had outlawed, consulting the spirits of the dead. He called on the skills of a medium or a woman with a familiar spirit. It is an indication of the nature of popular Israelite religion that Saul's servants had no difficulty finding such a woman. He visited her in disguise, promised her that she would suffer no harm, and asked her to bring back the spirit of Samuel (4 Samuel 28:8–10).

The scene is strange, but there is probably no society, including our own, which does not try to communicate with the dead. The incident at En-dor is typical of the intense longing that living people have for contact with those whom they knew who have died. The witch of En-dor was recognized as an authority or an expert, so Saul went to her with confidence.

There are comparable experts in other societies. In African society, for example, there were, and some would say there are, specialists, mediums, and diviners trained to link human beings with the living-dead and with spirits. One African scholar writes that while many traditional ideas are abandoned and modified, "the majority of our people with little or no formal education still hold on to their traditional corpus of beliefs and practices."[14] So it was in Israel long after the giving of the law, and it explains the rapid way in which Saul was able to arrange a meeting.

According to the text, when the ghost of Samuel appeared the medium knew that it was Saul who had visited her. But Saul was intent upon the spirit and its message, and when he saw Samuel he cried to him for help. Samuel's answer was totally without hope "Tomorrow you and your sons shall be with me; the Lord will give the army of Israel also into the hand of the Philistines" (1 Samuel 28:19). When Saul heard this he collapsed.

The woman, no longer possessed, showed an almost motherly concern for the king. He did not want to eat anything, but she persuaded him and cooked some food. The preparation must have taken some time, yet Saul and his servants waited. Finally they ate together; it was a strange last meal.

The battle the following day was a total victory for the Philistines. Saul's three sons were killed; Saul was wounded and took his own life to avoid capture. There was such a general rout that many of the Israelites abandoned their cities and the Philistines went in and occupied them (1 Samuel 31:7).

Saul ranks very low in the hierarchy of Israel's leaders. The long summary of famous men, the heroes of Israel, to be found in Ecclesiasticus 44:1–50:29 does not even mention Saul (Ecclesiasticus 46:20). Yet he was an unusual and admirable man and the record of that has been preserved in the text, though David is clearly the hero of 1 and 2 Samuel. Saul's quality can be measured by the devotion which others had for him despite his disturbed later years. When the Philistines decapitated his body and those of his sons, and nailed them to the wall of Bethshan, the men of Jabesh-gilead, who never forgot what the king had done for them, recovered the bodies, certainly at the risk of their lives, and gave them a proper burial (1 Samuel 31:11–13).

The great men of Israel are notable for their contentious and disloyal families, and this was especially true of David and Solomon. But there was no disloyalty in Saul's family. Jonathan loved David, and Saul came close to murdering Jonathan because of it. But when Jonathan had to make a decision he and his brothers chose to stay with their father in what they must have known was a hopeless fight. They died together.

Saul did not seek the monarchy, and it seems that the strains of that office were too much for his pragmatic and yet unusually sensitive nature. Nevertheless, he was held responsible and punished. In this one can compare him with Job; both were the victims of divine intention. But he was an inarticulate Job whose feelings were not recorded, and, unlike Job, for him there was no happy ending.

[14]John Mbiti, African Religions and Philosophy (London: Heinemann, 1969), pp. xi and 17
See also Geoffrey Parrinder, *Religion in Africa* (Baltimore: Penguin Books, 1969), p. 83, and Benjamin C. Ray, *African Religions* (Englewood Cliffs, N.J.: Prentice-Hall, 1976), pp. 72–74 and 225, where there is a bibliography on witchcraft.

QUESTIONS FOR DISCUSSION

e following questions refer to Chapters 7–9.

While the book of Judges contains many accounts of faithfulness and courage some of the material in the book is exceedingly unpleasant, and the writer of the concluding verse appears to be quite discouraged. What is the religious value of this book? What does it teach us about the nature of God and about the Israelites commitment to their religion?

The account of the inauguration of the monarchy is ambiguous. Is it saying that the monarchy was against God's will? If so, why did God allow it? Samuel's dire predictions certainly came to pass. It was the monarchy which brought the people of Israel to disaster. Yet could Israel have survived beyond the period of the Judges without a king? What would have been necessary for that to happen?

In light of the fact that David's absence from the Israelite army may have let to its defeat and the death of Saul, could it be argued that Saul's original suspicions of David, in 1 Samuel 18:8, were well founded? Or, seeing that God had already chosen David to replace Saul, were David's personal ambitions, if he had them, irrelevant?

What does the ready availability of a necromancer, the Witch of Endor, suggest about the nature of popular religion in Israel during the early monarchy?

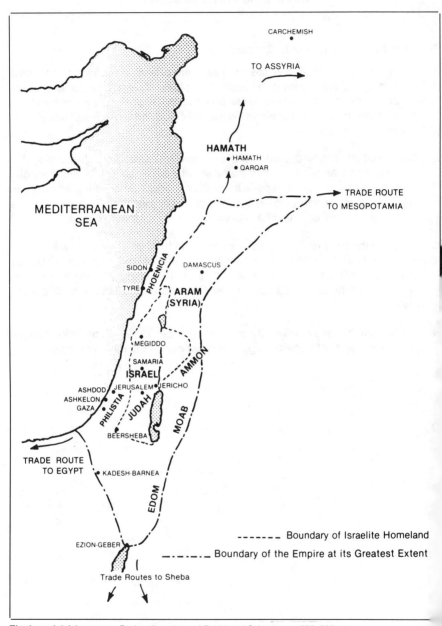

The Imperial Adventures. During the reigns of David and Solomon c. 1000–922 B.C.

CHAPTER 10
DAVID

DAVID, KING OF JUDAH

The battle of Gilboa was a disaster for Israel. The Israelites were scattered, their leader killed, much of their territory occupied once again by the Philistines. The outlook was very bleak. Yet within forty years this almost defunct nation had defeated the Philistines so that they were never again a serious threat. It conquered the smaller states of Edom, Moab, Ammon, and Amalek and extended its control through Zobah, north of Damascus. It concluded a long-lasting commercial agreement with Phoenicia and reached a friendly understanding with Hamath. From being marginal, Israel had become prosperous and secure.

This remarkable change was the work of David, whose personality and accomplishments have been of major importance in Jewish thought ever since. The city of Jerusalem, which he captured and made Israel's capital and the center of her worship, was known as the city of David, the earthly prototype of the heavenly city. His empire became the ideal to which generation after generation of Jews has wanted to return. His faith in God was regarded as the standard of righteousness to be expected of an Israelite monarch. And he himself, in real life a saviour of his country, became in both Jewish and Christian theology a symbol of the Messiah.

David's personality was complex and extreme. His grief at the news that Saul and Jonathan were dead was unrestrained:

How are the mighty fallen
　　in the midst of the battle!
Jonathan lies slain upon thy high places.
I am distressed for you, my brother Jonathan;
very pleasant have you been to me;
　　　your love to me was wonderful,
　　　passing the love of women.
How are the mighty fallen,
　　and the weapons of war perished! (2 Samuel 1:25–27)

It was genuine grief, but controlled grief. Unlike Saul, David grieved or was angry or repentant, and then he calculated his next best move. For example, after his second meeting and emotional reconciliation with Saul he observes coolly, "I shall now perish one day by the hand of Saul; there is nothing better for me than that I should escape to the land of the Philistines." (1 Samuel 27:1) Similarly, after his lament for Saul and Jonathan, he goes to Hebron, is anointed King of Judah and then, as soon as he hears about the rescue of the bodies, he sends the citizens of Jabesh-gilead a carefully political message which takes advantage of their loyalty to Saul to develop loyalty to himself.

May you be blessed by the Lord, because you showed this loyalty to Saul your lord, and buried him! Now may the Lord show steadfast love and faithfulness to you! And I will do good to you because you have done this thing.
Now therefore let your hands be strong, and be valiant; for Saul your lord is dead, and the house of Judah has anointed me king over them. (2 Samuel 2:5–7)

No one in Israel rivaled David as a leader. Abner "made" Saul's son Ishbosheth King over the northern tribes, and doubtless there was sympathy and potential loyalty but the people of Israel did not choose him nor did he act like a leader; he did not for example, send a message to Jabesh-gilead. His capital city Mahanaim lay across the Jordan in a remote part of Israel's territory. David, by contrast, was chosen and showed a characteristic initiative. He established himself at Hebron, a city much more at the center of the life of Israel than Mahanaim, and much closer to Israel's most obvious enemies, the Philistines. It is possible that by allowing himself to be proclaimed King of Judah while Ishbosheth was King of Israel (2 Samuel 2:9), David intensified the division between north and south;[2] on the other hand it was very natural for him to secure himself among his supporters. He must also have guessed that Abner was after the throne of Israel for himself.

[1]Ishbosheth, "man of shame," a contemptuous distortion of the name Eshbaal (Baal exists), intended no doubt to discredit Saul. Hertzburg suggests that the real name is referred to in 1 Samuel 14: as Ishyo, Man of Yaweh. 1 Chronicles 8:33 and 9:39 use the name Eshbaal. Hans Wilhelm Hertzburg *I and II Samuel*, 2d ed., J. S. Bowden trans. (Philadelphia: Westminster Press, 1960). p. 249.
[2]Yohanan Aharoni, *The Land of the Bible*, A. F. Rainey trans. (Philadelphia: The Westminster Press, 1967), p. 260.

Yet David did not want to alienate Saul's followers and he did not want to arouse the suspicion of the Philistines. From their point of view he was still a client king.

David's tactic was to wear down the opposition without destroying it so that, as the text explains, the house of David grew stronger and stronger and the house of Saul grew weaker and weaker. For example, at the skirmish beside the Pool of Gibeon, in which Abner killed Joab's brother Asahel, Joab called off the fight before it became too serious even though his men had the upper hand. The Pool of Gibeon is not far from Gibeah, Saul's fortress, which may have underlined how poorly Ishbosheth compared with his father, and so helped to further discredit him among his followers.

In addition to military tactics, David's marriage to Maacah, daughter of the King of Geshur, an Aramaean state east of the Sea of Galilee, may have been designed to secure an ally in Ishbosheth's rear (2 Samuel 3:3). Possibly for similar reasons he entered into friendly relations with Ammon (2 Samuel 10:2).

DAVID'S OPPONENTS

David was helped greatly by his opponents. Ishbosheth did not like his subservient position with Abner and wanted to challenge it. Abner, who had the power but not the authority, wanted to assert it. He did so in a particularly telling way by sleeping with Rizpah, one of Saul's concubines. The two men quarrelled and Abner deserted to David. Why he did that rather than overthrow Ishbosheth and take command himself the text does not explain. Possibly by then he realized that David was too strong, so he used the quarrel as an excuse to change sides.

The violence which followed was not David's responsibility, but it was to his advantage. He received Abner cordially, but Joab arranged a meeting with Abner too, and under guise of stepping aside for a private conversation stabbed him to death. David grieved loudly and publicly, possibly sincerely, and made Joab grieve publicly too, but he must have felt relieved. He pronounced an impressive curse upon Joab, which was probably as much to persuade the public as to castigate Joab. At any rate, it convinced the Israelites that David had not been involved and that he genuinely regretted Abner's death. It was another example of David's good fortune: first the death of Saul, then of Abner, finally of Ishbosheth, the unfortunate King whose murder removed the last serious opposition to David becoming King of all Israel.

Ishbosheth is one of several tragic figures in the two books of Samuel; another was his younger brother Mephibosheth. Ishbosheth's life was overshadowed by his brother, Jonathan; his kingship was manipulated by Abner, and he died a miserable and useless death. Although he quarrelled with Abner his courage failed when Abner went over to David, and "all Israel was dismayed." In this state of mind he took his midday rest in his tent with no one to guard him but an old woman who herself became drowsy and fell asleep. It was then that two of his officers crept into the tent, murdered him in his bed, and brought the unfortunate man's head to David hoping to gain an advantage. David treated them as he treated the Amalekite who claimed to have murdered Saul. He had them put to death and displayed their decapitated hands and feet beside the pool in Hebron, prompt action which no doubt helped to convince the people that, once again, David was not responsible for the death of a rival. We do not, however, read that David lamented the death of Ishbosheth as he had the death of Abner.[3]

THE CAPTURE OF JERUSALEM
AND THE DEFEAT OF THE PHILISTINES

The Philistines meanwhile tolerated David as their vassal king. He relieved them of having to garrison sections of the country and it was to their advantage that the Israelites were divided. They appear to have been rather easygoing compared with the days when they fought and almost defeated Egypt in fierce land and sea battles. They seemed content to control the country but not to occupy it with any thoroughness. That was an error on their part for it left David free to strengthen his influence among the northern tribes, and he no doubt took full advantage. One can imagine that he and Joab spent many hours discussing strategy. When he was ready he outwitted and outfought the Philistines with stunning efficiency.

It is not really clear just when David became king of the united nation. Ishbosheth was forty when he succeeded his father as king of Israel, and he reigned for two years. David ruled Judah for seven and a half years (2 Samuel 2:8–11), so that there appears to be a long period between the death of his rival and his succession as king of a united nation.

The biblical text gives the impression that the succession followed immediately after the death of Ishbosheth, but it also states twice that he ruled over Judah for seven and a half years (2 Samuel 2:11; 5:5).[4]

Once David was proclaimed king he required a base to secure himself against the Philistines. The obvious choice was Jerusalem, but if we think back to the time before it happened, capturing Jerusalem presented an almost impossible task. The Philistines were the strongest fighting force in Palestine and, as far as we know, they had not attempted to capture Jerusalem. Joshua's forces are reported to have killed the king of Jerusalem, Adonai-zedek (Joshua 10:1–27), but they did not capture the city. Later, the men of Judah are said to have captured it (Judges 1:8), yet in the same chapter we read that the Benjamites did not drive out the Jebusites of Jerusalem and the Jebusites have lived on in Jerusalem with the Benjamites till the present day (Judges 1:21).

At the time of David it was still an independent Jebusite city built on a lofty

---

[3]Marvin Noth, *The History of Israel*, 2d ed., revised translation by P. R. Ackroyd, (New York: Harper and Row, 1960), pp. 184–86.

[4]Hertzburg, *I and II Samuel*, p. 250.
Noth, *A History of Israel*, p. 194.

View of Jerusalem looking east toward the Dome of the Rock and the Mount of Olives. The original city of David was slightly south, just beyond the right of this photograph. Photo by Elizabeth Gordon.

spur of rock between the Kidron and Tyropoeon Valleys and defended by huge walls. The remains of the Jebusite walls have been excavated. They are 27 feet wide at the highest point and may be as much as forty feet wide at the base.[5] It was therefore extremely bold strategy on David's part to attempt to capture the city, and it is unlikely that either the Philistines or the Jebusites imagined that anyone would try. But it is also possible that the Philistines did not care to try, that the city was politically and economically so unimportant that they did not consider its capture worth the effort required to overcome its strong defenses.[6] This is a recent suggestion which might help explain why the city remained independent for so long. Had it been regarded as strategically important, the Philistines would have attempted to capture it.

When David assembled his forces the Jebusites were not alarmed; in fact they appear to have laughed at the Israelites' presumptuousness. The reference to the blind and the lame is obscure, except that it was certainly intended as an insult. But David and Joab knew that there was a tunnel cut through the rock from the Gihon spring

[5]G. Ernest Wright, *Biblical Archeology* (Philaelphia: The Westminster Press, 1962), p. 127.
[6]Michael M. Eisman, "A Tale of Three Cities," *Biblical Archeologist,* Vol. 41.2 (June 1978), p. 164.

to inside the city wall, and it was likely that in this way the Israelites entered, with Joab leading them, and captured the city.[7] The occupation was peaceful, certainly without much bloodshed or destruction. We read that David later bought a threshing floor, possibly the Temple Mount (2 Samuel 24:18–25), from Araunah the Jebusite who may have been the ruler of the city when David defeated it.

The value of Jerusalem to David was considerable. It not only provided him with a strong defensive base, but it provided him with a capital city not previously associated with any of the tribes. Jerusalem was indeed the city of David by right of conquest. It was also on the border of the northern and the southern tribes, and so avoided the appearance of being aligned with one or the other. Later he made it the religious center. He therefore controlled the religious, the political, and the military life of the nation from one place.

The Philistines were now aware of what was happening. They assembled a force to attack David and overran the Vale of Rephaim, southeast of Jerusalem, but David took refuge in the city. He then attacked, and the Philistines were defeated. They "left their idols there, and David and his men carried them away" (2 Samuel 5:21), which in a sense avenged the capture of the Ark years before (1 Samuel 4:11). The Philistines regrouped and attacked again. This time they were routed as far as Gezer by a flanking maneuver which took them by surprise in the rear. The text explains that the Lord himself was present at the battle. The Philistines were never again a serious threat to the safety of Israel, although there was continued fighting and on one occasion the Philistines actually captured David and nearly killed him (2 Samuel 21:15–17).

MILITARY AND DIPLOMATIC ACHIEVEMENTS

David's accomplishments were military, diplomatic, administrative, and religious, of which the religious were most important to the Old Testament writers. But the military accomplishments made the religious ones possible. The text deals with his victories in a rather summary fashion, and one may overlook the magnitude of what he did. Had David been a Pharaoh or an Assyrian king, he might be ranked among the great commanders in world history. Within a smaller arena he was consistently victorious. He defeated the Philistines in Israel and on the coast, the Moabites and the Ammonites in the East, the king of Zobah and the Aramaeans of Damascus in the north, and the Edomites in the south. He treated the Moabites with unusual cruelty, killing two out of three prisoners chosen by a length of cord (2 Samuel 8:1–2), an incident which must have occurred to King Mesha when, about a hundred years

---

[7]For an alternative explanation of how David captured Jerusalem see Gaaylah Cornfeld, *Archeolog of the Bible: Book by Book* (New York: Harper and Row, 1976), p. 96. This work is a compilation of material published in the *Biblical Archeologist*. The author refers to a thesis based on Benjamin Mazar's translation of 2 Samuel 5:9, which reads, "they struck and damaged the horizontal conduit" leading to the vertical shaft. With its water supply disrupted, the city could easily be taken by storm.

later, he recorded his victory against Israel on what we now call the Moabite Stone. David practiced genocide in Edom, where it is stated that Joab remained for six months until he had destroyed every male except Hadad, a young man of the royal house of Edom who escaped to Egypt with some of his father's servants (1 Kings 11:14–25).

There may be a reference here to particularly bitter and protracted fighting. At the southern tip of Edom was the fort of Elath; with that in their control the Israelites could trade from the Persian Gulf to the Mediterranean. The stakes were very high and the Edomites would not want to lose them; that may explain why Joab personally directed operations in Edom for half a year.

David was unquestionably a formidable warrior, but he made a practice when possible, and when it suited him, to develop friendly relations with nearby states. He did this with Toi the king of Hamath and with the Ammonites, until they quite needlessly insulted his messengers of goodwill (2 Samuel 10:1–5). Near the end of his reign he made a treaty with Hiram, the king of Tyre (2 Samuel 5:11), which began an association that lasted through the reign of Solomon.

By means of conquest and diplomacy David controlled territory that stretched from the Sinai desert to a sphere of influence as far north as the Euphrates Valley. It was a substantial empire.[8]

ADMINISTRATIVE POLICIES

With considerable territory to administer, David established a small bureaucracy (2 Samuel 8:15–18). It consisted of a commander-in-chief, Joab; a secretary of state, Jehoshaphat; two priests, Zadok and Abiathar, who had survived Saul's massacre at Nob; an adjutant general, Seraiah; Benaiah, the commander of the Philistine mercenary guards, the Kerethites and Pelethites, who would play an important role in the succession of Solomon; and Adoram (2 Samuel 20:23–26), in charge of the forced levy, an ominous indication of how the monarchy in Israel was developing. David may have taken his administrative model from the Canaanite cities he conquered, such as Jerusalem, and from Egypt, where there was considerable administrative experience. Perhaps he employed some of the bureaucrats he had captured, or even hired Egyptians. He may also have been influenced by his contact with Phoenicia, which was engaged in international trade.[9]

One administrative device which he used could have been the precursor of what is regarded as a radical innovation of Solomon's. Solomon replaced the ancient tribal

---

[8]Noth, *The History of Israel,* p. 197.
Walter Brueggemann, *In Man We Trust,* (Atlanta: John Knox Press, 1972), p. 31.

[9]John H. Hayes, *Introduction to the Bible* (Philadelphia: Westminster Press, 1971), p. 111.
At the time of David, administrative procedures had been practiced in the Near East for more than a millennium. In the Ur III dynasty, ca. 2060-1950 B.C., scribes used elaborate double-entry bookkeeping. Evidence would indicate "not only the antiquity of the modern bureaucracy but the modernity of the ancient." Clyde Curry Smith, "The Birth of Bureaucracy," *Biblical Archeologist,* Vol. 40.1 (March 1977), p. 24. With regard to Abiathar son of Abimelech see 1 Samuel 22:20 and 1 Samuel 21:2.

divisions with administrative divisions of his own, each under an administrator responsible to him. David did not go as far but, according to 1 Chronicles 27:16–22, which may have been a later reflection, he placed principal officers in charge of the tribes, which suggests a tightening of administrative control. This could have been related, as it was in the case of Solomon, to the requirements of the forced levy organized by Adoram.

DAVID'S RELIGIOUS POLICY

Saul was chosen by God but he acted with considerable independence of God. As we have seen he aroused Samuel's anger by ignoring the rules, and he thoroughly alienated the priests by murdering many of them at Nob (1 Samuel 22:9–23), when they unwittingly assisted David. Saul never attempted to give the Ark a better residence than it had at Kiarath-mearim and Baalath-Judah. David, however, brought the Ark to Jerusalem and restored it to the prominence it had at the time of Moses. He wanted to build a Temple, but the Lord reserved that privilege for Solomon, his son. Jerusalem then became the religious center of the Israelite people.

The procession of the Ark to the city is described in great detail; there were harps, lutes, tambourines, castanets, cymbals, singing and dancing, and making merry. Yet the strange incident of Uzzah, who attempted to steady the Ark and was immediately struck dead (2 Samuel 6:1–11), ended the rejoicing for that day. One can hardly understand this in terms of twentieth-century Western religion, by whose standards God's treatment of Uzzah was savage, but in ancient religion and many non-Western religions the holy is always dangerous. The standard phrase for the genuine or the canonical scriptures was that they defiled the hands because they were holy. Only priests, who were themselves holy, could touch the holy. It otherwise was like touching a high voltage line.

Uzzah's death delayed the transfer of the Ark for two months; it was then brought to the city with renewed celebrations. The text, however, includes another incident which tempered the rejoicing and reveals the hard side of David's character, and the vulnerable and dependent position of women at the time. Part of the bargain which David made with Abner when Abner decided to change sides was that he would return David's first wife Michal. Perhaps David thought he could strengthen his right of succession if he could have a child by Saul's daughter. At the beginning of David's career she had fallen in love with him and he had performed a great act of heroism to win her hand. Later, she saved his life by helping him to escape her father (1 Samuel 19:9–17). But since then she had been married to Paltiel and the evidence is that they loved one another. Abner returned Michal clearly against her husband's wishes. The text tells us that Paltiel followed Michal weeping as she was taken from him until Abner drove him off (2 Samuel 3:12–16). It may have been against Michal's wishes too. When she saw her royal husband dancing beside the Ark and exposing himself she was disgusted, and let David know it. His response was correct and brutal

The text states simply that "she had no child to the day of her death" (2 Samuel 6:20–23).

THE CHARACTER OF DAVID AND HIS FAITH

Michal did not understand her husband's religious enthusiasm, but it was genuine. He cared, probably more than any king of Judah and Israel, for the reality of his faith. God was very real to him. This side of David's character, his religious enthusiasm, his willingness to forgive, his devotion to friends, his ability to admit wrong and to confess and plead for forgiveness without reserve are, in a sense, personal accomplishments which have made him one of the best loved personalities in the Old Testament. For almost three thousand years he has been an ideal of ardent, faulty, human devotion to God, combining more virtues than faults in his multifaceted life, the "anointed of the God of Jacob" who was also, with his poetic and musical nature, "the sweet psalmist of Israel" (2 Samuel 23:1).

The darkest blot on David's career was the incident concerning Bathsheba and her husband Uriah. From a modern perspective his seduction of Bathsheba, while it broke a commandment, may be less odious than his cold-blooded murder of the trusting Uriah. This affair illustrates the curious relationship that existed between David and Joab. The king seems genuinely to have disliked his general's murderous efficiency, yet he relied on him for just that quality. It was Joab who led the capture of Jerusalem, Joab who killed Abner, a rival of David as much as Joab, it was Joab who killed Amasa, who briefly succeeded him, and who was not on the job when he should have been as commander-in-chief (2 Samuel 20:4–13). It was Joab who had Absalom killed against the king's orders (2 Samuel 18:9–17), and then Joab who criticized the king sharply for being a defeatist at a time of victory. Even in the midst of his grief the king recognized that what Joab said made good sense (2 Samuel 19:1–8). Perhaps it was those final two incidents which broke their relationship, so that at the end of David's life Joab backed the man who was not the king's favorite. But before then David found Joab exceedingly useful as, for example, in the incident of Bathsheba. Joab probably knew the whole story, could sympathize with the king, and was willing and able to do whatever was necessary without moralizing or asking questions. In some respects, in this incident, Joab was to David what, in the Naboth incident, Jezebel was to Ahab (1 Kings 21).

Uriah's death was handled expeditiously. Bathsheba became one of David's wives and bore him a son. Apart from some court gossip the incident was kept secret, but David was King of Israel, and Israel was committed by Covenant to a certain standard of behavior, which included not committing adultery or murder. There were similar prohibitions in other contemporary societies, but in Israel there was no exception for the king, not even for the most powerful king of his time.

It is possible that God told Nathan what happened, but it is also possible that, like a latter-day reporter, he found out all he needed to know by listening to soldiers in the field and women in the court and putting two and two together. He was then ready to confront David, and he did so in a superbly tactful and devastating manner. By telling David a story about a small man who is victimized by a great man, he so aroused David's anger that the king burst out, "As the Lord lives, the man who has done this deserves to die; and he shall restore the lamb fourfold, because he did this thing, and because he had no pity." Nathan's classic reply was, "You are the man." (2 Samuel 12:1–7)

There was a precedent for this in very ancient times. In Egypt, about a thousand years before the time of David, the prophet Ipu-wer blamed his Pharaoh Mur-Ka-Re (2100 B.C.) for the distressing conditions of the day. "Authority, perception, and justice are with thee, (but) it is confusion which thou wouldst set throughout the land."[10] It was a democratic vision which did not continue. Egyptian society changed, and the stories of Ipu-wer dropped out of currency. In Israel the role of the prophet became increasingly important. It was the prophets who reminded the people of their Covenant obligations, and who never let them forget that no matter how secular their society might become, their allegiance was always to God.

David's response to Nathan's strong criticism tells us why, despite his great faults, he was so admired. Psalm 51, traditionally ascribed to David, as are many Psalms, is a deeply penitent appeal to God for forgiveness, and is consistent with what we know of the long record of David's character left for us in the Old Testament. Although his sin was grave he was willing to accept criticism. One can compare this with Ahab's angry rebuttal of the prophet Micaiah (1 Kings 22), and the contemptuous manner in which Jehoiakim destroyed Jeremiah's prophecy (Jeremiah 36).

THE COURT HISTORY OF DAVID

The chapters that tell the story of Bathsheba and Nathan are part of a remarkable document (2 Samuel 9–20; 1 Kings 1 and 2). It deals largely with the events of David's personal life and with the murderous struggles between his children for the succession. The writing is graphic, convincing, and uncomplimentary to its hero. It bears the marks of a firsthand account written shortly after the events happened.

David was a great King of Israel, but he was a culpably bad father. The text softens that obvious fact by linking his family trouble to the solemn reprimand uttered by Nathan after David had murdered Bathsheba's husband Uriah. " 'Now therefore the sword shall never depart from your house, because you have despised me, and have taken the wife of Uriah the Hittite to be your wife.' Thus says the Lord: 'Behold I will raise up evil against you out of your own house...' " (2 Samuel 12:10–11).

The troubles began with David's eldest son Amnon, who developed a passion for his half sister Tamar. With the scurrilous help of his cousin Jonadab, Amnon tricked Tamar into coming into his bedroom, raped her, and then, with his love turned to

[10]John A. Wilson, *The Burden of Egypt* (Chicago: The University of Chicago Press, 1951), p. 115

"Absalom's Tomb" outside the walls of Jerusalem. Photo by Elizabeth Gordon.

hate, cast her out. Tamar was Absalom's sister, and as David did nothing about the incident Absalom nursed his anger for two years and then he murdered Amnon (2 Samuel 13: 1–33).

Again David took no action except to grieve that Absalom was in exile with his mother's family in Geshur, and when he returned, with Joab's help, the king would not see him for two years until, again with Joab's help, he formally received him (2 Samuel 14, 28–33).

We don't know what became of Tamar, but Absalom had a daughter whom he named Tamar (2 Samuel 14:27), "a beautiful woman," so we may suppose that he was still angered by the wrong done to his sister, and that that was a dominant reason for his deliberate and carefully managed plans to usurp his father's throne.

Although David was King of all Israel and had ruled for many years he could not assume the loyalty of all his subjects. The northern tribes still regarded him as an outsider, which became clear during Absalom's rebellion and Sheba's rebellion that followed it (2 Samuel 20:1). David took advantage of a complaint by the Gibeonites to have two of Saul's remaining sons and five of his grandsons put to death (2 Samuel 21:1–14), an action which he carried out so readily as to suggest that he feared a rival claim to the succession. There were other kinds of unrest, possibly associated with the census (1 Chronicles 27:24), and perhaps with the principal officers (1 Chronicles 27:16). It would seen that the people of Israel felt remote from their king and were ready to listen to and follow someone who promised a change. Absalom, therefore, sat himself at the city gate and ingratiated himself with the population by providing a return to an old style of leadership in which the leader had direct contact with his people. "Oh that I were judge in the land! Then every man with a suit or cause might come to me." (2 Samuel 15:4) In this way he "stole the hearts" of the Israelites (2 Samuel 15:6). But David did nothing to restrain them. From Amnon's rape of his half sister Tamar to Absalom's rebellion there were eleven years, and the king allowed matters to drift until he had to flee from Jerusalem into the Judean wilderness to escape his son. Only then did he seem to come to life with some of the energy and skill of his earlier years.

His tactics are clear; he did not want to be trapped into a wasting defense of the city. He preferred the open country which he knew better than probably anyone in Israel, and could use to greater advantage. His setting up of a spy system within the city (2 Samuel 15:24–25) was a tribute not only to his quick thinking, but also to the total loyalty of his immediate followers.

Absalom's rebellion was put down with the death of Absalom, and a more serious and widespread rebellion led by Sheba was dealt with firmly shortly after, but the resentments that caused both of them remained. Sheba's battle cry,

We have no portion in David,
we have no inheritance in the son of Jesse;
every man to his tents O Israel! (2 Samuel 20:1)

was repeated forty years later, after the death of Solomon.

The end of David's reign is an anticlimax, but that is less important than what he achieved. He had transformed the Israelites from an insecure conglomerate of tribes to a powerful small empire confident in its faith about its future. It was to continue, however, only through the lifetime of David's son.

CHAPTER ELEVEN
SOLOMON

THE SOURCES

Like the two books of Samuel, 1 and 2 Kings were originally one book. The text was divided in the Greek Septuagint (third century B.C.) and then in printed editions from the fifteenth century A.D.

An obvious reason for dividing the work was its length. Two scrolls are more convenient to handle than one. Yet long as they are, the books of Kings provide only a "skeletal account" of the history of Israel from Solomon to the destruction of Jerusalem.[1] There were other works to which the reader is referred: the Acts of Solomon (1 Kings 11:41), the Book of the Chronicles of the Kings of Israel (1 Kings 14:19), and the Book of Chronicles of the Kings of Judah (1 Kings 14:29). These contained more complete information than the author or editor of Kings wished to use; for example, at the conclusion of the account of Rehoboam, "Now the rest of the acts of Rehoboam, and all that he did, are they not written in the Book of the Chronicles of the Kings of Judah?" (I Kings 14:29) How complete the information was in those works, whether they were literary compositions or "dry and factual" lists[2] is not known

---

[1]Brevard S. Childs, *Introduction to the Old Testament as Scripture* (Philadelphia: Fortress Press, 1979), p. 288.

[2]John Gray, *I and II Kings,* second, fully revised edition (Philadelphia: The Westminster Press, 1970), p. 28.

for sure, although it is likely that both kinds of material were available to the author.

Other sources may have been used for the stories about Elijah and Elisha, such as sagas about the prophets and a hagiology, or sacred writings, which contained the more personal and miraculous incidents of their lives.[3]

PURPOSE OF THE BOOK

What was the editor's purpose in writing this work? While there are different answers,[4] it would seem that, as in the books of Samuel, the purpose was, in general, "definitely and deliberately religious."[5] The rise and fall of the Hebrew monarchy is presented as a long parable of what happens when a nation obeys or, most often in this account, disobeys the requirements of God. David is the ideal king, and Josiah is the hero because he attempted to reform the nations in accordance with the Deuteronomic law, that is, the Book of the Law found in the Temple in 621.[6] One writer[7] suggests that the author's aim is to be found in David's final charge to his son Solomon (1 Kings 2:2-4) "Be strong, and show yourself a man, and keep the charge of the Lord your God, walking in his ways and keeping his statutes, his commandments, his ordinances, and his testimonies, as it is written in the law of Moses."

This was not a new standard against which to judge all the kings, but a very old one.[8] It expressed, in effect, an original theocratic view of Israel in which the nation, from the king down, was subject to God.

The book of Kings was probably written about 600 B.C., nine years after the death of Josiah, thirteen years before the fall of Jerusalem, a time of fear and confusion. About fifty years later, about 550 B.C., the book was revised.[9] In its present form it is, to some extent, a homily on the consequence of religious neglect with the threat of final disaster connecting the various reigns "like a red thread."[10]

But while God punishes, he also forgives. Whether this is implied by the kind treatment of Jehoiachin at the end of the book (2 Kings 25:27-30) is uncertain. It is, however, the theme of God's entire revelation, of which the book of Kings is a part.

---

[3]Ibid., p. 29.

[4]Childs, *Introduction to the Old Testament*, pp. 285-287.

[5]Norman H. Snaith, "Introduction to I and II Kings," *Interpreters Bible*, Vol. III (New York: Abingdon Press, 1954), p. 7.

Gerhard Von Rad, *Old Testament Theology*, Vol. I, D.M.G. Stalker trans. (New York: Harper and Row, 1962), p. 337.

[6]Snaith, "Introduction to I and II Kings," p. 7.

[7]Ibid.

[8]Von Rad, *Old Testament Theology*, p. 336.

[9]Gray, *I and II Kings*, p. 7.
Interpreters Bible, Vol. III, pp. 3-4.

[10]Childs, *Introduction to the Old Testament*, p. 288.

SOLOMON'S CONSOLIDATION OF POWER

The book opens with a struggle for power between Adonijah and Solomon at the end of David's life. It is a tale of deceit and violence. The two rival factions involved priests, the military command, and the royal family. A few people may still have been alive who could remember the unpretentious style of the first king, Saul, and who could remember also that when David became King of all Israel it was by choice of the people. Solomon became king by palace intrigue.

The political unrest of David's reign was due to rivalry between his sons. His eldest son, Amnon (2 Samuel 3:2–5), had been murdered by his third son, Absalom (2 Samuel 13:23–29). Absalom was killed at Joab's order during the rebellion (2 Samuel 18:9–17). Adonijah was the fourth son, by Haggith, about whom we know nothing more than her name. Solomon was a younger son by Bathsheba, the king's best known wife. The affair which David had with her, and his murder of her husband, Uriah, led as we have seen to a dramatic confrontation between the king and Nathan the prophet (2 Samuel 11–12).

Adonijah, as the older son, may have felt that he should succeed his father. Solomon, as the most favored, evidently felt that he should succeed. The other sons did not contend.

David had become old, possibly senile, and was not alert to matters of state. Members of his household even found a beautiful young woman named Abishag to keep him warm. Perhaps, taking advantage of his father's condition, Adonijah decided to make a bid for the throne. He gained the support of Joab, who although an old man was evidently thinking of his position with the next monarch, and of Abiathar the priest. He then invited his royal brothers and "all the royal officials of Judah" (1 Kings 1:9) to a sacrificial banquet at En-rogel, a spring outside the city, where he proclaimed himself or was proclaimed king (1 Kings 1:5–10, 25–26). He did not invite Solomon, or Nathan, or Benaiah, who commanded David's bodyguard of Philistine mercenaries, the Cherethites and the Perethites. This was a basic weakness; Joab was apparentlay no longer the powerful figure he had been so that when the challenge came Adonijah's attempt at the throne collapsed.

It was Nathan who alerted Bathsheba to Adonijah's actions. Since his harsh denunciation of the king and his proclamation of God's punishment upon David and Bathsheba's first child, Nathan had remained a close supporter of the family. He told Bathsheba what was happening and advised her for her own safety, and for her son's safety, to see the king and say, "Did you not, my lord the king, swear to your maid-servant, saying, 'Solomon your son shall reign after me, and he shall sit upon my throne?' Why then is Adonijah king?" (1 Kings: 1:13–14). Bathsheba went to the king, but she made a slight change in the message. Instead of asking a question she stated a fact, "My lord, you swore to your maidservant by the Lord your God, saying, 'Solomon your son shall reign after me, and he shall sit upon my throne.' And now, behold, Adonijah is king, although you, my lord the king, do not know it." (1 Kings 1:17–18).

By prior arrangement Nathan entered while Bathsheba was speaking and, subtl
suggesting that it was David himself who had encouraged Adonijah, wondered wh
he and Solomon had not been told. This roused the old king. He ordered Zado
the priest, Nathan, and Benaiah to take Solomon to Gihon, a pool just outside th
city, closer than En-rogal, anoint him there, and acclaim him king.

The writer continues his narrative with a strong sense of drama: the surpris
and fear of Adonijah and his party, his brief reconciliation with Solomon, his incredibl
foolish request for Abishag and his death, the execution of Joab and Shimei. Th
events are crowded and confusing, but they are worth attention because they provid
a uniquely intimate glimpse of the passion and ruthlessness in an ancient Near Easter
court.

Solomon was not a warrior like his father, and he did not have to be. Durin
most of his reign Egypt was ruled by a weak, and therefore friendly, dynasty. Durin
David's reign Assyria, under Ashur-rabi II (1012–995), had lost part of its empir
to Syria. But David defeated Syria, that is Hadadezer of Aram, and so saved Assyri
from being overrun by the Syrians. Ironically, this saved or at least provided a respit
for the power that two centuries later was to destroy the Northern Kingdom of Israel.
Nevertheless, Solomon gave careful attention to his country's defense. He strengthene
a number of strategic towns: Hazor in the north, Megiddo in the northwest, Geze
southwest of Jerusalem, and Tamar south of the Dead Sea in the northern part c
Edom. He also strengthened Jerusalem and built various store cities and towns wher
he quartered his chariots and horses (1 Kings 9:15–19). His army included 1400 chario
and 12,000 horsemen (1 Kings 10:26). He was not threatened, but he was preparec
and so he was able to direct his energies to other matters than empire building an
defense. On every side, he said, "the Lord my God has given me rest. . .there is neithe
adversary nor misfortune." (1 Kings 5:4)

SOLOMON'S WISDOM

Tradition represents Solomon as a monarch of great wisdom. God appeared to hir
one night in a dream, asking him to name a gift that God might give him. His piou
reply was, literally, "Give to your servant a listening heart to judge your people, t
distinguish good from evil." God gave Solomon not only a listening heart but all th
benefits of peace and prosperity which most monarchs would have chosen fir
(1 Kings 3:5–15).

The most famous example of his wisdom, deciding who was the mother of th
disputed baby, exhibits cleverness rather than wisdom (I Kings 3:16–28). He solve
an awkward problem by quick thinking rather as Daniel solved a comparable prob
lem and saved Susanna's life.[12] It is claimed that Solomon uttered three thousan

---

[11]G. Ernest Wright, *Biblical Archeology*, 2d ed. (Philadelphia: Westminster Press, 1972), p. 12
Albert T. Olmstead, *History of Assyria* (Chicago: The University of Chicago Press, 1951), pp. 74–7

[12]The History of Susanna is one of the books of the Apocrypha, a group of writings produce
during the two centuries before the Christian era and not included in the Hebrew canon.

proverbs and his songs numbered a thousand and five. He talked about trees and beasts and birds and animals. People came from all parts of the earth to hear him (1 Kings 4:29–34). The book of Proverbs is ascribed to him, as are Ecclesiastes and the Song of Songs. While this is hyperbole (the Song of Songs, for example, was written over a very long period of several hundred years), the association of these works with Solomon suggests what was certainly true, that during his reign there was a great advance in appreciation of the arts.

One reason for this was the more active involvement of Israel with other societies. For example, the Phoenician craftsmen whom Solomon invited to his country had a lasting impact upon Israelite crafts and architecture. Phoenicia was also noted for its music, and in that respect, too, stimulated the musical life of Israel, although there was already a tradition of music in Israel through David. The Israelites were preeminent in literature, but Jewish literature similarly reflects the influence of surrounding nations.

In 1888 the British Museum obtained an Egyptian papyrus roll entitled "The Teaching of Amenemope," written originally in the thirteenth century B.C. It was a collection of proverbs divided into thirty chapters (compare Proverbs 22:20), some of which are so similar to passages in the biblical book of Proverbs that even if there were no direct borrowing it seems clear that they were related.[13] In one section (Proverbs 22:17, 22:24), the parallels are especially close:

> Give thine ears, hear what is said,
> Give thy mind to interpret them.
> To put them in thy heart is beneficial; It is detrimental for him who neglecteth them. (Amenemope)

> Incline your ear, and hear the words of the wise,
>   and apply your mind to my knowledge;
> for it will be pleasant if you keep them within you,
>   if all of them are ready on your lips. (Proverbs 22:17–18)

> Associate not with the hot-head
> Nor become intimate with him in conversation . . .
> Leap not to cleave to such a one,
> Lest a terror carry thee off. (Amenemope)

> Make no friendship with a man given to anger,
>   nor go with a wrathful man. (Proverbs 22:24)

It is possible that Solomon's Egyptian wife stimulated the Israelites to a greater appreciation of Wisdom Literature, a form of writing which had been popular in Egypt at least since the third millennium. Possibly too there was an international common stock of proverbial literature in the ancient Near East which the Israelites could have shared with their neighbors.[14]

[13]D. Winton Thomas, *Documents from Old Testament Times* (New York: Harper and Row, 1961), p. 176.
[14]Ibid., p. 172.

When God asked Solomon what he wanted he did not ask for wisdom as such but for the ability to listen (1 Kings 3:9). The Instruction of Ani, written earlier than Solomon, a set of instructions from Egypt given by a father to his son, states bluntly "Do not talk a lot. Be silent and thou wilt be happy."[15] One of the earliest Wisdom texts, the Instruction of Ptah-Hotep, who lived about 2450 B.C., urged the reader to "take counsel with the ignorant as well as the wise" and later in the text, "Every hearkener [is] an advantage, and hearing is of advantage to the hearkener. To hear is better than anything that is, [and thus] comes the goodly love [of man]."[16] An Akkadian Proverb of a later date counsels:

> As a wise man, let your understanding shine modestly,
> Let your mouth be restrained, guarded your speech.[17]

Compare this with Proverbs 13:3:

> He who guards his mouth preserves his life;
>   he who opens wide his lips comes to ruin.

Solomon's request is often interpreted as a sign of modesty and preference for the things of God rather than the things of the world. What we know of his life does not support that view. It could be argued instead that he asked for the ability to listen because it was traditionally a highly admired characteristic, a point, as we have seen, that is made in the Wisdom Literature again and again.[18]

SOLOMON AS A BUSINESSMAN

Solomon is distinguished from almost all Israelite monarchs as one whose accomplishments were other than war. There are exceptions, Josiah in the seventh century and Uzziah and Jeroboam II in the eighth, hundreds of years later than Solomon. But these monarchs lived at times when the Kingdom was divided, and potentially powerful enemies were never far away. Josiah was caught up in the clash between Egypt, Babylon, and Assyria; Uzziah and Jeroboam II devoted much of their energy to restoring the ancient borders of their countries. Solomon came to the throne at a proud moment in Israel's history. His task was not to restore power nor to achieve it but to maintain and develop it, and this he did largely through manufacture and trade.

[15]James B. Pritchard, *Ancient and Near Eastern Texts Relating to the Old Testament* (Princeton, N.J.: Princeton University Press, 1969), p. 420a.

[16]Ibid., pp. 412b, 414a.

[17]Ibid., 426b.

[18]James L. Crenshaw, *Old Testament Wisdom* (Atlanta: John Knox Press, 1981), pp. 42–54.

See the discussion on the value of silence in Henri Frankfort, *Ancient Egyptian Religion* (New York: Harper and Row, 1961), pp. 65–68.

In 1 Kings 9:26, we read that Solomon built (that is, had the Phoenicians build for him) a fleet of ships at Ezion-geber at the head of the Gulf of Aqabah. These were manned by Phoenician crews who sailed them to Ophir (possibly Somaliland, the identification is not clear)[19] returning with gold, almug wood and precious stones (1 Kings 10:11), ivory, apes, or monkeys, and peacocks (1 Kings 10:22). The journey took three years, one full year and part of two others.

Such trade, carried on through the Red Sea to the south of the Arabian Peninsula and the Horn of Africa, was not new, but until then it had been conducted mainly by Egypt. For example, in the fifteenth century, during the reign of the Egyptian queen Hatshepsut, an expedition sailed down the Red Sea to the Somali coast, known then as Punt, and returned with gold, ivory, rare woods, skins, incense, animals, and slaves.[20] But the activity of Israel in this area was new, and it impinged upon the trading operations of the Sabeans in South Arabia who sent caravans north to Palestine and Mesopotamia with gold, jewels, and spices. It was undoubtedly because of this that the queen of Seba (Sheba) paid a visit to Solomon with samples of her country's merchandise (1 Kings 10:1–10). The "hard questions" that she came with were quite likely as commercial as they were theological and metaphysical. The chronicler reports that "there was nothing hidden from the king which he could not explain to her" (1 Kings 10:3), which might be interpreted as meaning that the queen's visit was a success.

In 1 Kings 10:22 there is a reference to the king's "fleet of ships of Tarshish," ships designed by the Phoenicians for carrying copper which they mined in Cyprus and Sardinia. In all these enterprises the Phoenicians played a crucial part, and it is doubtful that Solomon could have achieved very much in the realm of large-scale trade and manufacturing without them. The Phoenicians were city people with little more than a strip of land along the coast (now Lebanon), but their "territory" was as extensive as the farthest port they could reach for trade. Ezekiel 27:12–25 provides a lengthy description of the range of their business enterprises at a later date: purple garments, fine linen, and black coral from Edom, wine from Damascus, spices, precious stones, and gold from Sheba, livestock from Arabia, colored fabric rolled up and tied with cords from Asshur and Media, silver, iron, tin, and lead from Tarshish, wheat, oil, and balsam from Judah and Israel, and so on. As Isaiah put it, "you were the merchant of the nations." (Isaiah 23:3) They were inveterate seafarers and traders, willing to take risks, rather like the Venetians and the Dutch and the British of 2500 years later, not particular whom they dealt with providing they could work out a profitable arrangement, as they apparently did with Israel.

The scope of this arrangement must have been as irresistible to Hiram as to Solomon. With the decline of Egypt, Phoenicia controlled the Mediterranean. Secure routes from their own ports through Solomon's territory to Ezion-geber would give the Phoenicians access to the Gulf of Aqabah and the Persian Gulf. They could then

[19]*Cambridge Ancient History,* Vol. II, part 2, pp. 526, 594.

[20]Robert W. July, *A History of the African People* (New York: Scribners, 1970), p. 33.

A reconstruction of the Temple of Solomon. Drawn by C. F. Stevens based on specifications of W. F. Albright and G. E. Wright. Reproduced from *The Westminster Historical Atlas of the Bible.* Revised edition edited by George Ernest Wright and Floyd Vivian Filson, Copyright 1956 by W. L. Jenkins. Used by permission of the Westminster Press, Philadelphia, Pa.

trade from the western Mediterranean to the east coast of Africa. The enormous profits attainable through such large-scale commerce explains why Hiram was so obliging to a still young empire. It was worth it to him to build a fleet of merchant ships for a nonseafaring nation, and to man the ships with his own men, because the return on his investment would be huge. And it was worth it to him to supply Solomon with the goods and services he needed for a major building program, and to be somewhat casual about the financing. Solomon himself would make a lot of money. It was only when Solomon, who proved in this respect not to be as wise as Hiram, outran his income that relations between the two monarchs became strained.

THE TEMPLE

From the chronicler's point of view, Solomon's major accomplishment was building the Temple, yet while Solomon instigated the building and paid for it, the construction and the design were Phoenician. Israel had no independent artistic traditions. It was therefore natural, when an especially magnificent structure was desired and native craftsmen were not sufficiently skilled to build it themselves, to call upon those who could.

Throughout the reigns of David and Solomon the affairs of Phoenicia and Israel were increasingly close-knit.[21] David's pact with Hiram helped to stabilize the as yet

[21]Brian Peckham, "Israel and Phoenicia," *Magnalia Dei* (Garden City, N.Y.: Doubleday, 1976), p. 224.

very insecure Kingdom. Hiram's support of Solomon's trading enterprises contributed to Israel's wealth, and the Temple, which was the glory of Solomon's reign and the center of Israel's worship until its destruction by the Babylonians, was built and designed by Hiram and his gifted and resourceful craftsmen. An exchange of letters between the two monarchs is recorded in the much later account of 2 Chronicles 2:1–16. Solomon requests Hiram to send him "a man skilled to work in gold, silver, bronze, and iron, and in purple, crimson, and blue fabrics, trained also in engraving, to be with the skilled workers who are with me in Judah and Jerusalem." He promises to send Hiram large supplies of wheat, barley, wine, and oil. The Phoenician king responds warmly. He will send Solomon what he wants and he looks forward to the supplies which Solomon had promised. Meanwhile his men will cut the trees in Lebanon (the Phoenicians were expert lumbermen, see verse 8 and 1 Kings 5:6), float them as rafts from Tyre south along the coast to Joppa, and from there ship them to Jerusalem.

It is not surprising that Hiram built what has been described as a typically Syrian temple, of a kind excavated at Tell Tainat in Syria[22] and Hazor,[23] the design of which was similar to that of Solomon's Temple, and it is not surprising that many pieces of temple equipment, such as lavers, shovels, and flesh hooks, have been found in various parts of Syria and Palestine, indicating not only that the instruments were similar but that the various temples were similarly equipped and possibly engaged in similar kinds of activities.

The most sacred place in the Temple was the Holy of Holies, a thirty-foot cube, unlighted except through the open door. There rested the Ark, and on either side of it two large cherubim made of olive wood and covered with gold leaf, fifteen feet high with a wing span of seven and a half feet, (see Isaiah 6:1–3). These cherubim were most likely the winged sphinx, a winged lion with a human face, which was a frequent motif in Canaanite art.[24]

Such interrelationship of Israelite and Canaanite (or Phoenician) religious motifs and practices undoubtedly helped to perpetuate the influence of Baal worship in Israel. Not only did it have the special attractiveness of polytheism (that is, one or another of the pantheon of nature gods, which we described in chapter 8, could be used by the worshipper or influenced by him as Yahweh could not), but the place of worship and manner of worship were similar. It is likely that many Israelites did not clearly know the difference.

Yet Hebrew religion was distinct. There could be no image of Yahweh. There was no embodiment of God in a king. The Israelite God could be approached through the Temple, but he did not reside in the Temple and was not dependent upon Temple offerings as were the Babylonian gods who, after the flood, in the Babylonian version,

[22]*Cambridge Ancient History,* Vol. II, part 2, p. 594.

Wright, *Biblical Archeology,* p. 137b.

[23]Yigael Yadin, *Hazor* (Jerusalem: Weidenfeld and Nicolson, 1975), Chapters 5 and 6, particularly p. 98.

[24]Roland de Vaux, *Ancient Israel,* Vol. 2 (New York: McGraw Hill, 1961), p. 319.

crowded round Utnapishtim's sacrifice like flies. Years later when God found the behavior of his people particularly objectionable, a prophet proclaimed that God would do away with sacrifices altogether (Amos 5:21–22).

Yahweh was totally independent of his people save that he was bound by a Covenant, and this is recognized in Solomon's prayer of dedication after the Temple was built.

> Then Solomon stood before the altar of the Lord in the presence of all the assembly of Israel, and spread forth his hands toward heaven; and said, "O Lord, God of Israel, there is no God like thee, in heaven above or on earth beneath, keeping covenant and showing steadfast love to thy servants who walk before thee with all their heart; who hast kept with thy servant David my father what thou didst declare to him; yea, thou didst speak with thy mouth, and with thy hand hast fulfilled it this day." (1 Kings 8:22–24)

The dedication of the Temple, a relatively small structure 90 by 30 feet, must have been a solemn and uplifting occasion. The promise to Abraham had been unquestionably fulfilled. All nations admired Israel, even the mighty and ancient Egypt. Israel was wealthy, powerful, and at peace, with a splendid house where God could meet his people and hear their prayers. Perhaps this moment was the climax of Israelite history.

THE WEAKNESSES OF SOLOMON'S REIGN

But Israel was not secure. Solomon spent seven years building the Temple (1 Kings 6:38). He spent another thirteen years building a house for himself (1 Kings 9:10) and for his enormous court and harem (1 Kings 11:3). As we have seen, he constructed and strengthened fortifications in different parts of the Kingdom: store cities, chariot cities, cities for his horsemen. He built whatever he wanted to build in Jerusalem, in Lebanon, and throughout his whole dominion (1 Kings 9:19).

At the commencement of this great enterprise Hiram declared that he was ready to do "all you desire" in the matter of cedar and pine, and reference to payment was dealt with in a polite and open way (1 Kings 5:6). But after twenty years Solomon had apparently outspent himself. He was obliged to sell to Hiram twenty cities of the land of Galilee for one hundred and twenty talents of gold. According to the text Hiram was not pleased with the cities (1 Kings 9:11–14); he called them the Land of Cabul, possibly fettered or sterile land. But this may have been a way of minimizing a painful loss. The land itself was not sterile.[25]

Not only were Solomon's building operations expensive, but so were the size and lavishness of the royal establishment. His use of gold was prodigal (1 Kings 10:14–17). Silver "was not considered as anything in the days of Solomon"

---

[25] Yohanan Aharoni, *The Land of the Bible,* A. F. Rainey trans. (Philadelphia: The Westminster Press, 1967), p. 277.

Kings 10:21). The expenses of an army equipped with fourteen hundred chariots, ch of which cost six hundred shekels of silver, only begins with the purchase of e military hardware.

According to the text Solomon had seven hundred wives and three hundred ncubines (1 Kings 11:3). They must have been a tremendous drain upon the resources the country. Solomon's provision for one day was "thirty measures (*cor* in Hebrew) fine flour, sixty measures of meal, ten fat oxen, twenty pasture-fed cattle, a hun- ed sheep, besides harts, gazelles, roebucks and fatted fowl." (1 Kings 4:22–23). A easure (or *cor*) was equivalent to approximately five U.S. bushels.[26] The scripture cords that Judah and Israel ate and drank and were happy.

Solomon's building projects must have given employment to thousands and mulated private enterprise. The use of the iron-tipped plough increased the pro- ictivity of the soil and led to a larger population. In other words, the lot of the in- vidual Israelite was generally improved, certainly at first. But the extent of Solomon's ojects eventually went beyond what the country could bear. Initially it appears that used non-Israelites and their descendants as slaves. "But of the people of Israel lomon made no slaves" (I Kings 9:22).

However, the time came when foreign slaves were not sufficient, and Solomon ised "a levy of forced labor" out of all Israel amounting to thirty thousand men Kings 5:13–14). They were required to serve one month out of every three. It must ave occurred to many of these men, and the women who remained at home, that od had rescued them from oppression in Egypt and now, scarcely three hundred ars later, they were virtually slave laborers in their own country conscripted to build, nong other things, a house for an Egyptian princess.

DMINISTRATION

) conscript and organize thirty thousand people requires considerable organiza- on. Both because of this and because of Solomon's complex commercial activities ere was need for a far larger administration than at the time of David or certainly ıul. Apart from his cabinet, which was not large (1 Kings 4:1–6), but included doniram in charge of forced labor, there were five hundred and fifty officers in charge the foremen (1 Kings 9:23) and three thousand three hundred foremen to superin- nd the laborers (1 Kings 5:16). There may have been a comparable number of remen and officers in the organization of his commercial activities, loading, ıloading, transporting, keeping accurate records and maintaining security.

To ensure that his people contributed their proper share of taxes and involun- ry services, Solomon organized the country into twelve districts, each with an of- :er in charge (1 Kings 4:7–19). It was a significant innovation. From earliest times

[26]O. R. Sellars, "Weights," *The Interpreters Dictionary of the Bible* (Nashville, Tenn.: Abingdon Press, 62), p. 835.

the people of Israel had consisted of twelve tribes descended traditionally from the sons of Jacob. Tribal loyalties were very strong and on occasion the tribes had fought against each other to protect their independence, even of one another. Throughout David's reign there was a latent north-south division, and perhaps to have more control he appointed principal officers in charge of the tribes (1 Chronicles 27:16–22), but he did not interfere with the tribes themselves. Solomon did. By organizing the country into twelve districts, even though several of the districts were similar to the tribal areas, he replaced one of the most revered traditions in Israel. That he got away with it indicates how thoroughly he controlled the population. The nation had become what it was never intended to be, an oppressive autocracy.

THEOLOGICAL CARELESSNESS

But it was not Solomon's social injustice, nor his extravagance and ostentation which disturbed the Lord. It was his theological carelessness. The scripture lays the blame on his wives. "For when Solomon was old his wives turned away his heart after other gods; and his heart was not wholly true to the Lord his God, as was the heart of David his father." As a consequence he was told that all but one tribe would be torn from his son and that would be left only because of David "and for the sake of Jerusalem which I have chosen." (1 Kings 11:4–13)

When Saul was confronted with a comparable charge he confessed his sin to Samuel (1 Samuel 15:24–31), and when David was confronted by Nathan (2 Samuel 12), he also confessed and asked for forgiveness. There is no record of Solomon's response; it was as if he had not heard or, at his late age, could not comprehend. Solomon's apparent silence may have been the responsibility of the final editor of the book of Kings, whose purpose it was to demonstrate royal neglect of God's requirements. But it may well have been the first step toward the disdain and anger which became the typical response of monarchs to the prophets in later years.

The biblical writer refers to certain adversaries whom the Lord raised up against Solomon. One of these was Hadad, an Edomite who survived Joab's massacre of the Edomites (1 Kings 11:14–25; 2 Samuel 8:14) and fled to Egypt. In the north, Rezon, another survivor of David's wars, captured Damascus and controlled all or part of Syria (1 Kings 11:23–24).

Most serious was the treason of one of Solomon's own courtiers, Jeroboam son of Nebat. He is described as an able young man to whom the king gave responsibility for forced labor in the tribal district of Joseph (1 Kings 11:28–29). While going about his business he was met by a prophet who tore his own new garment into twelve pieces, handed ten to Jeroboam and told him that he would be king over ten tribes. Solomon heard of this and tried to kill Jeroboam, but he escaped to Egypt where the Pharaoh, Shishak, gave him refuge (1 Kings 11:30–40).[27]

---

[27]According to one proposal, Jeroboam may have helped introduce to Shishak's court Solomon's system of taxation districts. Alberto R. Green, "Israelite Influence on Shishak's Court." *Bulletin of the American Schools of Oriental Research*, No. 233 (Winter 1979), p. 59.

At Solomon's death the empire was brittle: unchecked rebellion in Syria, potential rebellion in Edom and a contender for power supported by the prophets taking
refuge in Egypt. The resources of the country were strained, the mass of the people
exhausted, and a great number of them deeply antagonistic toward the way in which
they were being treated.

A wise monarch, a Josiah, an Uzziah, even an Absolom with an ability to listen
to the people, even an ordinary monarch who could have been influenced by popular
feeling could have saved the unity of the nation, but Solomon's son and successor
Rehoboam had no ability to rule anyone. He ignored his one chance and brought
the outwardly magnificent kingdom which his father had bequeathed to him to ruin.

QUESTIONS FOR DISCUSSION

The following questions refer to Chapters 10–11.

1. David is regarded in the Old Testament as the ideal Israelite king. Is this because
    all the other kings fall so far below what might be expected of them that David
    shines by comparison, or was David an exceptional monarch? While the Old Testa-
    ment writers do not hide David's murder of Uriah and his adultery with Bathsheba,
    is the seriousness of these offenses really admitted? David was a superb military
    leader and he had an impulsive faith and an attractive personality, but should that
    have been sufficient to make him so highly favored by the Old Testament writers?

2. A careful examination of Solomon's reign suggests that he was anything but wise.
    Why has the tradition of his wisdom persisted?

3. It has been argued that the promise to Abraham and the giving of the Covenant
    were a commitment by God to the people of Israel, whereas the promise made
    to David was a commitment to one family. The consequence of the promise to David
    was that the democratic ideal of the Covenant was changed into the aristocratic
    ideal of the house of David. This, it is claimed, led to the neglect of the Covenant,
    to the division of the kingdom, and eventually to the destruction of both Israel and
    Judah. What is the merit of this kind of analysis? Is it a case of reading into the
    Bible something that is not there?

4. It terms of twentieth century technology, how should we estimate the achievements
    of the craftsmen who built the Temple?

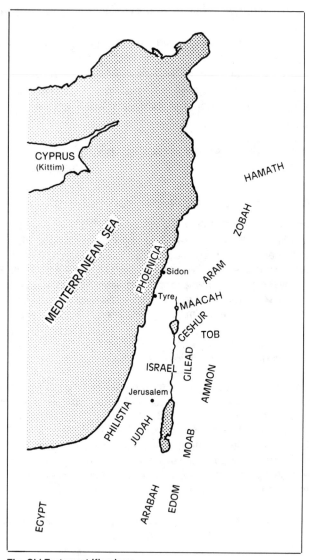

The Old Testament Kingdoms

CHAPTER TWELVE
THE DIVISION OF THE KINGDOM TO OMRI

After Solomon's death all Israel gathered at Shechem to make Rehoboam king. One might ask: Why Shechem when Jerusalem was the center of government and worship? But Jerusalem was a new city in Israel, whereas Shechem was part of Israel's earliest history with links that went back to the Patriarchs. Simeon and Levi, two sons of Jacob, had captured the city (Genesis 34); Joshua had summoned the people to Shechem to proclaim their obedience to the Covenant (Joshua 24); and Abimelech had made it his headquarters during a premature attempt to establish himself as king (Judges 9). It was also a northern city, and the bulk of the population identified itself with the north. By the time that Solomon died Jerusalem had become much more of a symbol of extravagance and servitude than of God's blessing. Shechem represented earlier and purer days.

Solomon was proclaimed king without reference to the wishes of the people. Presumably Rehoboam was his designated heir. After the death of Solomon, the people played a dominant role. They not only summoned Rehoboam to a place of *their* choice, but they also summoned Jeroboam, a rebel and a fugitive whom Solomon had tried to kill.[1] They then presented the heir apparent with an ultimatum. It is a tribute to the Israelites' character that their basic independence reasserted itself at the first real

---

[1]The references to Jeroboam in I Kings 12: 2.12.20 are not consistent. See the discussion in Joseph Robinson, *The First Book of Kings* (Cambridge: Cambridge University Press, 1972), pp. 151–52, and James Montgomery, *The Book of Kings,* International Critical Commentary (New York: Scribners, 1951), p. 253.

Shechem: Late Bronze Age gate (*1 Kings 12*). Photo by Elizabeth Gordon.

opportunity. The complex network of foremen and supervisors and the administra
structure devised by Solomon were powerless to prevent the people from taking
matter of succession into their own hands.

The text relates that "all the assembly of Israel came to Rehoboam and s
'Your father made our yoke heavy. Now therefore lighten the hard service of
father and his heavy yoke upon us, and we will serve you' " (1 Kings 12:4-5

Rehoboam asked for three days to consider an answer. He did indeed co
with some older advisors, and they instructed him to do as the people wanted, "s
good words to them when you answer them, then they will be your servants fore
(1 Kings 12:7). But his peers persuaded him to reply in a different way. With inc
ble foolishness he returned to the people and told them, "My father chastised
with whips, but I will chastise you with scorpions" (1 Kings 12:11); that is, a
ticular kind of lash called a scorpion.

The response was immediate, and revealed how strongly felt was the antago
of the northern tribes for Judah.

What portion have we in David?
We have no inheritance in the son of Jesse.

To your tents, O Israel!
Look now to your own house, David. (1 Kings 12:16)

It was Sheba's battle cry of perhaps fifty years before (2 Samuel 20:1). During all that time it had not been forgotten.

The chronicler deals with the actual division of the kingdom tersely. "So Israel departed to their tents. But Rehoboam reigned over the people of Israel who dwelt in the cities of Judah." (1 Kings 12:17) At first Rehoboam did not understand what had happened. He sent his commander of forced levies, Adoniram, certainly a tactless choice, to bring the people into line. They stoned him to death. Only then did the king realize that in the north he was no longer king. He took his chariot and returned to Jerusalem as fast as he could.

ISRAEL'S TRADITION
OF POLITICAL INDEPENDENCE

When the Israelites summoned Rehoboam they were continuing a tradition which began before David. Samuel had objected to Saul's elevation to king, but the people insisted upon a king (1 Samuel 8). Still earlier the people had rejected Eli's children in favor of Samuel (1 Samuel 2:24-25 and 3:10-18).

Even earlier, after Abimelech persuaded the city of Shechem to recognize him as king, it was the people of that city who changed their minds and precipitated his fall from power and his death (Judges 9).

This tradition of independence was supported by Israel's prophets, who played an important role in the political life of the nation both before and after the division. The prophets were the guardians of Israel's religious and political traditions, and they wielded both spiritual and secular power; for example, Nathan challenged David (2 Samuel 11-12) and helped ensure the succession of Solomon (1 Kings 1). Ahijah was instrumental in the breakup of Solomon's kingdom and the elevation of Jeroboam to the throne of the ten tribes (1 Kings 11). Ahijah also prophesied and so instigated the destruction of Jeroboam's family (1 Kings 14:1-20, and 15:25-30). In the books of Kings, we see that when a prophet withdrew his support from a monarch, that monarch could be, and frequently was, turned from office, often by assassination. That happened to the dynasty of Elah (1 Kings 16:1-14) and of Omri (2 Kings 9).

These were indications that the monarchy was not part of the basic structure of the Israelite nation, but was an additional feature "which never had the power to alter or supersede the ancient law of God by its own legislation."[2] This was much more the case in the north. In the south, the family of David had been promised that its kingdom would last forever (2 Samuel 7:12-16), but there too, as we shall see, the kings and those who supported them came under fierce prophetic criticism.

[2]Albrecht Alt, "The Monarchy in the Kingdoms of Israel and Judah," in *Essays on Old Testament History and Religion*, R. A. Wilson trans. (Garden City, N.Y.: Doubleday, 1968), p. 313.

A DIVIDED KINGDOM

Almost immediately the powerful empire of David and Solomon disintegrated into two weak states. The northern kingdom was known as Israel; it was also known as Ephraim, after its largest tribe, and as Samaria, after its capital city. The southern kingdom was called Judah. Rehoboam of Judah wanted to fight, but the prophet Shemaiah, who otherwise is unknown, dissuaded him, ostensibly because it was wrong to fight his kinsmen (1 Kings 12:21–24), but the odds were greatly in favor of the north. Five years later, however, about 917, Pharaoh Shisak struck both Judah and Israel with tremendous force (1 Kings 14:25–28). Shishak was an Ethiopian, descended from mercenaries who were originally hired by Egypt. In 935 he overthrew a weak dynasty which was friendly to Solomon (Solomon had married one of the Pharaoh's daughters, 1 Kings 3:1) and tried to disrupt Israel, first by harboring the fugitive Jeroboam and then by direct attack. An inscription at Karnak refers to over one hundred and fifty places which Shishak overran in all parts of Israel from Ezion-geber and towns in the Negeb in the south to Megiddo in the north, making no distinction between Judah and Israel.

Rehoboam seems to have bought Shishak off with a huge ransom from the Temple treasures, and so the Egyptians withdrew (1 Kings 14:25–26). But their aim was to control Palestine as they had controlled it four hundred years before. Shishak, however, died before he could consolidate his gains, and the Pharaohs who succeeded him were neither as capable nor as energetic. Asa, King of Judah, grandson of Rehoboam, is reported to have defeated an army which attacked Judah under the leadership of Zerah the Cushite (2 Chronicles 14:8–14), possibly a local Egyptian commander.

ESTABLISHING A NEW KINGDOM

The south was smaller and weaker than the north and its traditions were more recent, but they were established and well organized. Jerusalem was the strongest city in the two countries, the center of worship, with a magnificent temple and a functioning priesthood. It was also the seat of government with an efficient, even if oppressive bureaucracy. Rehoboam was an unsuitable ruler but the Davidic line had authority.

Jeroboam realized that if the Israelites in the north continued to regard Jerusalem as the center of worship, he would lose their loyalty and perhaps his life (1 Kings 12:27). He therefore established two shrines at opposite ends of his kingdom, Dan in the north near the border of Syria, and Bethel about ten miles north of Jerusalem. Bethel was already an ancient shrine associated with Abraham (Genesis 13:3) and Jacob (Genesis 35:1–15). Dan, formerly Leshem or Laish, had been captured by the tribe of Dan and renamed (Joshua 19:47). Jeroboam then "made two calves of gold. And he said to the people, 'You have gone up to Jerusalem long enough. Behold your gods, O Israel, who brought you up out of the land of Egypt' " (1 Kings 12:28). He also instituted an independent religious feast (1 Kings 12:32).

These innovations were a source of scandal to later historians, and king after king was measured against Jeroboam, son of Nebat, "who made Israel to sin." But this was the view of the Deuteronomic editors of the books of Kings, who had little sympathy for the breakaway northern kingdom. Archeological evidence suggests that it was common practice among Israel's neighbors, such as the Phoenicians and the Syrians, to represent their gods as riding on the backs of animals or enthroned upon Cherubim. That would be sufficient to reinforce the strong conviction which the Deuteronomists in the south, writing from the point of view of centralized worship in Jerusalem, had of Jeroboam's apostasy. Yet there is another side.

It seems unlikely that Jeroboam, who owed his title to God, would attempt deliberately to turn his people away from God. It is quite likely that the calves, or bulls, were not intended to represent gods or God, but the place of God's presence in the way that the Ark was the place of God's presence in the Temple.[3] One also gets a different picture of the northern shrines from a northern point of view. Dan and Bethel were not new shrines. They were, in fact, ancient. Compared with them, Jerusalem was a new shrine. Quite possibly Dan and Bethel may have seemed to many in the north much more in keeping with the Covenant tradition of Israel than was Jerusalem, associated as it was with a despotic monarchy.[4] The author of Kings, however, makes no allowance. The whole account of Jeroboam's reign is almost savagely critical. There seems to be no awareness of the incongruity between that portrait and his having been especially chosen by God.

JUDAH

The history of Judah up to the time of Uzziah (783–742) was much less eventful than that of Israel, which experienced almost continuous political turmoil and was exposed to attacks from Syria and later Assyria.

Rehoboam refrained at first from fighting his kinsmen in the north (1 Kings 12:21–24), but there was constant fighting between them throughout his reign 1 Kings 14:30). Abijam his son (915–913) and Asa his grandson (913–873) continued he conflict. During the reign of Asa, Baasha of Israel, who had murdered Jeroboam's son Nadab, invaded Judah and fortified Ramah about five miles north of Jerusalem "that he might permit no one to go out or come in to Asa King of Judah" 1 King 15:17). Asa was in a desperate situation and so he resorted to what was to become an attractive and a fatal solution in times of military peril, he appealed to foreign power, in this case Syria, which was allied to Israel. He offered Benhadad f Damascus a large bribe to attack Israel; Benhadad agreed. It was a treacherous rrangement on his part but he kept his bargain with Asa so that Baasha had to leave Ramah and take care of the unexpected danger in the north. Asa then promptly conscripted everyone in Judah to dismantle the half completed fortifications at Ramah

---

[3]Roland de Vaux, *Ancient Israel*, Vol. 2 (New York: McGraw Hill, 1961), pp. 333–336.

[4]Robinson, *The First Book of Kings*, p. 155.

A village near Tirzah, ancient capital of the northern kingdom of Israel (*1 Kings 15:21,33*). Photo by Elizabeth Gordon.

and use the materials to fortify Geba or Gibeah, about four miles north of Jerusalem and Mizpah which may have been the tremendously fortified city of Tell en Nasbeh The walls of the city were at some points twenty-six feet thick and plastered at the base to make it as treacherous as possible for an attacker to climb.[5]

This quasi civil war was a dangerous luxury which made both countries extremely vulnerable to outside attack. In addition, the government of the north followed a pattern of self-destruction. Jeroboam's son Nadab was murdered by Baasha (1 King 15:25–32). Baasha reigned for twenty-three years (900–877) and was succeeded by his son Elah (877–876). Elah was murdered by Zimri, a chariot commander who burst in upon the king when he was drunk at a party and killed him. He then exterminated the entire royal family (1 Kings 16:8–14). Both murders were instigated by prophets, by Jehu of Hanani in the case of Elah (1 Kings 16:7), by Ahijah in the case of Nadab (1 Kings 15:29). But Zimri reigned for only one week. When the Israeli troops who were attacking the Philistine city of Gibbethon heard about this they "made

[5]G. Ernest Wright, *Biblical Archeology* (Philadelphia: The Westminster Press, 1962), pp. 151–5

Omri, the commander of the army, king over Israel that day in the camp." (1 Kings 16:16)

Omri and his troops withdrew from Gibbethon and attacked Zimri in Tirzah, whereupon Zimri, seeing that the city had fallen, retreated to the keep of the royal palace, set it on fire, and perished (1 Kings 16:15-20).

For several years there was fighting between the followers of Tibni, a would-be successor to Zimri, and Omri. Omri finally proved stronger. Tibni was killed and Omri became king (1 Kings 16:21-22), a circumstance which probably saved the northern kingdom from early extinction.

CHAPTER THIRTEEN
OMRI AND AHAB:
A RELIGIOUS CRISIS

OMRI

The fighting between Tibni and Omri could have been the end of Israel, but with Omri the nation gained a first-rate leader. He so impressed the Assyrians that for about a hundred years they referred to Israel as the House of Omri, or Omri-land. Omri copied the policies of David. He sought internal peace, which meant friendly relations with Judah and close ties with the Phoenicians, and he maintained a firm position toward surrounding nations. He provided the country with a strategic and splendidly built capital, and he developed the armed forces so that in an anti-Assyria coalition formed after his death Israel was one of the strongest of the allied powers. Yet the Old Testament devotes only six verses to the reign of Omri (1 Kings 16:23–28) while dealing extensively with that of his son Ahab (1 Kings 16:29–22:53). "A sad loss to secular history that we possess only these few verses in record of the most capable of the North Israelite monarchs."[1]

The reason for such an imbalance is the intention of the ancient writer. Contemporary historians are trained to be impartial, and while they seldom have all the facts and generally cannot use all that they have, they endeavor to present their

---

[1]James A. Montgomery, *The Books of Kings,* International Critical Commentary (New York: Charles Scribners and Sons, 1951), p. 284.

148

View from the ancient city of Samaria, looking northeast. Photo by Elizabeth Gordon.

objectively and not manipulate them to make a point. But the Old Testament was not written primarily as an historical account but to present a point of view. History to the Old Testament chronicler was the record of God's activity in the world. Events which did not illustrate that were not regarded as important. The treatment of the life of Omri is an instructive example of this. Omri won respect from a great military power, but his achievements were not to the glory of God as understood by the chronicler. His life, therefore, merited little attention other than to comment that how he lived was wrong in the eyes of the Lord. Old Testament writers use a standard phrase, he "followed in the footsteps of Jeroboam the son of Nebat," that is, he was not a faithful, exclusive worshipper of Yahweh according to the Deuteronomic views of the author, that is, views based upon the Deuteronomic Code (Deuteronomy 12–26), which formed the basis for the religious reforms conducted by Josiah in Jerusalem in 621 B.C. For Omri political considerations came before religious, which resulted in a crisis for Israel during the reign of Ahab that threatened the existence of her covenant religion. The Old Testament account does mention, however, that Omri "bought the hill of Samaria from Shemer for two talents of silver; and he fortified the hill, and called the name of the city which he built, Samaria, after the name of Shemer, the owner of the hill." (1 Kings 16:24)

SAMARIA

The hill is gently sloping with a fine view of the country around. It was there that Omri built, or commenced the building of his capital, which rivalled Jerusalem in strategic importance and the quality of its construction. So closely fitting were the stones in the city walls that not even a knife could be inserted between them. Specific mention is made in 1 Kings 22:39 of the ivory house, or palace, which Ahab built, that is, a house decorated on the inside with ivories, which has been discovered by excavators. The remains of the city are also of interest in the history of architecture because of the Ionic columns used by the Phoenician builders in the forecourt to the city gate. This design was developed later by the Greeks and has become part of the architectural tradition of the Western world.[2]

Omri's reign was very short; he died in 869, and so was king for only seven years, but the change in the fortunes of Israel during that time was immense. Omri inherited, or rather won after a hard struggle, a country on the point of collapse. He bequeathed to his son Ahab a nation that was secure, at least it could put up a vigorous defense against Syria; it was on friendly terms with Phoenicia and Judah, and so, one presumes, could devote its energies to improving the condition of its life. The change came at a propitious time.

THE BATTLE OF QARQAR

The gradual emergence of Assyria as a superpower seems to have taken Israel and her contentious neighbors by surprise. They were so engrossed in their own quarrels that they did not realize until almost too late how strong Assyria had become. During the reign of David, Assyria had suffered defeats by the Arameans, but by the reign of Ahab it had become a formidable antagonist whose power stretched from central Mesopotamia almost to the Mediterranean.

In 859 Shalmaneser III ascended the throne of Assyria and soon became a serious threat to the independence of all the countries in the Syria-Palestine area. Realizing that no one of them could oppose Assyria alone they formed a coalition, pooled their military forces and fought the Assyrians at Qarqar (or Karkar) in northern Syria on the river Orontes about one hundred and fifty miles north of Damascus. This event (853) is not referred to in the Old Testament, but we have the details of the battle from Shalmaneser himself. Adad-idri of Damascus supplied 1,200 chariots, 1,200 cavalry horses, and 20,000 men. Irhuleni of Hamath supplied 700 chariots, 700 cavalry, and 10,000 men. Among the others Ahab supplied one of the largest forces with 2,000 chariots and 10,000 men. The total number of the allied side was huge: almost 4,000 chariots, 1,900 cavalry horses, 62,000 men, and 1,000 camels from Gindibu of Arabia. Shalmaneser's stele has left us a graphic account.

[2]Gaalyah Cornfeld, *Archeology of the Bible: Book by Book* (New York: Harper and Row, 1976), pp. 1? and 119.

They came directly toward me in close battle, (but) with the superior aid which Ashur the Lord had given, and with the mighty weapons which Nergal, my leader, had gifted me, I fought with them. From Qarqar to Gilzau I defeated them. I smote 14,000 of their men with weapons, falling upon them like Adad pouring down a hailstorm. I flung their bodies about, filling the plain with their scattered soldiery.[3]

Other Assyrian records give the casualities as 20,000, 25,000, and 29,000. Allowing for exaggeration the number of killed and wounded must have been very high not including the Assyrian. Shalmaneser claimed a victory, but in fact his army appears to have been stopped. It was another four years before he attacked Damascus again. The immediate threat to Syria and Palestine had been averted.

ELIJAH AND JEZEBEL

While ignoring these events the Old Testament chroniclers gave their attention to what they considered to be the much more significant struggle *within* Israel for and against the true faith. Rather than the battle of Qarqar, in which all the military strength of Israel and her allies was sufficient only to delay the advance of the Assyrians, the chroniclers, who must have known of the battle, describe in detail the "battle" of Carmel, in which one man acting for God overwhelmed all the prophets and followers of Baal.

This religious struggle was focused upon two powerful personalities, Jezebel and Elijah. Elijah is one of the greatest and one of the strangest figures in the Old Testament. He appeared from the desert dressed in a distinctive rough garment at a moment of peril in the history of Israel. He seemed to own nothing and he belonged to no one. He challenged the king and his family with unrelieved hostility, and he left the earth awesomely and abruptly after having appointed a successor who would help to bring about the total and brutal destruction of the family he detested.

Jezebel was the daughter of the Phoenician King Ittoba'al of Tyre. Omri had arranged her marriage to his son Ahab clearly to bind the two countries together to their mutual advantage. It is suggested that Omri was from a Canaanite family, long incorporated into Israel, and that his interest in Phoenicia was due partly to family connections.[4] But this otherwise quite normal act of international diplomacy had unexpected consequences. Jezebel was as powerful a personality as Elijah. She believed in her god, Baal, as Elijah believed in his God, Yahweh. She was determined that Israel would worship Baal. Elijah was determined that Israel would worship Yahweh. Jezebel had the advantage of royal power and the cultural superiority of her faith. Elijah had the advantage of divine power and the ancient traditions of Yahweh worship. Jezebel was willing to use violence to gain her ends, so was Elijah. Jezebel

[3]D. Winton Thomas, *Documents from Old Testament Times* (New York: Harper and Row, 1961), p. 47.

[4]John Gray, *I and II Kings,* second, fully revised edition (Philadelphia: Westminster Press, 1970), . 364.

Panoramic view of the plain of Jezreel from the summit of Mount Carmel (*1 Kings 18*). Photo by Elizabeth Gordon.

was courageous in the face of death. In this respect she proved to be more courageous than Elijah.

The setting for the conflict was a severe drought, mentioned in Phoenician records.[5] The Old Testament credits the drought to Elijah (1 Kings 17:1), as a punishment upon the land for Ahab's apostasy. Jezebel, the Princess from Tyre, not only brought her own cult, which was a normal procedure for a foreign princess, but proceeded to force it on the people by murdering the prophets of Yahweh (1 Kings 18:4) and replacing them by prophets of her own. Ahab did nothing to prevent this and seems to have supported it (1 Kings 18:11–15).

Conditions were especially severe for the poor people. The story of the widow of Zarephath (1 Kings 17) sketches vividly the suffering that was inflicted upon them by the drought. The widow and her son were reduced to absolute starvation when Elijah met them. The story also indicates their willingness to bear it. The widow never gave away Elijah's whereabouts, although it might have benefitted her, and this must have been the case throughout the drought for although he may have been supernaturally hidden, the quiet cooperation of a God-fearing people would make Elijah's immunity from capture appear supernatural. The fact that Obadiah "who was over the household," (1 Kings 18:3), hid a hundred prophets implies that opposition to Baalism was considerable, otherwise he would have been discovered. Elijah's statement (1 Kings 18:22) that he was the only prophet of the Lord may have been intended for Ahab, for the people would certainly have known that that was not true.

There are some dramatic incidents in this part of the text: Obadiah, who had risked his life for God, fearing that his encounter with Elijah would be his undoing (1 Kings 18:1–16); Ahab's bitter greeting to Elijah, "Is it you, you troubler of Israel?" (1 Kings 18:17); Elijah's no less bitter response, and then his challenge to the prophets of Baal which the listening crowd heard without comment (1 Kings 18:20–21).

[5]William F. Albright, *The Biblical Period from Abraham to Ezra* (New York: Harper and Row, 1963) p. 67.

Montgomery, *The Books of Kings*, p. 293.

THE CONTEST ON MOUNT CARMEL

Attempts to explain the supernatural elements of this event by reference to a natural phenomenon are not successful,[6] nor do they seem to be necessary. As in the crossing of the Red Sea, God intervened at a critical moment in the history of Israel, and with what appeared, in retrospect, to be miraculous power, the people were saved. The self-inflicted wounds and wild dancing of the prophets of Baal were typical of prophetic behavior of the time (compare the behavior of Saul and the prophets he met, 1 Samuel 19:20–24). It was not always admired. There is a note of contempt in the conversation between Jehu and his officers about the "mad fellow," the prophet, who had met him (2 Kings 9:11–12). But it was accepted behavior. The writer is therefore making a studied comparison between that and the calm assurance of Elijah.

How serious the religious situation was is at least open to question. It was quite normal for a foreign queen to be permitted the practice of her own religion. There is, it is claimed, no evidence that Baal worship was introduced anywhere other than in Jerusalem[7] and it is possible that Jezebel's massacre of Israel's prophet was in retaliation for an earlier massacre by the Israelites of her own prophets.[8]

The chronicler, however, saw the matter as a life and death issue for Israel, but writing with the assurance of a person who is confident of his religious position, he introduces a touch of humor into his account. It is, however, grim humor, for lives were at stake and perhaps also the religious future of Israel. Elijah was, in fact, wagering everything. He challenged the people to make a choice for Yahweh or for Baal. There was to be no split opinion, no tolerance. So they watched while the prophets of Baal called upon their god, and Elijah could not resist a dark jibe "Cry aloud," he said,

[6]Gray, *I and II Kings,* p. 401.
[7]Norman K. Gottwald, *All the Kingdoms of the Earth* (New York: Harper and Row, 1964), pp. 58–59.
[8]Ibid.

"for he is a god; either he is musing, or he has gone aside, or he is on a journ[
or perhaps he is asleep and must be awakened," (1 Kings 18:27).

And then, when Baal failed to act, Elijah began his preparations. It was r
a problem to him that the altar was in the northern kingdom, far from Jerusale
He took twelve stones, one for each of the tribes of Israel, and he soaked the offeri
with water, an extravagance when even the king had to search the country for fodc
for his animals (1 Kings 18:5), but it made the point clear that only fire from G
could consume that sacrifice.[9]

The fire came and Yahweh was vindicated. Elijah slaughtered the prophets
Baal (1 Kings 18:40), and when rain brought an end to the drought, at first w
a cloud no bigger than a man's hand (1 Kings 18:44), Elijah, still filled with the spi
and acting with superhuman energy, ran ahead of Ahab's chariot twenty or so mi
to Jezreel.

The incident that followed is completely unexpected. Elijah was seemingly
the height of his power and prestige, a prophet who could call upon God and
answered. But when Jezebel heard what had happened and sent a threatening messa;
Elijah ran for his life, a distance, from Jezreel to Beersheba, of about a hundred mil
When he got there he was so physically and mentally exhausted that he wanted or
to die. Very practically God provided him with food and he made his way, a furth
great distance, to the place of the beginnings of Israel, to Horeb, the Mount of Gc
There he met with God in a manner that was as strange as his own behavior, r
in a strong wind, or earthquake, or fire, but in a "still small voice," which repli
to his frightened and exaggerated complaints with quiet instructions (1 Kings 19:1:

Readers of the Bible have given to this passage a significance which perha
it may not warrant. But it reminds one of the much later comment of a prophe
"In quietness and in trust shall be your strength" (Isaiah 30:15) and is an early i
dication that although the authority of God was often expressed in power and destru
tion, and on occasions would continue to be, ultimately, the power of God is o!
different character.

NABOTH AND HIS VINEYARD

There is another incident in which Elijah is involved. It concerns not a religious matt
but one of individual rights at a time when the individual in the ancient Near Ea
was given little consideration, should his interests clash with those of a king.

It is the story of Naboth and his vineyard (1 Kings 21). Naboth was a local ma
He had a right to his property and he maintained his right. It is significant that a
that King Ahab could do in response to Naboth's refusal to sell his land was su!
The incident presents the king as petty, lacking courage in small things but willir
to go along with his wife. Yet his lack of courage revealed a grudging respect for tl

---

[9]Montgomery, *The Books of Kings*, p. 307.

traditions of his society. His wife was not necessarily more courageous. She had different traditions. According to her it was unthinkable that a king could not have his way, although it has to be kept in mind that Tyre was a trading city dependent for its success upon many ordinary people, and if their rights were too seriously interfered with by their monarch, the trading operations could not have prospered as they did. It is likely that even in her own country Jezebel would have been regarded as officious, and perhaps a religious fanatic. In relatively backward and conservative Israel she ignored all constraints. Yet even she was careful to preserve a bare minimum of legality in the way she disposed of Naboth. She arranged for two men to accuse him (1 Kings 21:10; Deuteronomy 17:6) and so secured the vineyard for her husband.

But the Lord was not pleased, and Elijah confronted Ahab with a ferocious curse:

> . . .because you have sold yourself to do what is evil in the sight of the Lord. Behold, I will bring evil upon you; I will utterly sweep you away, and will cut off from Ahab every male, bond or free, in Israel. . . And of Jezebel the Lord also said, 'The dogs shall eat Jezebel within the bounds of Jezreel.' Any one belonging to Ahab who dies in the city the dogs shall eat; and any one of his who dies in the open country the birds of the air shall eat." (1 Kings 21:20–24)

The shock of this appears to have stunned Ahab; for a time "he lay in sackcloth and went about dejectedly." or, in the New English Bible "muttering to himself." (1 Kings 21:27)

The Naboth incident is significant, not only as an occasion for Jehu's bloody revolution (2 Kings 9), but also because a matter of the rights of one man led to momentous events which involved a nation. The choice of what incidents to record indicates, too, what was important to the Israelite chronicler, not a great battle, not a reign that even the Assyrians admired, but the struggle of a prophet against apostasy and the rights of a small landowner to his family property. Ultimately it was this perspective that enabled Israel to survive military and political destruction. The greater nations which depended on material power had nothing to sustain them when that power failed.

CHAPTER FOURTEEN
FROM AHAB
TO JEROBOAM II

The concluding chapter of 1 Kings gives an account of Ahab's death in battle against the Syrians. After the battle of Qarqar in 853, the coalition of small nations, including Syria and Israel, which had halted the Assyrians, dissolved, and there was intermittent fighting between Syria and Israel in which first one country and then the other gained the advantage.

The hostilities ended with the defeat of Ben-hadad, king of Syria. Ahab spared Ben-hadad's life in return for territory and trade concessions. Perhaps Ahab felt pleased with his statesmanship, but his self-confidence was rudely shaken when an anonymous prophet declared that his own life would be forfeited because he had been so generous. "The king of Israel," we read, "went to his house resentful and sullen." (1 Kings 20:42–43).

Three years later the Syrians had apparently not kept part of their bargain, which was to turn over Ramoth Gilead, formerly the government seat of one of Solomon's administrative regions (1 Kings 4:13). Ahab, therefore, decided to attack the city, and invited Johoshaphat, the king of Judah, to help him.

Ahab was like Saul in not considering the religious implications of his military decisions. Jehoshaphat was, in this matter, more like Samuel. The approval of God was a first consideration (2 Chronicles 19:4–11). It is in character then that Jehoshaphat while agreeing to help Ahab, suggested that first they seek counsel from the Lord and when a large group of court prophets told the king rather obviously only what he wanted to hear, he asked if there were no other prophet of the Lord through whom they could seek guidance (1 Kings 22:7). Ahab's reply was that there was one more, Micaiah.

Elijah had complained to the people (1 Kings 18:22) that he alone remained as a prophet of the Lord. Yet we know that Obadiah hid a hundred of these prophets (1 Kings 18:13). Perhaps one of them was Micaiah, and perhaps Micaiah did not emerge as a powerful figure until after the vindication of God on Mt. Carmel. But he was well known to the king not long after, although there is no other reference to him, unless he was the anonymous prophet of the preceding chapter.[1] His personality appears to have been different from Elijah's, but in courage, dry humor, and total self-assurance the two men were much the same. Micaiah stood before the king with all the authority and presence of Elijah, and from him comes a rare account of a vision of God (1 Kings 22:19) reminiscent of Isaiah's vision (Isaiah 6:1–8) or of Stephen's (Acts 7:54–56).

The story of Micaiah tells us that prophets such as he and Elijah worked out of a prophetic context which was characterized at its best by great spiritual power. But the stories about Elisha, at the beginning of the second book of Kings, are folk tales which describe a prophet from the point of view of the ordinary Israelite. When a child is sick, when a family is in debt, when something valuable is lost, people need help, especially people without money or influence. The Elisha tales are the small person's wish come true, as nontheological as the crowds which followed Christ because he healed the sick and provided them with food.

WAR WITH MOAB

Ahab's son Ahaziah died as the result of an accident (2 Kings 1:1–17). He was succeeded by his brother Jehoram. Neither was equal in military ability to Ahab. Certainly the campaign against Moab (2 Kings 3:4–27) reflects no credit upon Israel, and while it appears from a nonbiblical source that Jehoram was not involved in this incident, the fact that it is ascribed to him suggests that the Old Testament chronicler had a low opinion of Jehoram's ability as a military commander.

The nonbiblical source is known as the Moabite Stone. It was discovered in 1868 at Diban, a few miles north of the river Arnon to the east of the Dead Sea. It was therefore in the territory of Reuben beyond the boundary of Moab not far from Ataroth, which is mentioned on the monument. Its great value to the student of the Old Testament is that it provides an account of a biblical incident from the point of view of the other side.

Israel and Moab were similar people and spoke a similar language. In Genesis 19:37 Moab is referred to as a son of Lot, but throughout their history the

[1]James A. Montgomery, *The Books of Kings,* The International Critical Commentary (New York: Scribners, 1951), p. 322.

two nations were enemies, except that shortly before Jerusalem's capture and destruction it appears that Judah and Moab attempted to make common cause against the Babylonians (Jeremiah 27:3). The Old Testament account in 2 Kings 3 records how the forces of Israel and Judah attacked Moab because Mesha had rebelled against Israel, and presumably stopped supplying the large quantity of wool and livestock required of him. The Old Testament account reports how, on their way to Moab, the allies ran out of water and would have perished but for Elisha's magical prowess. When the battle was joined the Moabites were close to defeat until, in desperation, Mesha sacrificed his eldest son on the city wall. The Israelites were filled with such consternation at this sight, that they withdrew and "returned to their own land" (2 Kings 3:27).

Military reporting is seldom objective, so we can assume exaggeration on both sides. On the Moabite Stone Mesha records that he attacked the Israelites in Ataroth and "slew all the people of the town, a spectacle for Chemosh," the God of the Moabites. The god then commanded Mesha to take the town of Nebo, which he did, fighting against it from break of dawn till noon. "I took it and slew all: seven thousand men, boys, women, and (girls) and female slaves, for I had consecrated it to Ashtar-Chemosh."[2] The incident is strikingly similar to many in the Old Testament which describe victorious Israelite battles, for example the capture of Ai (Joshua 8:18–29).

THE PROPHETIC REVOLUTION

Whether or not the Old Testament chronicler was attempting to emphasize Jehoram's ineptness, his officers appear to have had little confidence in him and were ready for a change. When one of Elisha's prophets secretly anointed Jehu king, his fellow officers accepted him with enthusiasm (2 Kings 9:1–13).

The role of the prophet in this instance was what we would now call subversive. It was direct political interference. Nathan had played a prominent part in stopping Adonijah from becoming king and securing the throne for Solomon, (1 Kings 1); Ahijah the prophet had instigated the rebellion which led to the division of the kingdom after the death of Solomon, (1 Kings 11:29–39); the prophet Jehu, son of Hanani, was involved in the destruction of Baash'a dynasty (1 Kings 16:1–7).

In all these cases the political action was motivated by a desire for religious purity in the nation. But it is a question, at least, whether in the long run this activity was not counterproductive. Did the prophets worsen the situation they were trying to improve? None of the monarchs whom they helped to establish lived up to expectations, that is, God's expectations. Such a question illustrates the difficulty of interpreting Old Testament history. One can deal with it in a secular way, as one might deal with the history of Assyria or Egypt, or one can regard Old Testament history as an expression of God's purpose. The one yields a somewhat deficient understand-

---

[2]D. Winton Thomas, *Documents from Old Testament Times* (New York: Harper and Row, 1961), p. 195

ing, for biblical history cannot be separated from its religious meaning. But the other is often too easy. God's purposes in events, after the fact, can be identified as readily as the patterns in rice thrown on a table. To identify his purpose in events, assumedly controlled by him, which appear to work against his purpose is a difficult task.

Jehoram of Israel and Ahaziah of Judah were both at Jezreel, Jehoram recovering from wounds he received fighting against the Syrians, and Azariah visiting him. Jehu went there directly after his encounter with the prophet and the acclamation of his fellow officers, driving his chariot furiously, and took both kings by surprise. Jehu killed them both and ordered Jehoram's body thrown onto the plot of land that had belonged to Naboth, so fulfilling the Lord's judgment against Ahab (2 Kings 9:25–26, 1 Kings 21:19); Jehu then went after Jezebel.

Jehu's actions were merciless, but they were directed against a family which had come as close as any to destroying the worship of God in Israel. He was in effect completing the work begun by Elijah, to root out apostasy from Israel and, in the case of Naboth, to protect the rights of the individual. The instigator of the apostasy and oppression and the particular object of prophetic wrath was Jezebel, who had remained a dominant figure in Israel's religion and politics. Baalism was still popular, clearly so in Samaria, where Jehu had no trouble gathering a large number of Baal priests and worshippers for what proved to be a fatal celebration (2 Kings 10:18–28).

Jehu destroyed Jezebel in an especially brutal way, but she showed more character than the man who killed her. Knowing or suspecting that the end had come "she painted her eyes, and adorned her head" and then asked the bitingly scornful question "Is it peace, you Zimri, murderer of your master?" Zimri had been king for only seven days. This really angered Jehu; he had Jezebel thrown from a window to the ground below where she was trampled by horses. He then "went in and ate and drank" (2 Kings 9:34).

The purge of his enemies was wholesale (2 Kings 9–10), although he acted with discretion toward the city of Samaria, treating it like an independent city-state.[3]

To his considerable advantage Jehu gained the support of Israel's most conservative religious figure, Jehonadab (2 Kings 10:15–16), leader of the Rechabites, whose followers lived in tents in the desert and maintained that what they believed were the ancient religious traditions of the nation.

Jehu acted with zeal but not with discretion. The murder of Jezebel, the wholesale slaughter of the priests of Baal, and the deliberate sacrilege of their Temple (2 Kings 10:27) alienated Phoenicia, which had been an ally and trading partner of Israel since the time of David. The murder of Ahaziah, King of Judah, and his friends and relatives alienated Judah; and the mass murder of the family of Omri and his friends robbed the country of leaders which, as events showed, it needed badly.

But Jehu did not abolish the rival sanctuaries of Dan and Bethel, nor did he act in an especially God-fearing way himself, (2 Kings 10:28–31). The country grew

---

[3]Albrecht Alt, *Essays on Old Testament History and Religion,* R. A. Wilson trans. (Garden City, N.Y.: Doubleday, 1968), p. 333.

Scenes from the Black Obelisk of Shalmaneser III. In the top panel Shalmaneser is receiving tribute from Jehu, king of Israel. (*Courtesy of British Library*).

weaker, losing control of territories east of Jordan to which Israel laid claim (2 Kings 10:32–36).

What the Old Testament does not mention and what was not discovered until 1847 was that Jehu had brought tribute to the Assyrian king, Shalmaneser III, the king whom Ahab and his allies had fought at Qarqar in 853. This information was on a black obelisk whose bas-reliefs and inscription "were as sharp and as well defined as if they had been carved but a few days before."[4] A. H. Layard, who found the obelisk, was unaware at first that the "prisoner" kneeling before Shalmaneser was Jehu, king of Israel, in the only known picture of an Israelite king. There is a great contrast between the savagery with which Jehu treated his religious and political opponents and his subservient posture before the great king, "In all the colorful stories about Jehu in the Bible no mention is made of this humiliating event of international importance."[5] The event seems to have taken place in 842. An inscription describes the scene. "The tribute of Jehu, Son of Omri; I received from him silver, gold, a golden saplu bowl, a golden vase with pointed bottom, golden tumblers, golden buckets, a staff for a king, and wooden puruhtu."[6]

CONSEQUENCES IN JUDAH

The prophetic revolution, as it is sometimes called, had repercussions in Judah. Ahaziah, king of Judah, whom Jehu had killed, was a son of Athaliah, one of Ahab's daughters or possibly his sister. Athaliah had a cruel and ambitious nature. When she heard that her son was dead she "arose and destroyed all the royal family," (2 Kings 11:1) and almost succeeded except that Ahaziah's sister hid her brother's son Joash (2 Kings 11:2). Athaliah established herself as queen of Judah for almost seven years but was then overthrown and killed by a carefully planned coup, and the young Joash was proclaimed king. So the house of David was preserved (2 Kings 11).

ISRAEL AND JUDAH AFTER JEHU

Jehu of Israel was succeeded by his son Jehoahaz (815–801). Israel meanwhile suffered greatly from Syrian attacks. Hazael, king of Syria, allowed Jehoahaz no armed force except "fifty horsemen and ten chariots and ten thousand footmen; for the king of Syria had destroyed them and made them like the dust," (2 Kings 13:7), a sad decline from the strong forces of Ahab's reign and particularly Solomon's.

[4]James B. Pritchard, *Archeology and the Old Testament* (Princeton, N.J.: Princeton University Press, 1958), p. 143.

[5]Ibid., p. 145.

[6]James B. Pritchard, *Ancient and Near Eastern Texts Relating to the Old Testament* (Princeton, N.J.: Princeton University Press, 1969), p. 281.

Jehoahaz' son Joash (801–786) (not the Joash just referred to of the souther
kingdom), was more fortunate than his father. In 805 the Assyrians unde
Adad-nirari III engaged in a long war with Syria, and by 802 the Syrians wei
defeated. In 801 when Joash came to the throne of Israel, he was able to defeat th
new Syrian king, Benhadad, and regain lost Israelite territories. The situation als
improved with regard to the Assyrians. Israel had to pay tribute to them, but Assyri
was greatly weakened by the war with Syria, and was threatened by the powerf(
neighboring state of Urartu which equalled Assyria in size. Assyrian leadership follov
ing Adad-nirari was not able to do more than protect the country from that threa
and so left Israel alone. Meanwhile, as soon as Assyrian pressure was relaxed, th
Syrian cities of Hamath and Damascus fought one another for control,[7] furth(
weakening themselves to the advantage of Israel.

Having won victories in Syria Joash was not disturbed when Amaziah, kin
of Judah, who had recently captured the Edomite town of Sela, proposed "to loc
one another in the face," that is to fight. In reply Joash sent Amaziah a parable abou
a thistle in Lebanon who wanted the daughter of a ceder in marriage to his son. Bu
"a wild beast of Lebanon passed by and trampled down the thistle. You have indee
smitten Edom," he continued "and your heart has lifted you up. Be content wit
your glory, and stay at home; for why should you provoke trouble so that you fal
you and Judah with you?" (2 Kings 14:8–10)

Amaziah would not listen. There was a battle and he was defeated and capturec
Joash destroyed a long section of Jerusalem's city wall, took treasures from the Lord
house and the palace, and some hostages, and went back to Samaria. The incider
is not elaborated upon, but it is an occasion when, had Joash wished, he could hav
united the two kingdoms under his own rule. Perhaps it was this humiliating adver
ture that led to Amaziah's murder in 783.

A NEW PROSPERITY

Then the fortune of the two kingdoms changed. Amaziah was succeeded by his so
Azariah, or Uzziah, whose long reign (783–742) was one of the most well ordere
and prosperous in Judah's history. Joash of Israel was succeeded by Jeroboam I
whose reign was equally prosperous and almost as long (786–746). Not only wei
the two monarchs extremely capable, but they cooperated with one another instea
of fighting. Their joint territories compared with those of Solomon, and trade coul
once again flow as it had at that time. With Syria and Assyria unable to interfer(
the two Israelite kingdoms enjoyed more than forty prosperous years. But they wei
years in which the spiritual commitments for which Israel had been founded wer
ignored and largely forgotten. The prosperity was therefore destructive. The shor

---

[7]Martin Noth, *The History of Israel,* revised translation by Peter Ackroyd (New York: Harper an
Row, 1960), pp. 249–50.

sighted material interests which caused the people to neglect the will of God, caused them also to neglect their own political interests, and that led to the ruin, first of Israel, and then of Judah. Assyrian "weakness" was nevertheless still dangerous for small states like Israel. Israel refused to recognize that, as she refused to recognize how far she had strayed from her Covenant obligations. But this was the moment when we come upon "the most astonishing phenomenon in the whole of Israel's history: at a time when Yahwehism was being increasingly undermined and indeed was not far short of distintegration, it was able once again to re-emerge, with almost volcanic force, in a completely new form—in the message of the prophets."[8]

QUESTIONS FOR DISCUSSION

The following questions refer to Chapters 12–14.

1. In later generations Jeroboam, the son of Nebat, became a byword for apostasy. Surely God must have foreseen this. Why then did he choose Jeroboam as the means of disciplining the family of David and Solomon? Is it possible that the biblical writers were unfairly biased against Jeroboam, and made him into a villain (rather like Shakespeare's Richard III), when the facts as we have them do not support that interpretation?

2. The Old Testament writers were remarkably honest in presenting the faults as well as the virtues of their political and religious leaders. Yet they wrote from a point of view. An example is their treatment of the reigns of Omri and Ahab. Given these two instances, are we justified in looking upon the history of the divided kingdom as a political religious tract, or is that too extreme a view on the basis of too little evidence?

3. Could it be argued, despite the clear point of view of the Old Testament writers, that Jezebel was one of the most admirable figures in the Old Testament, standing on a level with the greatest figures of Israel's faith?

4. It is claimed in Chapter 13 that the incident involving the death of Naboth revealed Israel's strong commitment to individual rights. Is there other evidence to support this view, and are we to suppose from the preaching of Amos that Israel's concern with individual rights was abandoned by the reign of Jeroboam II?

5. Far from helping to secure the religious and political stability of Israel and Judah, the activity of prophets such as Ahijah, Jehu son of Hanani, and Elisha seems to have been destructive and counterproductive. But as they were chosen by God and acted by his command that would seem to be a contradiction. What should we conclude?

[8]Gerhard Von Rad, *The Message of the Prophets* (London: SCM Press, 1968), p. 9.

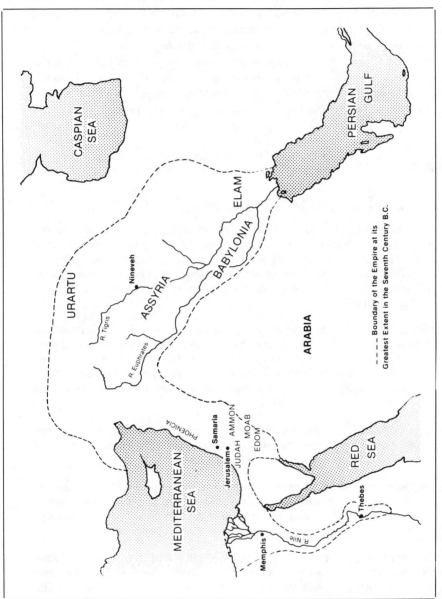

The **Assyrian Empire.**

CHAPTER FIFTEEN
THE PROPHET AMOS

As a phenomenon of history the eighth century prophets belong to the ancient world, but what urged them on, how they believed, and what they preached is relevant to all times including our own.

When anti-Viet Nam war protesters in the 1960s and the early 1970s burned their draft cards, poured blood over registration records, destroyed the American flag, sang songs and composed poetry about freedom, and disrupted campuses, large numbers of Americans were outraged. It seemed to them to be not only irrational and destructive behavior but treasonable as well. Yet the protesters were part of a very ancient tradition. In their view they were far from treasonable, it was the state itself which had failed to maintain its own ideals, and the "irrational" behavior was often deliberately symbolic, intended to make people aware of how far they had strayed from their original commitments. As a result, there were painful confrontations between the usually young protesters and those who believed that patriotism and morality are measured by obedience to the status quo.

The situation in Israel and Judah from the middle of the eighth to the end of the sixth century is analogous. The nation began as an original classless society, with only the Levites as a separate but not a governing elite. Theoretically, all Israelites were equal before God, with a Covenant and a larger code of law which they were expected to obey.

But after the introduction of the monarchy, Israel lost its egalitarian distinctiveness and became increasingly like the oppressive, status-conscious kingdoms surrounding her. Israel's early traditions were honored in theory but disregarded in practice. Liturgy became a substitute for religious commitment, and social injustice flourished while wealth and power became all-important. Conditions were so bad that except for the poor and powerless, who suffered directly, Israelite society as a whole did not appear to be aware that anything was wrong. From the perspective of material achievement, they were successful with God and man.

It was at that point in the eighth century that there arose a group of protesters or prophets. Their task was not, as is often misunderstood, to predict the future, but to confront their contemporaries with God's requirements. "He has showed you, O Man, what is good;" said Micah, "and what does the Lord require of you but to do justice, and to love kindness, and to walk humbly with your God." (Micah 6:8) The impact of these men upon their society can be measured by the reaction of their society to them. Amos was angrily ordered back to his own country and accused of conspiracy, Jeremiah was flogged, imprisoned, and accused of treason, Ezekiel was listened to, at times, with indulgence as if he were singing love songs, at other times confronted with angry words, and Uriah was put to death. The preaching and strange symbolic behavior of these prophets was often deliberately provocative, shrill, denunciatory, extreme, and disrespectful of authority. That is what society saw and heard. It did not see or care about the internal anguish of these men, whose preaching was not all angry, but who suffered the disappointments of God, whose own personalities were not aggressive, but who were compelled to act out of character under the force of a "mysterious compulsion."[1] It was a phenomenon which went far beyond what had been experienced in Israel before.[2]

We know about these prophets, what they said and did, and how they were treated because their preaching and descriptions of their lives were written down. That is why they were, until recently, called the writing prophets. In the case of Jeremiah, we know the name of his scribe, Baruch. Why the phenomenon of preserving the prophetic message in detail began we have no way of knowing. Perhaps someone listening to Amos, or a number of listeners, realized that here was a personality whose message should not be lost. Perhaps they memorized it first and wrote it later.[3] We must suppose that what was done for Amos seemed natural to do for Hosea, and then for the other prophets.

The result has been an immense enrichment of world literature, in particular of the Old Testament itself. It includes much of the greatest poetry written. These prophets provided not only a sustained critique of their society in terms of what was

---

[1]Gerhard Von Rad, *Old Testament Theology,* Vol. II (New York: Harper and Row, 1965), p. 70.

[2]Gerhard Von Rad, *The Message of the Prophets* (London: SCM Press, 1968), p. 33

[3]Johannes Lindblom, *Prophecy in Ancient Israel* (Oxford: Basil Blackwell, 1962), p. 235.

expected of it by God, but they also provided a searching examination of the nature of God, one which despite the great distance in time we also can share.[4]

The first of these prophets was Amos, who lived in Tekoa, a short distance south of Bethlehem. We are told that he was a herdsman and a dresser of sycamore figs. That is, he pricked the first fruit of sycamore trees to help it ripen faster (Amos 1:1, 7:14). At some point, he received a call from God to preach to the Kingdom of Israel in the north.

Our present book of Amos is what has been preserved of that preaching, together with biographical material probably written by someone other than Amos. There are different opinions about how much else was added to the original message, and over what period. It is possible that some editing took place and that material was added (perhaps the judgment against Judah, Amos 2:4–5 and the promise of salvation, Amos 9:11–15) until as late as the exile. In general, it is agreed that most of the book can be attributed to Amos, and so it provides us with a vivid contemporary account of the conditions in Israel during the reign of Jeroboam II.[5]

PROSPERITY AND SOCIAL INJUSTICE IN ISRAEL

From the accession of Joash in Israel in 801, when Israel's fortunes improved, following the destruction of Damascus and the beginning of a long period of Assyrian weakness, to the death of Jeroboam II in 746, the people of Israel could forget their humiliation under Jehu's son Jehoahaz. They could forget the coups and counter-coups and economic uncertainty of most of the 120 years from the division of the kingdom to the defeat of Damascus. People born at the beginning of the eighth century could look upon the deceptively favorable international scene as normal. The business of life had indeed become business, and for those who prospered, pleasure. Wealthy persons owned winter houses and summer houses as they still do in Syria and Lebanon. They enjoyed wine, for which the country was famous, and liked music. Many of their houses were finely decorated with ivory carvings and expensive furniture, and the women loved beautiful clothes and cosmetics.

While this could seem decadent to a prophet such as Amos, whose life had been lived as a shepherd and farmer, and whose interest was in the will and character of God, from a less intense point of view it was not evil in itself. David and Solomon enjoyed music and poetry, and the Temple, undoubtedly familiar to Amos who lived near Jerusalem, was a permanent exhibit of the best Phoenician art. Solomon engaged in large-scale business which extended from the Mediterranean to the east coast of

---

[4]Robert Scott, *The Relevance of the Prophets* (New York: Macmillan, 1947), p. 204.

[5]James Luther Mays, *Amos* (Philadelphia: The Westminster Press, 1969).

Brevard S. Child, *Introduction to the Old Testament as Scripture* (Philadelphia: Fortress Press, 1979), p. 397–99.

Lower courses of Ahab's wall in Samaria (*1 Kings 16:24*). Photo by Elizabeth Gordon.

Africa. As such these activities and interests were not evil. The evil consisted in the Israelites' failure to see that God must be involved in them.[6]

What angered the prophet and incurred the wrath of God was that the pleasant, well-to-do life of certain Israelites was enjoyed at the expense of the less fortunate. Success in business and pleasure had become ends in themselves, and when it suited their purposes, the wealthy and the powerful perverted justice to their own ends. The prophet's denunciation is blunt.

> O you who turn justice to wormwood,
>   and cast down righteousness to the earth! (Amos 5:7)

Twice there is reference to selling and buying the destitute for a pair of shoes (Amos 2:6, 8:6). The guiltless are persecuted, men held to ransom, the destitute (presumably trying to appeal) thrust out of court, or turned aside "in the gate" where judicial proceedings were held (Amos 5:12). There was blatant fraud, giving short measure, taking overweight, and dealing "deceitfully with false balances" (Amos 8:5).

The Israelites engaged in other kinds of objectionable behavior. "A man and his father go in to the same maiden," (Amos 2:7), and in direct violation of the law, creditors seized and kept their debtor's clothes (Amos 2:8, also Exodus 22:26–27). There was other deplorable behavior. "In the house of their God they drink the wine of those who have been fined" (Amos 2:8).

Nazarites, who took a vow not to drink any alcohol, were made to drink wine (Amos 2:12), and prophets were ordered not to prophesy, as Amos himself discovered (Amos 7:10–13).

In marvelously vivid language the prophet expresses his amazement at what the people were doing.

> Do horses run upon rocks?
>   Does one plow the sea with oxen?
> But you have turned justice into poison
>   and the fruit of righteousness into wormwood. (Amos 6:12)

FORMAL AND EMPTY RELIGION

Meanwhile the performance of formal religious obligations continued: the burning of thank offerings, the bringing of tithes (Amos 4:4–5). To the prophet this indicated a complete misunderstanding of the required relationship between Israel and God. Jeremiah, a prophet who lived and prophesied in Judah about a century after Amos, wrote "thou art near in their mouth and far from their heart" (Jeremiah 12:2).

---

[6]Theodore H. Robinson, *Prophecy and the Prophets in Ancient Israel,* 2d ed. (London: Gerald Duckworth and Co., 1953), p. 68.
Von Rad, *Old Testament Theology,* p. 137.

Amos found this abhorrent. With great sarcasm he exclaimed (New Englis Bible translation), "You love to do what is proper, you men of Israel," (Amos 4:5 He wanted no part of organized religion that would allow a person to believe he wa meeting the requirements of God while behaving in cruel and unjust ways.

> I hate, I despise your feasts,
>   and I take no delight in your solemn assemblies.
> Even though you offer me your burnt offerings and cereal
>   offerings, I will not accept them. (Amos 5:21–22)

The people of Israel had so forgotten what true worship was that they believe a day was coming, "a day of the Lord" (Amos 5:18), when God would bless then Yet the whole structure of their worship was not only morally objectionable, it wa apostate. The very act of worship at Bethel and Gilgal, rival shrines to Jerusalem was rebellion (Amos 4:4).

GOD'S JUDGMENT

The inevitable outcome was judgment, not only for what the people had done bu for the love that the people had ignored. The prophet reminded the people of the great history.

> Hear this word that the Lord has spoken against you, O people of Israel, against th whole family which I brought up out of the land of Egypt:
>
> You only have I known
>   of all the families of the earth;
> therefore I will punish you
>   for all your iniquities. (Amos 3:1–2)

Israel was Yahweh's people, but Yahweh was not Israel's God in any possessiv sense.[7] The people had ignored his love. Their fine way of life would be destroyec Summer houses, winter houses, houses of hewn stone, and pleasant vineyards woul be destroyed and taken by others (Amos 5:11). The proud and self-indulgent wome would be carried away on shields through breaches in the city walls and pitched o a dunghill (Amos 4:2–3). The false shrines of Bethel and Gilgal would be pulled dow (Amos 5:5).

> In all the squares there shall be wailing;
>   and in all the streets they shall say, "Alas! alas!"
> They shall call the farmers to mourning
>   and to wailing those who are skilled in lamentation. (Amos 5:16)

[7]Mays, *Amos,* p. 8.

Amos prophesies that a nation will be raised up against Israel that will harry the entire land, from Hamath to the Brook of the Arabah (Amos 6:14), that is, to the full extent of Jeroboam II's territories. Flight will not help, nor strength, nor weapons, nor horses, nor bravery (Amos 2:14–16).

> Not one of them shall flee away,
> not one of them shall escape. (Amos 9:1)

The enemy will be more terrible because it will act according to God's direction. There will be no escape from the enemy and no escape from God.

> Though they dig into Sheol,
>   from there shall my hand take them;
> though they climb up to heaven,
>   from there I will bring them down.
> Though they hide themselves on the top of Carmel,
>   from there I will search out and take them;
> and though they hide from my sight at the bottom of the sea,
>   there I will command the serpent, and it shall bite them.
> And though they go into captivity before their enemies,
>   there I will command the sword, and it shall slay them;
> and I will set my eyes upon them for evil and not for good. (Amos 9:2–4)

He paints strange and chilling vignettes of what will happen when the dead outnumber the living. There are two passages which seem to preserve the actual manner of Amos's dramatic preaching.

> And if ten men remain in one house, they shall die. And when a man's kinsman, he who burns him, shall take him up to bring the bones out of the house, and shall say to him who is in the innermost parts of the house, "Is there still any one with you?" he shall say, "No"; and he shall say, "Hush! We must not mention the name of the Lord." (Amos 6:9–10)

and in Chapter 8, in the New English Bible translation

> In that day, says the Lord God, the singing women in the palace shall howl, "So many dead men, flung out everywhere! Silence!" (Amos 8:3)

Such preaching stirred up angry opposition from the religious military establishment. Amos did not use caution. He preached at Bethel, the center of the religious life of Israel. His words were not only religiously but politically offensive; he prophesied that Israel would be overrun and that Jeroboam would die by the sword. Jeroboam died of natural causes but Israel was overrun by Assyria about fifty years later. Perhaps a clear-headed observer could see that Israel stood little chance in any event, for either Assyria would regain power and conquer the nations which lay between her and the Mediterranean, or her great rival the Kingdom of Uratu would do the same after defeating Assyria. Although the prophets valued Israel, meaning both Judah and Israel, and could see a glorious future as long as it obeyed God, they were realistic about its political and military weakness.[8] Amaziah, however, the priest of Bethel, regarded Amos's remarks as treasonable, and in a curiously contemporary way accused him of conspiracy (Amos 7:10). "The land," he declared, "is not able to bear all his words," which, according to one commentator suggests that "the man who wrote was a keen-eyed observer with real insight into the force of Amos's words."[9]

Amaziah ordered Amos to be off, to earn his living as a prophet in his own country. Amos's classic reply was that he was not a prophet nor a prophet's son. That is, he did not belong to a guild of prophets. He did not earn his living by prophecy. He was a farmer, but he had been called by God. This may have been an especially effective answer in the north where there was a long tradition of prophets who were summoned to a prophetic ministry in that way.

> You say, "Do not prophesy against Israel,
>   and do not preach against the house of Isaac."
> Therefore thus says the Lord:
> "Your wife shall be a harlot in the city,
>   and your sons and your daughters shall fall by the sword,
>   and your land shall be parceled out by line;
> you yourself shall die in an unclean land,
>   and Israel shall surely go into exile away from its land." (Amos 7:16-17)

These strong words are placed within a series of visions: of locusts devouring crops, of fire devouring all creation, of God setting a plumb line to the heart of his people. In the first two visions, Amos prays and God relents, but in the third, God declares "I will never again pass by them" (Amos 7:1-9).

DEVELOPMENT IN THE CONCEPT OF GOD

Amos's message was harsh and forbidding. In one respect he was like Isaiah who would later preach to a people who he knew would neither listen nor reform because their salvation depended upon a change of attitude which nothing suggested would take place.

> Hear this word which I take up over you in lamentation, O house of Israel:
> Fallen, no more to rise,
>   is the virgin Israel;
> forsaken on her land,
>   with none to raise her up. (Amos 5:1-2; also see Isaiah 6:9-12)

[8]Albert T. Olmstead, *History of Assyria* (Chicago: University of Chicago Presss, 1975), pp. 110-11, 166-67, 191-205.

[9]Von Rad, *Old Testament Theology*, p. 89.

The people to whom Amos's words were first addressed reacted with anger or indifference to the complaints, and were probably unaware of their particular significance. For example, the prophecy begins with a series of exclamations against Israel's neighbors: Damascus, Gaza, Tyre, Edom, Ammon, and Moab. Since the time of Moses, God's wrath had been directed against non-Israelite nations because of crimes against the Israelites.[10] In Amos the crimes referred to are committed by these nations *upon one another.* The Edomites are condemned because they hunted down their kinsmen, stifling natural affection. The Moabites are condemned because they burned the bones of the King of Edom to ash. God was concerned with behavior *as such* wherever it was. The passage in Amos 9:1–4 illustrating the universal sovereignty of God is, in this context, applicable to all people. There is no escape from God anywhere by anyone. God is not simply the God of Abraham and Isaac but of all creation and all people in it. He is not for one group and against others. He requires them all to meet the same standard, and punishes them all.

The consequences of this affected Israel in a particular way. If all people were to be held to the same standard and treated equally, the chosen people had no special claim upon God's providence.

"Are you not like the Ethiopians to me,
   O people of Israel?" says the Lord.
"Did I not bring up Israel from the land of Egypt,
   and the Philistines from Caphtor [Crete]
   and the Syrians from Kir?" (Amos 9:7)

Yet Amos himself had spoken of God's special care for Israel,

You only have I known
   of all the families of the earth. (Amos 3:2)

It was an unexpected and ominous contradiction, but it suggests now a development in understanding of the relationship between God and his people which was to continue throughout the Old Testament. The evolution of prophetic thought was towards the universality both of God's love and human responsibility. This is how best to interpret the often quoted passage from Hosea, Amos's younger contemporary.

When Israel was a child, I loved him,
   and out of Egypt I called my son. (Hosea 11:1)

Otherwise it might appear that Hosea was attempting to reaffirm what Amos appeared to deny.

In an important respect the preaching of Amos was not new. Like Elijah he

[10]Norman K. Gottwald, *All the Kingdoms of the Earth* (New York: Harper and Row, 1964), pp. 94–110.

argued that a person's standing with God and all that can be called success depend upon quality of life.

> Seek good, and not evil,
>   that you may live;
> and so the Lord, the God of hosts, will be with you,
>   as you have said.
> Hate evil, and love good,
>   and establish justice in the gate;
> it may be that the Lord, the God of hosts,
>   will be gracious to the remnant of Joseph (Amos 5:14–15)

From the time of Amos the importance of quality of life is a dominant theme in the message of the prophets. It is worth noting that this emphasis which attracts so much attention in the New Testament, most notably in the Sermon on the Mount, is a natural expression of the Old Testament.

AN INDIRECT SIGN OF HOPE

Despite the harshness of his message there is a note of hope in Amos of tremendous but indirect significance. It is in the vision which Amos had of a strange famine.

> not a famine of bread, nor a thirst for water,
>   but of hearing the words of the Lord. (Amos 8:11)

The land referred to is ostensibly Israel, but it could be anywhere, with men and women of all nations staggering from north to south, ranging from east to west looking for the word, the message of a prophet which they were presently rejecting. The vision is an especially painful one because Amos declares "they shall not find it," yet the note of hope is present because the vision makes the point that ultimately, no matter what other benefits in life there may be, people want one thing, a conviction that they are in touch with God. The fact of religious consciousness in human beings from the beginning of our knowledge of human life is an indication of this. Amos's frightening prophecy that people will go too far and lose touch with the word of the Lord may be an ultimate misinterpretation of God's love. We don't know. We should rather take the grim warning to heart. Yet there is good evidence that according to the Scriptures the love of God is never failing. This is the emphasis given by Amos's younger contemporary, Hosea, in the prophecy that bears his name.

CHAPTER SIXTEEN
THE PROPHET HOSEA

Hosea was born in the Northern Kingdom during the reign of Jeroboam II, but some years later than Amos. It is possible that he heard the older prophet preach. He certainly must have heard about him. Israel was a small country. The sudden appearance of the uncompromising southerner was probably a major topic of debate. Consider, for example, the angry reaction of Amaziah the priest of Bethel (Amos 7:10-14). One can only speculate that that is what helped direct Hosea toward his own career as prophet. But the main factor in his decision would seem to be his marriage. So prominent is his marriage in what we know about him that the beginning of his ministry as a prophet may indeed have been God's command that he marry Gomer.

The story of the marriage is found in the first three chapters of Hosea. The prophet is told to marry a prostitute (Hosea 1:2). He obeys and marries Gomer "a wife of harlotry." Three children are born, and they are given symbolic names: a son, Jezreel, which means "God sows," a daughter, Lo-ruhamah, which means "not loved," and another son, Lo-ammi, which means "not my people" (Hosea 1:4-10). In Chapter 3 Hosea's wife, not identified as Gomer, has deserted her family, but Hosea searches for her, brings her back, and, we assume, reestablishes their relationship.

These details seem clear enough in general outline, but examined more closely they pose a number of questions. There are two different accounts of the marriage. How are they to be reconciled, or should we first consider that the marriage, or one of the accounts of the marriage, was an allegory rather than a real event? That would relieve what has seemed to be a problem for some readers, that God would require one of his prophets to marry a prostitute. Was Gomer really a prostitute, and was there one woman, or were there two, and two marriages? There have been many attempts to answer these questions.[1] One commentator, for example, argues that the description of Gomer as a "wanton woman" or woman of adultery should be understood as we understood "man of unclean lips" in Isaiah 6:5. She would then not be wanton in the obvious sense, but only to the extent that she was part of the self-centered materialistic society of her time.[2] It is possible that later she proved false to Hosea, and that he then projected back to God the command to marry a wanton woman.[3]

Another writer proposes that Gomer was a prostitute at one of the Baal temples.[4] While abhorrent to the Israelites, temple prostitution, it is argued, was an accepted and essential institution to those who believed in the Baal nature myths. After a time, Gomer went back to the temple, but Hosea found her, redeemed her and brought her home. Hosea then did symbolically what Israel had done actually. The names of his children by Gomer added point to the meaning of his symbolic act. The result of consorting with Baalism was that the people of Israel were "not my people," that they were "not loved," that God "would sow" whatever grapes of wrath he chose to. The theory has lost some of its force however, since doubts have been raised about the practice of cultic prostitution, as we noted in an earlier chapter.

What makes the story of Hosea as appealing as any in the Old Testament is that, despite the unpromising start of his relationship with Gomer, however we interpret it, he loved her. Perhaps he grew to love her after they were married, but whatever the situation was, it suggests that, wanton or not, Gomer was a woman with lovable qualities. We know about Hosea's fidelity, and Gomer's lack of it, but given the prophet's continuing love it seems unlikely that the relationship was completely one-sided.

Perhaps that also was part of the divine plan. The marriage was symbolic of the evil consequences of apostasy. It was symbolic too of God's continuing love, which never failed, although it could be ignored or rejected. But it also symbolized that the people whom God loved were intrinsically worth loving, that people who act in unloving, self-destructive ways have the capacity to be what was intended by the term "a chosen people."

With regard to the two accounts of the marriage, it is possible that the book as we now have it was compiled from two collections.[5] One of these was very short

[1]James Luther Mays, *Hosea* (Philadelphia: The Westminster Press, 1969), p. 23. Mays summarizes various points of view and refers to Harold Rowley's discussion and bibliography in "The Marriage of Hosea," reprinted in *Men of God* (London: Nelson, 1963)

[2]Robert Gordis, "Hosea's Marriage and Message," in *Poets, Prophets and Sages* (Bloomington, Ind.: Indiana University Press, 1971), p. 233.

[3]Otto Eissfeldt, *The Old Testament*, P. R. Ackroyd trans. (New York: Harper and Row, 1965), p. 38

[4]Norman K. Gottwald, *A Light to the Nations* (New York: Harper and Row, 1959), pp. 297–9

[5]Theodore H. Robinson, *Prophecy and the Prophets in Ancient Israel*, 2d ed. (London: Gerald Duckworth and Co., 1953), p. 75.

consisting only of the first two chapters. At the beginning of each section was an account of the marriage, Chapter 1 in the third person, Chapter 3, beginning the longer second section, in the first person. This would exclude the hypothesis that the marriage was an allegory. "For the presence of two reports, one biographical and one autobiographical, can only be explained if we are dealing with a real event. It would, to say the least, be very strange if an allegory were related in this duplicate form."[6]

THE POLITICAL SITUATION

In 745, the year following the death of Jeroboam II, a leader came to the throne of Assyria, Tiglath-pileser III, who initiated a policy of expansion that brought the nation, under Esarhaddon (681–669) and Ashurbanapal (669–633), to the zenith of power. This by itself created a dangerous situation for the independent states of Syria and Palestine, but the danger was increased in Israel many times by the collapse of her own leadership.

Jeroboam II was the last capable monarch of the Northern Kingdom. He had indeed been fortunate. His reign coincided with a relatively quiet period in international politics, which allowed Israel to develop without interference. During that time he had neglected the religious traditions of his people, and he appears to have given little attention to the social injustices which flourished among them. But he was a strong ruler. He reconquered Syria, cooperated with Judah, and enabled his country to prosper (2 Kings 14:23–29). He was followed by men who were interested only in their personal ambition. His son, Zechariah, succeeded him and was murdered by Shallum six months later. So ended the dynasty of Jehu (2 Kings 15:8–12). Shallum had reigned for one month when he was killed by Menahem (2 Kings 15:13–15).

These savage coups and countercoups are probably referred to by Hosea.

They made kings, but not through me.
They set up princes, but without my knowledge. (Hosea 8:4)

Menahem remained in power until his death eight years later in 738, but he survived only by acts of extreme savagery against his own people (2 Kings 15:16), and by paying a heavy tribute to Assyria. He gave Tiglath-pileser "a thousand talents of silver, that he might help him to confirm his hold of the royal power" (2 Kings 5:19). He did not pay it himself. He taxed all the wealthy men fifty silver shekels. Undoubtedly they resented this, but they waited until after his death in 738 when he was succeeded by Pekehiah his son. This unfortunate monarch ruled for two years and then was murdered in the royal palace as the result of a conspiracy led by Pekah, his lieutenant, with the help of fifty Gileadites (2 Kings 15:25).

Pekah was anti-Assyrian, and presumably objected to the pro-Assyrian policies

[6]Eissfeldt, *The Old Testament*, p. 390.

of Menahem and his son, but his nationalistic fervor did not include devotion to Yahweh. Like Ahaz of Judah whom he attacked, he offered human sacrifice.

Pekah attempted to form a coalition with Rezin, king of Syria, and the Philistines against the now immense power of Assyria, but they needed the support of Judah.[7] Judah's young King Ahaz did not want to join. The allies, therefore, tried to persuade him by force, that is by attacking Jerusalem. Ahaz appealed to the Assyrian king, who attacked Syria, killed Rezin, and greatly reduced Israelite territories. During the attacks Pekah was killed by Hoshea who then became the last king of Israel (2 Kings 15:30).

HOSEA'S MESSAGE

Throughout all this Hosea railed against the frantic political intrigues of Israel, first with Egypt, then Assyria (Hosea 7:11). He preached to the people about the love and the knowledge of God. He pleaded with them to return as he had pleaded with Gomer to return. Yet his preaching must have appeared strange to many Israelites. We are acquainted with the leaders of Israel and the prosperous members of the state, but in all communities there are people who are neither especially wicked nor especially good, neither especially wealthy and powerful nor especially poor and dependent. These people would certainly not identify themselves with Gomer, but they could not be expected to understand the idealism of Hosea. They were moved by events and in the daily fears of enemy invasion and the daily injustice of unscrupulous fellow citizens their minds must have been filled with immediate practical concerns, not the far out images of the prophet. But he continued to preach from the conviction that the events that moved the people were not real, the practical concerns that filled their minds were an illusion. What they imagined they knew, they did not know, because *knowledge* was knowledge of God. It is what we might call Hosea's theory of knowledge, which he expressed in poetic images and which gave to this preaching its great power.

> Hear the word of the Lord, O people of Israel;
> for the Lord has a controversy with the inhabitants of the land.
> There is no faithfulness or kindness,
> and no knowledge of God in the land;
> there is swearing, lying, killing, stealing, and committing adultery;
> they break all bounds and murder follows murder. (Hosea 4:1-2)

Knowledge of God is regarded by Hosea as the basis of human relationship. Where there is no such knowledge the society breaks down, the people "are destroyed for lack of knowledge" (Hosea 4:6). Hosea regards the priests as particularly culpable

---

[7]Martin Noth, *The History of Israel*, 2d ed., revised translation by Peter R. Ackroyd (New York: Harper and Row, 1960), pp. 259-60.

Outside Jerusalem. "They shall return and dwell beneath my shadow," (*Hosea 14:7*). Photo by Elizabeth Gordon.

because instead of teaching the people about God, which is their duty, they reject knowledge of God (Hosea 4:6), and so teach another lesson to the people which they are very ready to learn.

> For the spirit of harlotry is within them,
>   and they know not the Lord. (Hosea 5:4)

The word "to know" used by Hosea, as one writer explains, denotes in most instances "an act involving concern, inner engagement, dedication, or attachment to a person. It means also to have sympathy, pity or affection for someone."[8] He gives examples of the use of the word in other parts of the Old Testament, where "know" is not an adequate translation of the Hebrew word. In Exodus 2:24–25, God heard the cry of the people, saw them and "knew" their condition. The sense here is to have pity. In Exodus 3:7 when God spoke to Moses he told him that he "knew" the sufferings of the people, that is, he had sympathy for and was affected by. There is quality of affection in such knowledge, illustrated by Hosea's own affection for Gomer. Therefore, when Hosea upbraids the people for not knowing, and calls upon them

[8]Abraham Heschel, *The Prophets,* Vol. 1. (New York: Harper and Row, 1969), p. 57. Heschel further discusses the use of the Hebrew word translated as "know" to describe sexual intercourse, as in Genesis 4:1, but see Ephraim Speiser's comments about this word in *Genesis* (New York: Doubleday, 1964), p. 32.

to know, he is urging more than the renewal of covenant relationship; he is calling for a quality of life characterized by a level of faith for which the Covenant is a necessary but not a sufficient condition. There could scarcely be a greater vision than that which Hosea had of an increasingly materialistic society conforming to this exalted ideal.

> Let us know, let us press on to know the Lord;
> > his going forth is sure as the dawn;
>
> For I desire steadfast love and not sacrifice,
> > the knowledge of God, rather than burnt offerings. (Hosea 6:3, 6)

ISRAEL'S INTRANSIGENCE AND GOD'S RESPONSE

The fact was that the society neither conformed nor desired to conform to this ideal. Even God found the people's intransigence impossible to overcome.

> What shall I do with you, O Ephraim?
>
> All their kings have fallen;
> > and none of them calls upon me.
>
> The pride of Israel witnesses against him;
> > yet they do not return to the Lord their God,
> > nor seek him, for all this. (Hosea 6:4, 7:7, 10)

Ironically, at those times when they felt the need for God's assistance, they claimed that they did indeed know him (Hosea 8:2). But no people who had knowledge of God as Hosea understood it would boast that they did not fear the Lord (Hosea 10:3).

God's response was twofold. First the people would get what they asked for they had sown the wind, they would reap the whirlwind (Hosea 8:7). They had ploughed wickedness into the soil, the crop would be mischief (Hosea 10:13). The Lord would punish the society for their misdeeds (Hosea 12:2), for their apostasy (Hosea 13:1-3), and for their rebellion (Hosea 13:16), and the punishment would be terrible (Hosea 9:13-17). But there is a poignancy in the book of Hosea about the pronouncement of God's judgment, which can be better understood in the light of the prophet's own experience of unappreciated love.

> When Israel was a child, I loved him,
> > and out of Egypt I called my son.
> The more I called them, the more they went from me;
>
> > I took them up in my arms;
> > but they did not know that I healed them.
> I led them with cords of compassion,
> > with the bands of love . . .
> > and I bent down to them and fed them. (Hosea 11:1-4)

God's other response was intimately connected with these pictures of family
e. It was the response of a father to his prodigal son, or of Hosea to the faithlessness
his wife. As Hosea never lost faith in Gomer, so God through the prophet never
 faith with his people.

Return, O Israel, to the Lord your God.

So you, by the help of your God, return,
    hold fast to love and justice,
    and wait continually for your God. (Hosea 14:1, 12:6)

In the social, political setting of the time, Hosea's message was exceptional.
hat the world regarded as important, as overwhelmingly crucial, was regarded by
 prophet as peripheral. Yes, there was danger from Assyria, and yes, the political
 ation in Israel was appalling, but that was not the problem. The problem was
 ack of knowledge of God. To illustrate, cancer research has progressed to the point
 being able to identify primary and secondary malignancies. The secondary
 lignancies are often easier to find and to treat, but until the primary malignancy
 dealt with there can be no cure. The people of Israel were afraid of and wanted
 ure for the secondary malignancies of their diseased society. They were ignoring
 e primary problem.

E FALL OF SAMARIA

 der Hoshea (732–724) Israel barely survived as an independent nation. Her only
 asonable course of action was to accept Assyrian control without protest. This she
 uld not do. In 727, Tiglath-pileser died. He was succeeded by Shalmaneser V,
 d in the political uncertainties and apparent weaknesses of the succession Hoshea
 cided to revolt, counting on the help of Egypt. We read that he sent messengers
 the king of Egypt and withheld tribute from Assyria (2 Kings 17:4). This was in-
 dibly foolish. Shalmaneser attacked, occupied what remained of Israel and besieged
 maria. Meanwhile Hoshea was captured or he gave himself up to the Assyrian
 g. Two years later (722–721), the city of Samaria fell and Israel became an Assyrian
 ovince. Sargon, who at that point succeeded Shalmaneser, lists 27,290 citizens who
 re deported to distant parts of the Assyrian empire as far away as Nineveh and
 edia. They were replaced by inhabitants from Babylon, Cuthah, Avva, Hamath
 d Sepharvaim, that is primarily Babylonia and Syria (2 Kings 17:24). Later,
 abians were settled there. The Northern Kingdom thereupon ceased to exist.[9]
    Hosea had been sent to warn the people of Israel. They would not listen and
 y perished. But Hosea's influence persisted. It is postulated that he escaped to
 dah after the fall of Samaria and his prophecies went with him.[10] There, his message

[9]Albert T. Olmstead, *History of Assyria* (Chicago: University of Chicago Press, 1975), Chapter
 I, "The Last Days of Israel."
[10]Mays, *Hosea*, p. 16.

could be seen not only as a warning about the future, but as a description of what had happened to Judah's nearest neighbor. If he was the first man in history to de-nounce militarism,[11] the people of Judah could see in the fate of Samaria how useless militarism proved to be. If he was the first to describe Israel's attraction towards Baalism as harlotry,[12] the people of Judah could see what terrible consequences followed from it.

But they might also have seen that Hosea offered a daring, unparalleled message of hope.[13] God would not give up his people (Hosea 11:8). If Israel would return, the Vale of Trouble would be a door of hope (Hosea 14:1, 2:15). Israel had rejected it and perished, but for Judah there was still time to respond with knowledge to the word of the Lord.

QUESTIONS FOR DISCUSSION

The following questions refer to Chapters 15–16.

1. What is a prophet? How would an ancient Israelite have known the difference between a true prophet of God and a false prophet?

2. What could account for the first appearance of prophets such as Amos and Hosea in the eighth century B.C. and not earlier? Why were there no prophets like that dur-ing the reign of Solomon when their influence might have been great enough to prevent the division of the kingdom? Did these prophets appear too late?

3. Every society suffers from unlawful and selfish behavior, but not everyone in a society acts unlawfully and selfishly. Is it possible that Amos, coming as he did from the spare life of a small farmer, applied unrealistic standards to the Northern Kingdom? If he didn't, what had happened in Israel for there to be such a breakdown of social morality? The Assyrians were cruel enemies, but among themselves, in their own cities, the record shows that they lived reasonably ordered and law abiding lives. Why should the Northern Kingdom not only have repudiated the commandments of God but violated common standards of decent behavior?

4. There is much discussion about the details of Hosea's marriage. Does any one explanation appear to you as more persuasive than the others? Apart from details of the marriage, did God manipulate Hosea and his wife for the purpose of making a point, and if so, isn't it contrary to the concern expressed in other parts of the Old Testament for the individual? Or are God's laws for the individual suspended when he calls a prophet? Was it not possible for God to have conveyed his message to Israel without using the painfulness or causing the painfulness of Hosea's marriage?

---

[11]Norman K. Gottwald, *All the Kingdoms of the Earth* (New York: Harper and Row, 1964), p. 13 footnote 55 quoting Yehezkel Kaufman, *The Religion of Israel,* translated and abridged by Moshe Greenber (Chicago: University of Chicago Press, 1960), p. 335.

[12]Gerhard Von Rad, *Old Testament Theology,* Vol. 1 (New York: Harper and Row, 1965), p. 14

[13]Ibid., p. 145.

CHAPTER SEVENTEEN
ISAIAH OF JERUSALEM

THE STRUCTURE OF THE BOOK

The title of the book of Isaiah implies that all sixty-six chapters were written by one author, and this was widely believed until late in the nineteenth century. The consensus now is that the book can be divided into three sections. The first, Chapters 1–39, is attributed to Isaiah of Jerusalem who lived in the eighth century, whose advice King Ahaz ignored in 732, and whose faith and courage were vindicated in 701 when the Assyrians retired from besieging Jerusalem. But these chapters themselves have been divided, and opinion differs as to whether they were independent units brought together by a later editor, or whether there was an original core of Isaianic material which was edited and expanded.[1]

The second section, Chapters 40–55, is attributed to an author, or authors, living during the exile, almost two centuries later, at the time when Cyrus, king of Persia, had become, or was becoming, the dominant power in the ancient Near East. He is referred to as "my shepherd" who will rebuild Jerusalem, (Isaiah 44:28), and as the Lord's "anointed" to carry out his divine purposes (Isaiah 45:1). Cyrus captured Babylon in 539 and shortly thereafter issued an edict permitting the Jewish

---

[1]The matter is discussed by Otto Eissfeldt, *The Old Testament,* Peter Ackroyd trans. (New York: Harper and Row, 1965), pp. 306–8.

Brevard Childs, *Introduction to the Old Testament as Scripture* (Philadelphia: Fortress Press, 1979), p. 318–21.

exiles to return to Jerusalem. Apart from the question of whether a prophet of God could foretell the future at such a great distance, that is, whether Isaiah of the eighth century could foretell the rise to power of Cyrus in the sixth, there seems to be no reason why in the eighth century Isaiah should have done so. It would seem to be consistent with prophetic activity elsewhere in the Old Testament, which did not engage in spectacular feats of foreknowledge, to posit an author who lived in the sixth century contemporary with the events he describes.

The third section, Chapters 56–66, is believed to have been written in the early days of the return from exile, when the Jews were attempting to resettle in their devastated city, and were occupied with such matters as the glory of the New Jerusalem, (Isaiah 60) and the importance of fasts and Sabbath keeping, (Isaiah 58). The author, or authors, of Third Isaiah made use of Second Isaiah, for example Isaiah 62:11, "His reward is with him; and his recompense before him," which repeats the words of Isaiah 40:10, and Isaiah 60:4 "Lift up your eyes round about and see; they all gather together, they come to you," which similarly repeats Isaiah 49:18.

The book of Isaiah as a whole is therefore a composite work, written over a long period by, possibly, three main authors, but most likely by several others until the work assumed its present form.

The final editor, however, who was surely aware of the complex nature of the Isaiah material, prefaces it with the statement, "The vision of Isaiah the son of Amoz, which he saw concerning Judah and Jerusalem in the days of Uzziah, Jotham, Ahaz, Hezekiah, kings of Judah" (Isaiah 1:1). This implies that the entire work was a "vision" of Isaiah of Jerusalem, who lived in the eighth century.[2] Unless the anonymous editor simply ignored the historical setting, and so had Isaiah of the eighth century refer to Cyrus of the sixth, or unless he was maintaining the ability of the prophet to foretell events at a distance of two hundred years, it is possible that he intended the reader to understand the book of Isaiah not in terms of its historical consistency but in terms of its theological purpose.[4] This is a view which, contrary to the claim that Isaiah's message is "unintelligible without an exact knowledge of contemporary history," proposes that, in the case of Second Isaiah, "The theological context completely overshadows the historical."[5] Instead of filtering the biblical text through a "historical critical mesh" the student is called upon to look closely at the text in its received form, that is, the form in which we have it in our Bible, in order to "discern its function for a community of faith."[6] According to this view the writing of the sixth century Second Isaiah, Chapters 40–55, was deliberately placed within the context of the eighth century prophet in order to free it from a specific historical period and direct it to the future. Its message could then relate "to the redemptive plan of God for all of history."[7]

---

[2]Otto Kaiser, *Isaiah 1–12*, R. A. Wilson trans. (Philadelphia: The Westminster Press, 1972), p.
[3]Eissfeldt, *The Old Testament*, p. 305.
[4]Childs, *Introduction to the Old Testament*, p. 326.
[5]Ibid., p. 83.
[6]Ibid.
[7]Ibid., p. 326.

A watchtower (*Isaiah 21:8*). Photo by Elizabeth Gordon.

The value of such an approach would seem to be that while it takes into account the textual history of a passage or a book, such as Isaiah, it also attempts to understand it for its theological purpose. The interpreter is then "forced to confront the authoritative text of Scripture in continuing theological reflection."[8] A possible danger of such an approach is that the interpreter would be tempted to neglect textual and historical considerations as being less important than the final, canonical form. A full understanding of the text certainly involves taking into account all these factors and neglecting none of them.

ISAIAH OF JUDAH

The first 39 chapters of Isaiah are primarily the work of the prophet of Judah whose ministry began the year that King Uzziah died (742) and continued through the reigns of Jotham, Ahaz, Hezekiah and perhaps Manasseh. His life spanned three great crises in the history of Judah: The Syro-Israelite coalition of 732, the fall of Samaria in

[8]Ibid., p. 83.
    Brevard Childs' Canonical approach is discussed in several articles in the May 1980 issue (No. 6) of the *Journal for the Study of the Old Testament.* For reference to a critical assessment of Childs' position, see Chapter 6 of this work, footnote 37.

721, and Sennacherib's invasion of Palestine in 701, which is discussed in a following chapter.

The preaching of Isaiah has been described as the "theological high watermark of the whole of the Old Testament."[9] But in 742 the prophet was commanded to preach, not only to a people who did not listen to what he had to say, but to people who could not listen. Isaiah received the strange order to speak to the people, and at the same time command them not to understand.

> And he said, "Go, and say to this people:
> 'Hear and hear, but do not understand;
> see and see, but do not perceive.'
> Make the heart of this people fat,
>   and their ears heavy,
>   and shut their eyes;
> lest they see with their eyes,
>   and hear with their ears,
> and understand with their hearts,
>   and turn and be healed." (Isaiah 6:9–10)

Whether these are the precise words which the prophet received, or whether they are his interpretation of God's commission after years of preaching to people who refused to take him seriously, we cannot say. We should no doubt be cautious about explaining away a divine command because it is difficult to understand. The hardening of the people's heart must be understood in terms of "the far-reaching nature of God's designs in history."[10] Nevertheless, the command does illustrate the painful contradiction of intellect and emotion that was a daily part of Isaiah's experience. His work had to go on despite evidence that it was useless. Isaiah believed that he *had* to proclaim the word of God, and he did so independently of what the results were. That, however, is true of other prophets, such as Amos, Hosea, Jeremiah, and earlier prophets such as Micaiah and Elijah, all of whom were obliged in a sense to fly blind, blind to the surroundings, but sensitive to the commands of God.

AN UNCONSCIOUS PRESUPPOSITION

From the side of the prophet the people appeared to be wilfully resistant to what he had to say. But this may be assuming too much self-consciousness on the part of the people. What we do not hear, or cannot, to use Isaiah's terminology, and what we do not do, is not always what we know we do not hear, or know that we do not do. The point is made by W. K. C. Guthrie in a book on Greek philosophy, quoting from A. N. Whitehead,

[9]Gerhard Von Rad, *Old Testament Theology*, Vol. II, D.M.G. Stalker trans. (New York: Harper and Row, 1965), p. 147.
[10]Ibid., p. 154.

When you are criticizing the philosophy of an epoch, do not chiefly direct your attention to those intellectual positions which its exponents feel it necessary explicitly to defend. There will be some fundamental assumptions which adherents of all the variant systems within the epoch unconsciously presuppose.[11]

All the people of Judah certainly "unconsciously presupposed" (so that it did not appear to them as an assumption) that they were chosen by God, and that their kingdom would continue forever. It was also, in the same way, no assumption that if they kept the commandments they would be blessed, and if they did not keep them they would be punished. It was, however, an unwarranted assumption to turn that piece of reasoning about, and argue that as they had not been punished they were keeping the commandments, and therefore a prophet like Isaiah was not to be taken seriously. It was an assumption, yet it was understandable. For forty years, more than an average lifetime in those days, the country flourished under the long and brilliant reign of Uzziah, 783–742. He built the city of Elath, near Ezion-geber; he fought and defeated the Philistines. His influence extended south towards Egypt and east to the Transjordan. He strengthened the fortifications of Jerusalem and "built towers in the wilderness" to protect outlying areas. He hewed out many cisterns for his large herds. He promoted farming and grape growing for "he loved the soil" (2 Chronicles 26:10). He strengthened his army and equipped it well. "He made engines invented by skilful men, to be on the towers and the corners, to shoot arrows and great stones" (2 Chronicles 26:15). Moreover, Uzziah's reign coincided with that of Jeroboam II in the north, and so the two kingdoms were as strong and prosperous as at any time since the reign of Solomon.

It would have been very difficult for the citizens of Judah to believe that God was not pleased with them and, as they were doing no differently from what they had done or intended to do, would not continue to bless them in the future. The absence of any visible disapproval from God over a long period, the tradition of their being a uniquely chosen people with a glorious future, coalesced into a self-satisfied view of their relations with God which became a fundamental assumption, so unconsciously presupposed that the people could not understand what the prophet was saying. They could not see with their eyes nor listen with their ears nor understand with their wits Isaiah 6:10). Their attitude could be summed up by an exasperated comment of Jeremiah, who prophesied in Judah about a hundred years later, "Were they ashamed when they committed abominations? No, they were not at all ashamed; they did not know how to blush." (Jeremiah 6:15)

THE GROWING POWER OF ASSYRIA

The people were blind to their own faults; they were also blind to what was happening in the world around them. The Israelites were more dependent than they cared

[11]William K. C. Guthrie, *The Greek Philosophers* (New York: Harper and Row, 1960), p. 11.

to admit upon external conditions. The united Kingdom of David and Solomon coincided with a period of international calm; so did the contemporaneous reigns of Uzziah and Jeroboam II. The three powers most likely to disrupt Israel, namely, Egypt, Syria, and Assyria, were not during that period able to do so, but one year after the death of Jeroboam II in 746 one of the greatest Assyrian monarchs, Tiglath-pileser III, came to the throne and began to interest himself in territories to the west, in Syria and Palestine, and the small nations of Transjordan.

About three years later, in 742, Uzziah of Judah died of leprosy. There is some indication that just before his death he brought together an anti-Assyrian coalition, without success. An Assyrian text from the *Annals* of Tiglath-Pileser III refers to an Azriau of Iuda who attempted to repel the Assyrians "by means of an attack with foot soldiers," but he and his allies were defeated.[12]

Jotham, Uzziah's son who succeeded him, was a capable ruler and continued his father's policies of building and fortifications and active warfare against the ancient enemies of Judah (2 Chronicles 27), but Jotham was succeeded in 735 by Ahaz, his twenty-year-old son, who was not equal to his immense responsibilities. The account in Chronicles records an unhappy reign of a king of Judah who had no apparent commitment to his nation's religion. He was one of the few persons in the Old Testament to engage in human sacrifice: he "burned his sons as an offering" (2 Chronicles 28:3). He had no ability as a military commander: he was defeated by the Edomites in the south, and the Syrians and Israelites in the north (2 Kings 16:5–6, 2 Chronicles 28:1–8). He is remembered especially, however, because at a moment of great crisis he was presented with an opportunity to affirm his faith in God by one of the greatest Old Testament prophets. It was an opportunity which he refused (Isaiah 7:12).

By 734 Tiglath-pileser was clearly intending to invade the western states. Syria and Israel decided to form an alliance, similar to the alliance against Shalmaneser of 120 years before in which Ahab had been a prominent member, and perhaps similar to the more recent alliance led by Uzziah. Pekah of Israel and Rezin, ruler of Damascus, called upon Ahaz to join them. Ahaz was young and inexperienced, he had been monarch for only about three years, but he was alert enough or frightened enough to realize that an alliance against Assyria could not succeed. The two kings thereupon attacked Judah, ravaged the countryside and besieged Jerusalem. King and people were shaken as "the trees of the forest shake before the wind" (Isaiah 7:2). Meanwhile the Edomites and the Philistines attacked Judah in the south and the west (2 Chronicles 28:16–18).

A SIGN FROM GOD

At this critical moment God spoke to Isaiah and told him to tell the young king to be on his guard but not to be frightened by "these two smoldering stumps

[12]James B. Pritchard, *Ancient and Near Eastern Texts Relating to the Old Testament* (Princeton, N.J.: Princeton University Press, 1969), pp. 282–83.

firebrands," that is Pekah and Rezin (Isaiah 7:4). They had not taken Jerusalem and they would not. Within a lifetime both nations would be destroyed.

Isaiah, accompanied by his son, who had been given the symbolic name of Shear-jashub ("a remnant will return") and speaking at the command of God, invited Ahaz to ask for a sign, but Ahaz refused. Perhaps he was frightened of the prophet or did not understand him. Perhaps he was too preoccupied, he was examining the city's water supply at the time. Nevertheless, Isaiah replied somewhat impatiently that the king would be given a sign anyway. A young woman was about to bear a son and his name would be Immanuel ("God with us"). Before the child was old enough to know the difference between right and wrong, the two attacking nations would be destroyed.

Isaiah later provided another sign through the birth of a child named Maher-shalal-hash-baz ("speed-spoil-hasten-plunder"). "Before the child knows how to cry 'My father' or 'My mother,' the wealth of Damascus and the spoil of Samaria will be carried away before the king of Assyria." (Isaiah 8:1–4)

But Ahaz did not believe God's sign. In that respect he was an example of those to whom Isaiah spoke, who "could not" hear. An appeal to divine protection means nothing to those who have no faith. Ahaz ignored the prophet and looked for the kind of help he could understand. He appealed to Assyria, "I am your servant and your son. Come up, and rescue me from the hand of the king of Syria and from the hand of the king of Israel, who are attacking me." (2 Kings 16:7) He took treasures from the temple and the palace to reinforce his appeal and sent them to Tiglath-pileser who was no doubt pleased to receive an invitation to do what he shortly intended to do. The Assyrians destroyed Damascus, killed Rezin its king, and deported the inhabitants. Meanwhile the Assyrians swept through Israel and occupied all its territory except Ephraim and western Manasseh. Pekah was murdered and replaced by Hoshea. Judah had been saved, but although she retained a nominal independence, it was at the cost of actual subservience to the wishes of Assyria.

Ahaz went to Damascus to meet Tiglath-pileser and returned, as one commentator put it, "a thoroughly disillusioned man." But it is possible that he felt a great deal more secure than he had, and his later enthusiasm for non-Jewish forms of worship suggests that he may not have remained disillusioned for long.

In secular terms Isaiah had been made to appear ineffectual, but that was a common experience of prophets. He warned the people that because they had rejected

> the waters of Shiloah that flow gently, and melt in fear before Rezin and the son of Remaliah; therefore, behold, the Lord is bringing up against them the waters of the River, mighty and many, the king of Assyria and all his glory; and it will rise over all its channels and go over all its banks; and it will sweep on into Judah, it will overflow and pass on, reaching even to the neck; and its outspread wings will fill the breadth of your land, O Immanuel. (Isaiah 8:6–8)

The people, perhaps at this point, boasted cynically that they had a covenant with death,

> We have made a covenant with death,
>   and with Sheol we have an agreement;
> when the overwhelming scourge passes through
>   it will not come to us. Isaiah 28:15

Possibly they were referring to a Canaanite god, but their cynical disregard of the reality of their condition as Isaiah saw it must have made him even more aware that the people indeed could not hear or understand. He replied with strong words but hardly with confidence that anyone would listen.

THE HOLINESS OF GOD

The intensity of Isaiah's preaching may be gauged by the climactic nature of his call. It was the year that King Uzziah died, 742, and the future had suddenly become bleak for the small country of Judah. Isaiah was in the Temple when he saw the Lord seated on a throne attended by seraphim, or burning creatures, with six wings. Perhaps the seraphim were the cherubim of Exodus 25:18, winged creatures that were part of the furniture of the Holy of Holies. To Isaiah it was the real awful presence of the Lord, and the building shook to its foundations and filled with smoke. His reaction was fear and an overwhelming sense of his own sinfulness. Then in his vision one of the seraphim took a glowing coal from the altar, touched his lips and told him that his iniquity had been removed, his sin wiped away (Isaiah 6:1–7).

From this experience one may trace Isaiah's preoccupation with the holiness of God as the standard to which the people of Judah had to conform.

But for one who had encountered it in the person of God himself, holiness could not be simply a standard, a measure applied to life to determine greater or lesser degrees of compliance; it had to be the total preoccupation of life. At the beginning of his ministry, but presumably after his vision, Isaiah is confident that if the people would discuss the matter reasonably with God they would change, and God would forgive them.

> Come now, let us reason together,
>   says the Lord:
> though your sins are like scarlet,
>   they shall be as white as snow. (Isaiah 1:18)

But the people had had no experience of God that was in any way like Isaiah's, which may be an additional reason, or perhaps the primary reason why they could not hear or understand. When life is filled with selfish concerns there is only a slight chance that profounder matters will get a hearing. The evidence from the book of Isaiah is that it was a very slight chance indeed.

A stream in the desert (Isaiah 35:6). Photo by Elizabeth Gordon.

THE MANNER OF LIFE
OF THE PEOPLE OF JUDAH

Amos castigated the Northern Kingdom for its luxury and greed, its unjust treatment of the poor and helpless, its perversion of law, its apostasy and, despite all that,
its self-righteousness. Isaiah likened Judah to a diseased body with not a sound spot
on it, nothing but "bruises and sores and bleeding wounds" (Isaiah 1:6). Perhaps
he was thinking of the physical condition of Uzziah, who had died of leprosy shortly
before. The image would be clear to everyone. But Uzziah was an honorable ruler;
the people of Judah dishonored God. "Your hands are full of blood" Isaiah charged
(Isaiah 1:15). The city of Jerusalem, once the home of justice and righteousness, was
a place of murderers (Isaiah 1:21). The people were trying to deceive God: "this people draw near with their mouth and honor me with their lips, while their hearts are
far from me and their fear of me is a commandment of men learned by rote" (Isaiah
29:13). God would therefore no longer accept their sacrifices and prayers:

> What to me is the multitude of your sacrifices?. . .
>
> even though you make many prayers,
>   I will not listen. (Isaiah 1:11, 15)

He excoriated the women of Judah for their vanity and wantonness, incidentally
providing us with an informative description of the personal jewelry and clothing
of the time.

> In that day the Lord will take away the finery of the anklets, the headbands, and the
> crescents; the pendants, the bracelets, and the scarfs; the headdresses, the armlets, the
> sashes, the perfume boxes, and the amulets; the signet rings and nose rings; the festal
> robes, the mantles, the cloaks, and the handbags; the garments of gauze, the linen
> garments, the turbans, and the veils. (Isaiah 3:18–23)

Isaiah was disgusted with priests and prophets who could not control their
behavior but

> reel with wine and stagger with strong drink. . .
> all tables are full of vomit. (Isaiah 28:7–8)

Repeatedly he utters a "Woe!" upon the people.

> Woe to those. . .who draw sin as with cart ropes. . .
> Woe to those who call evil good and good evil,
> who put darkness for light and light for darkness. (Isaiah 5:18, 20)

What God required of Judah was purity of religious commitment and purity
of life. If the people did not listen to him he would discipline them, for there was

a day of doom waiting (Isaiah 2:12), and he would strip Jerusalem and Judah of every prop and stay (Isaiah 3:1).

THE POLITICAL SITUATION IN THE NORTH

As we saw in the previous chapter the political situation of the Northern Kingdom at this time was desperate. The Assyrian invasion which rescued Judah left Israel with merely a remnant of its former territory. Pekah was killed and Hoshea, the last king of Israel, was allowed to keep his diminished kingdom only by paying Assyria a heavy tribute. His wisest course would have been to accept the situation and do nothing to arouse Assyrian anger. But he did the reverse; after the death of Tiglath-pileser he "sent messengers to So, king of Egypt" and withheld his annual tribute (2 Kings 17:1-4). This was a suicidal folly.[13] Egypt could not help Israel and probably had no intention of doing so, it was concerned with its own borders. Hoshea, who may have tried to explain himself to Shalmaneser, was arrested. The Assyrian army overran Israel and besieged Samaria. The biblical text (2 Kings 17:1-6) says little more than that the siege lasted for three years, and when the city was captured in 721 its inhabitants were deported to areas of Mesopotamia near Haran and Gozan and to Media. The Assyrian records are similarly terse.[14] But from what we know of the siege of Jerusalem we can imagine the suffering and terror and growing despair of the people in Samaria. We may also suppose that the inhabitants of Judah forty miles to the south were anxious, not only about their fellow Israelites, whom sectional loyalties had divided but who were all members of the family of Abraham and heirs of the promise, but about their own fate. If indeed the Lord would remove from them "every prop and stay" unless they changed their manner of life, was that not the strongest incentive to make a change? Perhaps some of them were thinking that, or perhaps some had concluded that nothing could protect them from such power as Assyria. Isaiah had another view.

GOD, LORD OF ALL NATIONS

From Isaiah's awareness of the holiness of God arose his deep conviction that in times of need there is only one place to go, that is to God. When Israel and Syria attacked Ahaz and threatened to overthrow him, Isaiah's advice was not to be afraid: "Take heed, be quiet, do not fear, and do not let your heart be faint because of these two smouldering stumps of firebrands" (Isaiah 7:4). The New English Bible translation

[13]Martin Noth, *The History of Israel*, 2d ed., revised translation by Peter Ackroyd (New York: Harper and Row, 1960), pp. 261-62.

[14]Pritchard, *Ancient and Near Eastern Texts*, pp. 284-85.

brings out a play on words, "Have firm faith, or you will not stand firm."[15] (Isaiah 7:9)

But Ahaz and his officers looked to troops and alliances in moments of danger. For them and their leaders survival depended upon military strength and clever diplomacy. Isaiah looked to God.

The prophet had in mind much more than the ability of God to protect his people, which had been demonstrated many times since the Exodus. Isaiah asserted the power of God over all nations in the world. The people of Judah were irrationally confident that Egypt would resuce them and were terrified of Assyria. To Isaiah that was a mistake. "The Egyptians are men, and not God;" he told them, "their horses are flesh, and not spirit" (Isaiah 31:3). Assyria was an instrument in God's hands and could do only what God permitted it to do. The people of Judah were afraid of the wrong power. "The Lord of Hosts...let him be whom you fear and let him be your dread." (Isaiah 8:13)

> Ah, Assyria, the rod of my anger,
>   the staff of my fury! (Isaiah 10:5)

Clearly the people to whom Isaiah spoke understood nothing of this. Using the term that Hosea had made so much of, the prophet deplored Judah's lack of knowledge with all that it implied about lack of love and lack of obligation. They were more profoundly ignorant than animals:

> The ox knows its owner
>   and the ass its master's crib;
> but Israel does not know,
>   my people does not understand. (Isaiah 1:3)

They had spoken and acted against the Lord in the manner of their religion (Isaiah 2:8, 8:19) and their manner of life (Isaiah 3:14, 10:1–2). In a grim phrase the prophet declares, "they have brought evil upon themselves" or, in the New English translation, "they have earned their own disaster." (Isaiah 3:9)

But they were not disturbed, and like those in our own time who buy newspapers which print only good news, the people of Jerusalem ordered accommodating preachers to tell them what they wanted to hear: "speak to us smooth things, prophesy illusions." (Isaiah 30:10) Perhaps that is what they got, but not from Isaiah.

> Thus says the Holy One of Israel,
> "Because you despise this word,
>   and trust in oppression and perverseness,
>   and rely on them;

---

[15]Von Rad, *Old Testament Theology,* p. 159.

To illustrate the play on words in the Hebrew text, the translator of Von Rad's work, D.M.G. Stalker, refers to an English north country phrase: If ye have not faith, ye cannot have staith. This is used by George A. Smith in *The Book of Isaiah I–XXXIX* (New York: A.C. Armstrong and Son, 1897) p. 106n.

therefore this iniquity shall be to you
> like a break in a high wall, bulging out, and about to collapse,
> whose crash comes suddenly, in an instant. (Isaiah 30:12–13)

THE REMNANT

When a tragedy takes place, the people who survive will sometimes discover that after all it isn't the end, that they can still hope. The harsh experience has reordered their lives; they see opportunities which they hadn't seen before and the way they see is different. But there are few who can anticipate disaster in all its grimness and see the hope beyond. To reach through disaster without having been there and imagine a welcoming landscape on the other side is rare. Isaiah knew that Judah would fall, the people "had earned disaster," and he knew what the suffering would be because he believed that God himself would inflict it. As the farmer did not spare his vineyard which produced sour fruit (Isaiah 5), so God would not spare his people. But Isaiah saw that out of the tragedy of destruction and exile the purpose of God would be carried toward fulfillment by those who survived, and that was the heart of his teaching about the remnant.

The mysteries of God are regarded as such because divine providence does not draw the distinctions which human intelligence is in the habit of drawing. The Old Testament presents God as gentle, harsh, loving, overwhelmingly stern, expansive, and jealous, contrasts not ordinarily expected in the same character. One set of contrasts is described as the problem of evil, the difficulty of reconciling the beneficence of God with human suffering. The fact that the problem persists suggests that reconciliation is not easily done, but attempts are made, and Isaiah's doctrine of the remnant appears to be one such attempt, his endeavor to reconcile the implacable discipline of God with his care for his people's future. He announced a day when, "the branch of the Lord shall be beautiful and glorious, and the fruit of the land shall be the pride and glory of the survivors of Israel. And he who is left in Zion and remains in Jerusalem will be called holy, every one who has been recorded for life in Jerusalem . . . ." (Isaiah 4:2–3)

So confident was Isaiah of this that he named one of his children Shear-jashub, which means "a remnant shall return" (Isaiah 7:3). He anticipated a time when the remnant would abandon those who could not help them and would turn to "the mighty God." (Isaiah 10:20–21)

Isaiah's teaching about the remnant can be regarded as a rather severe message of hope, but it can also be regarded as his endeavor to probe God's nature and grapple with the complexities of God's will. The prophets were more than preachers. They were in a sense spiritual and philosophical frontiersmen. Like the actual frontiersmen of the new world, who brought their own culture with them, the prophets of Israel worked from a prophetic tradition. But often their experiences went beyond tradition. Not surprisingly they suffered the fate of many explorers, whose marvelous tales appeared so alien to what their contemporaries "knew" about the world, that they were not believed.

IMMANUEL

Such an alien message, alien at the time and still not understood, was Isaiah's vision of God symbolized in the name of a child, Immanuel, that is, God with us. The identity of the child is not clear, perhaps it was Hezekiah, whose life is remembered as truly devout, or perhaps it was a reference to a mysterious savior or Messiah, whom Isaiah elsewhere described as a great light.

> The people who walked in darkness
>> have seen a great light;
> those who dwelt in a land of deep darkness,
>> on them has light shined.
> Thou hast multiplied the nation,
>> thou hast increased its joy;
> they rejoice before thee
>> as with joy at the harvest. (Isaiah 9:2-3)

Their enemies are to be destroyed and turned away.

> For to us a child is born,
>> to us a son is given;
> and the government will be upon his shoulder,
>> and his name will be called
> "Wonderful Counselor, Mighty God,
>> Everlasting Father, Prince of Peace."
> Of the increase of his government and of peace
>> there will be no end. (Isaiah 9:6-7)

In another passage the prophet writes about "a shoot from the stump of Jesse," that is, a descendent of David, whose knowledge and sense of justice will be perfect, defending the humble and the poor and striking down the wicked. He will reign over a world from which violence has been abolished, where no creature hurts another, and "the earth shall be full of the knowledge of the Lord as the waters cover the sea." (Isaiah 1:1-9)

If Isaiah's authorship of Isaiah 9:1-7 and 11:1-9 is questioned[16] one is still left

---

[16]Eissfeldt inclines toward accepting 9:1-7 but not 11:1-9. See *The Old Testament: An Introduction*, Peter Ackroyd trans. (New York: Harper and Row, 1965), pp. 318-19. In neither case, however, does he regard the evidence as positive.

Kaiser, *Isaiah 1-12*, accepts both passages as genuinely from Isaiah. Concerning 11:1-9 he writes, "Here we are dealing with a true prophecy," p. 155.

with the symbolic name, Immanuel, Isaiah 7:14. That alone suggest that the prophet, who all his life probed the depth of the nature of God, and in that attempt
developed a doctrine of the remnant, went further. A remnant is what is left, the
surviving part, but one can suppose that the man who encountered the glory of God
could not believe that his creator would be satisfied with less than the unity of all
he had created. Political forces were dividing God's people; that was only with God's
permission and for his purpose. One day the people would be gathered together, but
not just they, all nations. The chosen people of the promised land would be one among
them. In a sense the identity of the person referred to in these passages, whether a
Jewish king or Messiah or, as Christian commentators have believed, Christ, is less
important than the message it represents. Isaiah had what philosophers sometimes
call a synoptic view of existence; he saw things whole. Within the context of Judaism
that means that every existing thing and all that happens is related to the will of God.
An Assyrian invasion, the probable destruction of Jerusalem, and the remnant are
items in a total plan presided over by God's ultimate wisdom. "God with us" is the
symbol of a cohering and coordinating power.

   Isaiah's vision of total existence was not likely to be comprehensible to a little
nation living on its past. His reflections were meaningful only to later generations.
In his time they were mainly seeds on stony ground.[17]

---

[17]For a discussion of many aspects of the book of Isaiah see *Interpretation,* A Journal of Bible and
Theology, Vol. 37.2 (April 1982). This issue is devoted to the study of Isaiah.

CHAPTER EIGHTEEN
FROM HEZEKIAH
TO JOSIAH

The one hundred and six years from the beginning of Hezekiah's reign in 715 to the death of Josiah in 609 saw switchback changes in the religious attitudes of Judah's monarchs. Hezekiah did what he could to correct the religious excesses of his father, Ahaz. Manasseh and Amon, who followed Hezekiah, led the country through half a century of apostasy. Josiah, who succeeded Amon, attempted a number of far-reaching reforms in what proved to be the last attempt in Judah's history to return the country to the true worship of God.

Throughout most of this period the dominant power in the Near East was Assyria, which reached its zenith during Manasseh's reign with an empire that stretched from the Persian Gulf to Egypt. For the small nations of Syria and Palestine these were years of terror alternating with hope whenever it appeared that Assyrian power was declining or Egyptian power increasing. But the hope was always false. To those countries which submitted voluntarily, Assyria permitted limited freedom; those countries which tried to resist or which tried to break away were struck down with tremendous force, their cities destroyed, their populations often deported. To maintain an independent existence was practically impossible.

Political skills of the kind associated with secular governments were far from the minds of the Old Testament writers. The standard they used was obedience to

God, which meant purity of worship and life. By that standard Hezekiah "did what was right in the eyes of the Lord, according to all that David his father had done" (2 Kings 18:3). He removed the high places, that is, pagan shrines, and restored centralized worship in Jerusalem. (It was one of the sins of Jeroboam I that after the division of the kingdom he established rival centers of worship at Dan and Bethel. Any center other than Jerusalem was regarded as apostate.) He repaired the Temple and exhorted the priests to sanctify it. Second Chronicles 29–31 gives a long account of how he purified the house of the Lord and restored its services, and the writer declares with obvious enthusiasm that "every work that he undertook in the service of the house of God and in accordance with the law and the commandments, seeking his God, he did with all his heart, and prospered" (2 Chronicles 31:21).

Early in his reign ambassadors were sent by the Ethiopian king of Egypt, Piankhi, to persuade Hezekiah to join a revolt, possibly with Moab and Edom (Isaiah 18). Isaiah the prophet was strongly against it and saw nothing but harm. To emphasize the point he walked naked and barefoot through Judah for three years as an example of what would happen to those who rebelled against Assyria (Isaiah 20). Presumably Hezekiah took Isaiah's advice; the rebel towns were severely punished but Judah escaped. Nevertheless, Hezekiah did not give up the idea of independence at some time, and he made careful preparations. He gathered stores of food, built barns, strengthened the fortifications of Jerusalem and built a phenomenal underground tunnel from the Gihon spring outside the city to the Pool of Siloam within to ensure a continuous supply of water (2 Chronicles 32:27–30, Isaiah 22:10, 2 Kings 20:20). But as Isaiah comments sharply, Hezekiah was concerned with fortifications and water supply but did not look to the ultimate maker "or have regard for him who planned it long ago" (Isaiah 22:11). Although he had a commitment to the God of Abraham which his father, Ahaz, never had, Hezekiah was not willing to trust God only. He believed in practical preparations and in allies. We read that he sent letters to Ephraim and Manasseh, which were by then part of Assyrian territory, inviting them to keep the Passover at Jerusalem, but his messengers were laughed at (2 Chronicles 30:1–11). Elsewhere he acted more directly. He conquered the coastal region of the Philistines as far as the city of Gaza (2 Kings 18:8), and he invaded Edom (1 Chronicles 4:41).

These last actions, which amounted to open defiance of Assyrian authority, may have taken place after the death of Sargon in 705 and the succession of Sennacherib. The new Assyrian king was totally involved at first with the suppression of revolts in Babylon under Marduk-apal-iddina (also known as Merodach-baladan), and in Egypt under Shabako, that is, both ends of his realm. So it may have seemed to the subject states in Syria and Palestine that the time had come to make a bid for independence. Hezekiah took a leading part, even holding as prisoner in Jerusalem the king of Ekron who had refused to join the rebellion. It took Sennacherib three years to settle accounts with other parts of his realm and turn his attention to Palestine. When he did so Hezekiah's preparations were severely tested.

HEZEKIAH'S TUNNEL

In the final statement on Hezekiah's life in the book of Kings we read:

> The rest of the deeds of Hezekiah, and all his might, and how he made the pool and the conduit and brought water into the city, are they not written in the Book of the Chronicles of the Kings of Judah? and Hezekiah slept with his fathers; and Manasseh his son reigned in his stead." (2 Kings 20:20)

This brief passage hides the fact that the tunnel was a major engineering feat of its time. The workers dug underground through 1750 feet of limestone. The immensity of the project can best be appreciated by walking or wading through it with a flashlight. The cramped space and the smoking torches must have made it a difficult place to work, quite apart from the pressure which Hezekiah no doubt put upon the workmen to finish quickly, and the difficulty of knowing whether or not they were cutting in the right direction.

The tunnel is named for the man who authorized it. We could hardly expect to know very much after so long a time about the anonymous workers who actually cut through the rock, but in 1880 some boys who were playing at the Siloam end of the tunnel discovered an inscription which vividly recreates the final moment before the two sets of workers, who were cutting from opposite ends, broke through and met.

> And this is the story of the piercing through. While (the stone cutters were swinging their) axes, each towards his fellow, and while there were yet three cubits [the cubit was about 18 inches long] to be pierced through, (there was heard) the voice of a man calling to his fellow, for there was a crevice (?) on the right. . . . And on the day of the piercing through, the stone cutters struck through each to meet his fellow, axe against axe. Then ran the water from the Spring to the Pool for twelve hundred cubits, and a hundred cubits was the height of the rock above the head of the stone-cutters.[1]

The water still runs, and it must have given the people of Jerusalem great satisfaction and a feeling of security when the tunnel was completed and the water ran for the first time, especially when not long after the work was completed, Sennacherib came to Palestine to punish the states that had dared to challenge his authority.

SENNACHERIB'S CAMPAIGN

Sennacherib's campaign was a time of greatest peril for Judah. We admire Joshua, and Gideon before him, and Judas Maccabaeus centuries later. But none of those men faced the odds that Hezekiah faced in challenging Assyria. The likelihood of success was as minimal as the likelihood of his being killed and Jerusalem being destroyed was certain. The fact that he did succeed, that Jerusalem was not destroyed and the Assyrians withdrew, was regarded as an unchallengeable example of how

[1]D. Winton Thomas, *Documents from Old Testament Times* (New York: Harper and Row, 1961), p. 210

God loved his people and would rescue them from the most hopeless situation. Ironically, that experience contributed to Judah's later downfall when, during the Babylonian siege of Jerusalem, Jeremiah counselled the people to capitulate, but they, remembering the time when God rescued Judah from Sennacherib, decided that the prophet had to be wrong and rejected his advice.

The Assyrian force was very large. It proceeded down the Phoenician coast, captured Tyre, destroyed an Egyptian army at Eltekeh about forty miles west of Jerusalem, near the coast, then turned toward Judah. The *Annals* of Sennacherib report that the "prevailing army of Asshur. . . stunned" the fortified cities which he attacked "and they bowed to my feet."[2] The prophet Micah has left us what may be a contemporary account of the dismay and confusion of the people of Judah as the Assyrian army approached.

> For this I will lament and wail; I will go stripped and naked;
> I will make lamentation like the jackals,
>   and mourning like the ostriches.
> For her wound is incurable; and it has come to Judah,
> it has reached to the gate of my people, to Jerusalem. (Micah 1:8–9)

He describes various cities in the vicinity of Jerusalem.

> For the inhabitants of Maroth wait anxiously for good,
> because evil has come down from the Lord
>   to the gate of Jerusalem.
> Harness the steeds to the chariots,
>   inhabitants of Lachish; . . .
> Therefore you shall give parting gifts
>   to Moresheth-gath;
> the houses of Achzib shall be a deceitful thing
>   to the kings of Israel.
> I will again bring a conqurer upon you,
>   inhabitants of Mareshah. (Micah 1:12–15)

Hezekiah must have heard that Sennacherib had captured Lachish and was attacking Libnah (2 Kings 19:8). One can imagine the consternation in Jerusalem; Lachish was a heavily defended city with an inner wall that was twenty feet thick and an outer wall that was thirteen. It covered an area of eighteen acres, larger than Megiddo or Jerusalem, surrounded on all sides by valleys. What chance was there for the capital?

The violence of the siege and destruction of Lachish have been uncovered by archeologists. Eight feet of burnt debris separate the city which Sennacherib attacked from the next level of occupation. The defenders attempted to cut a shaft through

---

[2]Quoted in *The Macmillan Bible Atlas,* Yohanan Aharoni and Michael Avi-Yohah eds. (New York: Macmillan, 1968), p. 99. There are two maps of Sennacherib's campaign on the same page.

The city of Lachish. Photo by Elizabeth Gordon.

the rock to provide themselves with water, but they didn't finish in time. Outside the city were the remains of two thousand skeletons.[3]

Sennacherib was obviously proud of the campaign and has left both a pictorial record of reliefs carved in stone and a written account. One of the reliefs shows the actual siege of Lachish. At the front of the attacking forces are siege engines which were made of wood and protected by a leather canopy. Inside the canopy soldiers wield a large pointed battering ram against the city wall while the defenders throw down flaming brands to set the engines alight. But the attackers are equipped with long-handled ladles and buckets of water to douse the flames. Outside the walls Assyrian soldiers are impaling naked prisoners on upright stakes, and through a city gate women hurry to safety, clutching bundles of their belongings as they attempt to pass through the battle. The written account describes the mechanics of the siege and so provides an Assyrian version of the biblical event.

> But as for Hezekiah, the Jew, who did not bow in submission to my yoke, forty-six of his strong walled towns and innumerable smaller villages in their neighborhood I besieged and conquered by stamping down earth-ramps and thus by bringing up battering rams, by the assault of foot-soldiers, by breaches, tunnelling and sapper operations.[4]

[3]Gaalyah Cornfeld, *Archeology of the Bible: Book by Book* (New York: Harper and Row, 1976), p. 174. Among the skeletons were found three skulls with a square of bone "removed by a saw to reduce pressure on the head." This was an ancient surgical operation known as trephination.

[4]Thomas, *Documents,* p. 67.

The tunnels were built underneath the walls, supported by wooden posts. As the sappers withdrew they set fire to the posts, which collapsed and weakened and eventually collapsed the wall above. Earth ramps were mounds of earth thrown against the wall to enable the attackers to storm it at a higher level.

Judah at that point was entirely overrun, with Jerusalem standing like an island in the midst of occupied territory. The Assyrian record refers to this: "He [Hezekiah] himself I shut up like a caged bird within Jerusalem, his royal city."[5]

The Old Testament account describes what amounts to an ancient example of psychological warfare in which the Assyrian general calls upon Hezekiah and his city to surrender and, with unmistakable sarcasm, offers to give the king two thousand horses if he could find riders for them. "Do not let Hezekiah deceive you, for he will not be able to deliver you out of my hand. Do not let Hezekiah make you to rely on the Lord.... Make your peace with me and come out to me; then every one of you will eat of his own vine, and every one of his own fig tree, and every one of you will drink the water of his own cistern." (2 Kings 18:29-31)

At the end of his talk the people were silent "and answered him not a word" (2 Kings 18:36). They knew very well the fate of conquered cities; Lachish had been one of them, and also Samaria which held out for three years but was finally taken by the Assyrians and destroyed. But they must also have thought about the water tunnel and the promise given by God to David that his royal house would continue forever (2 Samuel 7:12-16).

Earlier in Hezekiah's reign Isaiah had counselled him not to join a rebel alliance or to seek help from Egypt:

> The Egyptians are men, and not God;
> > and their horses are flesh, and not spirit.
> When the Lord stretches out his hand,
> > the helper will stumble, and he who is helped will fall,
> and they will all perish together. (Isaiah 31:3)

The consequence of rebellion would be nakedness and bondage (Isaiah 20). But now, n Judah's moment of peril, Isaiah encouraged the people to be firm:

> Thus says the Lord concerning the king of Assyria, He shall not come into this city or shoot an arrow there, or come before it with a shield or cast up a siege mound against it. By the way that he came, by the same he shall return, and he shall not come into this city, says the Lord. For I will defend this city to save it, for my own sake and for the sake of my servant David. (2 Kings 19:32-34)

Isaiah's assurances were proven correct. The Old Testament records that "that ight," presumably the night following Isaiah's prophecy, "the angel of the Lord went orth, and slew a hundred and eighty-five thousand in the camp of the Assyrians; nd when men arose early in the morning, behold, these were all dead bodies. Then ennacherib king of Assyria departed and went home, and dwelt at Nineveh." (2 Kings

---

[5]Ibid.

19:35–36) Possibly the troops were stricken with a disastrous pestilence, or Sennacherib heard about troubles at home which made him decide to return, thinking that the rebel states had been taught enough of a lesson. Whatever it was that caused the Assyrian army to leave, Jerusalem and Judah were saved for another hundred years or so of precarious independence.[6]

According to the text, shortly after the mysterious withdrawal of the Assyrians, Hezekiah became very ill and sent for Isaiah. The prophet told him bluntly that he was a dying man. Despite his faithfulness to God, Hezekiah was not prepared for death. He turned his face to the wall and "wept bitterly," reminding the Lord of his devotion and pleading for extra days (2 Kings 20:1–11). The incident is described in such sharp detail that it must have made a considerable impression. Comparing it with Socrates' famous *Apology*, (that is, comparing outstanding representatives of Hebrew and Greek religious philosophy), one realizes how thin were the religious and philosophic resources of the most devout Israelite during the seventh and sixth centuries B.C. Isaiah was almost alone in his profound understanding of the nature of God and his courage in the face of hostile circumstances. The only other comparable religious personality of the time that we know of was Micah.

God answered his prayers, and Hezekiah recovered. He had not, however, learned the need for caution in the political crosscurrents of the time. Merodach-baladan visited Hezekiah, ostensibly to congratulate him on his recovery, but undoubtedly to encourage rebellion. The king naively showed him all his ornaments and all his treasures. Isaiah, who had far more political acumen than the king, was not pleased. "The days are coming," he is reported as saying, "when all that is in your house, and that which your fathers have stored up till this day, shall be carried to Babylon; nothing shall be left" (2 Kings 20:17).

MICAH

Micah was a younger contemporary of Isaiah who preached in Judah during the reigns of Jotham (742–735), Ahaz (735–715), and Hezekiah (715–687). His prophecy about the destruction of Jerusalem, "Zion shall be plowed as a field; Jerusalem shall become a heap of ruins," (Micah 3:12) is referred to by Jeremiah about a hundred years later (Jeremiah 26:18).

Micah came from Moresheth, so his reference to Moresheth-gath (Micah 1:14) would, perhaps, have been somewhat poignant. He stressed the importance of quality of life in words that are often repeated:

> He has showed you, O man, what is good;
> and what does the Lord require of you
> but to do justice, and to love kindness,
> and to walk humbly with your God? (Micah 6:8)

[6]There is a question about whether the events described in 2 Kings 18:9–19:37 refer to one invasion or two. The matter is dealt with in detail in John Bright, *The History of Israel*, 3d ed. (Philadelphia Westminster Press, 1981), pp. 296–308. See also Thomas, *Documents*, pp. 64–65.

The book of Micah was of particular interest to the early Christian church as it was believed to contain a prophecy about the birth of Christ.

> But you, O Bethlehem Ephrathah,
>   who are little to be among the clans of Judah,
> from you shall come forth for me one who is to be ruler in Israel,
>   whose origin is from old, from ancient days. (Micah 5:2, see Matthew 2:6; John 7:42)

MANASSEH (687–642)

The Lord granted Hezekiah fifteen years. Three years later his son Manasseh was born. It is an unobtrusive irony of the Old Testament that this child, born only because of an act of God's mercy, became one of the most thoroughgoing opponents of the covenant faith since Jezebel, and his reign was the longest of all the kings of Judah and Israel, forty-five years (687–642). Manasseh's position was certainly precarious. After political upheavals following Sennacherib's assassination (2 Kings 19:37), Assyria reasserted its control over its restless empire. Merodach-baladan was defeated and Manasseh undoubtedly placed under the same heavy obligations as his father and grandfather.

It is a "paradox of history" that if Manasseh had not accommodated himself to the political realities of the time, there might have been no book of Kings for us to judge him by. Josiah's reform might then not have been necessary. There would have been nothing to reform. "The same policies which made Josiah's reform necessary permitted it to take place."[7]

It does not follow, however, that political control meant religious subservience. It has seemed so. For example, when Ahaz visited Tiglath-pileser in Damascus, he sketched an altar which he saw there and sent it to Jerusalem. We read that Uriah the priest had a copy of the altar set up in the Temple for the king on his return. The king then worshipped there (2 Kings 16:10-15).

It has been widely accepted that this was the result of religious coercion, that Ahaz had no choice, that political control entailed religous control. Recent studies question this and argue that, to the contrary, providing that Assyria was satisfied with the political submission of its subjects, it "did not interfere with the continued performance of local cults."[8]

The religious apostasy of Ahaz, then of Manneseh and Amon, was therefore ot the result of Assyrian imperialism so much as those monarchs' own religious reference. The fact that Hezekiah, the reforming king, succeeded an apostate father, nd Josiah, who carried out sweeping reforms, came to the throne after the more

---

[7]James A Sanders, *Torah and Canon* (Philadelphia: Fortress Press, 1972), p. 40.

[8]Morton Cogan, *Imperialism and Religion: Assyria, Judah and Israel in the Eighth and Seventh Centuries C.E.* (Missoula, Mont.: University of Montana, Society of Biblical Literature and Scholars Press, 1974), 111.

than forty years of Manneseh and Amon indicates that there were strong religious crosscurrents in Judah during this time.

Manasseh seems to have engaged in every kind of religious practice that would horrify a devout Israelite, including human sacrifice.

> He built altars for all the host of heaven in the two courts of the house of the Lord. And he burned his son as an offering and practiced soothsaying and augury, and dealt with mediums and with wizards (2 Kings 21:4–6).

Manasseh's activities were not only religious, he "shed very much innocent blood, till he had filled Jerusalem from one end to another" (2 Kings 21:16). He conducted a reign of terror, presumably against his religious and political opponents. An unsubstantiated tradition claims that Isaiah was put to death during this time by being sawed in two, which indicates the diabolical character attributed to that monarch.

AMON (642–640) AND THE COLLAPSE OF ASSYRIA

However harshly Manasseh is remembered, he maintained good relations with Assyria. He may have been involved in a plot, which would explain the reference to his being brought to Babylon in chains (2 Chronicles 33:10–13), but otherwise the forty-five years of his reign were peaceful. He was succeeded by his son Amon, who continued his father's policies for two years. It was not, however, an internal peace. Amon's courtiers, feeling that they could take action against the son which they had not dared to take against the father, murdered him in his house. They misjudged popular feeling because "the people of the land"[9] killed all the conspirators and made Amon's son Josiah king in his place (2 Kings 21:23–24).

The almost half century between the death of Hezekiah and the accession of Josiah saw the beginning of what must have been to the people of the time an unimaginable change. Twenty years before the death of Manasseh in 663, Assyria reached the limit of its territorial expansion with the conquest of Upper Egypt by Asshurbanapal. But even during his reign Egypt broke free, and for years Asshurbanapal was engaged with large-scale insurrections throughout his empire Egypt, Babylon, Asia Minor, Syria, Palestine, Edom, and Moab. He subdued them all except Egypt, and at the end of his reign found time to develop a great library which, when discovered during the nineteenth century, revolutionized our knowledge of ancient Mesopotamia.[10] But twenty years after Asshurbanapals' death in 627 th Assyrian empire had vanished. Centuries of warfare, civil war, and the increasing power of Babylon led to the end of what is remembered as the world's most hated power

---

[9]The term "People of the Land" is used in different ways in the Old Testament. In 2 Kings 21:23–2 it refers to Israelites, perhaps in that passage a popular gathering, or in Genesis 23:12 as a representati body. In Ezra 4:4 and 10:2 the term refers to non-Israelites. The distinction is made clear in Ezra 9 "The people of Israel . . . have not separated themselves from the peoples of the lands."

[10]Aristotle, the Greek philosopher who lived about three hundred years later (358–322), mak a scathing comment about Asshurbanapal, *Nicomachean Ethics*, Book 1, Chapter 5. He refers to him a "monster of sensuality" under the name of Sardanapalus, which was a by-word for extravagant livir

ZEPHANIAH

Asshurbanapal was still vigorously subduing revolts when Josiah came ot the throne as a boy of eight in 640. But thirteen years later, as the Assyrian empire began to disintegrate, the Israelites found themselves in a power vacuum. Josiah, who was just twenty-one, moved to take advantage of the situation, religiously and politically.

It is possible that the child Josiah was influenced by the prophet Zephaniah, whose ministry is identified with that king's reign. Even though the people of Israel killed Amon's assassins, there may have been by then popular dissatisfaction with the policies of political and religious subservience they had lived with for fifty years. Zephaniah may therefore have had a strong influence upon the young king.

His prophecy refers to a "day of the Lord" (Zephaniah 1:7), when Judah will be punished for its iniquities. God will search Jerusalem with a lantern (Zephaniah 1:12). He will bring "distress on men" (Zephaniah 1:17) for their sin against the Lord. He therefore advises the nation to seek the Lord.

> seek righteousness, seek humility;
> perhaps you may be hidden
> on the day of the wrath of the Lord. (Zephaniah 2:3)

Regarding the future he is optimistic, and this is partly because the survivors of the day of the Lord will no longer do wrong or speak lies (Zephaniah 3:13), but also because the Lord will destroy Israel's foes (Zephaniah 3:14–15).

At some point the prophet saw that Assyria was in mortal trouble. Whether he anticipated this in a prophetic manner or wrote after the direction of events was clear, it nevertheless meant that it was no longer a political necessity to be subservient to Assyria, and so he had an opportunity to press home the value of religious reform in a way that was different from every other prophet. The normal context of prophecy in the Old Testament was the threat of political and military disaster. Amos and Hosea knew that the prosperous times in the Northern Kingdom could not last; all the others lived under the shadow of a great power. Zephaniah alone, with the possible exception of Nahum, was able to preach within a context of imminent freedom, and we can suppose that he did all that he could to encourage the young king to take advantage of it.

Another unusual factor about Zephaniah's preaching is that in the case of all the other prophets pragmatic considerations were against them. There were generally good practical commercial and political reasons why the prophets should be ignored. In the case of Zephaniah the practical reasons worked the other way. One of the most disturbing arguments used by Sennacherib's commander in chief, when the Assyrians

---

Aristotle is remembered among his other accomplishments for having developed the first catalogued library in the ancient world. He might have been more generous to Asshurbanapal had he known that too gathered a great library, one of the greatest in the ancient world. It contained 22,000 clay tablets among which were Babylonian accounts of the Flood and the Creation. This is evidence that there was another side to the character of that greatly hated people.

surrounded Jerusalem and it seemed to have no chance of escape, was that the gods were on Assyria's side (2 Kings 18:33–35). It was therefore only common sense for Jerusalem to capitulate. But Assyria had collapsed, or was collapsing. The gods were not on its side. It was therefore a matter of common sense not to trust in them but to trust in the God whose nation had survived. The practical argument for honoring the covenant relationship was as strong as it had been during the time of Ahaz for honoring the Assyrian god (2 Kings 16:1–20).

Zephaniah, therefore, was given a wonderful opportunity.

> Sing aloud, O daughter of Zion; shout, O Israel!...
> The Lord has taken away the judgments against you,
>   he has cast out your enemies...
> The Lord, your God, is in your midst,
>   a warrior who gives victory...
>   he will renew you in his love;
> he will exult over you with loud singing
>   as on a day of festival. (Zephaniah 3:14–18)

THE DISCOVERY OF THE BOOK OF THE LAW

Josiah accepted Zephaniah's words wholeheartedly, but it was not a sudden decision. According to 2 Chronicles 34:1–7, he sought the guidance of God at the beginning of his reign when he was a child of eight, which probably means that as all young children are susceptible to strong direction, Josiah was no exception.

By 621 he had been on the throne for nineteen years, he was twenty-seven years old, and he decided to purify the nation's worship. It would require, however, a major effort. For half a century the country had almost no experience of the covenant faith. Many would have lived and died without it, and while the religious climate changed after the death of Amon, knowledge of the faith must have been rudimentary.

Josiah decided therefore to begin with the practical task of cleaning and repairing the Temple. We read (2 Kings 22:3–6) that in the eighteenth year of his reign Josiah sent his adjutant-general to the Temple to arrange for payment of workers who were carrying out the repairs. It was directly after this that the high priest Hilkiah told the adjutant-general that he had "found the book of the law." The book was called to the attention of the king, and when he heard what it contained, and presumably realized how far from meeting its requirements the people of Judah were, he rent his clothes, a symbolic act of intense displeasure or grief, and ordered the priests to find out from God what he and the nation could do.

The question is asked whether Josiah's religiosity led to his repairing the Temple, which seems to be implied by 2 Chronicles 34:1–7, or whether his repairing of the Temple and the subsequent discovery of the book of the law led to his religiosity. The two positions may not be exclusive of one another. What may have been a since but low-key program of religious change could have been transformed into a crusade by finding the book.

It is difficult to appreciate the significance of this event, except perhaps to imagine that in some great civil disruption the United States Constitution was lost and forgotten, but after a change of administration it was found and reintroduced to the nation as if it were a new document.

The lengthy catalogue of shrines dismantled and images destroyed (2 Kings 23:4–20) makes clear that the nation had drifted a long way from its covenant beliefs and obligations in the forty-seven years of the reigns of Manasseh and Amon. The culmination of the reform was a great Passover like no one had kept "since the days of the judges who judged Israel, or during all the days of the kings of Israel or of the kings of Judah" (2 Kings 23:22).

This passage indicates a return to the traditions of Moses and a movement away from the traditions of David and the monarchy. The long-term consequences was that when the monarchy disappeared, the premonarchic Mosaic traditions and the literary work of the reformers helped to provide Israel with a base to carry on, even when they were exiled from Jerusalem.[11]

THE BOOK OF THE LAW

What was the book that Hilkiah found? Probably it was Chapters 12–26 of the present book of Deuteronomy. A comparison of the reforms carried out by Josiah with the requirements in Deuteronomy shows a number of similarities, such as the destruction of cult objects (Deuteronomy 16:21; 2 Kings 23:4 and 14) and high places (Deuteronomy 12:1–3; 2 Kings 23:8 and 19) and the restoration of the Passover (Deuteronomy 16:1–8; 2 Kings 23:21–23). It is argued that the book originated in the Northern Kingdom, but after the fall of Samaria in 721 it was brought to Jerusalem and possibly developed during the long reign of Manasseh into something like its present form. If that were so, one wonders why it was not brought to Josiah's attention earlier.

The name Deuteronomy, *deuteros nomos* ("second law"), is taken from a Greek translation of Deuteronomy 17:18. While the meaning of the Hebrew is "copy of this law," there is a sense, as one writer suggests, that it is a second giving of the law, "the opening of an opportunity for Moses to speak directly to an apostate age."[12]

Josiah's ambition was not only to purify the nation but to restore the boundaries which it had at the time of Solomon. He had a real chance. There was no longer a Northern Kingdom; Samaria had been a province of Assyria for a hundred years, but there was no Assyria. In 621 the mighty empire was fighting its last battles and Egypt had not yet reasserted itself in Palestine and Syria. It must have seemed to the ardent young king like a God-given opportunity. He moved into the Assyrian province and destroyed and desecrated the idolatrous altar at Bethel, where Amos was been insulted and charged with conspiracy, and he suppressed all the hill shrines

[11]Sanders, *Torah and Canon*, p. 44.
[12]Norman K. Gottwald, *A Light to the Nations* (New York: Harper and Row, 1959), p. 335.

in the cities of Samaria which the kings of Israel had set up. It would not be surprising if Josiah had had visions of a restored nation united under God, and had it been possible, had Josiah been less ardent, less convinced perhaps that God was with him, more cautious, and more political, the subsequent history of Judah could have been profoundly different. It was not to be. Josiah destroyed himself by attempting to intervene in the three-way conflict between Assyria, Egypt, and the new power, Babylon. Egypt and Assyria had long been enemies, but Egypt, deciding that it now served its interests to support a weakened Assyria against the new enemy, sent a force to help the Assyrians who were fighting the Babylonians at Haran. Josiah, deciding that it was to his advantage to support the Babylonians, tried to stop the Egyptians at Megiddo (2 Kings 23:29). The attempt failed. His army was defeated and he was killed. The date was 609. As, on a grander scale, the death of Asshurbanapal led to the collapse of Assyria, so the death of Josiah led in twenty-two years to the destruction of Jerusalem and the total dissolution of the Kingdom of Judah.

A NOTE ON ASSYRIAN CRUELTY

Assyria had a reputation for extreme cruelty; Lord Byron's often quoted line, "The Assyrians came down like a wolf on the fold" is still taken as fairly representing the behavior of that greatly feared people. There are many stone reliefs which serve as gruesome reminders that when the Assyrians conquered a city its people suffered to an unusual degree. The bodies of prominent citizens are quite regularly shown hanging on wooden posts outside the captured city walls; there are piles of decapitated heads, long lines of miserable prisoners. Assyrian brutality appears to have been excessive even by the savage standards of the time.

> Assyria was the nest of a bird of prey whence, during nearly ten centuries, set fort the most terrible expeditions which ever flooded the world with blood. Ashur was it god, plunder its morality, material pleasure its ideal, cruelty and terror its means. N people was ever more abject that those of Ashur; no sovereigns were ever more despoti more covetous, more vindictive, more pitiless, more proud of their crimes. Assyria sum up in itself all the vices. Aside from bravery it offers not a single virtue.[13]

This view is echoed elsewhere.[14]

Nevertheless there is another side, and the point of presenting it is not minimize the cruelty of Assyria but to take account of the facts. "It is rare," commen one writer, "to find any attempt to look at Assyrian warfare and imperialism as whole in its perspective."[15] He draws attention to the many examples of ferocity be found in the Old Testament, the wholesale massacres of religious and politic opponents, for example by Baasha (1 Kings 15:25–29); Zimri (1 Kings 16:8–13); a

---

[13]De. Morgan, *Premieres Civilisations,* 1909, p. 340, quoted in A. T. Olmstead *History of Assy* (Chicago: University of Chicago Press, 1975), p. 645.

[14]Abraham Heschel, *The Prophets, An Introduction* (New York: Harper and Row, 1962), pp. 162–

[15]H.W.F. Saggs, *Everyday Life in Babylonia and Assyria* (London: B.T. Batsford, 1965), p. 99.

Jehu (2 Kings 9 and 10). One could add to this David's very cruel treatment of the Moabites (2 Samuel 8:2), and the savagery of Menahem, who attacked one of his own cities and "ripped up" all the pregnant women (2 Kings 15:16).[16] The point is that the infamous cruelty of Assyria was not a rare phenomenon in ancient times.

In the last fifty years a large number of letters have been excavated from Nineveh and Calah and other Assyrian cities.[17] These were correspondence addressed to the king, often from provincial governors, and show that "far from being simply a despotic militarism holding down conquered races by mere brutal harshness, Assyrian imperialism owed much of its success to a highly developed and efficient administrative system, and to the attention of an energetic bureaucracy to the day-to-day trifles of government."[18] For example, an official of the city and province of Kakzu in the east of Assyria was accused by the central authority of settling farmers on land subject to flooding. His defensive reply makes clear that the interests of farmers were taken seriously and he knew it. In another instance a local official named Ashur-matka-gur was resettling some Aramaeans whom he provided with provisions, clothes, shoes, and oil. But he also planned to provide them with Assyrian wives. Here, however, he ran into a problem because the marriage customs of the women were different from those of the men. The Assyrian women expected a payment when they were married. The Aramaeans either would not or could not pay. In his letter to the king Ashur-matka-gur writes: "About the Aramaeans of whom the king said 'They are to be married off,' the women say 'We find that the Aramaean men are unwilling to give us money,' and 'Not until they give us money!' " Ashur-matka-gur's suggestion to the king was that the men be given the money so that they would be acceptable to the women. This may have been less a humanitarian consideration than a practical one to ensure the stability of the resettled population, "none the less, attention to such details must have alleviated many hardships."[19] Other letters deal with the administration of conquered cities, complaints from aggrieved citizens and even possibly non-Assyrians. They indicate that the sweeping condemnation of Assyria as a lion that "filled his caves with prey and his dens with torn flesh" (Nahum 2:12) is not a balanced account.

The Assyrians do not emerge as a kindly people, especially in their conquered territories, but the evidence does not support the stereotyped image any more than evidence supports similarly stereotyped images of the Egyptians and the Canaanites.[20]

---

[16]H.W.F. Saggs, *The Greatness that was Babylon* (New York: Hawthorne Books, 1962), p. 224.

[17]Leroy Waterman, *Royal Correspondence of the Assyrian Empire* (Ann Arbor, Mich.: University of Michigan Press, 1930–36).

A. Leo Oppenheim, *Letters from Mesopotamia* (Chicago: University of Chicago Press, 1967).

[18]Saggs, *The Greatness That Was Babylon,* p. 240.

[19]Ibid., pp. 245–46.

[20]Olmstead, *History of Assyria,* p. 645.

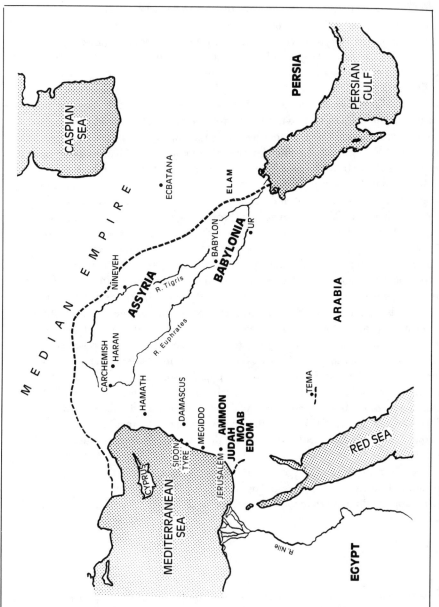

The Babylonian Empire, 605–538 B.C. The southern boundary of the Babylonian Empire was not clearly defined, but it included ... Nabonidus spent most of the last ten years of his reign.

CHAPTER NINETEEN
THE PROPHET JEREMIAH

THE POLITICAL BACKGROUND

The death of Manasseh, the murder of his son Amon and the accession of the young king Josiah signalled great changes for Judah. As the king grew to manhood he attempted to turn his nation back towards its fundamental religious commitments. And as Assyria was then in its last decline the chance of success seemed reasonably good. Judah, if not actually free, was left to take care of herself. She could repudiate not only Assyrian political authority but Assyrian religion. Manasseh and Amon had preferred it to their own, but not Josiah. He instituted a major religious reform and took advantage of Assyrian preoccupation with the Medes in the north and Chaldeans in the south in order to control parts of the former Northern Kingdom and carry out religious changes there (2 Kings 23:15–20).

For nine years after Josiah found the Book of the Law, Assyria fought with decreasing strength against her enemies. Then in 612 B.C. her capital city Nineveh fell. There is an exultant and ferocious burst of rejoicing preserved for us by the prophet Nahum.

> Woe to the bloody city,
> all full of lies and booty—
> > no end to the plunder!

The crack of whip, and rumble of wheel,
    galloping horse and bounding chariot!
Horsemen charging, flashing sword and glittering spear,
hosts of slain, heaps of corpses...
Behold, I am against you, says the Lord of hosts...
And all who look on you will shrink from you and say,
Wasted is Nineveh; who will bemoan her?
    whence shall I seek comforters for her? (Nahum 3:1–7)

At the end of his book Nahum writes:

There is no assuaging your hurt, your wound is grievous.
All who hear the news of you clap their hands over you.
For upon whom has not come your unceasing evil? (Nahum 3:19)

Judah, however, was not free. After the death of Josiah Egypt assumed control of the Palestine-Syria area and replaced Josiah's son Jehoahaz with his brother Jehoiakim and deported Jehoahaz to Egypt (609 B.C.). Yet as long as there was a balance of power between Egypt and Babylonia, Judah had more opportunity to live independently than ever under Assyria.

But in 605 the balance was tipped. The Egyptians were totally defeated by the Babylonians at Carchemesh and a new world power emerged in place of Assyria. The anguished response to this is recorded by Habakkuk.

O Lord my God...
why dost thou look on faithless men,
    and art silent when the wicked swallows up
    the man more righteous than he? (Habakkuk 1:12–13)

For years Jeremiah preached and pleaded with the city and its inhabitants, wept for them, stirred up their anger, and risked his life. His ministry stretched from the last days of Assyria and the last high hopes of Judah to the presence of a new great power Babylon, the defeat of his country, the destruction of Jerusalem and the exile of his people.

JEREMIAH: PERSONALITY AND CALL

We know more about the life of Jeremiah than of any other Old Testament prophet. Not only do we have considerable biographical material about what he did, much of it attributed to his secretary and companion, Baruch, but we have numerous passages, sometimes called the "confessions" of Jeremiah, which reveal to us his inner feelings with the directness and intensity of the confessions of St. Augustine, written about a thousand years later. Jeremiah's personality may have been one of his most important contributions to the history of Hebrew religion.[1] It helps us to understand, as no other Old Testament record does, the personal cost required of those who attempted to serve God in the prophetic ministry. Hosea suffered, and we know a small amount about that, but we do not have, as in the case of Jeremiah, a personal account of what he felt, not only his struggles with the people who misunderstood him, but his struggles with God.

He was born near Jerusalem, in the town of Anathoth, where his father Hilkiah was a priest. It was the town to which Abiathar had been banished after his support of Adonijah's unsuccessful attempt at the throne (1 Kings 2:26–27). It is at least possible that Jeremiah was connected with Abiathar's family.

At any rate one can assume that Jeremiah grew up in a family environment constantly aware of the presence of God.

THE STRUCTURE OF THE BOOK

The book of Jeremiah has three sections and an appendix. The first section, Chapters 1–25, consists of poetic oracles from Jeremiah himself. In the first twenty-two years of his ministry, from 627, it would seem that his preaching was preserved orally, but in 605, the fourth year of Jehoiakim, Jeremiah was instructed by God to dictate his message to Baruch, his scribe, so that it could be preserved in writing (Jeremiah 36:1). This was done twice. After Jehoiakim had destroyed the first scroll, God commanded that it be rewritten, "and many similar words were added to them." (Jeremiah 36:27–32)

The second section, Chapter 26–45, consists of biographical data about the prophet, written probably by Baruch. Baruch was more than Jeremiah's secretary and scribe. He was a friend and colleague, possibly with high standing at court which he gave up in order to share the prophet's difficult and often dangerous life. At the end he was forcibly taken with Jeremiah to Egypt (Jeremiah 43:6).[2]

The third section, Chapters 46–51, consists of prophecies against foreign nations, headed significantly by Egypt, which had played a deceitful and destructive role in the affairs of Judah during Jeremiah's lifetime, and including Israel's ancient enemies. Assyria is not among them because by then it no longer existed.

The appendix, Chapter 52, quotes from II Kings 24:18–25 and 25:27–30. The literary sources of the book correspond partly to the sections just described. There are poetic oracles of the prophet, sometimes designated as A material.[3] There is

---

[1] James Philip Hyatt, "Jeremiah," *Interpreter's Bible,* Vol. 5 (Nashville, Tenn.: Abingdon Press, 1956), p. 782.

[2] Nahman Avigad, "Baruch the Scribe and Jerahmeel the King's Son," *Biblical Archeologist,* Vol. 42.2 (Spring 1979).

A report of a seal impression which has been positively identified as belonging to Baruch, Jeremiah's scribe. This is the first time that the owner of a seal impression has been positively identified with a person mentioned in the Bible. The author of the article discusses Baruch's status at court.

[3] Robert R. Wilson, *Prophecy and Society in Ancient Israel* (Philadelphia: Fortress Press, 1980), p. 231.

biographical prose, much of it attributed to Baruch, described as B material, and there is a prose source, C, scattered throughout the book. A number of scholars believe that C is the work of postexilic Deuteronomic editors who also added the oracles against the nations and the excerpts from II Kings. Others have argued that the C passages can be linked to Jeremiah. One writer is of the opinion that despite possible expansion of the prophet's words and adaptation of his thought, "the prose tradition of Jeremiah is in itself no late tradition, but one that developed on the basis of his words and apparently sought to present his message as his followers understood it."[4] It is possible that this material exerted an influence on Ezekiel, who was in Babylon at the time of the fall of Jerusalem, which would argue against late dating.[5]

JEREMIAH'S CALL AND EARLY MINISTRY

The words of the Lord came to Jeremiah in the thirteenth year of the reign of Josiah (627), six years before the discovery of the Book of Law.[6] God told him that he had been appointed a prophet to the nations. The circumstances of his call were not as obviously dramatic as Isaiah's, but the impact on the young Jeremiah was considerable. He did not welcome the idea. "Ah, Lord God! Behold, I do not know how to speak," he answered "for I am only a youth." (Jeremiah 1:6)

Modesty can be as unacceptable to God as arrogance. The Lord had chosen Jeremiah before he was born. It was not a matter for him to decide. "Do not say, 'I am only a youth'; for to all to whom I send you you shall go, and whatever I command you you shall speak. Be not afraid of them, for I am with you to deliver you, says the Lord." (Jeremiah 1:7–8)

Nevertheless, despite God's assurance, the commission was a hard one: ". . . gird up your loins; arise, and say to them everything that I command you. Do not be dismayed by them, lest I dismay you before them." (Jeremiah 1:17) Or more bluntly in the New English Bible translation, "Brace yourself, Jeremiah; or I will break you before their eyes."

In modern terms that is tough talk, especially when one considers the gentle and sensitive nature of the man whom God had called. By preference it seems that he would rather have spent his life as a recluse. "Oh that I had in the desert" he wrote "a wayfarers' lodging place, that I might leave my people and go away from them!" (Jeremiah 9:2) He did not have the opportunity. It is not stated directly that Jeremiah supported Josiah's efforts, but we know that he had a high regard for Josiah (Jeremiah 22:15–16), and so he presumably would have supported the king's religious

[4]John Bright, "Jeremiah," *Anchor Bible* (Garden City, N.Y.: Doubleday, 1965), pp. lxxii–lxxxii. See the discussion in Otto Eissfeldt, *The Old Testament* (New York: Harper, 1965), p. 348.

[5]Brevard S. Childs, *Introduction to the Old Testament as Scripture* (Philadelphia: Fortress Press, 1979) pp. 344–45.

[6]Hyatt, *Interpreter's Bible*, disputes this. The matter is discussed by John Bright, *Covenant and Promise* (Philadelphia: The Westminster Press, 1976), p. 142 note 2. Bright favors the traditional view.

policies. Some of those who were closely associated with the reform, Ahikam, Gemariah, and Elnathan (2 Kings 22:12; Jeremiah 26:24, 36:11–12), stood by Jeremiah when he was in trouble. This tells us "nothing directly of Jeremiah's attitude toward the reform, but it tells us a great deal regarding the reformer's attitude toward Jeremiah!"[7] It also tells us that despite the obstinacy, the misguided patriotism, the selfishness, the cowardice, and the fear that gripped almost all the nation's leaders, there were some who listened to the Word of God as proclaimed by Jeremiah. One wonders whether even he could have survived physically, mentally, or spiritually without the presence of a few people who supported him and encouraged him in what he was attempting to do.

It is suggested that Jeremiah was deliberately silent during the reform and for some years after to allow it to prove itself.[8] When it became obvious that the changes were merely superficial, he began to preach again. It seems unlikely, however, that he would have refrained from exercising a call given to him in such an uncompromising fashion. It is also suggested that his prophecies about a "foe from the north" (Jeremiah 4–6) refer to an anticipated Scythian invasion which failed to live up to its dire predictions. The prophet was thereby discredited and remained discretely silent. But the Babylonians also came from the north, from the Haran-Carchemesh area, so the prophecies could have referred to them.[9]

At some point Jeremiah began to preach, perhaps after the death of Josiah. He denounced strongly the religious apostasy of Judah under Jehoiakim which threatened to destroy all that the reform had done. Like Hosea, Jeremiah used the allegory of marriage in which the faithless wife Israel and her faithless sister Judah have defiled the land with thoughtless harlotry and idolatrous worship of wood and stone (Jeremiah 3:9–10).

JEREMIAH AND JEHOIAKIM

Jeremiah had an obvious contempt for Jehoiakim who was simply a puppet ruler, directed by Egypt. In the midst of an international crisis which, even before Carchemesh, threatened the security of Judah, Jehoiakim set about building himself a new palace. Not only that, he resorted to fraud and extortion to build it.

> Woe to him who builds his house by unrighteousness,
>   and his upper rooms by injustice;
> who makes his neighbor serve him for nothing...(Jeremiah 22:13)

And then with biting irony the prophet adds

[7]Bright, *Covenant and Promise,* p. 144.
[8]Gerhard Von Rad, *Old Testament Theology,* Vol. II (New York: Harper and Row, 1965), p. 196.
[9]Bright, *Covenant and Promise,* pp. 145n, 148.

A contemporary potter's house (*Jeremiah 18:2*). Photo by Elizabeth Gordon.

Do you think you are a king because you compete in cedar? (Jeremiah 22:15)

The relations between Jeremiah and Jehoiakim and those who supported the king were unremittingly hostile. Jeremiah's preaching was harsh and condemnatory to an extreme. His sermon at the Temple gate at the beginning of the reign of Jehoiakim in 609, infuriated those who heard it. If the king's officers had not arrived to investigate, Jeremiah might have been lynched. But he was not frightened and he was not silenced.

> But as for me, behold, I am in your hands. Do with me as seems good and right to you. Only know for certain that if you put me to death, you will bring innocent blood upon yourselves and upon this city and its inhabitants, for in truth the Lord sent me to you to speak all these words in your ears. (Jeremiah 26:14–15)

Jeremiah's life was spared partly because of his courage, but also because he had influential friends. Another prophet who dared to speak the truth was executed (Jeremiah 26:20–24).

On a different occasion Jeremiah was flogged and put into the stocks (Jeremiah 20:1–6). In the fourth year of Jehoiakim he and his scribe Baruch had to go into hiding to save their lives (Jeremiah 36:19–26). This was the year in which the Egyptians were defeated. Perhaps it was because of this that the word of the Lord came to Jeremiah to take a scroll and write on it "all the words that I have spoken to you against Israel and Judah and all the nations, from the day that I spoke to you, from the days of Josiah until today." (Jeremiah 36:2) The political situation was as uncertain for Judah as at any time during the previous hundred years. The king might have been expected to listen to a prophet whose preaching, though unpleasant, was genuine, and was motivated only by concern for his people. But when the scroll was finally read to Jehoiakim in December of 604, he treated its message with insolent disdain. As the scroll unwound to the floor the king took a knife, and despite the appeals of his officers, Elnathan, Delaiah, and Gemariah, who begged the king not to burn the scroll, he cut off pieces of three or four columns and burned them until there was nothing left.

JEREMIAH'S PERSONAL ANGUISH

Jeremiah was promised by God that he would be given extraordinary power.

> And I, behold, I make you this day a fortified city, an iron pillar, and bronze walls, against the whole land, against the kings of Judah, its princes, its priests and the people of the land. (Jeremiah 1:18)

Later God repeated his promise. "I will make you to this people a fortified wall of bronze" (Jeremiah 15:20), and so it seemed. No man spoke with greater courage, with more bluntness and with less regard for his own safety than Jeremiah. But his bold, unflinching exterior attitude concealed the acute anguish of his interior life. Possibly his small circle of friends knew what lay behind the wall of bronze, and perhaps it was Baruch the scribe who preserved Jeremiah's expressions of despair, of his anger against God, his fear and loneliness, his hopelessness. God had made him a wall of bronze to others, but not even God could make him a wall of bronze to himself.

In Chapter 15, after an almost savage outburst against Jerusalem, he cries

> Woe is me, my mother, that you bore me, a man of strife and contention to the whole land! I have not lent, nor have I borrowed, yet all of them curse me. (Jeremiah 15:10)

In the same chapter he continues,

> Why is my pain unceasing,
> my wound incurable,
> refusing to be healed? (Jeremiah 15:18)

He knew that his preaching was resented, but it hurt him to be the object of resentment.

I have become a laughingstock all the day;
    every one mocks me.
For whenever I speak, I cry out,
    I shout, "Violence and destruction!"
For the word of the Lord has become for me
    a reproach and derision all day long. (Jeremiah 20:7–8)

He was surrounded by people who were trying to destroy him and discount his message.

For I hear many whispering.
    Terror is on every side!
"Denounce him! Let us denounce him!"
    say all my familiar
    friends, watching for my fall..
"Perhaps he will be deceived,
    then we can overcome him,
    and take our revenge on him." (Jeremiah 20:10)

The trickery amounted to outright perjury.
"Come, let us make plots against Jeremiah . . . let us not heed any of his words." (Jeremiah 18:18), an odd comment as they were indeed paying attention to his message. The people of Anathoth, his home town, threatened him. "Do not prophesy in the name of the Lord or you will die by our hand." (Jeremiah 11:21)[10]
His family turned against him but he was not allowed to have a wife or children of his own (Jeremiah 16:2).[11] Jeremiah protested against the injustice of all this, and he confronted God directly.

Righteous art thou, O Lord, when I complain to thee;
    yet I would plead my case before thee.
Why does the way of the wicked prosper?
    Why do all those who are treacherous thrive? (Jeremia 12:1)

He called upon God to take vengeance for him upon his persecutors (Jeremiah 15:15) and on another occasion he prayed that his persecutors would be foiled (Jeremiah 17:18). But what is most extraordinary about Jeremiah is that he directed some of his most violent accusations against God himself.

God was to him like a brook that is not to be trusted, whose waters fail Jeremiah 15:18. Elsewhere he cries

[10]Wilson, *Prophecy and Society,* p. 245. Wilson suggests that rather than Jeremiah's immediate famil "men of Anathoth" refers to "some of Jeremiah's priestly relatives who were still occupying importa positions in Jerusalem's religious establishment."

[11]Bright, *Covenant and Promise,* p. 149. Bright suggests that Jeremiah may have felt a compulsic against marriage given his grim view of the future.

O Lord, thou hast deceived me, and I was deceived;
thou art stronger than I, and thou hast prevailed. (Jeremiah 20:7)

The word translated as "deceived" is used also in Exodus 22:16, "if a man seduces a maiden who is not betrothed. . ." and in I Kings 22:20, "The Lord said 'Who will entice Ahab'. . .'that is, encourage him to attack Syria. It is therefore a strong term.[12] At different times Jeremiah decided that he would stop preaching, but he was not able to.

If I say, "I will not mention him,
        or speak any more in his name,"
there is in my heart as it were a burning fire
        shut up in my bones,
and I am weary with holding it in, and I cannot. (Jeremiah 20:9)

AN ABORTIVE REBELLION

Jeremiah's interior struggle was hidden from the people to whom he preached. They would undoubtedly have used it against him had they known. But the prophet's stern warnings that the nation's only salvation lay in accepting Babylonian authority showed only "the wall of bronze." It was that which the people attacked. Yet Jeremiah's advice was almost self-evidently true. Babylon had destroyed Assyria and defeated Egypt. What could Judah do? She had tried once to fight a great power and had been badly defeated. Babylon was stronger than Egypt, Jehoiakim weaker than Josiah. The only reasonable course was to accept the situation. This Jehoiakim would not do.

Perhaps he could not. He seems to have been incapable of understanding Jeremiah. His officers believed that the patriotic Judaean should strive for independence by all possible means. We admire the Greeks because they stood up to the Persians against impossible odds, and they won. Had they lost we would still admire them. The difference was that the Greeks had a competent army and a powerful navy. They had also a number of tactical advantages which they used with skill. This was not the case with Judah. Judah was only as strong as Jerusalem could withstand a siege, and her military resources were very small compared with those of Babylon and its allies. Perhaps this lent weight to Jeremiah's warnings. But in 601 Egypt defeated Nebuchadnezzar, and it must have seemed to Jehoiakim and his officers that despite the warnings of Jeremiah the time had come to make a break with Babylon, so he rebelled.

[12]Heschel translates, the passage
        O Lord, Thou hast seduced me
        And I am seduced;
        Thou hast raped me
        And I am overcome.
Abraham Heschel, *The Prophets* (New York: Harper and Row, 1969), p. 113.

The Egyptian victory secured Egypt from Babylonian attacks upon her own territory, but it did not diminish the presence of Babylon elsewhere. Judah was immediately attacked by raiding parties of Chaldeans, Aramaeans, Moabites, and Ammonites. Undoubtedly they were ordered to attack by Babylon, but the account in 2 Kings 24:2 is that the Lord sent these peoples against him. Meanwhile Jehoiakim died and was succeeded by his son, Jehoiakin, who was left with the consequences of his father's policy. Nebuchadnezzar advanced on Jerusalem and besieged it. Jehoiakin did not attempt to resist. He surrendered the city in 597, and he and his family and large numbers of the people together with a great quantity of treasure were taken to Babylon. Nebuchadnezzar then appointed Mattaniah, a twenty-one year old son of Josiah, and changed his name to Zedekiah.

ZEDEKIAH

Zedekiah was king but not ruler. He allowed his policies to be determined by his nationalistic officers. Perhaps there was too much confidence in the memory of Sennacherib's miraculous defeat outside Jerusalem a hundred years before.[13] At the moment of greatest peril for Judah Isaiah had predicted about the king of Assyria

> He shall not come into this city
> or shoot an arrow there. . .
> I will defend this city to save it,
> for my own sake and for the sake of my servant David. (Isaiah 37:33–35)

These predictions were not less unlikely than those of Hananiah, who declared that within two years the exiles would return from Babylon with all the vessels of the Lord's house that had been taken by Nebuchadnezzar (Jeremiah 28:1–9). Jeremiah was disdainful, yet his somber predictions and his willingness to accept Babylonian control must have appeared not only treasonable but religiously false. He had been told by God to wear a yoke on his neck to indicate that Judah must submit to Nebuchadnezzar (Jeremiah 27:1–11). Hananiah challenged Jeremiah publicly, took the yoke from his neck and broke it (Jeremiah 28:10–17). Jeremiah accused Hananiah of being a false prophet and told him that he would die within the year, which he did. It was an angry exchange. Jeremiah then wrote a letter to the exiles in Babylon advising them to settle down in Babylon for at least seventy years and not listen to prophets who promised that they would be delivered sooner (Jeremiah 29:1–10). This provoked a letter in reply from Shemaiah in exile, to Zephaniah, in Jerusalem, implying that Jeremiah was a madman who should be flogged and put in the stocks. Jeremiah replied promptly invoking God's punishment upon Shemaiah and his children (Jeremiah 29:24–32). It is very clear that Jeremiah was thoroughly disliked and mistrusted.

[13]John Bright, "Jeremiah," *Anchor Bible* (Garden City, N.Y.: Doubleday, 1965), p. CIV.

THE SIEGE AND FALL OF JERUSALEM

Had Jeremiah's advice been taken, Jerusalem would not have fallen. Jehoiakim's rebellion might be excused as too optimistic a response to an Egyptian victory. But the lesson that Judah did not stand a chance against the Babylonians was ignored by Zedekiah. The Lord told Jeremiah to wear a yoke because representatives from Edom, Moab, Ammon, Tyre, and Sidon were in Jerusalem to discuss rebellion. That was in 594. Zedekiah did not take part, perhaps because of Jeremiah, but four years later he rebelled, and Nebuchadnezzar moved against Jerusalem, determined, it seems, to destroy the city and put an end to a troublesome and unreliable vassal state. According to Ezekiel, who was in Babylon, Nebuchadnezzar used divination to decide how he would attack Jerusalem (Ezekiel 21:18-23). He first besieged Lachish and Azekah (Jeremiah 34:7), and then surrounded the city with watchtowers, battering rams and siege ramps (Ezekiel 21:22). Ezekiel had prophesied in Babylon that the end would come.

> An end! The end has come upon the four corners of the land. Now the end is upon you, and I will let loose my anger upon you, and will judge you according to your ways. . . . Thus says the Lord God: Disaster after disaster! Behold, it comes. An end has come, the end has come; it has awakened against you. (Ezekiel 7:1-6)

The siege lasted two years. There is a vivid account of the suffering of Jerusalem in Lamentations, written most likely shortly after the event, of the violence, the desecration, the humiliation, of the children fainting in the streets crying for their mothers, of mothers eating their children, of priests, prophets, young men and women lying slaughtered in all parts of the city.

In Ezekiel there is an even more painfully drawn picture "The sword is without, pestilence and famine are within . . . If any survivors escape, they will be on the mountains, like doves of the valleys, all of them moaning, every one over his iniquity." The New English Bible translates the conclusion of this passage "while their hands hang limp and their knees run with urine." (Ezekiel 7:15-17)

But in the books of Kings and Chronicles the destruction of Jerusalem is dealt with in a summary fashion, and in the prophecy of Jeremiah the details of the siege and the destruction are barely mentioned. The action and the emotion of the events taking place are presented through the personalities of Jeremiah and the irresolute king. Three times the prophet is called into the king's presence. Jeremiah is undeviating in his insistence that Judah must accept the fact of Babylonian power, and he is unsympathetic to the king. Yet Zedekiah, who was very young, very frightened, and very alone obviously longed for someone to talk to. He did not have the power or the will to protect Jeremiah when his officers tried to kill him, but at the end he had Jeremiah brought to him secretly to hear once again what he was too afraid to do. He did not have the courage to surrender. "I am afraid" he said "of the Jews who have deserted to the Chaldeans, lest I be handed over to them and they abuse me." Jeremiah 38:19) His fear brought upon him a terrible punishment. When finally the city gave in, Zedekiah tried to escape, but he was caught and brought before Nebuchadnezzar, who had no pity. He killed Zedekiah's sons "before his eyes" and then had his eyes put out. (2 Kings 25:1–7)

Jerusalem was destroyed, and all but the poorest class of people were deported. Nebuchadnezzar put Gedeliah, a Jew, in charge of the city. Jeremiah was personally granted the freedom to go where he wished. Even in these tragic conditions there remained a remnant of God's people under the leadership of Gedeliah. But still there were extremists who believed that they must strike in some way against Babylon. Gedeliah was assassinated and the assassins fled to Egypt, taking Jeremiah with them against his will.

A COMPLEX PERSONALITY

Jeremiah is one of the more complex personalities of the Old Testament. The sensitivity and anguish of his personal life contradict altogether his abrasive public life. By nature he coveted affection, by calling he turned people against him. He presented the word of the Lord in an uncompromising way, and for that we admire him. But how effective was it, or did it help to bring about what it predicted? He loved his people, and longed for their return to God, but his advice was to give in to the enemy. The people in Jerusalem deserve our sympathy. Surrender and be saved is almost universally a contradiction as long as there is a shred of hope. Assyria did not surrender, she fought to the last. Hezekiah and the people who listened to the Rabshakeh's beguiling arguments did not surrender, and because of it they were saved. The king's officers who called for Jeremiah's death were genuinely indignant; they were patriots too. Jeremiah alone, apart from Gedeliah, was given privileged treatment by the Babylonian authorities after the city fell. To the people in Jerusalem he must have been controversial and enigmatic, and so he may be to us as we dwell on his long and unsuccessful ministry. No one devoted himself so completely to his calling as a prophet, and no one, on the face of it, achieved so little.

A NEW EFFORT OF THINKING

But there is an aspect of Jeremiah's ministry which makes clear that from one point of view he achieved a great deal. Militarily the defeat of Judah was a small event on the international scene. But it was a religious disaster.

The city of Jerusalem was the city of God, the place of the Temple and God's presence. And this was because the people of Israel and Judah were the people of God. They had been given a promise, they were partners to a Covenant. As a people they were to celebrate the Passover forever. Continuation of the royal line would be "for ever" (2 Samuel 7:12–16).

Jeremiah interpreted events differently. The power of God was still active. The events which happened to Israel and then to Judah were according to his will. They were punishment for the nation's sin, for not keeping the Covenant.

But if the nation were the embodiment of the promise, and the nation were destroyed, how would the promise be sustained? What meaning would be left in the Covenant? This was a religious crisis. Had God let his people down? If not, and if all the ways by which the relationship with God had previously been maintained were destroyed, what was left?

The fact that Judaism continued may persuade us now to think that there was no question of its continuing, and on the assumption that what God had promised he would fulfill, there was no real crisis. But the human believer, struggling to relate his faith to the circumstances of life, can seldom take the divine point of view. From that perspective the result is not self-evident.

In such a situation the believer faces hard questions about the continued existence of his faith. If faith is to be retained it may be that it cannot be retained in the same way. There may have to be a different understanding of it, and its relation to life. One writer, discussing what he calls intellectual impediments to religious belief, concludes that the present religious situation can be met, "if it is to be met at all, only by a new effort of thinking." This, he declares, is one of the tasks of philosophy of religion.[14]

Jeremiah is not ordinarily regarded as a philosopher, but in this respect he can be because, confronted with the chaotic circumstances that followed the death of Josiah, he not only prophesied the disaster about to occur and appealed to his people to repent, but he engaged in a new effort of thinking which provided a fresh understanding of the divine human relationship to serve the nation in the vastly changed conditions of life about to overtake it.

Job is often regarded as the one example in the Old Testament of a philosopher, because he asked searching questions about God and his dealing with men and women. That is a first step in philosophical thinking. As an expression of personal distress, however, it is more autobiography than philosophy. Jeremiah suffered too, and challenged God; he even, like Job, accused him of wrong. But the thrust of his questions went beyond that to an attempt at resolution. He arrived at a second stage of philosophic reasoning in which he proposed an answer that was independent of the personal situation and therefore could be applied to many situations. We may sympathize with Job, yet there is little in his recorded experience to carry our thought or develop our faith beyond the point where he was. Jeremiah provided a new way by which those who grasped it could go far beyond the situation of Job, or for that matter, Jeremiah.

There was strong sentiment in Jerusalem for the inviolability of the city and the continuation of the Davidic line. Jeremiah did not share this.[15] His understand-

[14]H. J. Paton, "The Modern Predicament," in Keith Yandell, ed., *God, Man and Religion* (New York: McGraw Hill, 1973) p. 176.

[15]Von Rad, *Old Testament Theology*, p. 192.

ing of the relationship between God and Israel was governed not by place, Jerusalem and the Temple, and the Davidic monarchy, but by the ancient commitment made at Sinai, the Covenant, reaffirmed by Josiah and forgotten again.

Jeremiah stressed the point about Israel's original commitment very plainly in his sermon at the Temple gate. "Do not trust in these deceptive words: "This is the temple of the Lord, the temple of the Lord, the temple of the Lord!'. . . Add your burnt offerings to your sacrifices, and eat the flesh. For in the day that I brought them out of the land of Egypt, I did not speak to your fathers or command them concerning burnt offerings and sacrifices. But this command I gave them, 'Obey my voice, and I shall be your God, and you shall be my people.' " (Jeremiah 7:4, 21–23)

Jeremiah conceived of a renewal of relationship between God and the people by superseding the structures of law, liturgy, and bureaucracy which had come between them. There was to be a new Covenant which would make possible an unimpeded relationship.

> Behold, the days are coming, says the Lord, when I will make a new covenant with the house of Israel and the house of Judah, not like the covenant which I made with their fathers when I took them by the hand to bring them out of the land of Egypt, my covenant which they broke, though I was their husband, says the Lord. But this is the covenant which I will make with the house of Israel after those days, says the Lord: I will put my law within them, and I will write it upon their hearts; and I will be their God, and they shall be my people. And no longer shall each man teach his neighbor and each his brother, saying, "Know the Lord," for they shall all know me, from the least of them to the greatest, says the Lord; for I will forgive their iniquity, and I will remember their sin no more. (Jeremiah 31:31–34)

All that the old Covenant provided would be retained in the new. In that respect it was not new. The newness consisted in the way by which its promise would be achieved. It would be written on people's hearts, their will to obey God would proceed from within, from an intimate spiritual communion. The destruction of the city, the dissolution of the monarchy, the scattering of Israel, which seemed to be such a disaster, an unimaginable breaking of the link between a fondly remembered past and whatever might lie in the future, was not a disaster. The new Covenant provided a spiritual link between God's historic intentions and their fulfillment in spite of the fall of Jerusalem. And because all people who are in communion with God are in communion with one another, there would be a new community in "this place," Jerusalem. God would bring them back to live with "one heart and one way, that they may fear me for ever. . .[and] I will rejoice in doing them good." (Jeremiah 32:39–41)

Jeremiah's preaching was largely ignored at the time, except in a negative way. But Ezekiel, a contemporary prophet ministering in Babylon, developed the idea of a spiritual relationship between God and his people in his own prophecy (Ezekiel 36:26–27, 37:1–14). Many years later the concept of the new Covenant provided an interpretation of a new faith, Christianity (1 Corinthians 11:25), whose writings, the New Testament, are literally the New Covenant.

Jeremiah's influence, not only through this passage but the entire scope of his preaching and the quality of his life, has been extensive. One commentator has written that of all the great men of that time, including Nebuchadnezzar, only one has survived "as a real and living personality, whose influence is not dead, and who has meaning for us today no less than for his own time." This man, from one of the smallest of the ancient states, was Jeremiah of Anathoth.[16] That judgment is substantially correct, although it overlooks Ezekiel. But Jeremiah did not stand alone. He was the inheritor of a prophetic tradition which undoubtedly provided him with a model and with inspiration.

Elijah and Micaiah long before, and Amos about a century earlier, had set an example of proclaiming God's word which Jeremiah seems to have been consciously aware of, (Jeremiah 26:14-15; see 1 Kings 18:17-18, 22:13-14). Part of his preaching is clearly a reflection of Hosea (Jeremiah 3; Hosea 1-3; Jeremiah 31:16-22; Hosea 11:1-9). Similarly we find in Jeremiah Hosea's concern for knowledge of God (Jeremiah 4:22, 9:24; see Hosea 4:1-5, 6:3). And as Amos challenged the false assumptions which the Israelites made about the Day of the Lord (Amos 5:18), so Jeremiah challenged the false confidence of the wise, the valiant, and the rich (Jeremiah 9:23-24).

Jeremiah would seem to have been part of a Deuteronomic tradition whose major attempt at reform under the leadership of King Josiah coincided with the early years of the prophet's ministry. He certainly had a high regard for Josiah (Jeremiah 22:15-16).

The point is that while Jeremiah's achievement as a prophet was immense, and in certain respects unique, like all great creative thinkers he drew from those who preceded him.[17]

[16]Theodore H. Robinson, *Prophecy and Prophets in Ancient Israel*, 2d ed. (London: Gerald Duckworth and Co., 1953), p. 121.

[17]For a discussion of many aspects of the Book of Jeremiah, see *Interpretation*, A Journal of Bible and Theology, Vol. 38.2 (April 1983). This issue is devoted to the study of Jeremiah.

QUESTIONS FOR DISCUSSION

The following questions refer to Chapters 17–19

1. Why was the discovery of the Book of the Law so great a surprise? Even though there had been a half century of apostasy under Manasseh and Amon, would not one expect there to be some knowledge of God's law? Could the discovery have been engineered by those who saw a chance for religious reform under Josiah? Is there any evidence of an underground movement of faithfulness to God's law in a society which had largely neglected it?

2. The call of Isaiah is one of the great events in the Old Testament. It is frequently cited as an example of a mystical experience. Do you see any connection between the nature of Isaiah's call and the message that he was given to preach?

3. Jeremiah was possibly the least successful of all the writing prophets. His life's work appeared to end in complete failure. Yet one might argue that in the long run his preaching was highly influential, and continues to be so. How would you assess the work of Jeremiah? Did it have any political value during his own time? Is its religious value entirely posthumous?

4. Assyria did not acquire its savage reputation for no reason. Might it be shown that the arguments of Saggs and Olmstead are a case of special pleading from the safe distance of 2500 years?

CHAPTER TWENTY
THE PROPHET EZEKIEL

The last forty years have made us unhappily familiar with scenes of wartime destruction and of terrified refugees. Even within a few weeks of writing these lines there were such scenes from the Middle East on the evening news, so one can fairly well imagine the smouldering devastation through which the Israelite captives passed under Babylonian guard, and their despair as they left their homes. The author of Lamentations 2, perhaps using eyewitness reports, writes:

> The Lord has destroyed without mercy
>   all the habitations of Jacob;
> in his wrath he has broken down
>   the strongholds of the daughter of Judah;
> he has brought down to the ground in dishonor
>   the kingdom and its rulers.

Then, with evident bitterness, the author continues:

> The Lord has become like an enemy
>   he has destroyed Israel; (Lamentations 2:2, 5.)[1]

[1]Although attributed to Jeremiah, Lamentations is thought not to be by him, and to be by more than one author. Chapter 2, quoted here, and Chapter 4 seem to be eyewitness accounts of the suffering of Jerusalem.

The number of captives was not large. According to Jeremiah, who may have used a Babylonian source, less than a thousand persons were deported from Jerusalem with Zedekiah in 587 (Jeremiah 52:30), though that number might be increased two or three times to include dependents. But thousands must have died in battle, or of starvation and disease, and many would have been executed and others no doubt fled.[2]

The stern words of Isaiah to Hezekiah, when he discovered that the king had entertained emissaries from Merodach-baladin and had shown him "all his treasure house, the silver, the gold, the spices, the precious oil, his armory, all that was found in his storehouses" (2 Kings 20:13) came to pass over a hundred years later. "The days are coming," the prophet had warned, "when all that is in your house, and that which your fathers have stored up till this day, shall be carried to Babylon; nothing shall be left." (2 Kings 20:17)

A thousand years or so earlier Abraham and his family had traveled from Haran to the Promised Land. Now his descendants were returning with all their great achievements apparently wiped out.

LIFE IN EXILE HAD SOME COMPENSATION

Yet the situation of the exiles was not totally bleak. There had been an earlier deportation eleven years before when, Jehoiakim having rebelled against the Babylonians, Nebuchadnezzer besieged Jerusalem. The Israelite king then died, leaving his young son Jehoiakin to face the consequences of rebellion. Jehoiakin surrendered to Nebuchadnezzer and was taken captive, but he continued to be treated as king of Judah. This we know from texts excavated from Babylon which give details of provisions supplied to Jehoiakin "King of Judah" and his sons.[3] Zedekiah, Jehoiakin's uncle, who had been put in Jehoiakin's place, was therefore only a regent. This is even more clear because while he reigned in Judah Jehoiakin's steward was also in Judah looking after the crown properties, which would explain why Zedekiah was treated with such extreme harshness after Jerusalem fell, and also why he could not control his military leaders before. Understandably, with this attitude the exiles in Babylon believed that they and King Jehoiachin would soon return to Jerusalem with all the sacred vessels that had been taken from the Temple. When Jeremiah told them to settle down for seventy years, he provoked a furious reply (Jeremiah 29:1–9).[4] Yet Ezekiel, the prophet who was among the first exiles, lived in his own house (Ezekiel 3:24), and there were a number of sites in the area south of Babylon where the Jews lived together in their own communities. Jeremiah's advice to "build houses and live in them; plant gardens and eat their produce" must have been based on knowledge of what was being done (Jeremiah 29:5).

[2]Martin Noth, *The History of Israel,* Stanley Godman trans. (New York: Harper and Row, 1958) pp. 280–87.

[3]D. Winton Thomas, *Documents from Old Testament Times* (New York: Harper and Row, 1961), pp 84–86.

[4]*Cambridge Ancient History,* 3d ed., Vol. III (Cambridge: Cambridge University Press, 1973), p. 399

So the captives would have known as they walked the hundreds of miles from Jerusalem to Babylon, along the perimeter of the Fertile Crescent, that conditions in the foreign land could be bearable, even comfortable, except that nothing can replace a person's own home when he wants to live there.

THE CITY OF BABYLON

Whatever they thought, and whatever they had heard or read about Babylon, they were probably not prepared for the magnificence which they found. "The time of Babylon's greatest material wealth and splendour, and the period which is reflected in much of the later tradition about Babylon, was the reign of Nebuchadnezzar, 605–562."[5]

As the exiles approached the capital city the first building they would see would be Etemenanki, the "House of the platform of Heaven and Earth," a seven-storied ziggurat 300 feet high and 300 feet at each side at the base. This structure was possibly the inspiration of the Genesis story of the Tower of Babel (Genesis 11:1–9). As they came closer they would have seen the huge walls of the city, surrounded by a wide moat fed from the water of the Euphrates, which divided the city. One of the most well-known pictures of the ancient world is the reconstruction of the great Ishtar Gate, named after the goddess who was the personification of Venus, the morning and evening star. The gate was decorated with reliefs of animals in different colored glazes,[6] and in the bright sun must have appeared dazzlingly splendid. The gate led to the Processional Way which, like other streets in Babylon and like streets in our own cities, had a name. This was called "may the enemy not have victory." It led past the Temple, or Esagila, and the Palace with the fabled Hanging Gardens which, according to tradition, were constructed by a king to please a Persian concubine who grew tired of the flat Mesopotamian landscape. There is some evidence to support the view that the gardens really did exist, but more importantly the structure which might have been the base of the gardens contained the room where the tablets referring to Jehoichin were found.[7]

The exiles had come to a place which made their own capital look small and provincial. At the time of its defeat Jerusalem covered an area of about 14 acres. It is estimated that Babylon covered a thousand acres. Its streets were at right angles, like a modern American city, with houses three or four stories high, and with probably as many as 200,000 inhabitants;[8] free men, slaves, priests, and laity drawn from all parts of the ancient Near East. It was consequently a great trading center with ships coming from distant parts right into the city center. "Next to the city," writes

[5]H.W.F. Saggs, *Everyday Life in Babylonia and Assyria* (London: B.T. Batsford, 1965), p. 156.
[6]Ibid., pp. 162–63.
[7]Ibid., pp. 161–62.
For the tradition about the Hanging Gardens see *Interpreter's Dictionary of the Bible*, Vol. I (Nashville, Tenn.: Abingdon Press, 1962), p. 137a.
[8]Saggs, *Everyday Life,* p. 164.

A reconstruction of Ancient Babylon in the times of Nebuchadnezzar. Used with permission of the Oriental Institute of the University of Chicago.

Herodotus, "the Armenian boats for navigating the Euphrates are most wonderful."[9] They were made from leather stretched over a frame of willows, lined with reeds, and were round. They floated downstream with the current and could carry a cargo, often casks of palm wine, of as much as 60 tons, sometimes twice that. The merchants caried an ass on board, because when they had sold their cargo, as they couldn't float back against the current, they would auction off the willow ribs, pile the leather skins on the asses, and return by land.

Outside the city were farms, many of them owned by the Temple. They were in open country but were secure during the reign of Nebuchadnezzar, and there was a network of canals, like capilliaries, irrigating water throughout the land which could not survive without them. It was on the banks of one of these canals, the Chebar, in the small town of Tel Abib, that Ezekiel received his vision from God.

EZEKIEL'S VISION

The prophet was watching a storm as it came from the north. There was a heavy cloud with lightning flashing through it and "in the midst of the fire, as it were, gleaming bronze." (Ezekiel 1:4) Then he saw what appeared to be four animals.

> Each had four faces, and each of them had four wings. Their legs were straight, and the soles of their feet were like the sole of a calf's foot; and they sparkled like burnished bronze. Under their wings on their four sides they had human hands. And the four had their faces and their wings thus: their wings touched one another; they went every one straight forward, without turning as they went. As for the likeness of their faces, each had the face of a man in front; the four had the face of a lion on the right side, the four had the face of an ox on the left side, and the four had the face of an eagle at the back. Such were their faces. And their wings were spread out above; each creature had two wings, each of which touched the wing of another, while two coverd their bodies. And each went straight forward; wherever the spirit would go, they went, without turning as they went. In the midst of the living creatures there was something that looked like burning coals of fire, like torches moving to and fro among the living creatures; and the fire was bright, and out of the fire went forth lightning. (Ezekiel 1:6-13)

The vision was strange enough at that point, but it continued. Ezekiel looked at the animals and saw wheels on the ground beside them. The wheels glittered as if they were made of topaz and chrysolite. The rims of the wheels had eyes all the way round and they moved with the animals in separate directions. When the animals moved the wheels moved; when the animals stopped the wheels stopped, for the spirit of the animals was in the wheels (Ezekiel 1:15-21).

Above the animals, or living creatures, was a "likeness of a firmament, shining like crystal, spread out above their heads" (Ezekiel 1:22). Two of the animals' four wings were spread out, and as they moved they made a sound like the sound of the Almighty, or like a storm or a camp. Then Ezekiel saw above the glittering vault what looked like a sapphire throne, and upon the throne a human form of burning brass

[9]Herodotus, *History*, Book 1, paragraph 194. There are many editions of this work.

encircled with light like "the appearance of the bow that is in the cloud on the day of rain." (Ezekiel 1:23–28)

With fear and awe, Ezekiel threw himself on the ground. But a voice spoke to him; it told him to stand up, and gave him a commission not unlike that of Jeremiah's. He was to speak to the Israelites, "whether they hear or refuse to hear, for they are a rebellious house." Ezekiel was not to be afraid. "Be not afraid of them, nor be afraid of their words." (Ezekiel 2:1–8)

Next, the prophet saw a hand holding a scroll. The hand unrolled the scroll and Ezekiel saw that it had "written on it words of lamentation and mourning and woe." A voice said to him, "Son of man, eat what is offered to you; eat this scroll, and go, speak to the house of Israel." So Ezekiel ate it and it tasted sweet as honey. (Ezekiel 2:9–3:3)

The voice continued. Ezekiel was not being sent to foreign nations whose speech is "hard" but to Israelites. Yet, if he had been sent to those nations they would have understood before the Israelites because the Israelites are brazen and will refuse to listen. But, continued the voice, "I have made your face hard against their faces." Whether they listened or not Ezekiel was to say, "Thus says the Lord God." (Ezekiel 3:4–11)

Then, in the climax of his vision, the spirit lifted him up. Behind him he heard a fierce rushing sound "as the glory of the Lord rose from his place." He heard the wings of the four living creatures brushing against one another, the sound of the wheels, a tumultuous shouting. He was full of exaltation, and the hand of the Lord was strong upon him (Ezekiel 3:12–14). So he came to the exiles at the Tel-abib and for seven days he stayed with them, stunned and dumbfounded.

INFLUENCES ON EZEKIEL'S MINISTRY

Some details of Ezekiel's visions were certainly influenced by his surroundings. He had come to Babylon five years before[10] (Ezekiel 1:1–3), and would have seen the strange monumental figures called Karibu, reminiscent of our word cherub (Exodus 25:18), with the head of a man, the body of a lion, the hooves of a bull, and the wings of an eagle, which stood on guard outside the palaces in Babylon. Such detail would attract Ezekiel because as a priest he was trained to be observant (Ezekiel 1:3), and symbolism was part of his life.[11]

When Ezekiel wrote about the spring of water that flowed from his ideal Temple (Ezekiel 47:1), he most likely had in mind the river Euphrates that flowed from north to southwest past the Temple in Babylon, and the perfect symmetry of Ezekiel's plans for the Temple, the new city of Jerusalem, and the precisely divided restored Israel suggest that he was much impressed by the large-scale symmetry of the city of Babylon.

[10]Gerhard Von Rad, *Old Testament Theology*, Vol. 2, D.M.G. Stalker trans. (New York: Harper and Row, 1965), pp. 220–221.

[11]Brevard S. Childs, *Introduction to the Old Testament as Scripture* (Philadelphia: Fortress Press, 1979) pp. 361–362.

Had Ezekiel been only a priestly intellectual, his work would have lacked the immense power which it now possesses. But he was a gifted poet, whose analysis of the sins of Israel and feelings of horror about its apostasy achieved literary power. There is, however, another factor, possibly independent of all these. Ezekiel has been described as an epileptic and paranoid schizophrenic.[12] But one should expect an individual's personality to be affected when God uses him to convey his message. In E. M. Forster's book *The Ship,* a certain character, who is unusually strong, attempts to save some of his fellow crew members. The ship has been struck by a torpedo and is on fire. In order to free some of his friends he has to open a large bulkhead door by turning a round steel handle. The handle is red hot. He grasps the handle and he turns it and opens the door, but his hands are burned almost to the bone. The impact of God may have a comparable effect upon a personality.

COMPOSITION AND STRUCTURE OF THE BOOK

Critical opinions about the book of Ezekiel have varied widely, from accepting it in its present form as the work of Ezekiel, to denying that he was the author at all. One view places the composition of the book in the late third century, about 350 years after Ezekiel is believed to have lived. Another view places the composition in the time of Manasseh, about a hundred years before the prophet is thought to have lived.[13]

More moderate opinions recognize that the text of Ezekiel has had a long and complex history, and that a number of hands were involved in its writing and editing, but that "in the main," the text achieved by critical research must be regarded as the work of Ezekiel himself.[14]

The book is carefully dated, covering a period of about twenty-three years in Ezekiel's life from 593 (Ezekiel 1:1), when he began his ministry, five years after leaving Jerusalem as an exile, to 571 (Ezekiel 40:1).

There appear to be two series of dates, which correspond to divisions within the book. Chapters 1–24 consist of prophecies delivered before the destruction of Jerusalem. Chapters 33–48 are concerned again with Judah and Jerusalem. The dates proceed chronologically in the first and third parts, but are interrupted by another chronological series of dates in the oracles against foreign nations, which suggests that Chapters 25–32 were not originally in their present position.[15]

Yet although questions of composition and chronology are important, the study of the text of Ezekiel must be, at least in part, a study of a process of the prophet's

---

[12]Karl Jaspers in *Ezekiel a Pathological Study,* referred to by Walther Eichrodt in *Ezekiel, A Commentary,* Cosslett Quin trans. (Philadelphia: The Westminster Press, 1975), p. 26. Eichrodt disagrees with Jaspers, Never, at any point in this history of so radical an inward transformation do we find any trace of mental abnormality or even disease. . . . Ezekiel's message is everywhere seen to be well thought out and directed towards a single end, which is in keeping with his conception of God, of the world, and of human nature."

[13]Otto Eissfeldt, *The Old Testament,* Peter Ackroyd trans. (New York: Harper and Row, 1965), p. 370.

[14]Walther Eichrodt, *Ezekiel,* Cosslet Quin trans. (Philadelphia: The Westminster Press, 1970), p. 13.

[15]Ibid., p. 18.

thinking as much as the study of a document. This is indicated by his recapitulation of Israel's history in Chapter 20, which convicts the people for their behavior in Egypt *before* the Exodus, and then describes God as giving the people *bad* commandments because of their wickedness (Ezekiel 20:25). According to Ezekiel, the people "deserved judgment."[16] That was the point which the prophet wished to make. The actual details of time and place were not essential. Hence, for example, in connection with Ezekiel's visit to Jerusalem (Ezekiel 8:3), whether he literally flew or made a special visit or did not go there at all but imagined that he did, was incidental to his purpose. He had a "different understanding of reality,"[17] which was not bound by ordinary temporal and physical rstraints but was governed by theological concepts. Similarly, whether the book is from the seventh century, the sixth century, or the third, its importance is its theological message.

EZEKIEL'S SYMBOLIC ACTS

Ezekiel's prophecy was directed primarily toward the inhabitants of Jerusalem, the "rebels" who set themselves against God. He began his ministry six years before the city was destroyed (Ezekiel 1:2). He may have hoped that the people would change if they listened both to him and to Jeremiah, who was in Jerusalem. Yet, like Isaiah, he was told to speak to a people who would refuse to listen to his message because they would refuse to listen to God (Ezekiel 2:7, Isaiah 6:9-10). Perhaps, to shock them into listening, his message was strange and harsh.

We read that at first he was struck dumb (Ezekiel 3:15, 25-27) and that he was unable to speak until the destruction of Jerusalem (Ezekiel 24:26-27, 33:21-22). This may explain why the first of his recorded messages were symbolic acts. He took a clay tile, drew a picture on it of Jerusalem, then besieged it with a trench and earth works and miniature battering rams like a child besieging a toy castle. He took an iron griddle and put it between himself and the city. It was a sign (Ezekiel 4:1-3). He lay on his left side for 390 days and then on his right side for 40 days to symbolize the length of time of the sufferings of the people, and he was tied with a rope so that he could not turn from one side to the other before the appointed time (Ezekiel 4:4-8). He was restricted to rough food and to a sixth of a hin of water a day, not much more than half an American quart (Ezekiel 4:9-12), scarcely sufficient if he were outside in the sun all day, to symbolize that the people of Jerusalem would eat bread "with fearfulness" and drink water "in dismay." (Ezekiel 4:16-17)

All this he did without complaint, but when God ordered him to cook his food on dried human dung he protested that he had never eaten anything unclean. God relented and allowed him to use cow dung, which was a normal cooking fuel (Ezekiel 4:12-15).

[16]Walther Zimmerli, *Ezekiel: A Commentary*, Vol. 1, Ronald E. Clements trans. (Philadelphia: Fortress Press, 1979), p. 418.
[17]Childs, *Introduction to the Old Testament*, p. 361.

ARSH COMMISSION

er his first overwhelming vision Ezekiel lay stunned for seven days; then God spoke
im:

> Son of man, I have made you a watchman for the house of Israel; whenever you hear
> a word from my mouth, you shall give them warning from me. If I say to the wicked,
> "You shall surely die," and you give him no warning, nor speak to warn the wicked from
> his wicked way, in order to save his life, that wicked man shall die in his iniquity; but
> his blood I will require at your hand. (Ezekiel 3:17–18)

should reflect on how we might feel were we confronted by God with such a respon-
lity. It was more ominous even than the warning given to Jeremiah which was
say to them everything I command you. Do not be dismayed by them, lest I dismay
before them." (Jeremiah 1:17). That made him responsible for his own standing
ore God; if he failed he would be punished. But if Ezekiel failed and the sinners
om he did not warn died for their sins, he would be responsible for them. The
ct of that somber announcement coming immediately after his vision, and seven
s of shock may well have determined for him that there would *never* be a person
) did not hear and was not warned, and to ensure that they could not mistake
message he cast it into the most harsh and offensive terms. The people had to
r. But they would not hear if what he said were polite or delicate. They had to
e it beaten into them until they accepted his message and were saved. Then, if
/ rejected it and died in their sin he could not be held responsible.

VIDUAL RESPONSIBILITY FOR SIN

, possible that this terrible concern contributed to his teaching about personal
onsibility for sin.

> The word of the Lord came to me again: "What do you mean by repeating this proverb
> concerning the land of Israel, 'The fathers have eaten sour grapes, and the children's
> teeth are set on edge'? As I live, says the Lord God, this proverb shall no more be used
> by you in Israel. Behold, all souls are mine; the soul of the father as well as the soul
> of the son is mind: the soul that sins shall die." (Ezekiel 18:1–4)

Ezekiel was quite explicit: the wicked son of an upright man will not be saved
is father's uprightness. He will die for his sin. But if he has an upright son, that
will not be affected by his father's sin; he will live. Yet, continues the prophet,
e house of Israel says, 'The way of the Lord is not just.' O House of Israel, are
ways not just? Is it not your ways that are not just? Therefore I will judge you,
ouse of Israel, every one according to his ways" (Ezekiel 18:29–30).

Personal responsibility was not a new concept in the Old Testament. Amaziah,
g of Judah (800–783), put to death his father's murderers, but spared their children
Kings 14:6) in deference to the command to be found in Deuteronomy 24:16, but

doubtless part of a more ancient code.[18] "The fathers shall not be put to death for the children, nor shall the children be put to death for the fathers; every man shall be put to death for his own sin."

The doctrine of personal responsibility for sin was also a currently held view in Ezekiel's time. Jeremiah had quoted the same proverb and added that "every one shall die for his own sin; each man who eats sour grapes, his teeth shall be set on edge." (Jeremiah 31:30) But Ezekiel made a special point of it, perhaps again because of his stern commission, so that no one would be able to appeal to his forefathers either as an excuse for present shortcomings or to claim by inheritance the benefits of secondhand righteousness. The fact that some Israelites did complain about the Lord's "injustice" suggests they were indeed trying to avoid responsibility.

A MESSAGE OF HOPE

Despite his terrible allegories, despite the savage judgments attributed to God, Ezekiel's prophecy includes an element of hope. An indication of this is the other side of Ezekiel's stress upon personal responsibility, that a sinner would be forgiven if he changed. He was not to be held guilty for wrongs he had overcome:

> But if a wicked man turns away from all his sins which he has committed and keep all my statutes and does what is lawful and right, he shall surely live; he shall not die None of the transgressions which he has committed shall be remembered against him for the righteousness which he has done he shall live. (Ezekiel 18:21-22)

He calls to the Israelites:

> Repent and turn from all your transgressions, lest iniquity be your ruin. Cast away fro you all the transgressions which you have committed against me, and get yourselve a new heart and a new spirit! Why will you die, O house of Israel? For I have no pleasu in the death of any one, says the Lord God; so turn, and live. (Ezekiel 18:30-33)

Jeremiah looked forward to a righteous branch from David's line who wou rule with wisdom and justice over an Israel restored to its own land (Jeremiah 23:5-8 Similarly, Ezekiel declares in the name of the Lord: "I will gather you from the people and assemble you out of the countries where you have been scattered, and I will gi you the land of Israel (Ezekiel 11:17). How much was Ezekiel influenced by Jeremiah preaching? It is possible that hearing about the destruction of Jeremiah's prophe scroll by Jehoiakim (Jeremiah 36), Ezekiel deliberately made use of what he kno of Jeremiah's teaching in order to preserve it. In both prophets one finds a conce that goes beyond opportunity for repentance and hopes for the future. Jeremiah h written in a letter to the exiles, which Ezekiel must have seen:

[18]John Gray, *I and II Kings,* second, fully revised edition (Philadelphia: The Westminster Pre 1970), p. 604.

Then you will call upon me and come and pray to me, and I will hear you. You will seek and find me; when you seek me with all your heart. (Jeremiah 29:12–13)

We can only surmise about cause and effect. Elsewhere in his prophecy Jeremiah expressed the constant, unfailing nature of God's love (Jeremiah 31:3). Ezekiel appears almost to be complementing his fellow prophet's teaching when he writes:

I will give them [The Israelites] one [a new] heart, and put a new spirit within them; I will take the stony heart out of their flesh and give them a heart of flesh, that they may walk in my statutes and keep my ordinances and obey them; and they shall be my people, and I will be their God. (Ezekiel 11:19–21)

God will transform the lives of those who may not have the strength to do it for themselves but are willing to allow it to be done.

THE VALLEY OF DRY BONES

This is the background of thought to the activity of the spirit that is so evident in the teaching of Ezekiel. It was a spirit who gave him instructions during his vision (Ezekiel 2:2), a new spirit that was to be the regenerative power in the repentant sinner (Ezekiel 11:19), and the spirit that was to give life to a nation so devoid of life that it could be likened only to a valley filled with dried human bones.

Ezekiel's macabre imagery of this valley may not have been as strange to those who first heard or read it as it is to us. For example, excavators have discoverd a large burial site outside the ruins of Lachish containing two thousand skeletons, some of them burned, probably the victims of Sennacherib's destruction of the city in 701.[19] The Assyrian record of the battle of Qarqar reports 14,000 of the enemy (Israel and its allies) killed, "I flung their bodies about," wrote Shalmaneser, "filling the plain with their scattered soldiery."[20] Throughout the Old Testament there are accounts of battles with a prodigious number of casualties. One can suppose that respects were paid to the dead as far as possible, but even in modern times those respects may be scant as, for example, in Henri Barbusse's grim story of the First World War, *Under Fire*. In ancient times, when battle followed battle and survivors fled, and conquering armies moved on to fresh victories; there must have been bodies that were just left to decompose and be eaten by wild animals. Ezekiel's vision may therefore have been an unpleasantly familiar sight in some form to many of the people for whom he wrote. See Ezekiel 39:15)

The hand of Yahweh which had carried him to Jerusalem took him away again, this time to a valley full of bones. "There were very many upon the valley; and lo, they were very dry." Yahweh spoke to him, "Son of man, can these bones live?" The

---

[19]Gaalyah Cornfeld, *Archeology of the Bible: Book by Book* (New York: Harper and Row, 1976), p. 174.
[20]Thomas, *Documents,* p. 47.

prophet hedged, "O Lord God, thou knowest." Then the Lord ordered him to prophesy so that the bones could live, and as he did so they gradually came to life. First the bones joined together, then sinews covered them, and finally skin, but the bodies were not alive. There was no breath in them. So the Lord Yahweh spoke again, "Come from the four winds, O breath, and breathe upon these slain that they may live." Ezekiel prophesied as he had been ordered, the breath entered the bodies; and they lived, "and stood upon their feet, an exceedingly great host." (Ezekiel 37:9–10)

The significance of the parable is given by Ezekiel in the verses that follow. Israel without hope is like a valley full of bones, but the Lord will put his spirit in them and they will live and he will resettle them in their own land (Ezekiel 37:11–14). Ultimately this would include all the people of Israel, including the lost tribes of the Northern Kingdom. God will cleanse them and David will reign over them, one shepherd for all. The promise is a very strong one. "I will make a covenant of peace with them; it shall be an everlasting covenant with them; and I shall bless them and multiply them, and will set my sanctuary in the midst of them for evermore." (Ezekiel 37:26)

This promise is beautifully expressed in one of the gentler passages of Ezekiel (Chapter 34), where the Lord denounces shepherds of Israel who are no shepherds, and declares that he himself will be their shepherd. At the same time he will raise up David to pasture them and be their shepherd. They will live in peace, without fear, and the trees and the land will bear abundantly. It was an idyllic scene, with only one detail lacking, and Ezekiel supplied it.

EZEKIEL'S TEMPLE

One of Ezekiel's prophecies, which must have sounded unusually harsh to the Israelites, was a vision of God in all his glory leaving the Temple and the city of Jerusalem (Ezekiel 11:23). It would seem to have been a final abandonment.

But Ezekiel, as a priest, was committed to the importance of the Temple. If Israel were to be ruled by a restored Davidic monarchy then there would have to be a Temple.

Ezekiel's visionary plans were on a gigantic scale. Once again the hand of God carried him in a mystical way from Babylon to Jerusalem and he was instructed to look closely and listen carefully and tell the Israelites all that he saw.

The preparations were grand by Jerusalem standards. The Temple area with its buildings and an inner and outer courtyard was 875 foot square, with three large and complex gates. Three gates then led from the outer to the inner courtyard and to the Temple itself, which resembled very closely what we know of the Temple of Solomon, where Ezekiel had served as priest.

This Temple was to be kept pure, and one can sense Ezekiel's continuing disgust at the profanities he had witnessed during his earlier vision. Only Jews were allowed to enter and only the sons of Zadok were permitted to officiate in the sanctuary. Zadok was the priest who remained loyal to David during the attempt by Adonijah to claim the throne (1 Kings 1:32–34, 2:27–35). Other Levites were to perform the lesser tasks, such as guarding the gates and killing the sacrificial animals (Ezekiel 44:10-14). Presumably these restrictions were enough to guarantee the purity of the Temple, enough for God to appear in all his glory and a voice to say "Son of man, this is the place of my throne and the place of the soles of my feet, where I will dwell in the midst of the people of Israel for ever." (Ezekiel 43:1-7)

Ezekiel's vision revealed to him not only plans for the Temple, but for the whole country, which he saw divided neatly into horizontal strips, one strip for each tribe, extending from the Mediterranean coast to the eastern border without regard to tribal traditions or geography. The central strip contained the Temple and the city of Jerusalem and an area to the east and west of the city for the prince (Ezekiel 45:1-9). The secular ruler in this restored community was closely restricted. Samuel had warned the people long before what would happen if they chose a king, and it happened (1 Samuel 8). This time the king was to be kept in bounds.

As the Temple was the place of God, it was appropriate that from under the Temple would flow a river of life. The water, which grew deeper as it moved from its source, was so pure and life-giving that along its banks fruit trees grew with leaves that never withered and fruit that never failed; they bore new fruit every month because the water came from the sanctuary, and when it flowed into the Dead Sea it brought the dead waters to life (Ezekiel 47:1-12).

The final paragraph in the book describes the gates of Jerusalem. There were twelve in the city walls, one for each tribe, and the name of the city in future was to be: "The Lord is there" (Ezekiel 48:30-35).

Ezekiel's description of the great new Temple in a restored and reorganized kingdom must have pleased his fellow exiles hugely. It is what they would most hope for, the restoration of what had been lost. It reaffirmed what they most wanted to believe, that with the power of the Almighty a little nation was superior to them all. In his sermon on Gog and Magog (Ezekiel 38), Ezekiel makes clear in a bold allegory that the mightiest power on earth will not prevail against Israel. The only portion of the land of Israel which even its greatest enemy will occupy will be graves for its dead (Ezekiel 39:11-16). Understandably, the elders of Israel in Babylon sought Ezekiel's advice. After the fall of Jerusalem he was the one person to whom they could turn. He gave to his people something specific to hope for, and with the help of the liberal policy of Cyrus and the devotion and persistence of Ezra and Nehemiah, Ezekiel's vision of a Temple-centered, exclusive religious community came to pass, and it survived. The Jews who fled from Jerusalem to Egypt and established a community in Elephantine created a hybrid style of worship which had little continuing influence. Ezekiel, on the other hand, can be regarded as the originator and inspirator of postexilic Judaism, which by ordinary calculations should not have survived. The odds against the Jews—decimated, scattered, disheartened—retaining any distinctiveness of race or religion were massive. It can be argued that Ezekiel made possible that continuation of the promise at a time when it appeared to have failed.[21]

[21]For a discussion of many aspects of the Book of Ezekiel, see *Interpretation*, a Journal of Bible and Theology, Vol. 39.2 (April 1984). This issue is devoted to the study of Ezekiel.

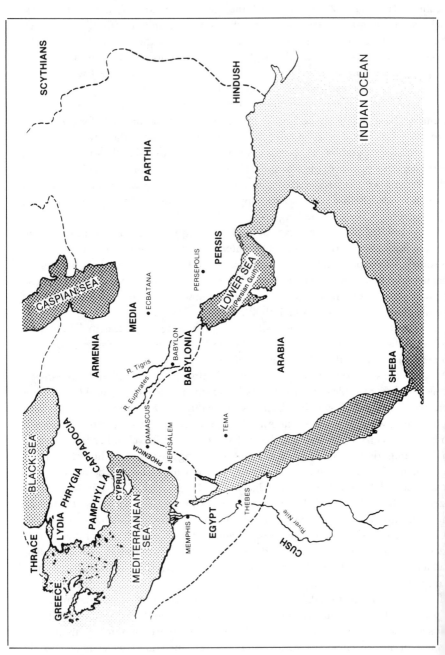

SCYTHIANS

HINDUSH

INDIAN OCEAN

PARTHIA

PERSIS

CASPIAN SEA

MEDIA • ECBATANA

PERSEPOLIS •

LOWER SEA (Persian Gulf)

ARMENIA

R. Tigris

BABYLON

BABYLONIA

R. Euphrates

DAMASCUS •

ARABIA

SHEBA

PHOENICIA

JERUSALEM •

TEMA •

BLACK SEA

THRACE

LYDIA

PHRYGIA

PAMPHYLIA CAPPADOCIA

CYPRUS

MEDITERRANEAN SEA

GREECE

MEMPHIS •

• THEBES

EGYPT

River Nile

CUSH

...... marks the limit of the Empire.

CHAPTER TWENTY-ONE
THE FALL OF BABYLON

abylon defeated Assyria in 612; it had was conquered the unconquerable. But in
ss than seventy-five years Babylon was conquered by Persia. The reasons for this
dden decline are known to us in some detail. They seem also to have been known
Ezekiel, for he writes about some of them individually in his prophecy. An exam-
e of this is in connection with the siege of Tyre.

He describes Tyre as a ship, perfect in beauty (Ezekiel 27:3), riding the sea
if it were a god (Ezekiel 28:2). He gives a brilliant account of its worldwide trade,
jewels, spices, precious metals, embroideries, horses, wheat, and wine. Tyre was
ilt on a rocky island just off the coast and so was difficult to besiege, but it would
destroyed by the Babylonians and reduced to naked rock, scraped bare, a place
fishermen to spread their nets (Ezekiel 26:4–5).

Given the military weakness of Phenincia and the immense power of Babylon
ekiel could have been fairly certain that that is what would happen. But in
apter 29 we find he has amended his predictions. Tyre proved difficult to defeat;
vithstood a siege for thirteen years. He writes:

Son of man, Nebuchadnezzar king of Babylon made his army labor hard against
Tyre; every head was made bald and every soldier was rubbed bare; yet neither
he nor his army got anything from Tyre to pay for the labor that he had
performed against it. (Ezekiel 29:18)

Ezekiel declared that God would give Egypt to Nebuchadnezzar as recompense to pay off his army and reward his efforts against Tyre.

THE MILITARY LOGISTICS OF BABYLON'S FAILURE

The reason for the strange ineffectiveness of the Near East's greatest and most recently victorious power was partly a logistical one, and it indicates, by comparison, the thorough grasp which the Assyrians had of the art of warfare.

The Assyrians, although a warlike society, did not keep a standing army in the field. It restricted its campaigns to a few months of the year. Babylon, however, kept its armies in the field for years at a time,[1] in the case of Tyre for thirteen years, and that created a tremendous strain on its manpower and its finances. For such a protracted and unsuccessful campaign, Babylon required revenue to pay off its troops. Ezekiel's comment is so direct that one wonders whether he had heard gossip around the capital and incorporated it into his writing. If so, he would have certainly learned that there was an important practical reason why the Babylonians wanted to capture Tyre. Its capture would help to compensate, far more than looting Egypt, for the loss of trade routes to the east and northeast, which were controlled by the Mede and the Persians. Through them came the raw materials which Babylon did not have but needed.[2] Its own ports at the head of the Persian Gulf were silting up,[3] so that despite the grandeur of its armies and its cities, Babylon was hemmed in on two sides. Tyre, which Nebuchadnezzar eventually captured, gave the empire an outlet to the west, and Nabonidus, the last king of Babylon, made vigorous efforts to develop trade routes from Arabia in the southeast; this was an economic problem which the Babylonians never really solved.

THE PROBLEM OF SUCCESSION

But there was another weakness over which Nebuchadnezzar had no control, and which affected Babylon in an especially serious way, and that was the problem succession. After Nebuchadnezzar's death there were three rulers in six years. The first, Amel Marduk, Nebuchadnezzar's son, was murdered within two years of succeeding his father. Amel Marduk was the Evil-merodach who released Jehoiach from prison (2 Kings 25:27, Jeremiah 52:31-34). His successor, Nebuchadnezzar's son-in-law, died or was killed within four years. That ruler's son was superseded by a man who had served Nebuchadnezzar as a diplomat, Nabonidus. He was to be the last king of the Babylonian empire.

---

[1]H.W.F. Saggs, *The Greatness That Was Babylon,* Sidgwick and Jackson, London 1962, p. 26
[2]Ibid., pp. 267-268.
[3]Ibid., p. 143.

NABONIDUS

Nabonidus's has been described as the first archeologist, and a learned antiquary. It is suggested that he wasn't quite sane. This may be what lies behind the story of the madness ascribed to Nebuchadnezzar in Daniel 4:28–33.[4] The king was reputedly punished by God for his self-esteem, and lived like an animal for seven years, letting his hair and nails grow long and eating grass. His behavior was certainly strange for an ancient king, for he seems to have almost wilfully disregarded the military and political dangers which threatened his kingdom.

Nabonidus's mother or grandmother had been a high priestess of the god Sin in Haran; and so we may suppose that he was prejudiced in that god's favor. But the tactless manner in which he attempted to supplant the prevailing senior deity Marduk with his favorite god Sin created much resentment. Nabonidus encroached upon a sensitive area when he began to tamper with the eminence of Marduk. There were riots in the cities. He therefore removed himself and his court to Tema in Arabia, about four hundred miles across the desert southwest of Babylon.

Nabonidus stayed in Tema for ten years, leaving his son Bel-shar-usur, the Belshazzar of the book of Daniel (5:22, 7:1, 8:1), as regent of Babylon. Nabonidus did not return until Cyrus had become an unstoppable threat to his empire.

THE NEED FOR A SOUTHERN TRADE ROUTE

Nabonidus's long stay in Tema may be explained as a sustained effort to deal with the economic problems of his empire by controlling the trade routes from Arabia. He moved to Tema around 550. During the preceding ten years, inflation had driven up prices by 50 percent,[5] and Nabonidus may have decided that something had to be done. It may have been a shrewd excuse to get away from the angry recriminitions of the worshippers of Marduk.

A FARSIGHTED RELIGIOUS POLICY

Nabonidus's religious policy can also be explained as statesmanship.[6] It is possible that he was aware of new religious ideas among the Jews and the Persians. The Jews were living in and around Babylon, at the heart of his kingdom, and there was, as we shall see, at least one great creative religious thinker among them during his lifetime. Among the Persians was the growing influence of Zoroaster, who may have lived about

[4]Albert T. Olmstead, *The History of the Persian Empire,* University of Chicago Press, Chicago, IL, 7th printing, 1978, pp. 55–56.

[5]Saggs, *Greatness,* p. 147.

[6]Ibid., p. 145.

five hundred years earlier (ca. 1000 B.C.).[7] Zoroaster's teaching was dualistic: the good spirit Ahura Mazda, creator of heaven and of mankind, was eternally in conflict with the evil spirit, the Lie, and ultimately proved victorious.

This doctrine was gradually moving to the forefront of religious thought among the Persians at a time when the ancient religion of Mesopotamia had reached the end of its vitality. Nabonidus wanted a diety that could be more universally accepted than was Marduk, who was not recognized by the Arabs or by the Syrians. Both groups recognized the moon god Sin. There were therefore good reasons for what Nabonidus was trying to do.

THE RISE OF CYRUS

But Nabonidus did not have political tact, and was perhaps really more of an antiquary, perhaps more of a thinker than the ruler of an empire could afford to be. A kingdom maintained its independence in those days only by superior military strength. While Nabonidus was pursuing his policies in a seemingly leisurely way Cyrus, the ruler of the small kingdom of Anshan, defeated the Medes, a powerful empire that was a potential threat to Babylon. Nabonidus may, in fact, have helped him. Four years later, in 546, Cyrus defeated Croesus, king of Lydia. By then Cyrus controlled a huge empire stretching from Asia Minor to north India. The fall of Babylon was a matter of time.

When Babylon defeated Assyria, the difference for subject peoples was incidental. One cruel and despotic power had been replaced by another. The Babylonians were as feared as the Assyrians; both nations practiced a policy of destruction. But when Cyrus rose to power he followed a quite different policy. Instead of deporting people from their homelands he allowed them to remain under Persian administration; insted of looting and destroying their temples he allowed the people to continue their own worship. Where they were scattered he allowed them to return and resume their normal lives.

The expectations this aroused among the exiles from Jerusalem can be measured by the despair they felt when they were first deported. Jeremiah had promised that they would return, Chapter 31, so had Ezekiel; (Ezekiel 39:25) but in the immediate aftermath of defeat these must have seemed to many of the Israelites unlikely promises. Now it appeared that the words of the prophets were about to be fulfilled.

ORDINARY CONCERNS AND THEIR SPIRITUAL CONTEXT

A number of times we have mentioned that the Old Testament is written from a point of view. It is an account of the activity of God among his people as he seeks to bring about his will. There is therefore always a tension between the ordinary human con-

[7]Robert Charles Zaehner, *The Teachings of the Magi,* New York, Macmillan, 1956, pp. 10–11.

cerns of safety, comfort, property, ambition, and the unvarying concern of God that life is not complete unless a person takes account of its spiritual context.

The Bible presents this through the prophets. Time after time at moments of importance, when people were absorbed with their immediate dangers or their immediate opportunities, a prophet would remind them that the obvious concern was a lesser concern, that the one they were ignoring was the one that mattered. When the Assyrians surrounded Jerusalem and there seemed to be no alternative to defeat, Isaiah told the king to trust in God. When the Northern Kingdom was caught up in a euphoria of prosperity, Amos warned that unless the people changed their lifestyle, there would be disaster. Elijah, Micaiah, Nathan, Jeremiah, and Ezekiel pointed to the universal, spiritual implications of particular current events. To them the practical details of life could not be understood apart from that larger context. So, during the few years after the defeat of Croesus of Lydia by Cyrus, and before Cyrus conquered Babylon, when anticipation and speculation must have been an all-absorbing interest, a prophet appeared, once again to present the spiritual context of what was taking place.

CHAPTER TWENTY-TWO
SECOND ISAIAH

No one knows the name of the prophet whom we call Second Isaiah, but in depth of spiritual understanding and literary brilliance his work is regarded as among the greatest of all Old Testament writings, "the noblest literary monument bequeathed to us from semitic antiquity."[1] We know nothing about the writer as a person, but we know a lot about him as a poet, as a thinker, as an exile, who cared for his fellow exiles, who was strong enough to encourage them, and faithful enough to convey a message of responsibility as well as consolation.

The message of Second Isaiah begins with consolation, the familiar "Comfort, comfort my people" (Isaiah 40:1). He was speaking to a people who had suffered and who were in bondage, but whom God had forgiven and would shortly lead back to Jerusalem. It would be a second Exodus along a great highway stretching across the desert, mountains leveled and valleys filled. The people of Israel would trave safely under the protection of God himself. He would care for them like a shepherc who gathers his lambs in his arms (Isaiah 40:11).

THE HISTORICAL SITUATION

The historical situation to which Second Isaiah refers is very different from that c his predecessor. Isaiah of Jerusalem lived in the eighth century when Assyria wa

[1]James Muilenburg, "Second Isaiah," *Interpreter's Bible,* Vol. 5 (Nashville, Tenn.: Abingdon Press p. 382.

dominant power. His prophecy concludes with an account of Sennacherib's inva-
n of Judah (701) and his mysterious withdrawal from Jerusalem. The final chapter
a short description of how Hezekiah naively showed his entire armory and his
asures to envoys from the king of Babylon, much to Isaiah's disgust.

Second Isaiah lived in the sixth century. This we can gather from his reference
Cyrus (Isaiah 44:26–45:1), who sprang into prominence with the unexpected defeat
Lydia in 546. With that, the fall of Babylon was almost certain. Second Isaiah
'ers to a time when Babylon had not yet fallen but her defeat was imminent (Isaiah
:3). Cyrus's generous religious policies were well enough known for the prophet
hope that he would allow Jerusalem to be rebuilt (Isaiah 44:26–28). The date of
iting, therefore, would seem to be about 540.

The historical reasons for distinguishing between the first two parts of Isaiah
supported by theological reasons.[2] It is thought unlikely that the eighth century
ιiah would have offered forgiveness to an unrepentant nation (Isaiah 40:1–2). It
quite appropriate to offer forgiveness to a nation which has experienced defeat and
ιle.

The difference between the Messiah of Isaiah 9:1–6 and 11:1–9, who will wield
minion and strike down the ruthless, and the servant of Chapters 40–55 is so great
it it is "hard to attribute them to the same person."[3]

Yet, from one point of view, to lay too much stress on such differences is to
ss the theological importance of interrelatedness. The vision of peace in Chapters 9
d 11 is not incompatible with the character of the servant passages. According to
s perception the two Isaiahs were placed together by the canonical editors not
cause of an accident but by deliberate intent. The historical content of Second Isaiah,
:luding the references to Cyrus, is not strong, compared with the first part of Isaiah
with Amos or Jeremiah. Understood within the context of the eighth century
ɔphet, Second Isaiah is released from its historical situation and refers not primarily
the needs of the exiles but "to the redemptive plan of God for all history." First
ιiah spoke of judgment, Second Isaiah preached forgiveness. While historically they
separate, theologically they are inseparable. That is the understanding which the
ιonical editors wished to convey by bringing together the two prophecies under
heading of the eighth century prophet.[4]

But with regard to the historical situation only, the changed conditions of the
wish people resulted in a changed tone in the prophetic message directed to people
ιo could not hear because they did not want to. They refused to believe that the
ɔphetic word applied to them. They were proud, self-confident, religiously indif-
ent, oblivious of their real danger—although they had many warnings—casually
·tain that, no matter how they behaved, because they were God's people, God would
ɔtect them. The message of the prophets was therefore often harsh and
ιdemnatory.

---

[2]Brevard S. Childs, *Introduction to the Old Testament as Scripture* (Philadelphia: Fortress Press, 1979),
27.

[3]Muilenburg, "Second Isaiah," p. 382.

[4]Childs, *Introduction to the Old Testament,* p. 327.

The Wilderness of Judaea (*Isaiah 41:19–20; Matthew 3:1*). Photo by Elizabeth Gordon.

But in 540 the Israelites had been exiled for almost fifty years. Many of the original exiles were undoubtedly dead, many born in exile, Israel still humiliated. Her country and her people were all but destroyed.

To such an audience, Second Isaiah directed a message of comfort and salvation whose opening passages are among the most gentle and loving in the Old Testament.

GOD'S ANOINTED

The theme is comfort and tenderness, good news and reward. The dispirited exile will return to Jerusalem under the care of God himself. God had been angry, bu that was past.

"For a brief moment I forsook you, but with great compassion I will gathe you" (Isaiah 54:7). The power to do this belonged to God, but his means would b Cyrus, king of Persia, whose outstanding victories and lenient policies clearly inspire Second Isaiah to the greatest admiration.

Who stirred up one from the east
> whom victory meets at every step?
. . .he tramples king under foot;
he makes them like dust with his sword. (Isaiah 41:2)

Cyrus is described as God's anointed (Isaiah 45:1), a term that carried with it implications from the earliest Israelite monarchy, when God anointed first Saul and then David (I Samuel 10:1, 16:12–13). The anointed of God was the specially chosen one, which was true of Cyrus though unknown to him because he worshipped other gods. But that was unimportant. The initiative belonged to God independently of Cyrus. Nevertheless, although Cyrus was only an instrument of God's will, he was loved by God.

Assemble, all of you, and hear!
> Who among them has declared these things?
The Lord loves him;
> he shall perform his purpose on Babylon,
> and his arm shall be against the Chaldeans. (Isaiah 48:14)

As the object of God's love he was the unwitting bearer of that love as God's "shepherd" who would fulfil his whole purpose (Isaiah 44:28).

THE UNIQUENESS OF GOD

Second Isaiah was concerned with the plight of his countrymen, and perhaps the direct occasion of his prophecies was the stirring of hope which followed Cyrus's victories. But his prophecy as a whole has a wider concern than the end of the Exile. He is credited with being the first person to present an unambiguous doctrine of ethical monotheism, the first person to state with absolute clearness that there is no other God than Yahweh, that he alone is God. All values, all knowledge, existence in its entirety proceed from, are dependent upon, and subject to God:

Thus says the Lord, the King of Israel
> and his Redeemer, the Lord of Hosts;
"I am the first and I am the last;
> besides me there is no God." (Isaiah 44:6)

The prophet imagines an assize at which those who wish can challenge God's claim. Babylon was filled with gods at the time, Bel and Marduk prominent among them, represented by wooden statues, often richly jewelled. As the military situation worsened, Nabonidus brought in the captured gods of other nations until there was a kind of celestial population explosion.

The prophet poured scorn upon them all.

Who is like me? Let him proclaim it,
> let him declare and set it forth before me (Isaiah 44:7)

With heavy sarcasm the prophet describes a workman, fashioning an idol from part of a piece of wood, lighting a fire and cooking his meal with the other. The same wood that prepares his food he bows down to; indeed, "He feeds on ashes." (Isaiah 44:20)

The prophet reiterates the majesty of God throughout his prophecy.

I am the Lord, who made all things,
> who stretched out the heavens alone,
> who spread out the earth—Who was with me? (Isaiah 44:24)

And in a passage which combines both God's uniqueness and his power:

I am the Lord, and there is no other,
> besides me there is no god.
> I give you, though you do not know me,
> that men may know, from the rising of the sun, and from the
> west that there is none besides me (Isaiah 45:5-6)

A LIGHT TO THE NATIONS

Second Isaiah's concept of God was an important development in religious thought. It must have pleased the Jewish exiles in Babylon that such a unique and omnipotent being was on their side. But the prophet made clear that the love of such a God involved those whom he loved in a responsibility.

The exiles, understandably, were thinking of themselves, and no doubt they interpreted God's loving-kindness in terms of what they wanted or they needed. None of the nations surrounding them had taken their side. Why should the exiles be concerned about them? The prophet, speaking in the name of God, had a different view. In effect he offers an interpretation of history. The people of Israel were called by Abraham. The prophet now gives the reason for that call.

I am the Lord, I have called you in righteousness
I have given you as a covenant to the people,
a light to the nations. (Isaiah 42:5-6)

Later, the charge is repeated

I will give you as a light to the nations,
that my salvation may reach to the end of the earth. (Isaiah 49:6)

The responsibility is specific. The Israelites are not to regard themselves as the sole recipients of God's love. They are the means by which that love is conveyed to all people, just as Cyrus was the means by which the exiles would be set free. The prophet broadcasts his message beyond the confines of Babylon, or even of the ancient Near East,

> Turn to me and be saved,
>> all the ends of the earth!
>> For I am God, and there is no other. (Isaiah 45:22)

This is a vision that stretches beyond the ancient world, as far as our own, to a time when everyone will acknowledge the sovereignty of God.

> By myself I have sworn,
>> from my mouth has gone forth in righteousness,
>> a word that shall not return:
> To me every knee shall bow,
>> every tongue shall swear. (Isaiah 45:23)

This is not mass conversion.[5] The reference to every knee and every tongue implies that men and women will enter as individuals, and as the reference is to *every* knee and *every* tongue, non-Jews are included too. Here is a quiet elaboration of Jeremiah's vision of religion as a pesonal, nondoctrinaire commitment. The passage has been described as one of the high peaks of Old Testament religion.[6]

THE SERVANT PASSAGES

Four passages in Second Isaiah are generally treated separately and as a group. These are Isaiah 42:1–4, 49:1–6, 50:4–9, and a longer passage at 52:13–53:12. They are called the Servant Songs because of the figure of the Servant who appears in each of them. The Servant is often described as the Suffering Servant, because of his experiences and his gentle character, but who he was remains unknown despite many interpretations.

In the first passage (Isaiah 42:1–4), we read that the Servant has been chosen by God. He is gentle, but not weak, for he will carry out the formidable task of taking God's law to all nations no matter what the difficulties.

In the second passage (Isaiah 49:1–6), we read that he was chosen before his birth. His strength is in his message and the spiritual illumination he will bring to all people.

In the third passage (Isaiah 50:4–9), we read that he is given the special ability

[5]Christopher R. North, *Isaiah 40–55* (London: SCM Presss, 1956), p. 94.
[6]Ibid.

to speak God's word. He receives careful instruction, but what he says incites great resentment. He is attacked, spat upon, yet does not resist. He is physically damaged, but is untouched by the insults. He will be defended by God himself, and vindicated. His accusers, however, will not be attacked; they will fall apart from their own weakness like cloth eaten by moths.

In the final song (Isaiah 52:13–53:12), the servant has been brutally treated and disfigured beyond recognition. We learn that his prolonged and intense suffering is borne on behalf of others. The God who chose him has placed upon him the world's guilt. In this manner he becomes responsible for evil he has not committed, and is put to death so that those who are responsible can be healed and have peace. He accepts his punishment without complaint, meanwhile suffering for those whom he is dying to save.

The Servant is believed by some to be an individual, and by others to be a corporate personality, such as Israel. On each side, the question of who the Servant was has received a "bewildering variety" of answers.[7] One writer remarks that recent treatment of the problem is marked by "the tendency for the boundaries between the different methods of interpretation to be more and more obscured and for them to merge increasingly in one another." He adds that "the division between the individual and collective interpretations has become very thin."[8]

In favor of the collective interpretation is the identification elsewhere in Second Isaiah of the Servant with Israel; for example, "But you, Israel my servant, Jacob whom I have chosen" (Isaiah 41:8). The song in Isaiah 42:1–6 is followed by a reference to God's people, who will be a light to the nations, which seems clearly to be identified with the Servant of Isaiah 42:1. As if to confirm this identity, in the second Servant Song the Servant is addressed directly as Israel, "You are my servant, Israel, in whom I will be glorified." (Isaiah 49:3)

But the identification is not clear unless a distinction is intended between an ideal Israel and an actual Israel. In verse 5 of Chapter 49, the Servant is referred to as separate from Israel. It is also puzzling that if the Servant is intended to be a corporate personality he should be described in the Servant Songs with increasingly individual characteristics. These characteristics are not to be readily transferred to Israel.

In the last two Songs the Servant suffers voluntarily and uncomplainingly for other people's sins. Israel the nation did suffer, but it was for her own lack of faith in God, not to redeem others. In fact, even in Second Isaiah there is undisguised delight at the downfall of Babylon (Isaiah 47). It is difficult to find any occasion when Israel performed a corporate saving function, except indirectly and unwittingly through the force of her religious convictions as they were grasped and interpreted by other nations.

Attempts to identify the Servant with an individual have included Hezekiah

---

[7]Ibid., p. 29.

[8]Otto Eissfeldt, *The Old Testament,* Peter Ackroyd trans. (New York: Harper and Row, 1965), p. 335.

Isaiah, Jeremiah, Moses, even Cyrus and Job. Jeremiah certainly suffered many of the indignities of the Servant. But he did not suffer them patiently.[9] Parallels have been drawn between the experience of the Servant and the myth of Tammuz, one of several deities in the ancient Near East who annually died and rose again.[10] But while that establishes a possible contemporary influence upon the writer of the Songs, it does not establish an identity with the figure of the Servant.

Among Christians the Servant has been very widely taken as a prophetic portrait of Christ. For Jews, of course, the Old Testament is the whole Bible so identifying the Servant with Christ in the New Testament is not an optional interpretation. To Christians, however, it is a lively issue. Christ is specifically identified with the Servant in Matthew 12:17, and again in Luke 2:32, where Simeon describes the infant Christ as "a light for revelation to the Gentiles" (see Isaiah 49:6). There is striking coincidence of detail between the last two Servant Songs and what we know of the suffering and the atoning death of Christ. But there is no logical entailment which leads us to accept this interpretation. It is a decision of faith. It is not impossible that the accounts of Christ's passion were written with the Servant Songs in mind, and details were emphasized which supported the identification and details which did not were left out.[11]

The spiritual achievements of Israel and the atoning work of Christ are of no less value if we cannot identify either with the Servant. But both may be considered more profoundly if we do so through the Servant metaphor, which suggests that it is not as important that the Songs be interpreted as Israel, or Christ, or Jeremiah, or Cyrus, or Second Isaiah himself, as that we try to understand what it was that the prophet had to teach us.

QUESTIONS FOR DISCUSSION

The following questions refer to Chapters 20–22.

1. Why is it that an empire, Babylon, which destroyed the most feared and powerful military force in the ancient Near East, Assyria, collapsed so swiftly? Were the reasons primarily political, military, economic, or religious? If none of the reasons was primarily to blame, was one reason more influential than the others? Try to assess their relative importance.

[9]North, *Isaiah 40–55,* p. 31.

[10]Thorkild, Jacobsen, *Toward an Image of Tammuz* (Cambridge, Mass.: Harvard University Press, 1970), pp. 45–46.

[11]See the reference to S. Mowinckel, "He That Cometh," in Harold H. Rowley, *The Servant of the Lord* (Oxford, Basil Blackwell, 1965), p. 57.

2. Does the section of the text which deals with the Suffering Servant give undue prominence to any one interpretation, or does it raise critical objections to one less than it does to the others? Which of the varying interpretations do you consider has most merit in terms of the Old Testament?

3. In certain respects the teaching of Ezekiel is similar to that of Jeremiah. But in other respects Ezekiel's concept of the nature of the Israelite community is profoundly different. Is it accurate to say that two strands in the development of Israelite religion are represented by these two prophets? If it is accurate, can one identify subsequent biblical writers as belonging to one position or the other?

4. Is the experience which Ezekiel records in Chapter 1, the vision of the wheels, of the same kind that Ezekiel records in Chapter 37, the valley of dry bones? Is either of them factual? If so, in what way? If neither is factual should we conclude that Ezekiel's visits to Jerusalem, when he was lifted up by the spirit and brought to the city, were not factual?

CHAPTER TWENTY-THREE
THE RETURN: HAGGAI AND ZECHARIAH

Babylon fell to the Persians without a battle. Its massive walls were no defense against the complete dissatisfaction of the Babylonians with their king. At the last moment Nabonidus returned to the city, took part in the New Year's Festival, and attempted to prepare for the invasion. But he seems to have relied mainly on the physical presence of the gods of his various cities which he transported to the already divinely crowded capital in such numbers that there was a general outcry.

Cyrus had shown that he could be unusually tolerant, but when he chose he could be as savage as the Assyrians. He burned the inhabitants of one Babylonian city alive. So the Babylonians were both corrupted by hope of better treatment and terrified by examples of brutality.

The city of Babylon was taken by Gobryas, one of Nabonidus's own governors who defected to Cyrus. Herodotus, a Greek historian who lived in the fifth century, states that the Persians diverted the Euphrates and then entered by the dry river bed.[1] Herodotus, however, is not reliable. It is possible that the city gates were opened by Persian sympathizers. Cyrus, in whatever way the Persians entered, ensured that the city was treated with respect. There was no looting, no destruction, and the sanctity of the Temple of Marduk, the Esagilia, was respected.

The Persian account of the conquest, written on what is known as the Cyrus

---

[1]Herodotus, *History*, Book 1, paragraph 191.

cylinder, explains how Nabonidus oppressed the people and offended the gods until Marduk, who looked through all the nations for a righteous ruler, chose Cyrus.[2] This proclamation was most likely written for the educated. An account was written in verse for the illiterate,[3] which in typical propaganda style presented Nabonidus in the worst possible light, and ended triumphantly:

> To the inhabitants of Babylon a (joyful)
>   heart is given now
> They are like prisoners when the prisons are opened
> Liberty is restored to those who were surrounded by oppression
> All rejoice to look upon him (Cyrus) as King![4]

THE RETURN

In the cylinder inscription there was a significant comment:

> I (also) gathered all their (former) inhabitants and returned (to them) their habitations. Furthermore I resettled upon the command of Marduk, the great Lord, all the gods of Sumer and Akkad whom Nabonidus has brought into Babylon to the anger of the lord of the gods, unharmed in their (former) chapels, the places which make them happy.[5]

Not among these gods in a physical sense, but present with the captive worshippers, was Yahweh, the God of the Israelites, whom Cyrus described as "the Lord, the God of heaven" (Ezra 1:2).

Rather like Elizabeth 1 of England, Cyrus's religion was respectful but political. He could see that subject peoples are more ready to accept a ruler who honors their religion and expresses a sympathetic appreciation of it. His proclamation to Israel was therefore consistent with a general policy: "Thus says Cyrus king of Persia: The Lord, the God of heaven, has given me all the kingdoms of the earth, and he has charged me to build him a house at Jerusalem, which is in Judah." (Ezra 1:2)

Another version of the proclamation, from a set of Aramaic documents, gives the dimensions of the Temple, describes its materials, and orders that the gold and silver vessels taken by Nebuchadnezzar be returned, and the expenses of the rebuilding and of the daily sacrifices be paid from the royal treasury (Ezra 6:3-5). The longed for restoration of the Temple and the city, which both Ezekiel and Second Isaiah had prophesied in vivid and inspiring detail, could now take place.

But there was no massive, joyful return of all the Israelites to Jerusalem. The

---

[2]James B. Pritchard, *Ancient and Near Eastern Texts Relating to the Old Testament* (Princeton, N.J Princeton University Presss, 1969), p. 315.

[3]Albert T. Olmstead, *History of the Persian Empire* (Chicago: University of Chicago Press, 1978), p. 5

[4]Pritchard, *Ancient and Near Eastern Texts,* p. 315. Compare Isaiah 61:1.

[5]Ibid., p. 316.

had left their previous captivity in Egypt only because conditions were unbearable, and the events of the plagues and Moses' leadership gave them enormous incentive. There was no such incentive for the exiles to leave Babylon; in fact, after sixty years from the first deportation they were comfortably settled.[6] those who thought of leaving faced an 800-mile journey along the perimeter of the Fertile Crescent, most of it on foot. When they got there, there was little to hope for about the place itself, only what it would become, what they could make of it.

Yet despite inducements to stay, and good practical reasons against returning, there were those who did return. We have a parallel to this in modern times in the migration of Jews from all over the world to Israel. Though many had comfortable homes and secure jobs in North America, Britain or other countries, they decided to go to Israel and recreate what they believed to be their homeland, accepting voluntarily loss of possessions and friends for an ideal. Similarly, those who were born in Babylon but were familiar with the prophecies of Ezekiel and Second Isaiah may have become imbued with the desire not only to learn about their tradition but, like Moses, to become a part of it.

JERUSALEM

The return from Babylon in 539 was led by Sheshbazzar, (Ezra 1:8) who was possibly the Shenazzar referred to in 1 Chronicles 3:18 as a son of Jehoiachin. If that is so, he was the legitimate heir to the throne of David.[7] One can imagine that the hopes of this first adventuresome group were high.

According to a letter sent years later to Darius, Sheshbazzar laid the foundations of the house of God in Jerusalem (Ezra 5:16).[8] We may suppose that they began as soon as they arrived, but they did not get very far. It seems that everything went wrong. There was drought and blight and hail, unseasonable cold, prices rose faster than wages until it seemed to the laborers that they put their money into a bag with holes (Haggai 1:6). Haggai declared that this was because the people built houses for themselves and neglected the house of the Lord (Haggai 1:3-4).

[6]Josephus, *Antiquities,* xi, 1.3 writes that many Jews stayed in Babylon because they were not willing to leave their possessions.

[7]See, however, Peter R. Ackroyd, *Exile and Restoration* (Philadelphia: Westminster Press, 1968), 143, where he takes an opposite view.

[8]D. Winton Thomas prefers the testimony of Haggai and Zechariah to that of Ezra because it as written much closer to the events which it describes. He notes that although Ezra writes that Sheshbazzar id the foundations of the Temple (Ezra 3:8-13), neither Haggai nor Zechariah indicates any knowledge attmepts to rebuild the Temple in 537. "The writings of these two prophets make it certain it was ly begun in 520." "Introduction to Haggai," *Interpreter's Bible,* Vol. 6 (Nashville, Tenn.: Abingdon Press, 56).

The matter is also discussed in Jacob M. Myers, *Ezra, Nehemiah* (Garden City, N.Y.: Doubleday, 65), p. xxvii.

A street in old Jerusalem. Photo by Elizabeth Gordon.

You have looked for much, and, lo, it came to little; and when you brought it home, I blew it away. Why? says the Lord of hosts. Because of my house that lies in ruins, while you busy yourselves each with his own house. (Haggai 1:9)

But the people had to live somewhere. They may have felt that the prophet was unreasonable. How could they build a Temple when sheer existence was a problem and their leader, Sheshbazzar, had either died or failed to lead?

Haggai, who wrote eighteen years later in 520, complained not only that the Temple was not yet built but that the people were saying, "The time has not yet come to rebuild the house of the Lord." (Haggai 1:2) From a practical point of view they may have been right. Perhaps the funds promised by Cyrus never came, and the money and valuables collected from the Jews in Babylon were used up. The journey from Babylon to Jerusalem was undoubtedly an expense.

But there was another reason why the people were discouraged. According to the text, after the building was resumed the "people of the land" offered to help (Ezra 4:4).[9] These people were not true Israelites. They were Jews living in Jerusalem, Judah, and Samaria who had not been exiled and were mixed with the local population. One need not suppose that their offer was insincere, but they were snubbed, and their help refused as brusquely as could be.

Zerubbabel and Jeshua (who had taken over leadership of the returned Jews) and the rest of the heads of families in Israel made their attitude very clear. "You have nothing to do with us in building a house to our God; but we alone will build to the Lord, the God of Israel, as King Cyrus the king of Persia has commanded us" (Ezra 4:3). This incident has been described as "the actual moment of birth for postexilic Judaism" which may have been more decisive in the formation of the Jewish community than the rebuilding of the Temple.[10]

It is not surprising that the people of the land "discouraged the people of Judah, and made them afraid to build." (Ezra 4:4) The returned exiles' blunt response brought out all the latent suspicion, hostility, envy, and memories, perhaps, of past antagonisms between north and south which the resident Jews had for those who returned. We read that they bribed officials at the Persian court to "frustrate their purpose." This they did through the reign of Cyrus and into the reign of Darius (Ezra 4:5).

HAGGAI

By 520, the second year of the reign of Darius, the year of Haggai's prophecy, the Temple was still unfinished. Even as far as it had gone it was a discouragement. Those who were old enough to remember Solomon's house wept at the modest dimensions

[9]For a comment on "the people of the Land" see Chapter 18 of this text, note 9.
[10]Brevard S. Childs, *Introduction to the Old Testament as Scripture* (Philadelphia: Fortress Press, 1979), p. 465.

of the new structure (Ezra 3:12–13). It was far from Ezekiel's grand vision. But Haggai refused to let them be discouraged. He may have been intransigent but he got them going. "Take courage, all you people of the land, says the Lord; work, for I am with you, says the Lord of hosts." (Haggai 2:4)

The people had been punished because of their neglect, but now God had a glorious future for them not only in Jerusalem, but everywhere.

> I will shake the heavens and the earth and the sea and the dry land; and I will shake all nations, so that the treasures of all nations shall come in, and I will fill this house with splendor, says the Lord of hosts. The silver is mine, and the gold is mine, says the Lord of hosts. The latter splendor of this house shall be greater than the former. (Haggai 2:7–9)
>
> Speak to Zerubbabel, governor of Judah, saying, I am about to shake the heavens and the earth, and to overthrow the throne of kingdoms; I am about to destroy the strength of the kingdoms of the nations, and overthrow the chariots and their riders; and the horses and their riders shall go down every one by the sword of his fellow. On that day, says the Lord of hosts, I will take you, O Zerubbabel my servant, the son of Shealtiel, says the Lord, and make you like a signet ring; for I have chosen you, says the Lord of hosts. (Haggai 2:21–23)

In 520 these were extremely incautious words. For two years the Persian empire had been in revolt against the new king, Darius, himself an usurper. The Jews were not the only people who wanted to be independent, so when Cambyses, Cyrus's son, died in 522, reputedly by his own hand, Babylon, Media Elam, Egypt, and almost every section of the empire attempted to break away. Darius defeated them all, sometimes treating rebel leaders with great ferocity. One wretched man was mutilated, blinded, and displayed in that condition until Darius was ready to have him impaled.[11]

Whether or not Haggai knew about this incident, he must have known about the general disturbances of the previous two years. It is possible that he saw them as a sign of the final world catastrophe which would introduce the Messianic age.[12] This may have explained Haggai's zealousness in urging completion of the Temple in anticipation of the Lord's return to Jerusalem.

Yet he might also have guessed that Darius, barely established on his throne, would have little patience with other potential rebels. Probably Haggai did not think about it, or, if he did, believed that God who had manipulated Assyria in the eighth century, and used Cyrus in the sixth, would protect the Jews against Darius should he fail to recognize the Messianic king. Neither he nor his prophetic colleague, Zechariah, who was in Jerusalem at the same time, and whose prophecy was written in the same year, had the political shrewdness of Jeremiah or Isaiah. It was political folly to promote a Messianic ruler at the very time that much stronger people than the Israelites had been forced to acknowledge that there was only one ruler, the Persian king. Zechariah appears to allude to this at the beginning of his prophecy: "All the earth remains at rest" (Zechariah 1:11).

---

[11]Olmstead, *History of the Persian Empire,* p. 114.
[12]Thomas, "Introduction to Haggai," p. 1037.

ZECHARIAH

Zechariah's prophecy consists of the first eight chapters of the book of Zechariah. Largely in the first person, and carefully dated, they are an account of revelations he received in the years 520–518.

The remaining six chapters are generally regarded as belonging to another writer, or possibly more than one. References to Ephraim and Judah, (Zechariah 9:10–13, 10:6) and to Syria, (Zechariah 9:1) and Assyria (Zechariah 10:10) have suggested that this part of Zechariah was written in the eighth century. But references to the rampart at Tyre (Zechariah 9:3), which was built by Alexander the Great in 332 and enabled him to capture the city, and to Greece (Zechariah 9:13) have suggested a much later date.[13] Within the Greek period, proposed dates have varied from Alexander to the Maccabaean period in the second century.[14]

The prophecy (Zechariah 1–8) is introduced by an account of Zechariah's call. There follows a series of eight visions and then a concluding promise of joy and peace in a future age when the people of Israel will be respected once again. "And as you have been a byword of cursing among the nations, O house of Judah and house of Israel, so will I save you and you shall be a blessing. Fear not, but let your hands be strong." (Zechariah 8:13)

The visions are written in a style suggestive of Ezekiel, whose work may have influenced Zechariah. The images are strange and dramatic: two women with stork's wings (Zechariah 5:9), a measuring line to measure Jerusalem (Zechariah 1:16), mountains made of bronze, and four different colored horses galloping to the four corners of the earth (Zechariah 6:1–8), an enormous flying scroll, as large as a building (Zechariah 5:1–4), and a golden lampstand with golden oil in its bowl (Zechariah 4:1–3, 11–14).

This style of writing, which may be described as proto-apocalyptic (see Chapter 26) marked a change from that of the earlier prophets, earlier than Ezekiel, whose prophecies were in general the direct revelation of a message. They did indeed employ certain poetic images and dramatic visions—Jeremiah's vision of the basket of figs (Jeremiah 24:1–3) and Amos's vision of a famine, "of hearing the words of the Lord" (Amos 8:11)—but not as a primary method of conveying God's words. Zechariah's prophecy is more indirect than these earlier prophets. In the first vision he sees a man seated on a horse standing in deep rooted myrtle, and an angel explains the meaning (Zechariah 1:8–9). In his second vision he sees a man standing with a measuring line, and the first angel is joined by a second angel who reports to Zechariah the words of Yahweh (Zechariah 2:1–9), and so on in each of the eight visions.

The prominent role that Zechariah gives to angels makes his prophecy important in the development of what is called angelology, a science which became very

[13]Otto Eissfeldt, *The Old Testament* (New York: Harper and Row, 1965), p. 437.
Childs, *Introduction to the Old Testament,* pp. 475–76,.
The use of Ephraim and Judah could be anachronistic; see 9:13, where there is a reference also to Greece.
[14]Thomas, "Introduction to Zechariah," p. 1053.

popular during the following centuries and was widespread at the time of Christ. Angels announced Christ's birth to the shepherds (Luke 2:8–14) and angels took care of him after his temptation (Matthew 4:11).

Zechariah is also one of the first Old Testament writers to refer to Satan (Zechariah 3:1-2), whose identity became increasingly more clear and widespread along with angels.

Zechariah's primary interest was rebuilding the Temple, but he looked toward the restoration of the political and spiritual eminence of Israel. He saw a dual leadership. Zerubbabel, whom he called the Branch, would assume royal dignity and would "sit and rule upon his throne. And there shall be a priest by his throne." The priest was to be Joshua (Zechariah 6:10-13). There was no political likelihood of this. Yet if he was influenced by the experience of Isaiah of Jerusalem, he may have hoped for divine intervention.

Faced with the power of Assyria and the always meddlesome power of Egypt, Isaiah's word from the Lord had been "In returning and rest you shall be saved; in quietness and in trust shall be your strength." (Isaiah 30:15)

Perhaps this was on Zechariah's mind when he wrote concering Zerubbabel, "not by might, nor by power, but by my spirit, says the Lord of hosts, (Zechariah 4:6). In a divine context he was correct, but in relating his views about Zerubbabel to the immediate contemporary situation he was incorrect. There was no way in which Zerubbabel would overthrow Darius.

We don't know whether Zerubbabel was arrested, or killed, or died, or quietly withdrew. He is not heard of again. But the Temple was built and dedicated in 515.

THE TEMPLE

Zerubbabel is described as the governor or high commissioner of Judah (Haggai 2:21), but he was subordinate to Tattenai, the Satrap of Transeuphrates, an area which included Judah (Ezra 5:3). A Satrap was literally "protector of the kingdom."[15] and had the authority of a monarch under the Persian king. He was, therefore, a person of eminence. Tattenai found out that the Jews were rebuilding their Temple and wanted to know who gave them authority to do so. He allowed them to continue building, but he sent a letter to Darius describing the questions he asked the Jews and their reply, namely that Cyrus had given them the authority about eighteen years before. He did not refer to the preaching of Haggai and Zechariah, perhaps in his view it was not important enough to take up with the king. But he treated their claim about Cyrus very seriously.

> Therefore, if it seem good to the king, let search be made in the royal archives there in Babylon, to see whether a decree was issued by Cyrus the king for the rebuilding of this house of God in Jerusalem. And let the king send us his pleasure in this matter (Ezra 5:17).

[15]Olmstead, *History of the Persian Empire*, p. 59.

When Darius received this letter he ordered a search to be made in Babylon. Nothing was found there and so the search was continued in Ecbatana, "the capital of Media" and the summer residence of the Persian kings. There, in the archives of the royal residence, the decree was found.

Darius then sent a reply acknowledging that, indeed, his predecessor had given the Jews permission to rebuild the Temple at royal expense, confirming that expenses would be paid for the building and for a supply of sacrifices, and warning Tattenai not to interfere:

> Also I make a decree that if any alters this edict, a beam shall be pulled out of his house, and he shall be impaled upon it, and his house shall be made a dunghill (Ezra 6:11).

With this encouragement the rebuilding went ahead and was completed on the twenty-third day of the month Adar, in the sixth year of King Darius (Ezra 6:15), that is on April 1, 515.

PERSIAN ADMINISTRATION

This incident is instructive, not only as an account of how the people of God overcame doubts and discouragement and official interference, but how evenhanded were the administrative policies of the Persians at this time. Tattenai could have stopped the rebuilding by his own authority, and the matter would have gone no further; Jerusalem was a very small part of a very large empire. Darius could have refused to be bothered, or, after no record of Cyrus's claim was found in Babylon, could have sent the matter back to Tattenai. Neither man did that, and from the account given it seems that it did not occur to them to do so. They acted with impartial efficiency, rather like an officer of the IRS dealing with a claim for a deduction. The decision would depend upon regulations and supporting evidence. It is also worth noting that while the biblical text implies that Tattenai was put in his place, it gives a complete enough account so that the reader is not left with a one-sided picture.

DEDICATION OF THE TEMPLE

The Temple was dedicated with a massive series of offerings in which the people were purged from their sin and the priests and Levites reestablished in their official positions and made ritually clean. But it was a selective celebration. "It was eaten by the people of Israel who had returned from exile, and also by every one who had joined them and separated himself from the pollutions of the peoples of the land to worship the Lord, the God of Israel." (Ezra 6:21-22)

Haggai and Zechariah are sometimes credited with being the founders of Judaism because they insisted that the Jews as a society should be ceremonially pure. But as we shall see, the people needed a much more profound reformation. This was provided later by Ezra.

CHAPTER TWENTY-FOUR
THIRD ISAIAH AND MALACHI

Our knowledge of life in Jerusalem between the rebuilding of the Temple, completed in 515, and the rebuilding of the city walls and the religious reforms under Nehemiah and Ezra, a period of over fifty years, is dependent upon the writing of two prophets: the author of Isaiah 56–66, known as Third, or sometimes Trito, Isaiah, and Malachi. Another prophet, Obadiah, also wrote during this period, but his prophecy is mainly a ferocious denunciation of Edom.

Isaiah 56–66 is probably not by one author.[1] For example, Isaiah 57:1–13 appears to describe conditions in Jerusalem before the Exile, although they could refer to conditions after the Temple was built as described by Malachi, whereas the remaining verses in the chapter refer to God's consolation after a period of judgment. Isaiah 63:7–19 seems to refer to the late exile or early return, when the Temple was still desecrated and reconstruction had not begun. Chapters 60 and 62, and possibly 61, are so like the writing of Second Isaiah (Isaiah 40–55), that they may have been written by him or by a close disciple.

There is no complete agreement about authorship nor about when the various

---

[1]Otto Eissfeldt, *The Old Testament* (New York: Harper and Row, 1965). Eissfeldt writes that "literary problems are hardly present in the book."

passages were written during the period after the Temple was rebuilt and before Nehemiah rebuilt the city walls:

> And your ancient ruins shall be rebuilt;
>> you shall raise up the foundation of many generations;
> you shall be called the repairer of the breach,
>> the restorer of streets to dwell in. (Isaiah 58:12)

Later in this section we read, "Foreigners shall build up your walls" (Isaiah 60:10), and then "They shall build up the ancient ruins, and they shall raise up the former devastations" (Isaiah 61:4), though that passage may not refer specifically to Jerusalem.

However, by reading Chapters 56–66, we can gain some impression of life in the city for the half century after the Temple was completed, and we find both disappointment and anger at what was taking place, and fervent hope for what the people and the city could become.

SPIRITUAL AND SOCIAL CORRUPTION

The leaders of Judah were not performing well: "They are all dumb dogs, they cannot bark; dreaming, lying down . . ." (Isaiah 56:10) As in the days of Amos, though with far less security and prosperity, the people were engaged in selfish and possibly vicious activities, rushing headlong into crime and leaving a trail of ruin and devastation (Isaiah 59:7). Again like Amos (Amos 4:5), the people were doing the proper thing but without the spiritual or religious content. People were assuring God that they wanted to know his ways, that they wanted his laws, and delighted, so they said, in approaching him. But they found excuses for not fasting, and the whole issue of fasting led to wrangling and strife and hitting "with wicked fist" (Isaiah 58:4). Why was this? There must have been a large amount of ill feeling, of "pointing of the finger" (Isaiah 58:9).

What God wanted were people who genuinely delighted in God's law, for whom fasting was not even abstention from food, but was an attempt to help people who needed help.

> Is not this the fast that I choose:
>> to loose the bonds of wickedness,
>> to undo the thongs of the yoke,
> to let the oppressed go free, and to break every yoke?
> Is it not to share your bread with the hungry,
>> and bring the homeless poor into your house;
> when you see the naked, to cover him,
>> and not to hide yourself from your own flesh? (Isaiah 58:6–7)

THE VALUE OF GENTLENESS

Like Second Isaiah, the writer of these passages values gentleness, bringing good news to the humble, binding up the broken hearted (Isaiah 61:1-2).

> But this is the man to whom I will look,
>> he that is humble and contrite in spirit,
>> and trembles at my word. (Isaiah 66:2)

> I dwell in the high and holy place,
>> and also with him who is of a contrite and humble spirit,
> to revive the spirit of the humble,
>> and to revive the heart of the contrite. (Isaiah 57:15)

In this section of Isaiah occurs an unusual characterization of God for the Old Testament. A long time before, when Moses was pressed almost to distraction by the petulant and complaining Israelites whom he was trying to lead to a new land, he cried out, "Am I their mother?" (New English Bible), or literally "did I become pregnant with" or, (Revised Standard Version), "conceive all this people." (Numbers 11:12) In Isaiah 66:13, God is likened to a mother. We read, "As one whom his mother comforts, so I will comfort you."

This quality of gentleness, which, as we saw, was an important part of the writing of Second Isaiah, is one of the reasons why it is thought that the later prophet was at least influenced by the earlier. Perhaps there was a school of prophets who shared a common view of the nature of God, and shared also a common love for poetry.

The beginning of Isaiah 60, "Arise, shine; for your light has come, and the glory of the Lord has risen upon you," is enough like the beginning of Isaiah 40 "Comfort, comfort my people, says God. Speak tenderly to Jerusalem . . ." to suggest a close literary and religious association between the two writers.

A QUALIFIED UNIVERSALISM

Like Second Isaiah, who had a vision of all nations included in the love of God (Isaiah 42:6, 49:6), the later writer declares that foreigners "who join themselves to the Lord . . . these I will bring to my holy mountain, and make them joyful in my house of prayer; their burnt offerings and their sacrifices will be accepted on my altar . . ." (Isaiah 56:6-7).[2] Yet in this instance communication with God was conditional on the foreigners keeping the Sabbath undefiled, a particularly Jewish institution. Moreover the benefits to Jerusalem would involve not only blessings to it and its inhabitants but tribute from other nations.

[2]James Muilenburg, "Introduction to Third Isaiah," *Interpreter's Bible,* Vol. 5 (Nashville, Tenn.: Abingdon Press, 1956); p. 381. Muilenburg describes the prophet's reflections upon the Temple and its cult in this passage as "among the most remarkable in the Old Testament."

Foreigners shall build up your walls,
>   and their kings shall minister to you. (Isaiah 60:10)

Just as in Zechariah 8:23, "In those days ten men from the nations of every tongue shall take hold of the robe of a Jew, saying 'Let us go with you, for we have heard that God is with you,' so the nations shall come to your light, and kings to the brightness of your rising." (Isaiah 60:3) Jerusalem shall be the center of worldwide tribute, material and honorific. But those who refuse to acknowledge the preeminence of Jerusalem will be dealt with severely. "For the nation and kingdom that will not serve you shall perish; those nations shall be utterly laid waste." (Isaiah 60:12)

EDOM

Third Isaiah is particularly bitter about Edom, the country to the southeast of Israel, long an enemy and always ready to take advantage of Israelite misfortunes. The prophet pictures the Lord, his clothes stained with blood from having taken vengeance upon the people of Edom (Isaiah 63:1–6). Obadiah, whose twenty-one verses are the shortest book in the Old Testament, writes about Edom with an animosity to be compared only with Nahum's savage outburst of the news of Assyria's downfall.

A NEW HEAVEN AND A NEW EARTH

Third Isaiah, however, goes beyond the benefits to be enjoyed by Israel and the defeat of her enemies. God's spirit and his word will remain with the people forever (Isaiah 59:21), and there will be a new heaven and a new earth. The past will not be remembered (Isaiah 65:17), so there will presumably be a different understanding of Judaism, which greatly values the past. But the new creation, as this prophet visualized it, will be distinctly Jewish. Jerusalem will be called Joy, and her people Gladness. The people will live as long as trees and they will wear out what they have made. Their race will be blessed by God. "Before they call I will answer, while they are yet speaking I will hear." (Isaiah 65:17–24)

Thus, borrowing from Isaiah of Jerusalem who lived perhaps 350 years before and whose work he must have read, he writes:

The wolf and the lamb shall feed together,
>   the lion shall eat straw like the ox;
>   and dust shall be the serpent's food.
They shall not hurt or destroy
>   in all my holy mountain,
>   says the Lord. (Isaiah 65:25)

MALACHI

Third Isaiah's contemporary, Malachi, was less visionary and far more blunt about the behavior of the people. Malachi means "my messenger," so it may be a pseudonym, (see Malachi 1:1 and 3:1).

The reference to the governor (Malachi 1:8; see Haggai 1:1) indicates a time after the conquest of Jerusalem. The unsuitable sacrifices were therefore being offered at the second Temple whose great doors are described in Malachi 1:10. The date of the book is also indicated by the reference to Edom (Malachi 1:2–5), which had been laid waste by the Arabs and was itself pushing into southern Judah, events that took place in the latter half of the fifth century. The most likely date would seem to be immediately preceding the work of Nehemiah. This would be about 450.[3]

RELIGIOUS FRAUD AND BOREDOM

After the first return in 539, work on the Temple languished (or did not even begin) for eighteen years until Haggai and Zechariah stirred the people on. With the Temple built, the Jews fell into another period of lassitude. It was not only that the strong and the wealthy oppressed the weak, particularly the widow and the orphan, but they engaged in what one might describe as grubby kinds of religious fraud. Jezebel was once an enemy of Israel but she was a woman of character and conviction. However wrong she and her priests and prophets were, they really believed in Baal. But what Malachi describes is the lowest level of so-called religious belief, comparable to some of the more odious habits of the church in prereformation Europe.

The priests in Jerusalem had become bored with what they were doing, "What a weariness this is" (Malachi 1:13). So they offered diseased and blind animals for sacrifice (Malachi 1:7–8). Worshippers vowed to offer a male, presumably "without blemish," from their flock and then offered a blemished animal (Malachi 1:14). This indifference towards formal cultic requirements was a sign of a general indifference towards God. There was widespread evasion of tithing, yet the people protested innocence of any cheating (Malachi 3:6–12).

Personal behavior suffered, with a proliferation of divorce. Divorce was not difficult for a man to obtain during Old Testament times, and so was open to abuse. Malachi was the first Old Testament writer to come down strongly against the practice; "I hate divorce" (Malachi 2:16).

Such behavior among his fellow Jews was contrasted with the respect that non-Jews gave to God.

> For from the rising of the sun to its setting my name is great among the nations, and in every place incense is offered to my name, and a pure offering; for my name is great among the nations, says the Lord of hosts. (Malachi 1:11)

[3]Robert C. Dentan, "Introduction to Malachi," *The Interpreter's Bible*, (Nashville, Tenn.: Abingdon Press, 1956), p. 1117.

The prophet must have known that, as a matter of fact, the nations were not offering gifts to Yahweh. That was not their intention. But what he clearly means is that the divine sacrifices of heathen worshippers were, in effect, offerings to God. This has been described as a more far-reaching expression of universalistic monotheism than any other passage in the Old Testament.[4]

While the heathen were offering pure gifts, acceptable to God, the people, chosen by God, who were to be a light to the nations, were neglectful of all interests but their own. The implication, at least, was that, failing in their responsibility, it would be taken from them. Amos had said as much to the Israelites of the eighth century (Amos 9:7-8).

According to Malachi a day would come when "all the arrogant and all evildoers will be stubble." They will be set ablaze and left with neither root nor branch (Malachi 4:1-2). The evildoers were the people of Israel. But, he adds, for those who fear the Lord's name, "the sun of righteousness shall rise, with healing in its wings."

There is an impressive realism in the thought of men such as Malachi, "who do not oversimplify the problems of their time, and whose recognition of human failure and divine promise is held together in soberness and confidence."[5]

The book of Malachi was regarded as important by the early Christian church. It is quoted (with part of Isaiah 40:3) at the beginning of Mark (Mark 1:2), Matthew and Luke to refer to Malachi in connection with John the Baptist, the messenger going before (Matthew 11:10, Luke 1:17-76; 7:27). In Revelation 6:17, the day of vengeance of the Lamb is predicted. "Who," asks the writer "can stand before it?" This is an oblique reference to Malachi 3:2, "who can endure (or abide) the day of his coming?" (a familiar passage to those who sing or listen to oratorios)

[4]Ibid.
[5]Peter R. Ackroyd, *Exile and Restoration* (Philadelphia: The Westminster Press, 1968), p. 231.

CHAPTER TWENTY-FIVE
THE PROPHETS
EZRA AND NEHEMIAH

THE MURASHU FAMILY

About eighty years ago our knowledge of Jewish life in Babylon was greatly enlarged by the discovery of several hundred cuneiform clay tablets written during the reigns of Artaxerxes 1, Darius II, and Artaxerxes II (465–358). These were the records of a Babylonian commercial family named Murashu which did a considerable business for several generations, and included among its customers a number of Jews.

The family itself was not Jewish, and it is not possible to identify from the lists of names who of its customers were and were not Jews. As one writer remarks, "There are in the Murashu documents more names of Jews than Jewish names."[1] Nevertheless, some of these customers have been identified as Jewish. We therefore get a glimpse of the conditions of life among the exiles, which suggests that they were as much a part of Babylonian society as their descendants from Europe were a part of the life of New York City twenty-four hundred years later.

Among the cuneiform tablets is a contract between several members of the Jewish family of Tob Yaw and the sons of Murashu to rent an irrigation canal, with a field and marshes, for three years at 700 Kur of barley per year, plus a surcharge

[1]Michael David Coogan, *West Semetic Personal Names in the Murashu Documents* (Chico, California: Scholars Press, 1976), p. 121.

of two grazing bulls and twenty grazing rams. The land was owned by absentee landlords who invested it with the Murashu family for a guaranteed percentage return. This is the same procedure as our depositing money in a bank for so much interest, and the bank using the money to make a profit. One Jew, El-Yadin, was co-creditor with a member of the Murashu family. He must therefore have been a wealthy man. It is possible that some Jewish fathers gave their children two names: a Babylonian or Babylonian-sounding name for legal and perhaps professional purposes, and a Jewish name. For example, Esther is a Babylonian name derived from the name of the Goddess Ishtar. Her Jewish name was Hadassah, which means myrtle (Esther 2:7). But there is no evidence of discrimination on religious or ethnic grounds. The Jews were free to worship as they wished and conduct such business as they wished. In this respect Babylon in the Persian empire was more advanced than societies many centuries later.

Jeremiah had told the Jews in Babylon to settle down for a long exile and become a part of their new city.

> Thus says the Lord of hosts, the God of Israel, to all the exiles whom I have sent into exile from Jerusalem to Babylon: Build houses and live in them; plant gardens and eat their produce. Take wives and have sons and daughters; take wives for your sons, and give your daughters in marriage, that they may bear sons and daughters; multiply there, and do not decrease. But seek the welfare of the city where I have sent you into exile, and pray to the Lord on its behalf, for in its welfare you will find your welfare. (Jeremiah 29:4–9)

From the evidence of the Murashu tablets the Jews may have become integrated into the economic life of Babylonian society more than Jeremiah intended. Was that a factor in the events described in Ezra 10? One Jew, however, who had not become integrated to that extent was Nehemiah.

AUTHORSHIP AND DATE

The book of Nehemiah and its companion volume Ezra, which precedes it, are the continuation of 1 and 2 Chronicles. As if to make the point clear to the reader, the last two verses of 2 Chronicles are the first two verses of Ezra. There is general agreement that one author/editor was responsible for the whole work, and that he drew upon a variety of sources: the personal memoirs of Ezra and Nehemiah (Ezra 7:28, Nehemiah 2:11), third person accounts (Ezra 10:2, Nehemiah 3:16), and official documents (Ezra 7:11). Parts of Ezra were written in Aramaic (Chapters 4:7–6:18, :12–26). There has been much discussion about when these parts were written and how historically reliable they are. It is possible that Ezra himself was the author/editor.[2]

[2]Jacob M. Myers, *Ezra, Nehemiah* (Garden City, N.Y.: Doubleday, 1965), p. Lxiii.
Jacob M. Myers, *I Chronicles,* 2d ed. (Garden City, N.Y.: Doubleday, 1965), p. Lxxxvi.

The main work was probably completed about 400 B.C. This is indicated in the royal genealogies of 1 Chronicles 3:17–24 and the list of high priests in Nehemiah 12:10–11. Had there been further names, they would have been included, especially of the high priests. The list presumably ends at the time of writing, about 400.[3]

NEHEMIAH

The condition of life of the Jews in Jerusalem was vastly more difficult than that of the Jews in Babylon. One of the major problems was physical safety. In 445 the city wall was broken and the gates destroyed by fire (Nehemiah 1:3). The city was then open territory to any who wanted to plunder it, and although there was a Persian administration, the local authorities were not at that time friendly.

The incident in Ezra 4:6–23 tells us that the people began to rebuild the walls without permission, for self-defense.[4] This provoked a hostile reaction from Rehum, the Persian high commissioner. He accused the city of attempted rebellion, and sent a letter of complaint to King Artaxerxes, who agreed with the commissioner and ordered that the work be stopped, which it was, by force of arms (Ezra 4:23).

Meanwhile the land suffered from locusts and drought. It must have seemed to the beleagured people that everything was contrary. No wonder they were discouraged, no wonder their divorce rate was high. There is a touch of real indignation in their reply to Malachi's complaints: "You have wearied the Lord with your words. Yet you say, 'How have we wearied him?' By saying, 'Every one who does evil is good in the sight of the Lord, and he delights in them.' Or by asking, 'Where is the God of justice?' " (Malachi 2:17)

It is difficult to remain a steadfast believer when every effort seems to fail. Priests and lay alike in Jerusalem were despondent, fearful and without confidence in God or in themselves.

Reports from the city were therefore understandably upsetting to someone like Nehemiah who, though he lived and worked hundreds of miles away, regarded Jerusalem as his spiritual home. When his brother, Hanani, arrived from Judah and described the conditions there, particularly in Jerusalem, Nehemiah sat down and wept (Nehemiah 1:4).

Nehemiah, however, was in a position to do something. As the king's cupbearer that is, as a high court official (something like a White House advisor) (Nehemiah 2:1) he had direct access to the king. But the task was a delicate one. Reconstruction of the wall had already been stopped by the king's order (Ezra 4:17–24). Nehemiah could not simply ask him to reverse his decision. But with considerable tact this is what he succeeded in having the king do.[5] Artaxerxes, therefore, appointed Nehemiah

[3]Myers, *Ezra, Nehemiah*, p. Lxx.

[4]Ezra 6–23 describes an incident in the building of the walls in the midst of an account of the building of the Temple, which took place about seventy years earlier.

[5]Albert T. Olmstead, *History of the Persian Empire* (Chicago: University of Chicago Press, 197_ pp. 314–15. Olmstead gives an imaginative but plausible description of how Nehemiah achieved his objective, based on Nehemiah 2:1–8.

governor of Judah (Nehemiah 5:14), with authority to requisition building materials, and he allowed him an agreed-upon time for a leave of absence.

The rebuilding of the walls is one of the stirring sagas of the Old Testament, and is a tribute to Nehemiah's courage, faith, and resourcefulness. After arriving in Jerusalem he waited for three days without explaining why he had come. He then rode around the walls at night, examining their gaps and burnt-out gates, and finally spoke to the people of the city: "You see the trouble we are in, how Jerusalem lies in ruins with its gates burned. Come, let us build the wall of Jerusalem, that we may no longer suffer disgrace." (Nehemiah 2:17)

He assigned different parts of the wall and different gates to different groups of Jews: the Fish Gate was built by the sons of Hassenaah, the Valley Gate was repaired by Hanun and the inhabitants of Zanoah. The men of Tekoa repaired a section of the wall from a point opposite the great projecting tower as far as the wall of Ophel (Nehemiah 3:3), and so on.

OPPOSITION

Nehemiah's problems were not with the construction of the wall. That went ahead surprisingly well, considering what had to be done with unskilled volunteers. It was the sustained opposition which included almost every type of harassment and intimidation except an outright assault on the city.

Sanballat is known from papyrus texts written by Jewish settlers in Elephantine, Egypt, as governor of Samaria, a larger territory of which Judah was a part. He probably objected to Nehemiah taking away some of his authority, and he and his colleagues did everything they could to prevent the walls from being rebuilt. At first they resorted to ridicule. "What are these feeble Jews doing? Will they restore things? Will they sacrifice? Will they finish up in a day?. . .Yes, what they are building— if a fox goes up on it he will break down their stone wall!" (Nehemiah 4:2–3) Sanballat then threatened to attack the volunteers and apparently made some preparations, enough to alarm them. His threats added mental stress to already physically exhausting work. How serious they were is hard to determine. Nehemiah did have royal authority, and he was an important official, so his opponents could not have gone too far. But Nehemiah took no chances. From then on, while half of his men were working on the wall the other half stood guard. If danger threatened at any point a trumpeter would sound an alarm,[6] and workers and guards from other sections of the wall would run to help (Nehemiah 4:16–23).

The work progressed rapidly despite opposition, and the walls were completed. But before the gates had been installed Sanballat attempted to allure Nehemiah from the city to "confer" with him; more likely, as Nehemiah suspected, to do him harm, perhaps to murder him (Nehemiah 6:1–4). When that failed his antagonists, and there were many in the city itself, accused Nehemiah of trying to make himself king. He was not disturbed and told them plainly that they were lying. "For they all wanted to frighten us" he wrote, "thinking, 'Their hands will drop from the work, and it will not be done.' " (Nehemiah 6:9)

It is possible that Nehemiah's description of Sanballat was unfair. In terms of the political realities of the time, Sanballat may have had valid cause to suspect Nehemiah of engineering a rebellion,[7] yet attempts at rebellion amounted to suicide unless they had some chance of success. Walls built in less than two months were not militarily significant, and in any case Nehemiah had been authorized to build them by Artaxerxes himself. One may assume that Sanballat, though he was genuinely alarmed at what Nehemiah was doing (if rebellion broke out in Judah he might be held responsible), knew that his charge of rebellion was farfetched. He might have taken Nehemiah's visit as an indirect royal rebuke for not caring properly for one of the cities in his territory. It is possible that, coming from the central administration of the empire, Nehemiah did not think it necessary to explain his activities to the local officials, hence his self-assurance, if not his imperial attitude towards his opponents, and the intense but nevertheless restrained antagonism on the part of Sanballat and his fellows.

Their final stratagem is an example of that restraint. It was a subtle attempt to play on Nehemiah's piety. They reasoned that although he was suspicious of them he might pay attention to a prophet, so they bribed Shemaiah to warn Nehemiah that he must take refuge in the Temple sanctuary and shut the doors, "for they are coming to kill you, at night they are coming to kill you." (Nehemiah 6:10)

> But I said, "Should such a man as I flee? And what man such as I could go into the temple and live? I will not go in." And I understood, and saw that God had not sent him, but he had pronounced the prophecy against me because Tobiah and Sanballat had hired him. For this purpose he was hired, that I should be afraid and act in this way and sin, and so they could give me an evil name, in order to taunt me (Nehemiah 6:11–14)

None of their efforts worked. The wall was built in fifty-two days, and Nehemiah wrote proudly: "And when all our enemies heard of it, all the nations round about us were afraid and fell greatly in their own esteem; for they perceived that this work had been accomplished with the help of our God." (Nehemiah 6:16)[8]

NEHEMIAH'S REFORMS

The walls gave the city physical security, but the Jews who lived in the city were not secure in their faith and their responsibilities as a Covenant people. The walls allowed the people to survive; much more serious work had to be done to restore them spiritually. Nehemiah attempted some reforms, but it was Ezra, with his rough discipli

[6]According to Josephus there was a trumpeter every 500 feet. Flavius Josephus, *Antiquities of Jews*, XI 5.8. There are many editions of this work.

[7]Olmstead, *History of the Persian Empire*, p. 316.

[8]Myers, *Ezra, Nehemiah*, p. xxxiv.

and ethnic and religious exclusivism, who really succeeded. It is ironic that the Jewish people, for centuries the victims of discrimination, were saved from possible oblivion only by a rigid policy of discrimination against others.

Nehemiah did what he could when he was presented with a problem but he did not enforce long-term rules. Many Jews had fallen into debt to their fellow Jews, a number of whom not only took all their property but the debtors themselves, or their children, as slaves. With great indignation Nehemiah excoriated such a practice.

> "The thing that you are doing is not good. . . Return to them this very day their fields, their vineyards, their olive orchards, and their houses, and the hundredth of money, grain, wine, and oil which you have been exacting of them." Then they said, "We will restore these and require nothing from them. We will do as you say." And I called the priests, and took an oath of them to do as they had promised. (Nehemiah 5:9–12)

However, this may be regarded as another instance of Nehemiah's overzeal-ousness. While enslaving fellow countrymen is bad, legitimate business must cease if all contracts are voided.[9] Because there are serious abuses in a system it does not follow, as it did for Nehemiah, that the system should be abolished.

At some point, possibly after returning from the court, Nehemiah discoverd that Aliashib, the priest, had provided a room in the sanctuary for Tobiah, a subordinate of Sanballat and a notable enemy of the Jews. Nehemiah simply threw out all of Tobiah's belongings and had the room purified (Nehemiah 13:6–9).

He was equally direct in other matters. He objected to business activities taking place on the Sabbath. He thereupon ordered the city gates shut on the Sabbath and threatened legal action against merchants who camped outside the gates (Nehemiah 13:15–22).

He greatly objected to mixed marriage and regarded it as an abomination that some of the children of Jews could not speak Hebrew.

> In those days also I saw the Jews who had married women of Ashdod, Ammon, and Moab; and half of their children spoke the language of Ashdod, and they could not speak the language of Judah, but the language of each people. And I contended with them and cursed them and beat some of them and pulled out their hair; and I made them take oath in the name of God, saying, "You shall not give your daughters to their sons, or take their daughters for your sons or for yourselves." (Nehemiah 13:23–25)

Almost the final comment of Nehemiah was "Thus I cleansed them from everything foreign." (Nehemiah 13:30)

THE CHRONOLOGY OF EZRA AND NEHEMIAH

According to the biblical text, Ezra came to Jerusalem in the seventh year of King Artaxerxes, 458 (Ezra 7:8). He carried with him a letter from the king requiring the

---

[9]Olmstead, *History of the Persian Empire,* p. 345.

people, on pain of death, banishment, confiscation, or imprisonment, to obey the Law of their God (Ezra 7:11-16).

Nehemiah arrived in Jerusalem in the twentieth year of Artaxerxes, thirteen years later, 445 (Nehemiah 2:1), as the result of the very discouraging report he received from his brother Hanani who had just returned from Judah (Nehemiah 1:1-4). Nehemiah stayed in Jerusalem for twelve years, returning to Persia in 433, the thirty-second year of Artaxerxes (Nehemiah 13:6). Some time before the king died in 424, Nehemiah came back to Jerusalem and corrected a number of abuses which had developed or had grown noticeably worse during his absence.

It is not clear when Ezra carried out his reforms. He went to Jerusalem during a dangerous time, without a guard, because he was ashamed to ask the king for an escort, having said so much about the power of God to protect his own people. This is one of the most candidly human insights that the Scriptures give us about Ezra (Ezra 8:21-24). It would seem that the reforms would naturally have taken place as soon as possible after he arrived, and that is how it appears in the book of Ezra. In Nehemiah, however, the reforms appear to have taken place after the building of the wall in 545 (Nehemiah 8:1), thirteen years later.

The chronology, based on the biblical text, is problematical. Nevertheless "until new material is presented, the evidence would suggest that Nehemiah preceded Ezra; the former being active in the reign of Artaxerxes I and the latter in the reign of Artaxerxes II. This provisional solution has been widely accepted. . . ."[10]

EZRA'S REFORMS

The debate does not alter the main point, that through the efforts of Nehemiah and Ezra, the Jewish community in Jerusalem, which was in danger of disintegration, was pulled together into a tough and enduring group of Covenant believers. The measures insisted upon by Ezra were draconian, but they worked. More gentle, compassionate measures would probably not have worked.

The primary task of Ezra was to confront his people with their responsibility to the Covenant and the law, and then to insist upon extremely painful reforms. The book of Nehemiah describes how Ezra read the law to the people from early morning until noon. As they listened to what they were supposed to do, and were not doing, they wept (Nehemiah 8:1-10).

What disturbed Ezra more than anything else was the extensive intermarriage between the Jewish community and surrounding nations. It seemed to him that if it continued, the Jews would be lost as a separate people, just as the ten northern tribes were lost, and he was right. The only recourse was to stop intermarriage completely, and to break ties between the foreign wives and children and their Jewish

---

[10]John J. Hayes and J. Maxwell Miller, *Israelite and Judaean History* (Philadelphia: Westmintste Press, 1977), p. 509.

Samaritan teacher with the Samaritan Pentateuch. Photo by Elizabeth Gordon

husbands. This basically cruel act—and it certainly does not seem to be consistent
with the teaching of a God of love, (see Leviticus 19:18)—was justified by regarding
the foreign wives and children as unclean, particularly because some foreign religious
practices might influence their husbands. It was not assumed that the strength of
a husband's belief in God could be stronger than the strength of his wife's belief in,
say, Chemosh.

> And Ezra the priest stood up and said to them, "You have trespassed and married foreign
> women, and so increased the guilt of Israel. Now then make confession to the Lord the
> God of your fathers, and do his will; separate yourselves from the peoples of the land
> and from the foreign wives." Then all the assembly answered with a loud voice, "It is
> so; we must do as you have said." (Ezra 10:10–12)

There were only four men who objected, Jonathan, Jahzeiah, Meshullam, and
Shabbethai (Ezra 10:15). The majority prevailed. A case-by-case inquiry was carried
out (Ezra 10: 16–17), perhaps to mitigate the hardship involved for the women who
had married in good faith and were suddenly declared unclean and unwanted. A
list is given of men who had married foreigners, and the book of Ezra ends with the
comment: "All these had married foreign women, and they put them away with their
children." (Ezra 10:44)

The extreme nature of the measure helps to explain why its results were enduring. One cannot believe that all the Jewish husbands were so inspired by religious enthusiasm that they had no regrets. There must have been many very agonized partings.

Having divorced their foreign wives, the break was not only personal but also
social and political. The Jewish husbands would certainly have aroused intense hostility
on the part of their former wives' own families. If the Jews had enemies before, they
would have had many more after.

There were therefore strong incentives not to backslide. Furthermore, such
matters as Sabbath observance and financial responsibility to the Temple, which had
been a continuing problem in the past, would be comparatively minor after the sacrifice
of the marriage relationship.

To destroy a family in the name of God is to pay a price which can be justified
only if the purpose of the destruction, the purity of the nation, is shown to be more
precious than the family. Having taken that step, the Jewish people were psychologically
and emotionally obligated to make it work.

QUESTIONS FOR DISCUSSION

The following questions refer to Chapters 23–25.

1. What happened to the Jews who fled to Egypt after the fall of Jerusalem, taking Jeremiah with them? What happened to the Jews who remained in Babylon after the return? Does their history provide any indication of what might have happened to all the Jews, had some not returned to Jerusalem?

2. "The winning enthusiasm and amusingly naive self-appreciation of Nehemiah's memoirs cannot blind us to the fact that Sanballat and his colleagues had a good prima facie case." (A. T. Olmstead, *History of the Persian Empire*) Olmstead's claim must be judged in terms of the evidence he uses to support it. Assuming that the claim is correct, is it possible that he was interpreting the evidence in one way and that another person could interpret the same evidence in a different way?

3. How justified do you think were the drastic reforms initiated by Ezra? Consider an argument that only such measures could have preserved the people of Israel and their religion from extinction. Consider another argument, that these reforms resulted in an ethnic and religious exclusiveness inconsistent with such biblical texts as Second Isaiah, Ruth, and Jonah. What are the merits of these two arguments?

4. It has been claimed that the biblical story of the Jews during the two hundred years after the fall of Jerusalem becomes a vitally new history when viewed against its contemporary Persian background. What is contributed by a knowledge of Persian history, and how does it make this period of Jewish history new and vital?

CHAPTER TWENTY-SIX

THE BOOK OF DANIEL AND THE HELLENISTIC AGE

HISTORICAL BACKGROUND

The events of the book of Daniel are set for the most part in the reign of Nebuchadnezzar. The opening chapter provides a brief acount of the capture of Jerusalem in 598 and the first deportation, when Jehoiakim, king of Judah, was taken to Babylon with numerous other prisoners, including Daniel (Daniel 1:1-6).

But it is evident that the writer was not familiar with the details of the history of that period. He confuses Nebuchadnezzar, the first Babylonian king, with Nabonidus, the last. He represents Belshazzar as Nebuchadnezzar's son (Daniel 5:1-2) when in fact he was Nabonidus's son. He describes Belshazzar as king (Daniel 5:1) but Belshazzar never was king, although he represented his father in Babylon; and he credits the overthrow of Babylon to Darius the Mede, who is not an historical figure (Daniel 5:30-6:1), when it was Cyrus who defeated Babylon.

The historical details in the book are nevertheless precise and accurate from the conquests of Alexander to the reign of Antiochus Epiphanes. This would be understandable if the author were writing about his more recent past, and about contemporary events. In fact, it is generally considered that the book of Daniel was written during the latter end of that period, the reign of Antiochus, a time of great peril for the Jews.

In 334–333 the Persian Empire, which had lasted for just 200 years, was conquered by Alexander the Great. After Alexander's sudden and early death about ten years later, his huge territories, which stretched from Greece to northern India, were divided into four parts ruled by four of his generals. The book of Daniel refers to this:

> Then a mighty king shall arise, who shall rule with great dominion and do according to his will. And when he has arisen, his kingdom shall be broken and divided toward the four winds of heaven, but not to his posterity, nor according to the dominion with which he ruled; for his kingdom shall be plucked up and go to others. (Daniel 11:3–4)

One of the generals, Ptolemy, gained control of Egypt, and established his capital at Alexandria, a city founded by Alexander in 332 to commemorate his conquest of Persia. Another general, Seleucus, took control of Babylonia, Syria, and Persia. Both Ptolemy and Seleucus wanted to control Palestine for the same reasons that Egypt and the Hittites had wanted to control it a thousand years before. It was militarily strategic and economically valuable. For about a century Palestine, and with it Jerusalem, was subject to the Ptolemies until 198 when Antiochus the Great, ruler of the Seleucid empire, defeated Egypt at Panium, near Dan, and Palestine became a part of his dominion.

With the acquisition of Palestine Antiochus ruled a huge empire, comparable to Alexander's except that it did not include Greece or Egypt. But having conquered so much he was certain he could conquer more. The Romans had just defeated Carthage. The Carthaginian general Hannibal fled to the Seleucid court and apparently persuaded Antiochus to invade Greece. That was a disastrous error. The Seleucid empire was far larger than the Roman. It did not, however, compare in military strength. Antiochus suffered a humiliating defeat. He was required to pay a huge indemnity, give up considerable portions of his territory and his military and naval forces, and send his son to Rome as a hostage (Daniel 11:7–19). It was this son who, as Antiochus IV Epiphanes, created the situation which led some unknown patriot to write the book of Daniel.

ANTIOCHUS EPIPHANES

Antiochus is universally and rightly condemned for his brutal treatment of the Jews. Self-interested, cruel, insensitive, he became their total enemy.

He twice "sold" the office of High Priest which was held by Onias, something no one had done before. But it was the brother of the High Priest himself, Jason, who made the offer to Antiochus. Three years later Antiochus gave the office to a more generous bidder, Menelaus, who was put up to it, it is believed, by a rival leading Jewish family. Menelaus therefore displaced Jason as Jason had displaced the rightful High Priest Onias. But he went even further; he had Onias murdered and attempted to plunder the Temple to pay his debt to Antiochus, (2 Maccabees 4:23–34).

Antiochus was not particular about the theological politics of one of his many cities. He had the authority to make and unmake high office; the Jewish High Priesthood was not sacrosanct to him. He may not have even heard of Moses and Aaron and the long priestly tradition. If he had, he could not have thought it important when two leading Jewish families were trying to destroy one another, motivated not by the tradition they were obligated to preserve but by the crassest kind of power politics. Antiochus was familiar with political power; he had used it himself to get the throne. He was not to know from his experience with Jason and Menelaus that the High Priesthood was genuinely regarded as sacred by the Jews, and that Jewish belief in one creator God could not be compromised.

The story of the worsening relations between Antiochus and the Jews is told with great intensity in 2 Maccabees 4–5. Jason, the deposed usurper, hearing a rumor that Antiochus was dead, attacked Jerusalem and took the Temple, but he committed such atrocities that he was driven out by his own people. Antiochus, however, regarded what Jason had done as a Jewish rebellion. He reestablished Menelaus and plundered the Temple.

THE GROWTH OF HELLENISM

Antiochus, who was Syrian, not Greek, was undoubtedly encouraged in his hard attitude toward the Jews by the fact that many of them adopted Greek ways. Jason, for example, who usurped his brother's position, not only wanted to be High Priest, he also wanted to establish Greek ideas in Jerusalem.[1] Jason built a gymnasium in Jerusalem, which created a scandal because it was the custom for Greek athletes to exercise nude, and nudity was abhorrent to the Jews. But although some Jews were shocked, there were others who embraced Greek culture with enthusiasm, who were ashamed of their circumcision and tried to remove it. We read (2 Maccabees 4:11-15), that Temple priests became more interested in a wrestling school than in the Temple, more concerned with Greek honors than with serving God.

The incident of the gymnasium is an example of how the conflict between Jew and Greek was not just a matter of sports appealing to young people more than their parents' old ways. That happens probably in every generation. The issue was both more general and more precise.

Greece and Palestine had traded with one another and exchanged ideas long before the appearance of Israel. It is argued that Alexander did not introduce Greek culture to Palestine when he conquered the ancient Near East in the fourth century, "he found it there."[2] What we call Hellenization, a process which affected Greece

---

[1]Louis H. Feldman, review of M. Hengel, *Judaism and Hellenism* in *Journal of Biblical Literature*, Vol. 96.3 1977, pp. 371–82. Hengel's book is a lengthy argument in favor of the widespread and early influence of Greek language and culture upon the Jews in Palestine "at least a century earlier than the Maccabean revolt of 168." Feldman challenges this argument. He is supported by Norman W. Porteous *Daniel* (Philadelphia: The Westminster Press, 1965), pp. 19–20. However, see Morton Smith, *Palestinia Parties and Politics That Shaped the Old Testament* (New York: Columbia University Press, 1971).

[2]Smith, *Palestinian Parties*, p. 61.

Hellenistic tower in Samaria. Photo by Elizabeth Gordon.

as well as the Near East, has been described as "a vast tissue of change, in which innumerable strands of independent, but parallel development are interwoven." The result was not simply the spread of Greek culture as such but the creation of a new culture, the Hellenistic, "no less different from classical Greek culture than from the culture of the more ancient Near East."[3]

Antiochus would therefore not have regarded Jason's enthusiasm for Greek ways

[3]Ibid., p. 76.

as anything other than the ordinary expression of a contemporary interest shared widely by the Hellenistic, Greek-Oriental society in which they all lived, and so, presumably, by all but a few intransigent Jews.

For the strict Jews, however, those to whom the reforms of Ezra were important, Hellenistic society presented as great a danger as Canaanite society had presented in the early days of the settlement. Cultural assimilation was a serious challenge. If Antiochus had not provided the Jews with a cause which aroused their religious and ethnic nationalism, the distinctiveness and the influence of Judaism could have waned during the following two centuries.[4] But Antiochus's tactlessness and cruelty, and his ardent support of Greek ways stirred the Jews to champion their own ways with equal ardor, and to separate themselves from a culture which until then they accepted widely.

A CONFLICT OF IDEOLOGIES

The Greeks, it has been said, were the first people to be in love with play.[5] They had an enthusiasm for life, a zest, a spirit in striking contrast to the general seriousness of the ancient world. Of course Egyptians, Jews, Assyrians, and Persians laughed and relaxed, but that was incidental to the main business. For the Greeks, in an elusive fashion, it was the main business, not play in place of work, but as an attitude to work and what they attempted and accomplished.

However, games, in the form of athletics were not only play, they were part of Greek religion. The Olympic games, the ultimate level of Greek athletics, were held in honor of Zeus. Other great athletic festivals were held to honor Athena and Apollo and took place on sacred ground. Their objective, the objective of all physical training among the Greeks, was to develop a particularly Greek quality called *arete,* which is often translated as virtue, but means much more than the modern usage of the term. In Aristotle's phraseology it was all the potential of a human actualized in thought and behavior. So the Greeks' delight in physical exercise, their admiration of physical beauty, was part of their belief in the wholeness of life, to be rejoiced in religiously as much as aesthetically or physically.

The conservative Jews were fully aware of the implications of this, and it greatly disturbed them, for in Hellenistic culture they encountered the same self-confident superiority that characterized their own. The Greeks in general were not vainglorious, but they knew that they were superior in intelligence, in literature, in art, in government, in religion, and in war. To be a Greek was to be a superior person blessed by

[4]However, it is argued that in the Seleucid realm Hellenistic Greek culture was actually in danger of being submerged by oriental culture. According to this, Antiochus was not trying to institute and encourage but to revive Hellenism. See *Cambridge Ancient History,* Vol. VII, p. 189.

[5]Edith Hamilton, *The Greek Way* (New York: Avon Books, 1973), p. 19.

the special providence of Zeus and, in Athens, protected by Athena. That view was still latent in Hellenistic society three hundred years after Pericles.

The Jews were not vainglorious, but they knew that the God of all the earth had called them to be his people. They were intelligent, yet to them the fear of the Lord was the beginning of wisdom. They were unself-consciously aware of their achievements in theological thought and literature. To be a Jew was to be a chosen person, chosen from among all people, bound by a Covenant, assured of God's special care.

Alexander the Great not only conquered the ancient Near East, he was in some sense a missionary for Greek ideas and Greek ways. Throughout his empire he established replicas of Greek cities with gymnasiums and theaters, where the ideals of Greek culture were encouraged by thousands of Greeks who emigrated from their country, and this policy of acculturation or Hellenization was continued by the generals who succeeded him.

The Jews did not have a missionary zeal of that kind but they knew that through them all nations would be blessed (Genesis 12:1–3), that they were the light to all nations, that they and they alone would bring salvation "to the end of the earth" (Isaiah 49:6).

To the Greeks all non-Greeks were barbarians, not because they were primitive and uncultivated—the Egyptians, for example, were neither—but because they did not speak Greek. Non-Greek languages sounded like a meaningless "ba, ba, ba," hence the word "barbarian." But it was not only a matter of not speaking Greek; the barbarian was one who did not understand or appreciate Greek ways, he belonged to that section of the world which was non-Greek and so despite itself was in some sense inferior. In Hellenistic society, the upper classes spoke Greek. Semitic speakers belonged to a lower class, and that included most Jews.[6]

To all Jews all non-Jews were Goiim, or Gentiles. Often they were more cultured than the Jews, such as the Egyptians and the Phoenicians. Even as late as the building of the second Temple in 515, the Jews had to rely on Phoenician craftsmen, but that was of little account compared with the fact that the Jews were a chosen people, and others were not.

Hence for the first time since they left Egypt, the Jews came into conflict with a people who were as convinced as they were of their special status, and were as unwilling to yield on any matters they considered essential to their way of life. The gymnasium represented the Greek way, as the Temple represented the Jewish way, and just as the Jews did all that they could to banish the gymnasium from Jerusalem, so the Greeks, most unworthily represented by Antiochus Epiphanes, did all that they could to discredit and even to destroy the Temple.

---

[6]Humphrey Kitto, *The Greeks* (Baltimore: Penguin Books, 1957), pp. 7–12. Kitto offers this explanation of the origin of the word "barbarian" and discusses the Greek attitude toward non-Greeks. Smith, *Palestinian Parties,* p. 79.

THE FIRST RELIGIOUS PERSECUTION

With ample justification, the writer of Daniel describes Antiochus IV as a "contemptible person" who came to the throne by intrigue and who "broke" the Prince of the Covenant, that is, he abetted the murder of Onias (Daniel 11:21–22). The text is cryptic but it describes Antiochus's career quite clearly. The "king of the south" (Daniel 11:25) was the young king of Egypt, Ptolemy Philometor, who was defeated by Antiochus and captured. Antiochus invaded Egypt again and defeated Philometor's successor. But within striking distance of Alexandria he was met by the Roman legate C. Papillius Laenas, who told him bluntly to get out of Egypt. Antiochus asked for time to think about it, but the legate drew a circle round him on the ground and told him that he would not leave the circle until he had made up his mind. Infuriated and humiliated he returned to Palestine and vented his anger on Jerusalem. The book of Daniel describes what happened.

> At the time appointed he shall return and come into the south; but it shall not be this time as it was before. For ships of Kittim shall come against him, and he shall be afraid and withdraw, and shall turn back and be enraged and take action against the holy covenant. He shall turn back and give heed to those who forsake the holy covenant. Forces from him shall appear and profane the temple and fortress, and shall take away the continual burnt offering. And they shall set up the abomination that makes desolate. (Daniel 11:29–31)

The books of Maccabees describe how Antiochus sent Apollonius to Jerusalem with an army of 22,000 which tore down the walls, burned part of the city, massacred and enslaved the inhabitants, and fortified and garrisoned a citadel called the Acra that overlooked the Temple. Antiochus, in fact, treated Jerusalem as an enemy city, and he determined not only to break the people physically, but to destroy their faith (1 Maccabees 1:29–36, 2 Maccabees 5).

Like Alexander himself Antiochus assumed a divine status. His coinage bore the words, Theos Epiphanes ("god manifest," or "revealed"), a pretension not to be taken too seriously by the majority of his subjects. But to the Jews it was blasphemy. Perhaps they could have ignored it had he left them alone; his explicit orders made that impossible. The first book of Maccabees gives a detailed description:

> The king then issued a decree throughout his empire: his subjects were all to become one people and abandon their own laws and religion. The nations everywhere complied with the royal command, and many in Israel accepted the foreign worship, sacrificing to idols and profaning the Sabbath. Moreover, the king sent agents with written orders to Jerusalem and the towns of Judaea. Ways and customs foreign to the country were to be introduced. Burnt offerings, sacrifices, and libations in the temple were forbidden; sabbaths and feast-days were to be profaned; the temple and its ministers to be defiled. Altars, idols, and sacred precincts were to be established; swine and other unclean beasts to be offered in sacrifice. They must leave their sons uncircumcised; they must make themselves in every way abominable, unclean, and profane, and so forget the law and change all their statutes. The penalty for disobedience was death. (1 Maccabees 1:41–50)

The most blasphemous act of all, "the abomination of desolation," was the construction of an altar to Zeus on top of the altar of the Lord in the Temple (1 Maccabees 1:54), an act intended to discredit the Jewish God.[7]

At their best the Greeks were moderates; "nothing too much" characterized their way of looking at life. But Antiochus was the reverse: almost all his behavior was immoderate. Extreme in giving gifts and extreme in causing pain, he listened to and followed his most extreme advisors and allowed himself to believe that the Jews who defied his orders, who objected to his attempt to turn the House of the Lord into a temple to Zeus, were a minority, that the majority of the Jews wanted Hellenistic culture and were willing to give up the uniqueness of their God. Resistance drove him on. He was not anti-Semitic as such, but he was furiously antagonistic to anyone who crossed him. The greater the courage and forebearance of his victim, the greater his efforts, and so he has left us, as a dark memorial, the first known instance in history of religious persecution.[8]

His method was thorough; he instructed his officers to visit every town and village in his large dominion and require that the inhabitants offer a sacrifice to Zeus. One of the villages was Modin, about twenty-five miles northwest of Jerusalem. The officer who went there spoke to Mattathias, a priest, and ordered him to be the first to offer sacrifice. Mattathias answered boldly, "Though all the nations within the king's dominions obey him and forsake their ancestral worship. . .yet I and my sons and brothers will follow the covenant of our fathers. Heaven forbid we should ever abandon the law and its statutes. We will not obey the command of the king, nor will we deviate one step from our forms of worship" (1 Maccabees 2:19–22). Perhaps Mattathias thought that his fellow villagers would take courage and defy the king's Officer in the same way. He was mistaken. As soon as he had finished, a Jew stepped forward and attempted to offer the pagan sacrifice. Mattathias, thereupon, in an immense passion, killed the Jew and the officer, and with his five sons fled to the nearby hills. That was the beginning of the Maccabean revolt, 167 B.C.

The book of Daniel takes the story to that point, to where "the people who know their God shall stand firm and take action" (Daniel 11:32). The writer expresses quiet confidence: Antiochus will be unchecked, but only "for a time" (Daniel 11:24), some of the Jewish leaders will fall victims (Daniel 11:33–34). Yet Antiochus "will come to his end, with none to help him" (Daniel 11:45), and that is roughly what happened. But the account of an invasion by a "king of the north," the appearance of Michael the archangel, the sealing up of sacred words, and the iteration of mysterious numbers make no reference to the great victories of Judas Maccabeus or to the rededication of the Temple in 167, which would certainly have been mentioned, as were other recent historical events, had they occurred when the book was written.

---

[7]Arthur Jeffrey, "Introduction to Daniel," *Interpreter's Bible*, Vol. 6 (Nashville, Tenn.: Abingdon Press, 1956).

[8]Yohanan Aharoni and Michael Avi-Yonah, *The Macmillan Bible Atlas* (New York: Macmillan, 1968), p. 118.

290 The Book of Daniel and the Hellenistic Age

If this is correct, the date of composition would have been shortly before the death of Antiochus Epiphanes and the rededication of the Temple, ca. 165–164 B.C.[9]

The author's response to these events was to write a stirring, though cryptic, account of a sixth century Daniel in the court of an alien monarch. Like Joseph long before, he proved to be more able than all the native subjects in courage, resourcefulness, and knowledge. This, of course, was due to the continuous help of God, and the final result was that God's people were honored, and his teaching held in high repute.

DATE AND UNITY

There is wide agreement about the second century date of the book. One scholar refers to it as an "assured position of scholarship,"[10] another scholar writes about the "amazing consensus" which, by the end of the nineteenth century, accepted "unequivocally the Maccabean dating of the book."[11] Yet there remain differences of opinion about its unity.

Was Daniel written by one author or by more than one? The reasons for multiple authorship seem clear from the book itself. The first six chapters are simple stories about Daniel, written in the third person. The last six chapters are an account of complex visions in the first person, as if he had written them himself. Chapters 2:4–7:28 are written in Aramaic. The remainder of the book is in Hebrew. [12] Were there two authors writing in different languages?

It has been proposed as highly probable that Chapters 1–6 were written in the third century and edited into their present form during the Maccabean period.[13] The possibility that Daniel 1–6 are drawn from earlier and perhaps non-Jewish sources is increased by the difference in attitude to authority in the earlier section and the later section. In 1–6 Nebuchadnezzar, Belshazzar and Darius are represented as reasonable people, willing ultimately to acknowledge the authority of God. This, it is argued, would scarcely have been possible had these chapters been written by the author of Chapters 7–12, for whom Antiochus was simply contemptible.[14]

Yet the unity of the work is strongly supported.[15] As one commentator put it, "the fact that so many suggestions have been made to explain the text is itself an indication of the uncertainty attaching to any theory."[16]

[9]Porteous, *Daniel,* p. 170.

[10]Otto Eissfeldt, *The Old Testament,* Peter Ackroyd trans. (New York: Harper and Row, 1965), p. 517.

[11]Brevard S. Childs, *Introduction to the Old Testament as Scripture,* (Philadelphia: Fortress Press, 1979), p. 612.

[12]Harold H. Rowley, "The Unity of the Book of Daniel," *The Servant of the Lord* (Oxford: Basil Blackwell, 1965), p. 250.

[13]Louis F. Hartman and Alexander A. DiLella, *The Book of Daniel* (Garden City, N.Y.: Doubleday, 1978), p. 13.

[14]Raymond Hammer, *The Book of Daniel* (Cambridge: Cambridge University Press, 1976), p. 7.

[15]Rowley, *The Servant of the Lord,* p. 250.

[16]Hammer, *The Book of Daniel,* p. 7.

THE CHARACTER OF THE BOOK OF DANIEL

In the last chapter of Daniel the prophet is commanded, "But you, Daniel, shut up the words, and seal the book, until the time of the end." (Daniel 12:4)[17]

Secrecy, or anonymity, was a characteristic of apocalyptic writing. Typically, it was a message from God, a divine truth, but presented in strange, sometimes fantastic images. The truth is revealed, but in such a way that only those equipped with an understanding of apocalyptic writing can interpret it. This is the character of much of the book of Daniel.[18] The vision of Daniel in Chapter 7 is an example.

A second-century Jew reading the book when it first appeared would have known that the four beasts referred to coming "up out of the sea" were four empires: the Babylonian, the Median, the Persian, and the Greek, that is, the Hellenistic Greek empire of Alexander the Great. This interpretation could be derived from Chapter 2, where Daniel explains to Nebuchadnezzar the meaning of his disturbing dream in which he saw a mighty image whose head was gold, breast and arms silver, belly and thighs bronze, legs iron, and feet a mixture of iron and clay. Nebuchadnezzar is the head of gold, and the other metals represent subsequent kingdoms, the feet of iron and clay being those of Antiochus Epiphanes. In Chapter 7, given the clue of the preceding chapter and the interpretation of the vision in Chapter 8, verses 20–22, the fourth beast is meant to symbolize the kingdom of Alexander seen not from the point of view of the enlightenment it brought to the nations it conquered, but from the point of view of the nations for whom Alexander's rule was like being crushed by great iron teeth (Daniel 7:19). The ten horns were intended to be the Seleucid rulers who succeeded Alexander. The little horn undoubtedly was Antiochus Epiphanes. Perhaps the horns, which had long been a symbol of divinity in the ancient Near East, were an oblique reference to the legend of Alexander the Great in which he is called "Alexander of the double horns." An Egyptian coin represents him with two horns protruding from his head.[19] The Seleucid kings claimed divine status, and so did the "contemptible" Epiphanes, who is described as a "little" horn with "eyes like the eyes of a man, and a mouth speaking great things." (Daniel 7:8)

Apocalyptic history is cosmic history divided into great periods; its protagonists are angels and demons, God and Satan, light and dark, good and evil. Its disasters are on a large scale, its resolutions are cataclysmic interventions by divine power. The apocalyptic world is transcendental, mythological, mysterious; its teaching is revealed and hidden. Its literary images are elusive in their attempt to confuse the uninitiated, bizarre and extravagant, remote from the human individual. These various "marks" are not found in all its writings, but in whole or in part they "build

---

[17] Jeffrey, *Interpreter's Bible.*
[18] Porteous, *Daniel,* p. 14.
[19] Eissfeldt, *The Old Testament,* p. 528.
[19] Gaalyah Cornfeld, *Archeology of the Bible: Book by Book* (New York: Harper and Row, 1974), p. 233.

up an *impression* of a distinct kind which conveys a particular *mood* of thought and belief.[20]

The "impression" and "mood" are like those one meets in movies such as *2001* and *Close Encounters of a Third Kind* and in science fiction stories where something ominous and puzzling but hopefully wonderful is to be found. The contrast with the writings of the earlier prophets is very great. Apocalyptic writing addressed itself to the rise and fall of nations, to aeons, to events on the largest scale. Prophets like Amos addressed themselves to people, to their specific faults and what should be done to correct them. Apocalyptic writing dealt with spiritual powers in high places; the prophets dealt with men and women in the market places.

The strange symbolic visions of apocalyptic texts were a means of inspiration for people who were spiritually and physically exhausted. After the Maccabean revolt had achieved its initial success with the rededication of the Temple in 165, but before the Jews had encounterd the main Seleucid army, they were undoubtedly apprehensive about the immediate future. The story of Daniel daring to be true to his faith in the court of a heathen king, passing through a fiery furnace, surviving the wild beasts, knowing from God what the king's own wise men could not know, defeating all his enemies and concluding his life in peace and honor was a message of what they could hope for even though the power ranged against them was immeasurably greater than they.[21]

RESURRECTION

The book of Daniel is notable for containing the clearest affirmation of resurrection to eternal life to be found in the Old Testament.

Jewish beliefs about life after death were not joyous. The most that a person could hope for was a quasi existence in Sheol. In an appeal to his tormenting "friends," Job cries out:

> Let me alone, that I may find a little comfort
> before I go whence I shall not return,
>   to the land of gloom and deep darkness,
> the land of gloom and chaos,
>   where light is as darkness. (Job 10:20–22)

[20]David S. Russell, *The Method and Message of Jewish Apocalyptic, 200 BC–AD 100.* (Philadelphia: Westminster Press, 1964), pp. 17–18.

John J. Collins, "The Jewish Apocalypses," *Semeia* 14, 1979, p. 21, provides a schematic description of Jewish apocalypses as a literary genre, and a definition of apocalypse. " 'Apocalypse' is a genre of revelatory literature with a narrative framework, in which a revelation is mediated by an otherwordly being to a human recipient, disclosing a transcendent reality which is both temporal, insofar is it envisages eschatological salvation, and spatial insofar as it involves another, supernatural world."

[21]Ibid., p. 16.

Porteous, *Daniel*, p. 14.

No matter how mighty an earth, in Sheol the dead were weak. When the king of Babylon died he was met by "all who were leaders of the earth" who greeted him with the words:

> You too have become as weak as we!
> You have become like us! (Isaiah 14:10)

Job feared Sheol; to him it was a hideous place where the shades "tremble" (Job 26:5), consequently any form of life was better than death. According to Ecclesiastes, "a living dog is better than a dead lion," because a living man still has hope, ". . . the dead know nothing, and they have no more reward; but the memory of them is lost." (Ecclesiastes 9:4–6)

But the sufferings inflicted by Antiochus Epiphanes were a challenge not only to human endurance but to what could be expected from God. Ecclesiastes' gloomy statements might be acceptable in almost all circumstances excepting those of Antiochus's persecution. When faithful people died horrible deaths there had to be a reward. Sheol could not be the ultimate journey's end. God had to have in mind some other future than a place of darkness and fear. It became then imperative that the matter so long debated should be resolved "now." It was an intellectual, theological crisis that demanded immediate attention. The author of Daniel, assuming the unity of the book, gave his attention to that crisis and affirmed unambiguously that there was a personal resurrection, and that those who served God in their lifetime would be blessed, and those who did not would be punished. Michael, the angelic captain, he wrote, would appear at the moment of greatest distress, the people would be delivered, and every one whose name shall be found in the book. "And many of those who sleep in the dust of the earth shall awake, some to everlasting life, and some to shame and everlasting contempt." (Daniel 12:1–2)

It is as if in the fearful circumstances of the time, he had studied the evidence of his traditions, evaluated them in terms of the love of God, and so reached a conclusion.

THE SON OF MAN

The embattled Jews who first read the book of Daniel must have welcomed the assurances that God would redress the wrongs of those who died. They must also have taken heart from the cryptic message, very plain to them, that the present political power was to be destroyed and replaced by the direct rule of God. Written in plain language this would have been obvious sedition and could have drawn a quick and no doubt brutal response from the authorities. One can supose that the strange symbolism of the book escaped them. Perhaps it is fortunate that brutality isn't often accompanied by sharpness of wit. In 1944 the French playright Jean Anouilh produced his version of the Greek play "Antigone" in Paris. Ostensibly it was Sophocles' tragic story about a young girl's defiance of her uncle who had ordered that her brother's body should not be buried but left to rot where it fell in battle. To the great majority of Frenchmen, mostly Parisians, who saw the play, Creon, the uncle, was the embodiment of the occupying Nazi power, and Antigone, the girl, was the embodiment of French resistance. To the French people who saw it, it was an inspiring play. Surprisingly, the Germans did not prevent it from being performed and it continued to be played until the Liberation.[22]

In Daniel's symbolism, Antiochus Epiphanes was the little horn which spoke words. "As I looked" explains the writer

> thrones were placed
> > and one that was ancient of days took his seat;
> his raiment was white as snow,
> > and the hair of his head like pure wool;
> his throne was fiery flames,
> > its wheels were burning fire.
> A stream of fire issued
> > and came forth from before him;
> a thousand thousands served him,
> > and ten thousand times ten thousand stood before him;
> the court sat in judgment,
> > and the books were opened. (Daniel 7:9-10)

Attention is sometimes drawn to the similarity between this and Ezekiel's vision of the appearance of the glory of the Lord in human form, seated upon a sapphire throne (Ezekiel 1:26-28), surrounded by wheels and flames of fire, (Ezekiel 1:4, 15-21). It is a clue that the writer of the book of Daniel was familiar with Hebrew religious texts and influenced by them. The "thousands upon thousands" attendant upon the "ancient in years" was no doubt appropriate encouragement to people in an undefended city who were being brutalized by twenty-two thousand of Antiochus's troops.

The proud speaking little horn is judged and killed along with the whole context of empire. The beast that supports it is destroyed by fire. There follows then an enigmatic passage.

> I saw in the night visions,
> and behold with the clouds of heaven
> > there came one like a son of man,
> and he came to the Ancient of Days
> > and was presented before him.
> And to him was given dominion
> > and glory and kingdom,

Israeli checkpoint at the Western Wall.

that all peoples, nations, and languages
    should serve him;
his dominion is an everlasting dominion,
    which shall not pass away,
and his kingdom one
    that shall not be destroyed. (Daniel 7:13–14)

The term "son of man" is introduced without explanation. From the interpretation given to the writer in his vision, the son of man seems to be an embodiment of the saints of the most high (Daniel 7:27). But why the writer should use a term which implies an individual if he meant a collective personality is not clear. While it seems to be unlikely that the author intended "son of man" to be a Messianic figure,[23] as years passed and the Jews came under the control of Rome, the "son of man" became in popular Jewish imagination a supernatural figure who would deliver them from their bondage. The prophecy of Daniel offered what seemed to be the only way in which they could be free. It was therefore of utmost significance when, in the

---

[23]Porteous, *Daniel,* p. 11.
Hartman and DiLella, *The Book of Daniel,* p. 219.

politically tense and religiously unsettled period of the turn of the millennia, Christ applied the term to himself (Mark 2:10).

A CONCLUSION

The conclusion of the book of Daniel is the conclusion of the Old Testament record. There were other Jewish books written afterwards, but they did not become part of the Hebrew canon.

During the 165 years or so between the beginning of the Maccabean wars and the birth of Christ, the Jewish people freed Jerusalem from the Seleucids, rededicated the Temple, and with extraordinary courage, skill, and perseverance, established an independent state. It lasted, however, for less than a century and then disintegrated from within. The conquest by Rome in 63 B.C. was a case of a great power moving into a situation which the incumbents could not control; but the Romans could not control it either. The disastrous revolt that culminated in A.D. 70 with the destruction of the Temple was followed by a second revolt which lasted from 131–135. The Jews were banished from Jerusalem altogether and the city was given a Roman name. The Jews of the dispersion were then no longer different from those who lived in Jerusalem; they were all dispersed.

By then the Jews were confronted with what seemed to many an especially dangerous challenge, the rise of a new faith which developed out of Judaism and seemed at first indistinguishable from it. In the early days the only Christians that there were were Jews, and that is indicative of the fact that the relationship between the two faiths is so close that it is really not possible to grasp the fullness of Christianity without a knowledge of Jewish scriptures.

Christ's ministry began with a reference to himself as the fulfillment of a prophecy in Daniel.[24] His death and resurrection were explained as part of God's plan foretold in the Scripture (Luke 24:25–27). The earliest Christian theologian built the doctrine of the new faith upon the teaching of the old. But the divergences since then have been great. To the Christian, the universalism implicit in the teaching of the prophets and the meaning of the new covenant find their fulfillment in a faith where there is no question of "Greek and Jew, circumcised and uncircumcised" (Colossians 3:11). This to the Christian seems to be consistent with the desire of God that the light of his salvation should illuminate the whole world. The Jew sees a particular spiritual value in being a Jew. The faithful observance of Jewish tradition and maintaining a Jewish identity in a Gentile world is regarded as God's requirement of his chosen people.

Despite these differences, the adherents of both faiths worship the same God and that may be the point to dwell upon. With such a shared commitment, whatever the opinion of individual Jews and Christians, their past, their present, and their future are inextricably bound together.

[24]See also the "little apocalypse" in Mark 13:5–27, Luke 21:8–28, Matthew 24:4–31. Note Matthew 24:30, "Then will appear in heaven the sign that heralds the Son of Man."

QUESTIONS FOR DISCUSSION

The following questions refer to Chapter 26.

1. If the book of Daniel was written not as history or prophecy but to encourage people during a time of persecution, what value does it have (other than an antiquarian value) now that the persecution is over?

2. What is the difference in character between prophecies such as in Amos and Jeremiah and apocalyptic works such as Daniel, Enoch, and Jude? Are there any examples of apocalyptic writing in Israel before the second century B.C.? Why do we not find writers like Amos in the second or first centuries B.C., or writers like Daniel in the eighth century B.C.?

3. Until the persecution of Antiochus there was considerable acceptance of Hellenistic Greek culture in Palestine. Could it be argued that had Antiochus not acted as he did the process of assimilation would have continued to the point of great danger for Judaism? If that is possible could the persecution, horrible as it was, be regarded as beneficial to Judaism in the long run?

4. The text states that "it is really not possible to grasp the fullness of Christianity without a knowledge of Jewish scriptures." What half dozen specific instances in the New Testament could be cited to support that claim?

APPENDIX: CHRONOLOGICAL CHARTS

From Before the Patriarchs to the Initial Settlement of the Israelites in Canaan

	Egypt	Mesopotamia	
		First dynasty of Ur, ancestral home of Abraham	2600–2360
		Wooley's Royal Cemetery artifacts from this period	
		Ebla, the remains of the capital city of a hitherto forgotten kingdom, discovered in Syria, A.D. 1976	2400–2200
		Sargon of Akkad, founder of one of the first great empires	2400–2250
		Laws of Ur Nammu, third dynasty of Ur, and Eshnunna	2100–1800
		Amorite invasions: Hammurapi and Abraham's family from Amorite or west Semitic stock, also the Canaanites and the Phoenicians	2000
		Babylonian flood story from this period	2000–1800
		Abraham may have lived at this time but there are wide disagreements about the date, also about his actual existence.	1900–1400
		Joseph and his family may have entered Egypt at the beginning of this period.	
		Laws of Hammurapi, sixth king of first Babylonian dynasty.	1728–1686
		Babylonian creation epic from this period	1750–1400
2600–2180	Old Kingdom		
	Pyramids		
	Instruction of Ptah-hotep possibly written during this period.		
2180–2000	First Intermediate Period, sometimes called a "Dark Age"		
	"Dispute Over Suicide" written during this period		
2000–1780	Middle Kingdom		
1780–1580	Second Intermediate Period		
	Hyksos invasion		
1552–1557	Amosis expels the Hyksos, possibly the Pharaoh "who knew nothing of Joseph." (Exodus 1:8)		

Aten, the sun, regarded as the first attempt at monotheism

Hymn to Aten (Psalm 104)

1305–1290	Seti I
1290–1225	Rameses II
1280–1250	Cities of Pithom and Rameses built using Israelite slave labor (Exodus 1:11)
	The Exodus, the Covenant, conquest of Transjordan states and beginning of settlement in Canaan under Joshua
1225–1211	A stele inscribed by Pharaoh Mereneptah makes first historical reference to Israel, suggesting that although they were in Canaan they were not yet a settled people.

From the Settlement in Canaan to the Division of the Kingdom

Sea People from the Aegean area attack Egypt and the Hittite Empire.	Mereneptah 1225–1211
Mereneptah and Rameses III repel the invaders, but the Hittite Empire is destroyed.	
The movements of the Sea People, and consequent disturbances, may have been caused by widespread drought.	Rameses III 1183–1069
Iron comes into general use, although the Philistines, a branch of the Sea People, try to keep it from the Israelites. (1 Samuel 13:19–22)	
Judges: local Israelite leaders who rally their people against various adversaries.	1200–1020.
The Philistines take advantage of the military unpreparedness of Israel and extend their conquests. They capture the Ark of God. Eli dies when he hears the news. (1 Samuel 4:12–22)	1040
Samuel becomes Priest and Judge of Israel, subdues the Philistines. (1 Samuel 7)	
The Israelites demand a king. Saul anointed first King of Israel. (1 Samuel 8–10)	1020
Saul cut off by God because of disobedience. (1 Samuel 13 and 15) David chosen as a "better man." (1 Samuel 15:28–29)	
Saul and his sons killed in battle with the Philistines. (1 Samuel 28)	1000
David anointed King of Judah. (2 Samuel 2:4)	
Jerusalem captured by David and becomes the political and religious center of Israel. (2 Samuel 5:6–6:19)	
Solomon succeeds David after an abortive attempt by Adonijah to seize the throne. (1 Kings 1–2)	961
Solomon rebuked by the prophet Ahijah. (1 Kings 11)	922
The kingdom divides into two parts when the northern tribes revolt against Rehoboam, Solomon's son and assumed successor. (1 Kings 12)	

From the Division of the Kingdom to Omri

922   The Division of the Kingdom. Rehoboam King of Judah, in the south, Jeroboam I, King of Israel, in the north. (1 Kings 12:1–20)

Israel

Date	Israel
922–901	Jeroboam establishes rival religious centers in Dan and Bethel (1 Kings 12:25–33)
	Shishak, King of Egypt, invades Judah and Israel causing much destruction ca. 918 (1 Kings 14:25–26)
901–900	Nadab is murdered by Baasha (1 Kings 15:25–32)
900–877	Baasha (1 Kings 15:33–16:7)
877–876	Elah is murdered by Zimri (1 Kings 16:8–14)
876	Zimri rules for one week, then commits suicide (1 Kings 16:15–20)
876–869	Omri, a notable monarch, builds the city of Samaria (1 Kings 16:21–28)

Judah

Judah	Date
Rehoboam (1 Kings 14:21–31)	922–915
Abijam (1 Kings 15:1–8)	915–913
Asa attacked by Baasha / Asa bribes Syria to attack Israel (1 Kings 15:9–24)	913–873

*Solid lines represent breaks between dynasties.

Omri and Ahab

	Israel	Judah	
876–869	Omri defeats Tibni and becomes King of Israel.	Asa (1 Kings 15:9–24)	913–873
	Omri builds Samaria, capital city of the Northern Kingdom.	Jehoshaphat (1 Kings 15:24, 22:41–50)	873–849
	Omri marries his son Ahab to Jezebel, a Phoenician princess from Tyre. (1 Kings 16:21–28)		
869–850	Ahab takes part in the battle against Shalmaneser III at Karkar (853), which halts the Assyrian army: this event is not referred to in the Old Testatment.	Shalmaneser III, King of Assyria	859
	Jezebel, Ahab's wife, attempts to force the worship of Baal on Israel in place of God.		
	Elijah challenges the prophets of Baal on Mount Carmel (1 Kings 18)		
	Ahab and his family are rebuked and cursed by Elijah in connection with Naboth's death (1 Kings 21)		
	Ahab is confronted by Michaiah. (1 Kings 22:1–28)	Jehoshaphat fights with Ahab against the Syrians. (1 Kings 22)	
	Ahab is killed in battle against the Syrians. (1 Kings 22:29–38)		

From Ahab to Jeroboam II and Uzziah. The reigns of Jeroboam II and Uzziah were a time of great prosperity, rivaling the days of Solomon. Assyria and Egypt were weak and not able to interfere with Israel or Judah.

Israel

869–850	Ahab is killed fighting the Syrians. (1 Kings 22:29–38)
850–849	Ahaziah dies as result of an accident (2 Kings 1:1–18)
849–842	Jehoram. (2 Kings 3:1–3)
842–815	Jehu murders Jehoram, Ahaziah, and Jezebel. (2 Kings 9:1–10:36)
	Black obelisk shows Jehu doing obeisance to Shalmaneser III, Elisha (859–824)
815–801	Jehoahaz is attacked by the Syrians. (2 Kings 13:1–9)
801–786	Joash defeats a weakened Syria. (2 Kings 13:14–24)
786–746	Jeroboam II (2 Kings 14:23–29)

Judah

873–849	Jehoshaphat (1 Kings 22:41–50)
849–842	Jehoram or Joram
	Edom gains independence from Judah. (2 Kings 8:16–24)
842	Ahaziah is murdered by Jehu. (2 Kings 8:25–9:28)
842–837	Athalia, Ahaziah's mother related to Ahab as sister or daughter, attempts to destroy the royal line, usurps the throne. (2 Kings 11:1–16)
837–800	Joash (Jehoash) pays large tribute to attacking Syrians, and is murdered (2 Kings 12:17–21)
800–783	Amaziah defeats Edom, picks a quarrel with Israel, and is defeated himself, later murdered. (2 Kings 14:1–22)
783–742	Uzziah (2 Kings 15:1–7)

Elijah

Elisha

Adad-nirari III 811–784 defeats Syria, but Assyria is weakened

From Jeroboam II to the Fall of Samaria

	Israel	Judah	

Judah

783–742 — Uzziah (Azariah) (2 Kings 15:1–7)

}Amos

This was a time of peace and prosperity in both Israel and Judah, but it was also a time of injustice and apostasy.

750–742 — Jotham (as regent)
742–735 — Jotham (as king) (2 Kings 15:32–38)

735–715 — Ahaz
Ahaz appeals to Tiglath-pileser III (745–727) for help against Pekah and Rezin. The Assyrian king invades both Israel and Judah. (2 Kings 16:1–20, Isaiah 7:1–17)

Isaiah of Jerusalem

Hosea

715–687 — Hezekiah

703 — Syria and Judah Invaded

Israel

786–746 — Jeroboam II (2 Kings 14:23–29)

746–745 — Zechariah murdered by Shallum (2 Kings 15:8–12)

745 — Shallum is king for one month, then murdered by Menahem. (2 Kings 15:13–15)

737–732 — Pekah forms anti-Assyrian coalition with Rezin, King of Syria; they attack Jerusalem because Ahaz will not join them; Pekah is murdered by Hoshea. (2 Kings 15:27–31)

732–724 — Hoshea (2 Kings 17:1–6)

722–721 — Fall of Samaria, end of the Northern Kingdom

Judah Only From Hezekiah to Josiah

687–642	Manasseh	Manasseh not in sympathy with Israel's faith (2 Kings 21:1–18)
642–640	Amon	Amon continues the policies of his father, murdered. (2 Kings 21:19–26)
640–609	Josiah	Josiah succeeds to the throne at the age of eight, carries out sweeping reforms, is killed in an abortive attempt to stop the Egyptian army at Megiddo. (2 Kings 22:1–23:30) Zephaniah prophecies ca. 620

Jeremiah

640–609	Josiah	Josiah carries out a religious reformation in Judah, 621, but it does not last. He takes over part of the Assyrian province of Samaria, Assyria at the point of collapse. (2 Kings 22:1–23:30)
		Habakkuk prophesies ca. 600
		Jeremiah called to be a prophet. (Jeremiah 1)
		Fall of Ninevah, capital of Assyria, 612, the prophecy of Nahum exults over this
		Josiah defeated and killed at Megiddo by Pharaoh Necho, 609. (2 Kings 23:28–30)
609	Jehoiahaz	Jehoiahaz reigns for three months, taken by the Egyptians to Egypt and replaced by his brother Jehoiakim. (2 Kings 23:31–24:6)
609–597	Jehoiakim	Defeat of the Egyptians by the Babylonians at Carchemesh, 605
		Jehoiakim rebels against Babylon but dies as Nebuchadnezzar attacks Judah
598	Jehoiakin	Jehoiakin surrenders to the Babylonians. Jerusalem is captured, Jehoiakin and many Israelites, incuding the prophet Ezekiel are taken to Babylon in the first deportation, 598. (2 Kings 24:8–16)
598–587	Zedekiah	Zedekiah another son of Josiah, his name changed from Mattaniah, rebels against Babylon. Jerusalem is beseiged captured a second time, and destroyed. Zedekiah is blinded his sons killed, second deportation. (2 Kings 24:17–25:30)
587	Fall of Jerusalem	Gedaliah installed as governor of Judah, but murdered b extremists who flee to Egypt taking Jeremiah with them agains his will. (2 Kings 25:22–30, Jeremiah 43:1–9)

From the Exile to the Roman Occupation of Palestine

587	Exile of the Israelites from Jerusalem to Babylon, second deportation
	Ezekiel already in Babylon, prophesies during the first years of the Exile. Second Isaiah (Isaiah 40–66) prophesies in Babylon near the end of the Exile
539	Cyrus, King of Persia, defeats Babylon
538	Cyrus issues an edict allowing the Jews to return. (Ezra 1:2–4, 6:3–5)
	The Jews return under Sheshbazzar, Prince of Judah. (Ezra 1:8) Foundations of the Temple laid
520	Work on the Temple recommences under Zerubbabel after an 18-year delay with strong encouragement from the prophets Haggai and Zechariah
515	New Temple completed and dedicated. (Ezra 6:13–18)
	The religious and social level of life in Jerusalem declining as indicated by the prophet Malachi and in the memoirs of Nehemiah
445	Nehemiah appointed governor of Judah by Artaxerxes, 465–424. (Nehemiah 2:1–10)
440	Walls of Jerusalem rebuilt. (Nehemiah 2:11–6:19)
	Ezra carries out religious reforms, dates of Ezra's activities are debated
427	Ezra's work possibly completed, 427. (Nehemiah 8–10, Ezra 7–10)
333	Persia defeated by Alexander
323	Alexander dies, his empire divided between his generals
301	Palestine comes under the control of Ptolemy
	The Old Testament translated into Greek, the Septuagint (LXX), for Greek-speaking Jews
223–187	Antiochus III (the Great), Seleucid ruler
198	Antiochus annexes Palestine after the battle of Panium
190	Antiochus defeated by Rome
175–163	Antiochus IV Epiphanes (grandson of Antiochus III) sells high priesthood, held by Onias, to Onias' brother Jason, later sells it to a higher bidder, Menelaus
	Antiochus issues an edict forbidding the practice of Judaism
67	The Temple defiled by "the abomination of desolation." (Daniel 11:31)
	Beginning of Maccabean revolt by Mattathias and his sons
64	Jerusalem freed and the Temple purified, origin of festival of Hanukkah (dedication)

From the Exile to the Roman Occupation of Palestine (continued)

142	Independent Maccabean kingdom established
	Antiochus oppression and the Maccabean wars described in the two books of Maccabus.
63	Jerusalem besieged and captured by Pompey
	Palestine comes under control of Rome

BIBLIOGRAPHY

The reference works listed here are necessary tools for the study of the Old Testament. In fact, anyone seriously interested in studying the Bible should own at least a Bible Atlas, a Bible Dictionary, a One Volume Commentary, and a Concordance. This is not a large investment and it will last.

For reading and studying the Bible several excellent translations are available in up-to-date English, such as the Revised Standard Version, the New English Bible, the Jerusalem Bible, The Good News Bible, as well as the greatly revered King James Version which is now over 350 years old. Bibles in paperback are not expensive, so that one can form a small collection of different translations without great cost. Comparison of different translations when studying a passage is instructive.

The books and articles listed in the various sections are primarily those referred to in the text, with some additions. They are representative of many more works, dealing with all parts of the Old Testament and many detailed issues.

OLD TESTAMENT REFERENCE WORKS

Concordances

A concordance enables you to find a passage in the Bible providing that you know at least one word of the passage and something about it. If, for example, you wanted to find the verse which begins "In the year that King Uzziah died..." you could look up any of these words, for example, "year." The concordance lists every use of the word in the Bible, and part of the sentence in which it occurs. By turning to "year" in the concordance you would be able to find the passage you wanted listed as "In the year that King Uzziah. . ." (Isaiah 6:1).

Cruden's Concordance to the King James Version is the oldest; there are many editions. Nelson's Complete Concordance to the Revised Standard Version, prepared with a Univac I computer by J. W. Ellison (Nelson, 1957) is more useful than Cruden's for a modern translation. Young's Analytical Concordance to the Bible based on the King James Version has gone through many editions since it was first published in 1902. It is now published by William Eerdmans. It lists not only the English words but also the Greek and Hebrew originals. This is helpful to the student because the same English word may translate more than one Greek or Hebrew word, for example, "Spirit" in the Old Testament translates the Hebrew Ruach and Neshamah, and in the New Testament "Spirit" translates pneuma and phantasma.

Commentaries

A commentary, as the name implies, provides detailed comment upon the biblical books, chapters, and verses. Commentaries also include general explanatory articles such as "Hebrew Prophecy" or "Old Testament Weights and Measures." Some commentaries are multivolume such as the 12-volume Interpreters Bible, (Abingdon Press) or The Anchor Bible (Doubleday). There are also single-volume commentaries such as The Interpreters One Volume Commentary on the Bible (Abingdon Press, 1971), Peakes Commentary on the Bible, revised edition (Thomas Nelson, 1962) and the Jerome Bible Commentary (Prentice-Hall, 1968). For the New Testament only there is the New English Bible Companion to the New Testament by A. E. Harvey (Oxford and Cambridge University Presses, 1970).

Bible Dictionaries

These are reference works which are more like an encyclopedia than a dictionary. They list in alphabetical order the multitude of names, events, places and so on which are to be found in the Bible. The four-volume, The Interpreters Dictionary of the Bible (Abingdon Press, 1962) and Supplement (1976) are most comprehensive. There are one-volume dictionaries such as Harpers Bible Dictionary (Harper and Row, 1985) and the New Westminster Dictionary of the Bible (1982).

Maps and Atlases

Maps are an indispensible aid to Bible study. Many bibles have a set of maps bound with the text. In addition, there are Bible Atlases which provide maps, photographs, drawings, and an explanatory text. The Oxford Bible Atlas (Oxford University Press, 1984), 3rd edition, edited by Herbert G. May, revised by John Day and The Westminster Historical Atlas, edited by G. E. Wright and F. V. Filson (The Westminster Press, 1956) are examples. See also The Macmillan Bible Atlas, Yohana

Aharoni and Michael Avi-Yonah (Macmillan, 1968) and *Atlas of the Biblical World,* Denis Baly and A. D. Tushingham (World Publishing Co., 1971).

CONCORDANCES, COMMENTARIES, DICTIONARIES, ATLASES

AHARONI, YOHANAN,   *The Land of the Bible,* (2nd ed.). A historical geography. Translated and edited by A. F. Rainey. The Westminster Press, Philadelphia, 1980.

AHARONI, YOHANAN and MICHAEL AVI-YONAH,   *The Macmillan Bible Atlas.* Macmillan Publishing Co. Inc., New York, 1968.

BLACK, MATTHEW and H. H. ROWLEY,   *Peakes Commentary on the Bible.* Thomas Nelson and Sons, Ltd., London, 1962.

BALY, DENIS and A. D. TUSHINGHAM,   *Atlas of the Biblical World.* World Publishing Co., New York, 1971.

BROWN, RAYMOND SS, JOSEPH A. FITZMEYER, S.J., ROLAND E. MURPHY O CARM,   *The Jerome Bible Commentary.* Prentice-Hall, Englewood Cliffs, N.J., 1968.

BUTTRICK, GEORGE ARTHUR,   *The Interpreters Dictionary of the Bible.* Abingdon Press, Nashville, 1962.

BUTTRICK, GEORGE ARTHUR,   *The Interpreters Bible.* Abingdon Press, Nashville, 1952–1957.

CRIM, KEITH and others,   *The Interpreters Dictionary of the Bible,* Supplement. Abingdon Press, Nashville, 1976.

CRUDEN, ALEXANDER,   *A Complete Concordance to the Holy Scripture of the Old and New Testaments,* based on the Authorized Version. First published in 1737; reprinted many times by different publishers.

ELLISON, J. W.,   *Nelson's Complete Concordance to the Revised Standard Version.* Nelson, New York, 1957.

GEHMAN, HENRY SYNDER,   *The New Westminster Dictionary of the Bible.* Westminster Press, Philadelphia, 1982.

HARTDEGEN, FR. STEPHEN J.,   *Nelson's Complete Concordance of the New American Bible.* The Liturgical Press, Collegeville, Minn., 1977.

HARVEY, A.E.,   *New English Bible Companion to the New Testament,* New York, Oxford and Cambridge University Presses, 1970.

HASTINGS, JAMES, ed.   Revised edition by Frederick C. Grant and H. H. Rowley, *Dictionary of the Bible.* Charles Scribners Sons, New York, 1963.

LAYMON, CHARLES M.,   *The Interpreters One-Volume Commentary on the Bible.* Abingdon Press, Nashville and New York, 1971.

MAY, HERBERT G.,   *Oxford Bible Atlas,* ed. Third Edition, revised by John Day. New York, Oxford University Press, 1984.

McKENZIE, JOHN L.,   *Dictionary of the Bible.* Bruce Publishing Company, Milwaukee, 1965.

MILLER, MADELAINE S., and J. LANE MILLER,   *The New Harpers Bible Dictionary.* (8th ed.). Harper and Row, New York, 1973.

PRITCHARD, JAMES B.,   *Ancient Near Eastern Texts Relating to the Old Testament.* Princeton University Press, Princeton, 1969.

PRITCHARD, JAMES B.,   *The Ancient Near East in Pictures Relating to the Old Testament,* Second Edition with Supplement. Princeton University Press, Princeton, 1969.

TRONG, JAMES,   *Exhaustive Concordance of the Bible* (first published in 1890 by Abingdon-Cokesbury). Many editions availble.

THOMAS, D. WINTON,   *Documents from Old Testament Times.* Harper and Row, New York, 1961.

314   Bibliography

WRIGHT, G. E., *Biblical Archeology,* New and Revised Edition, Westminster Press, Philadelphia, 1962.
WRIGHT, G. E. and FLOYD V. FILSON, *The Westminster Historical Atlas to the Bible,* revised edition. The Westminster Press, Philadelphia, 1956.

OLD TESTAMENT TEXT AND CANON

BRUCE, F. F., *The English Bible, A History of Translations* (3rd ed.). Oxford University Press, Oxford, 1978.
HAYES, JOHN H., *An Introduction to the Old Testament Study.* Abingdon Press, Nashville, 1979.
HILLS, MARGARET, *A Ready Reference: History of the English Bible* (revised by Elizabeth J. Eisenhart). American Bible Society, New York, 1981.
KENYON, SIR FREDERICK, *Our Bible and the Ancient Manuscripts,* revised by A. W. Adams. Eyre and Spottiswoode, London, 1958.
MELLOR, ENID B., ed., *The Making of the Old Testament.* Cambridge University Press, Cambridge, 1972.
MILLARD, ALAN R., "In Praise of Ancient Scribes," *Biblical Archeologist,* Volume 45, Number 3, Summer, 1982, p. 143.
SANDERS, JAMES A., *Torah and Canon.* Fortress Press, Philadelphia, 1972.

The preface to the Revised Standard Version provides a brief and interesting summary of the history of the English Bible from the time of the work of William Tyndale to the publication of the Revised Standard Version in 1952.

THE OLD TESTAMENT AS A WHOLE

AHARONI, YOHANAN, *The Archeology of the Land of Israel,* trans. A. F. Rainey. Westminster Press, Philadelphia, 1982.
ALBRIGHT, W. F., *The Biblical Period from Abraham to Ezra, an Historical Survey.* Harper and Row, New York, 1963.
ALON, AZARIA, *The Natural History of the Land of the Bible.* Paul Hamlyn, London, New York, 1969.
ANDERSON, BERNHARD W., *Understanding the Old Testament,* (3rd ed.). Prentice-Hall, Englewood Cliffs, N.J., 1975.
BALY, DENIS, *The Geography of the Bible,* new and revised edition. New York, Harper and Row, 1974.
BRIGHT, JOHN, *The History of Israel* (3rd ed.). Westminster Press, Philadelphia, 1981.
Cambridge Ancient History, 12 Volumes. Various editors: Cambridge University Press 1971–1973. A detailed study of the entire period of the Old and New Testaments.
CHILDS, BREVARD, *Introduction to the Old Testament as Scripture.* Fortress Press, Philadelphia, 1979.
DE VAUX, ROLAND, *Ancient Israel,* two volumes. McGraw-Hill, New York, 1965.
EISSFELDT, OTTO, *The Old Testament,* trans. P. R. Ackroyd. Harper and Row, New York 1965.
Fauna and Flora of the Bible, Prepared in cooperation with the committee on Translations of the United Bible Societies., 2nd edition, New York United Bible Societies, 1980.
GASTER, THEODORE H., *Myth Legend and Custom in the Old Testament,* 2 Vols. New York Harper and Row, 1969.

GOTTWALD, NORMAN K., *A Light to the Nations*. Haper and Row, New York, 1959.
GRANT, MICHAEL, *The Story of Ancient Israel*, New York, Scribners, 1984.
HAYES, JOHN H., *Introduction to the Bible*. Westminster Press, Philadelphia, 1971.
HAYES, JOHN and J. MAXWELL MILLER, eds. *Israelite and Judaean History*. Westminster Press, Philadelphia, 1977.
HERMANN, SIEGFRIED, *A History of Israel in Old Testament Times*, trans. John Bowden. Fortress Press, Philadelphia, 1975.
Josephus, Flavius (1st century Jewish historian), *Antiquites of the Jews*, A history of the Jews from the creation to the war with Rome. There are many editions of this work.
KAUFMANN, YEHEZKEL, *The Religion of Israel* from its beginnings to the Babylonian Exile. Translated and abridged by Moshe Greenburg, Chicago, Chicago University Press, 1960.
KENYON, KATHLEEN, *Archeology and the Holy Land*. Ernest Benn Ltd., London, 1960.
LANCE, H. DARRELL, *The Old Testament and the Archeologist*. Fortress Press, Philadelphia, 1981.
LaSOR, WILLIAM SANFORD, DAVID ALLAN HUBBARD, FREDERIC WILLIAM BUSH, *Old Testament Survey: The Message, Form and Background of the Old Testament*, Grand Rapids, Wm. B. Eerdmans Publishing Company, 1982. This book represents an "enlightened conservative" or evangelical approach to the Old Testament. See the review by Bernhard W. Anderson, *Interpretation*, Vol. XXXVIII No. 4, October, 1984.
MAGNUSSON, MAGNUS, *BC The Archaeology of the Bible Lands*. Drawings and maps by Shirley Felts. The Bodley Head, London, Sydney, Toronto, 1977.
McCURLEY, FOSTER R., *Ancient Myths and Biblical Faith*. Fortress Press, Philadelphia, 1983.
McEVENUE, SEAN E., "Old Testament, Scripture or Theology," *Interpretation*, Vol. XXXVI, 3, July 1981, pp. 229.
MEYERS, ERIC M., "The Bible and Archeology," *Biblical Archeologist*, Vol. 47, No. 1, March 1985, p. 36.
MOOREY, ROGER, *Excavation in Palestine*. William B. Eerdmans, Grand Rapids, 1983.
NAPIER, DAVID, *Song of the Vineyard: A Guide Through the Old Testament*, revised edition. Fortress Press, Philadelphia, 1981.
PFEIFFER, ROBERT H., *Introduction to the Old Testament*. Harper and Row, New York, 1948.
ROWLEY, H. H., *The Growth of the Old Testament* (3rd ed.). Hutchinson's University Library, London, 1967.
SELLARS, O. R., "Weights," *Interpreters Dictionary of the Bible*, 4 vols., ed: George Arthur Buttrick, Nashville, Abingdon, 1962.
TULLOCK, JOHN H., *The Old Testament Story*. Prentice-Hall, Englewood Cliffs, N.J., 1981.
VON RAD, GERHARD, *Old Testament Theology*, Vols I and II, translated D.M.G. Stalker, New York, Harper & Row, 1962 and 1965.
WRIGHT, G. E., R. H. JOHNSTON, and J. B. PRITCHARD, *Great People of the Bible and How They Lived*. Readers Digest, Pleasantville, New York 1974.

ORIGINS

AHARONI, YOHANAN, "Nothing Early and Nothing Late: Rewriting Israel's Conquest," *The Biblical Archaelogist*, Vol. 39, 2, May 1976, p. 71.
BIGGS, ROBERT, "The Ebla Tablets: An Interim Perspective," *Biblical Archeologist*, Vol. 43, 2, Spring, 1980.
CORNFELD, GAALYAH, *Archeology of the Bible: Book by Book*. Harper and Row, New York, 1976.
DAVIDSON, ROBERT, *Genesis 1–11*, Cambridge: Cambridge University Press, 1973.

DAVISON, ROBERT, "Genesis 12–20," *The Cambridge Bible Commentary,* Cambridge University Press, 1979. Accompanies the text of the New English Bible.

DE VAUX, ROLAND, *The Early History of Israel,* trans. David Smith. Westminster Press, Philadelphia, 1978.

DEVER, WILLIAM G., "The Peoples of Palestine in the Middle Bronze I Period," *Harvard Theological Review,* 64, April–July, 1971, p. 226.

FREEDMAN, DAVID NOEL, ed., "Letter to the Readers," *The Biblical Archeologist,* Vol. 43.2, Spring, 1980, p. 76.

FRYMER-KENSY, TIKVA, "The Atrahasis Epic and Its Significance For Our Understanding of Genesis 1–5," *Biblical Archeologist,* Vol. 40, 4, Dec. 1977, p. 147.

GREENGUS, SAMUEL, "Sisterhood adoption of Nuzi and the 'Wife-Sister' in Genesis," *Hebrew Union College Annual,* Vol. XLVI (1975) p. 5.

GONEN, RIVKA, "Urban Canaan in the Late Bronze Period," *Bulletin of the American Schools of Oriental Research,* No. 253, Winter 1984, p. 61.

GOTTWALD, NORMAN K., *The Tribes of Yahweh.* Orbis Books, Maryknoll, New York, 1979.

HEIDEL, ALEXANDER, *The Babylonian Genesis,* (2nd ed.). The University of Chicago Press, Chicago, 1951.

HOLT, JOHN MARSHALL, *The Patriarchs of Israel.* Vanderbilt University Press, Northville, 1964.

JACOBSEN, THORKILD, *The Treasures of Darkness: A History of Mesopotamian Religion.* Yale University Press, New Haven and London, 1976.

JACOBSEN, THORKILD, *Toward an Image of Tammuz,* Cambridge, Harvard University Press, 1970.

LAMBERT, W. G., A R. MILLARD, *Atra-Hasis, The Babylonian Story of the Flood,* Oxford at the Clarendon Press, 1969.

MARSH, JOHN, "Numbers: Introduction and Exegesis," *Interpreter's Bible,* Vol. 2.

MATTHIAE, PAOLO, *Ebla: An Empire Rediscoverd.* Doubleday, New York, 1981.

MICHAUD, ROBERT, *Les Patriarches: Histoire et Theologie.* Les Editions Du Cerf, Paris, 1975.

MICKLEM, NATHANIEL, "Leviticus: Introduction and Exegesis, " *Interpreter's Bible,* Vol. 2.

MILLARD, A. R., "A New Babylonian 'Genesis' Story," Tyndale Bulletin 18.1967 1–18.

OPPENHEIM, A. LEO, *Ancient Mesopotamia,* revised edition completed by Erica Reiner. University of Chicago Press, Chicago, 1977.

OPPENHEIM, A. LEO, *Letters from Mesopotamia,* Chicago, University of Chicago Press, 1967.

PETTINATO, GIOVANNI, "The Royal Archives of Tell Mardikh-Ebla," *Biblical Archeologist,* Vol. 39, 2, May, 1976, p. 44.

PRITCHARD, J. B., *Archeology and the Old Testament.* Princeton University Press, Princeton, 1958.

RAST, WALTER E., "Bab Edh-Dhra and the Origin of the Sodom Saga," *To appear in a volume in memory of D. Glenn Rose,* Atlanta, John Knox Press, 1985.

RINGGREN, HELMER, *Religions of the Ancient Near East,* trans. John Sturdy. Westminster Press, Philadelphia, 1973.

RYLAARSDAM, J. COERT, "Exodus: Introduction and Exegesis," *Interpreter's Bible,* Vol. 1

SAGGS, H.W.F., *The Encounter With the Divine in Mesopotamia and Israel.* Athlone Press, University of London, London, 1978.

SAGGS, H.W.F., *Everyday Life in Babylonia and Assyria.* B. T. Batsford, London; G. P. Putnam New York, 1965.

SAGGS, H.W.F., *The Greatness That Was Babylon.* Hawthorne Books, Inc., New York, 1962

SKINNER, JOHN, *Genesis: The International Critical Commentary,* Edinburgh, T & T Clark 1930.

SPEISER, E. A., "Genesis," *Anchor Bible.* Doubleday, New York, 1964.

VAN SETERS, JOHN, *Abraham in History and Tradition.* Yale University Press, New Haven and London, 1975.

VAN SETERS, JOHN, "Jacob's Marriages and Ancient Near East Customs: A Re-examination," *Harvard Theological Review,* 62, October, 1969, p. 377.

VIGAMO, LORENZO and DENNIS PARDEE, "Literary Sources for the History of Palestine and Syria," *Biblical Archeologist,* Vol. 47, 1, March 1984, p. 6.

VON RAD, GERHARD, *Genesis,* revised edition. The Westminster Press, Philadelphia, 1972.

WESTERMANN, CLAUS, *Genesis 1–11: A Commentary,* translated by John J. Scullion, S.J., Minneapolis Augsburg Press, 1984.

WRIGHT, G. ERNEST, "Deuteronomy: Introduction and Exegesis," *Interpreter's Bible,* Vol. 2.

EGYPT AND THE EXODUS

ALBRIGHT, WILLIAM F., "Moses in Historical and Theological Perspectives," *The Mighty Acts of God,* eds. F. M. Cross, W. E. Lemke, P. D. Miller, Jr. Doubleday, New York, 1976.

ALT, ALBRECHT, "The Origins of Israelite Law," *Essays on Old Testament History and Religion,* trans. R. A. Wilson. Doubleday Anchor, New York, 1966.

ANDERSON, G. W., ed., *Tradition and Interpretation.* Oxford University Press, Oxford, 1979.

BRIGHT, JOHN, *Covenant and Promise.* Westminster Press, Philadelphia, 1976.

BROWNLEE, WILLIAM H., "The Ineffable Name of God," *Bulletin of the American Schools of Oriental Research,* No. 226, April, 1977, p. 39.

BUBER, MARTIN, *Moses,* New York, Harper and Row, 1958.

CASELLES, H., "The History of Israel in the Pre-Exilic Period," *Tradition and Interpretation,* ed. G. W. Anderson, Oxford University Press, Oxford, 1979.

CUNLIFFE-JONES, H., *Deuteronomy.* SCM Press Ltd., London, 1951.

DAVIES, G. HURTON, *Exodus.* SCM Press Ltd., London, 1967.

EICHRODT, WALTHER, *Theology of the Old Testament,* trans. J. A. Baker. The Westminster Press, Philadelphia, 1961.

FRANKFORT, HENRI, *Kingship and the Gods.* University of Chicago Press, Chicago, 1977.

FRANKFORT, HENRI, *Ancient Egyptian Religion.* Harper and Row, New York, 1961.

FRANKFORT, HENRI, and others, *The Intellectual Adventure of Ancient Man.* University of Chicago Press, Chicago, 1977.

GRUBER, MAYER, 'The Source of the Biblical Sabbath', *Journal of the Ancient Near East Society of Columbia University,* 1969.

HEATON, E. W., *Everyday Life in Old Testament Times.* Batsford Ltd., London, 1956.

McCARTHY, D. J., *Old Testament Covenant.* John Knox Press, Richmond, Virginia, 1972.

MENDENHALL, GEORGE E., "Covenant," *Interpreters Dictionary of the Bible,* ed. G. A. Buttrick. Abingdon Press, Nashville, 1962.

MENDENHALL, GEORGE E., "Law and Covenant in Israel and the Ancient Near East," Buttrick. Abingdon Press, Nashville, 1962.

MENDENHALL, GEORGE, "Law and Covenant in Israel and the Ancient Near East," Pittsburgh Biblical Colloquium, 1955, Pittsburgh, PA reprinted from *Biblical Archeologist,* Volume XVII, No. 2, May 1954, pp. 26–46 and No. 3, September 1954, pp. 49–76.

NOTH, MARTIN, *Numbers,* translated by James D. Martin, The Westminster Press, Philadelphia, 1968.

NOTH, MARTIN, *The Laws in the Pentateuch and Other Essays,* Trans by Dr. R. Ap-Thomas, Oliver and Boyd, Edinburgh and London, 1966.

NOTH, MARTIN, *Leviticus,* translated by J. E. Anderson, The Westminster Press, Philadelphia, 1968.

NOTH, MARTIN, *Exodus: A Commentary,* translated J. S. Bowden, The Westminster Press, 1962.

NOTH, MARTIN, *The History of Israel,* Trans: Stanley Godman, Harper and Bros., New York, 1958.

PHILLIPS, ANTHONY, *Deuteronomy.* Cambridge University Press, Cambridge, 1973.

PORTER, J. R., *Leviticus.* Cambridge University Press, Cambridge, 1976.

ROWLEY, H. H., *From Joseph to Joshua.* Published for the British Academy by the Oxford University Press, London, 1950.

SNAITH, N. H., ed., *Leviticus and Numbers.* Nelson, London, 1967.

STAMM, JOHANN JACOB and MAURICE EDWARD ANDREW, *The Ten Commandments in Recent Research,* studies in Biblical theology, second series, 2. SCM Press, London, 1967.

STURDY, JOHN, *Numbers.* Cambridge University Press, Cambridge, 1976.

VON RAD, GERHARD, *Exodus,* revised edition. The Westminster Press, Philadelphia, 1972.

VON RAD, GERHARD, *Deuteronomy,* trans. by Dorethea Barton. The Westminster Press, Philadelphia, 1966.

WACHOLDER, B. Z., "Sabbath" in *Interpreters Dictionary of the Bible,* supplementary volume, Keith Crim et al. eds. (Nashville, Tennessee: Abingdon, 1976).

WEIL, ERIC, "What is a Breakthrough in History?" *Daedelus,* Spring, 1975, p. 21.

WILSON, JOHN A., *The Culture of Ancient Egypt.* The University of Chicago Press, Chicago, 1951.

ZIMMERLI, W., "The History of Israelite Religion," in *Tradition and Interpretation,* G. W. Anderson ed. Oxford University Press, 1979.

THE PENTATEUCH

ALT, ALBRECHT, "The Origins of Israelite Law," in *Essays on Old Testament History and Religion,* trans. R. A. Wilson. Doubleday Anchor, New York, 1958.

ANDERSON, BERNHARD W., "Introduction," *A History of Pentateuchal Traditions.* Martin Noth, Prentice-Hall, Englewood Cliffs, N.J., 1972

CASSUTO, UMBERTO, *The Documentary Hypothesis and Composition of the Pentateuch,* Israel Abrahams trans., Jerusalem: The Nagnes Press, 1961.

CLEMENTS, R. E., "Pentateuchal Problems," *Tradition and Interpretation,* ed. G. W. Anderson. Clarendon Press, Oxford, 1979.

ENGNELL, IVAN, *Critical Essays on the Old Testament,* translated from the Swedish by John T. Willis with Helmer Ringgren, London SPCK, 1970.

HAHN, HERBERT F., *The Old Testament in Modern Research,* with a survey of recent literature by Horace D. Hummel. Fortress Press, Philadelphia, 1966.

HARRELSON, WALTER, *The Ten Commandments and Human Rights.* Fortress Press, Philadelphia, 1980.

HOOKE, S. H., "Introduction to the Pentateuch," *Peakes Commentary on the Bible,* ed. H. H. Rowley. Nelson, London, 1962.

HYATT, J. PHILIP, "The Compiling of Israel's Story," *The Interpreters One Volume Commentary on the Bible,* ed. Charles M. Layman. Abingdon Press, Nashville, 1971, p. 1082.

KITCHEN, KENNETH A., *Ancient Orient and Old Testament,* Chicago, Inter Varsity Press, 1966.

NORTH, C. R.,   "Pentateuchal Criticism," *The Old Testament and Modern Study,* ed. H. H. Rowley. Oxford University Press, Oxford, 1961.

NOTH, MARTIN,   *A History of Pentateuchal Traditions,* translated with an introduction by Bernhard W. Anderson. Prentice-Hall, Englewood Cliffs, N.J., 1972.

SANDERS, JAMES A.,   *Torah and Canon.* Fortress Press, Philadelphia, 1972.

CLAIMING THE PROMISED LAND

AHARONI, YIGDAL,   "Nothing Early and Nothing Late," *Biblical Archeologist,* Vol. 39, 2, May, 1976, p. 55.

ALT, ALBRECHT,   "The Settlement of the Israelites in Palestine," *Essays on Old Testament History and Religion.* Doubleday, Garden City, New York, 1975.

BARTLETT, JOHN R.,   *Jericho.* William B. Eerdmans, Grand Rapids, 1983.

BOLING, ROBERT C.,   *Judges.* Doubleday, Garden City, New York, 1975.

BRIGHT, JOHN,   "Joshua: Introduction and Exegesis," *Interpreters Bible,* Vol. 2.

CRISLER, B. COBBY,   "The Acoustics and Crowd Capacity of Natural Theatres," *Biblical Archeologist,* Vol. 39, 4, December, 1976, p. 128.

DeMOOR, JOHANNES C.,   *The Seasonal Pattern in the Ugaritic Myth of Ba'lu, According to the version of Ilimilku Alter Orient and Altes Testament Neukirchen-Vluyn: Verlag Butyon and Bercker Kevelaer, 1971.*

DEVER, WILLIAM G.,   "Asherah, Consort of Yaweh? New Evidence from Kuntillet 'Ajrud' ", *Bulletin of the American Schools of Oriental Research,* Number 255, page 21, Summer, 1984.

DEVER, WILLIAM G.,   "Archeological Method in Israel: A Continuing Revolution," *Biblical Archeologist,* Vol. 43, 1, Winter, 1980, p. 40.

GLUECK, NELSON,   *The Other Side of the Jordan.* American Schools of Oriental Research, Cambridge, Mass., 1970.

GOTTWALD, NORMAN K.,   *The Tribes of Yahweh.* Orbis Books, Maryknoll, New York, 1979.

GRAY, JOHN,   *Joshua, Judges, Ruth.* Nelson, London, 1967.

GRAY, JOHN,   *The Canaanites,* London, Thomas and Hudson, 1964.

GREEN, ALBERTO R. W.,   *The Role of Human Sacrifice in the Ancient Near East.* Scholars Press, University of Montana, Missoula, Montana, 1976.

KENYON, KATHLEEN,   *Amorites and Canaanites.* Published for the British Academy by the Oxford University Press, London, 1966.

KENYON, KATHLEEN,   *Digging Up Jericho.* Praeger, New York, 1957.

MALAMAT, ABRAHAM,   "Charismatic Leadership in the Book of Judges," *The Mighty Acts of God.* Doubleday, Garden City, New York, 1976.

MARTIN, JAMES D.,   *The Book of Judges.* Cambridge University Press, Cambridge, 1975.

McKENZIE, JOHN L., S.J.,   *The World of the Judges,* Englewood Cliffs, NJ, Prentice-Hall, 1966.

MENDENHALL, GEORGE E.,   "Social Organization in Early Israel,'' *Magnalia Dei:'* *The Mighty Acts of God,* Edited Frank Moore Cross, Werner E. Lemke, and Patrick D. Miller, Jr., Garden City, NY, Doubleday & Company, Inc., 1976.

MENDENHALL, GEORGE E.,   *The Tenth Generation.* The Johns Hopkins University Press, Baltimore, 1973.

MILLER, J. MAXWELL and GENE M. TUCKER,   *The Book of Joshua.* Cambridge University Press, New York, 1974.

MYERS, JACOB M.,   "Judges: Introduction and Exegesis," *Interpreters Bible,* Vol. 2.

ROLING, ROBERT G., "In Those Days There Was No King in Israel," *A Light Unto My Path*, ed. H. N. Bream, R. D. Heim, C. A. Moore. Temple University Press, Philadelphia, 1974.

SOGGIN, J. ALBERTO, *Joshua*. The Westminster Press, Philadelphia, 1972.

SOGGIN, J. ALBERTO, *When the Judges Ruled*. Association Press, New York, 1965.

YADIN, YIGDAL, "Further Light on Biblical Hazor," *The Biblical Archeologist*, Vol. 20, 2, May 1957, p. 34.

YADIN, YIGAEL, *Hazor*. Weidenfield and Nicholson, Jerusalem, 1975.

THE MONARCHY

ACKROYD, PETER R., *The First Book of Samuel*. Cambridge University Press, Cambridge, 1971.

ACKROYD, PETER R., *The Second Book of Samuel*. Cambridge University Press, Cambridge, 1977.

ANDERSON, ROBERT T., "The Michigan State University Samaritan Collection," *Biblical Archeologist* Vol. 47.1, p. 41, March 1984.

CAIRD, GEORGE B., "I and II Samuel: Introduction and Exegesis," *Interpreters Bible*, Vol. 2

COGAN, MORTON, *Imperialism and Religion: Assyria, Judah and Israel in the Eighth and Seventh Centuries B.C.E.* Society of Biblical Literature and Scholars Press, University of Montana, Missoula, 1974.

CRENSHAW, JAMES L., *Old Testament Wisdom*, Atlanta, The John Knox Press, 1981.

EISMAN, MICHAEL M., "A Tale of Three Cities," *Biblical Archeologist*, Vol. 412, June, 1978, p. 47.

GOTTWALD, NORMAN K., *All the Kingdoms of the Earth*. Harper and Row, New York, 1964.

GRAY, JOHN, *I and II Kings*, second fully revised edition. The Westminster Press, Philadelphia, 1970.

GREEN, ALBERTO R., "Israelite Influence at Shishak's Court?" *Bulletin of the American Schools of Oriental Research*, No. 233, Winter, 1979, p. 59.

HEATON, E. W., *The Hebrew Kingdoms*, New Clarendon Bible III. Oxford University Press, Oxford, 1968.

HERTZBURG, HANS, *I and II Samuel*, (2nd revised ed.) trans. J. S. Bowden. Westminster Press, Philadelphia, 1960.

JULY, ROBERT W., *A History of the African Peoples*, New York, Charles Scribners, 1970.

KORFMANN, MANFRED, "The Sling as a Weapon," *The Scientific American*, October, 1973, pp. 34-42.

KRAABEL, A. T., "New Evidence of the Samaritan Diaspora has been found on Delos," *Biblical Archeologist* Vol. 47, 1, March, 1984, p. 44.

LEMAIRE, ANDRE, "The Ban in the Old Testament and at Mari," *Biblical Archeologist*, Vol. 47.2, June 1984, p. 103.

MAZAR, AMIHAI, "Additional Philistine Temples at Tell Qasile," *Biblical Archeologist*, Vol. 40.2, May 1977, p. 82.

MBITI, JOHN, *African Religions and Philosophy*, London, Heinemann, 1969.

McCARTER, P. KYLE, JR., *I Samuel*. Doubleday Anchor, New York, 1980.

MENDELSOHN, ISAAC, "Samuel's denunciation of Kingship in the Light of the Akkadian Documents from Ugarit," *Bulletin of the American Schools of Oriental Research*, No. 143, October, 1956, pp. 17-22.

MEYERS, CAROL, "The Roots of Restriction: Women in Early Israel," *Biblical Archeologist*, Vol. 41, 3, September, 1978, p. 91.

MONTGOMERY, JAMES A.,   *The Books of Kings,* The International Critical Commentary. Charles Scribners, New York, 1951.

MYERS, JACOB M.,   *I Chronicles,* New York, Garden City, Doubleday and Company, Inc. Second Edition, 1965.

OLMSTEAD, A. T.,   *History of Assyria.* University of Chicago Press, Chicago, 1923, Midway Reprint, 1975.

ORLINSKY, HARRY M.,   *Essays in Biblical Culture and Biblical Translation,* "The Seer in Ancient Israel," New York, Ktav Publishing House, Inc., 1974.

PARRINDER, GEOFFREY,   *Religion in Africa,* Baltimore, Penguin Books, 1969.

PECKHAM, BRIAN,   "Israel and Phoenicia," *Magnalia Dei,* ed: Frank Moore Cross, et alia, Garden City, NY, Doubleday, 1976.

RAY, BENJAMIN C.,   *African Religions,* Englewood Cliffs, NJ, Prentice-Hall, 1976.

ROBINSON, J.,   *The Second Book of Kings.* Cambridge University Press, Cambridge, 1976.

ROBINSON, J.,   *The First Book of Kings.* Cambridge University Press, Cambridge, 1972.

SAGGS, H.W.F.,   *Everyday Life in Babylon and Assyria.* B. T. Batsford, London: B. P. Putnam, New York, 1965.

SMITH, CLYDE CURRY,   "The Birth of Bureaucracy," *Biblical Archeologist,* Vol. 40, 1, March, 1977, p. 24.

SNAITH, NORMAN H.,   "I and II Kings: Introduction and Exegesis," *Interpreters Bible,* Vol. 3.

STIEBING, WILLIAM H.,   "The End of the Mycenean Age," *Biblical Archeologist,* Vol. 43.1, p. 7, Winter, 1980.

THE PROPHETS

AVIGAD, NAHMAN,   "Baruch the Scribe and Jerahemeel the Kings Son," *Biblical Archeologist,* Vol. 42, 2, Spring, 1979, p. 114.

BRIGHT, JOHN,   "Jeremiah," *Anchor Bible.* Doubleday and Co., Garden City, New York, 1965.

CARLEY, KEITH W.,   *The Book of the Prophet Ezekiel.* Cambridge University Press, Cambridge, 1974.

CLEMENTS, RONALD E.,   *Isaiah 1–39.* New Century Bible Commentary. William B. Eerdmans, Grand Rapids, 1981.

EICHRODT, WALTHER,   *Ezekiel,* trans. Cosslet Quin. The Westminster Press, Philadelphia, 1970.

HERBERT, A. S.,   *The Book of the Prophet Isaiah, Chapters 40–66.* Cambridge University Press, Cambridge, 1975.

HERBERT, A. S.,   *The Book of the Prophet Isaiah, Chapters 1–39.* Cambridge University Press, Cambridge, 1973.

HESCHEL, ABRAHAM J.,   *The Prophets,* Vol I and II. Harper and Row, New York, 1962.

HYATT, JAMES PHILIP,   "Jeremiah: Introduction and Exegesis," *Interpreters Bible,* Vol. 5.

Interpretation, A Journal of Bible and Theology. Three issues devoted to the study of a prophetic book: Isaiah, Vol. 37, 2, April 1982; Jeremiah, Vol. 38, 2, April 1983; Ezekiel, Vol. 39, 2, April 1984.

JACOBSEN, THORKILD,   *Toward an Image of Tammuz.* Harvard University Press, Cambridge, Mass., 1970.

KOCH, KLAUS,   *The Prophets Vol. 1. The Assyrian Period,* translated by Margaret Kohl, Philaelphia, Fortress Press, 1983.

KAISER, OTTO,   *Isaiah 1–12.* trans. R. A. Wilson. The Westminster Press, Philadelphia, 1972.

MAY, HERBERT G.,   "Ezekiel: Introduction and Exegesis," *Interpreters Bible,* Vol. 6.
MAYS, JAMES LUTHER,   *Hosea,* Philadelphia, The Westminster Press, 1969.
MEEK, THEOPHILE J.,   "Lamentations: Introduction and Exegesis," *Interpreters Bible,* Vol. 6.
MOWINCKEL, S.,   "He That Cometh," in *The Servant of the Lord.* H. H. Rowley, Basil, Blackwell, Oxford, 1965.
MOWVLEY, HARRY,   *Reading the Old Testament Prophets Today.* John Knox, Atlanta, 1979.
MUILENBURG, JAMES,   "Second Isaiah," *Interpreters Bible,* Vol. 5.
MUILENBURG, JAMES,   "Isaiah 40–66: Introduction and Exegesis," *Interpreters Bible,* Vol. 5.
NICHOLSON, ERNEST W.,   *The Book of the Prophet, Jeremiah, Chapters 26–52.* Cambridge University Press, Cambridge, 1975.
NORTH, CHRISTOPHER R.,   *The Second Isaiah Chapters XL–LV.* Oxford, at the Clarendon Press, 1964.
NORTH, CHRISTOPHER R.,   "Isaiah 40–55," *Torch Bible,* SCM Press, London, 1956.
ROBINSON, THEODORE H.,   *Prophecy and Prophets in Ancient Israel* (2nd ed.). Gerald Duckworth and Co Ltd., London, 1953.
SCOTT, R.B.Y.,   "Isaiah, Chapters 1– 39: Introduction and Exegesis," *Interpreters Bible,* Vol. 5.
SCOTT, R.B.Y.,   *The Relevance of the Prophets.* Macmillan, New York, 1947.
SMITH, GEORGE ADAM,   *The Book of Isaiah,* Vol. I, I–XXXIX, Vol. II, XL–LXVI, New York, A. C. Armstrong & Son, 1893.
STALKER, D.M.G.,   *Ezekiel.* SCM Press Ltd., London, 1968.
VON RAD, GERHARD,   *The Message of the Prophets.* SCM Press Ltd., London, 1968.
WEVERS, JOHN W., ed.   *Ezekiel.* Nelson, London, 1969.
WILSON, ROBERT R.,   *Prophecy and Society in Ancient Israel.* Fortress Press, Philadelphia, 1980.
ZIMMERLI, WALTHER,   *Ezekiel: A Commentary,* trans. Ronald E. Clements. Fortress Press, Philadelphia, 1979.

THE MINOR PROPHETS

ANDERSON, BERNHARD W.,   *The Eighth Century Prophets, Amos, Hosea, Isaiah, Micah.* Fortress Press, Philadelphia, 1978.
ANDERSON, FRANCIS I., and DAVID NOEL FREEDMAN,   *Hosea.* Doubleday and Co., New York, 1980.
DENTAN, ROBERT C.,   "Malachi: Introduction and Exegesis," *Interpreters Bible,* Vol. 6.
DENTAN, ROBERT C.,   "Zechariah, Chapters 9–14," *Interpreters Bible,* Vol. 6.
FOSBROKE, HUGHELL E. W.,   "Amos: Introduction and Exegesis," *Interpreters Bible,* Vol. 6.
GORDIS, ROBERT,   "Hosea's Marriage and Message," in *Poets, Prophets and Sages.* Essays in Biblical Interpretation. Indiana University Press, Bloomington, 1971.
HESCHEL, ABRAHAM,   *The Prophets,* Vols. I and II. Harper and Row, New York, 1969
KRAELING, EMIL G.,   *Commentary on the Prophets,* Vols. I and II. Nelson, London, Camden N.J., 1966.
LINDBLOM, J.,   *Prophecy in Ancient Israel.* Basil Blackwell, Oxford, 1962.
MARSH, JOHN,   *Amos and Micah.* SCM Press Ltd., London, 1959.
MAUCHLINE, JOHN,   "Hosea: Introduction and Exegesis," *Interpreters Bible,* Vol. 6.
MASON, REX,   *The Books of Haggai, Zechariah and Malachi.* Cambridge University Press, Cambridge, 1977.

MAYS, JAMES LUTHER,   *Amos.* The Westminster Press, Philadelphia, 1969.
TAYLOR, CHARLES L., JR.,   "Habakkuk: Introduction and Exegesis," *Interpreters Bible,* Vol. 6.
TAYLOR, CHARLES L., JR.,   "Nahum: Introduction and Exegesis," *Interpreters Bible,* Vol. 6.
TAYLOR, CHARLES L., JR.,   "Zephaniah: Introduction and Exegesis," *Interpreters Bible,* Vol. 6.
THOMAS, D. WINTON,   "Haggai: Introduction and Exegesis," *Interpreters Bible,* Vol. 6.
THOMAS D. WINTON,   "Zechariah, Chapters 1–8," *Interpreters Bible,* Vol. 6.
THOMPSON, JOHN A.,   "Joel: Introduction and Exegesis," *Interpreters Bible,* Vol. 6.
THOMPSON, JOHN A.,   "Obadiah: Introduction and Exegesis," *Interpreters Bible,* Vol. 6.
SMART, JAMES E.,   "Jonah: Introduction and Exegesis," *Interpreters Bible,* Vol. 6.
VON RAD, GERHARD,   *The Message of the Prophets.* SCM Press Ltd., London, 1968.
WOLFE, ROLLAND, E.,   "Micah: Introduction and Exegesis," *Interpreters Bible,* Vol. 6.

EXILE AND RETURN

ACKROYD, PETER R.,   *Exile and Restoration.* Westminster Press, Philadelphia, 1968.
BROCKINGTON, L. H., ed.,   "Ezra, Nehemiah and Esther," *The Century Bible.* Nelson, London, 1969.
BRUEGGEMANN, WALTER,   *In Man We Trust,* Atlanta, John Knox Press, 1972.
COLLINS, JOHN J.,   "The Jewish Apocalypses," *Semeia,* 14, p. 21, 1979.
COOGAN, MICHAEL DAVID,   *West Semetic Personal Names in the Marushu Documents.* Scholars Press, Chico, California, 1976.
FELDMAN, LOUIS H.,   review of M. Hengel "Judaism and Hellenism," *Journal of Biblical Literature,* Vol. 96.3, pp. 371–382, 1977.
GRAY, G. B., and M. CARY,   "The Rein of Darius," Chap. VII, Vol. IV, *The Cambridge Ancient History,* ed. J. B. Bury, S. A. Cook, F. E. Adcock. Cambridge University Press, Cambridge, reprinted 1977.
HAMILTON, EDITH,   *The Greek Way,* New York, Avon Books, 1973.
HAMMER, RAYMOND,   *The Book of Daniel,* Cambridge, Cambridge University Press, 1976.
HARTMAN, LOUIS F., and ALEXANDER A. DiLELLA,   *The Book of Daniel,* Garden City, New York, Doubleday and Company, 1978.
HENGEL, MARTIN,   *Judaism and Hellenism,* studies in their encounter in Palestine during the early Hellenistic period, translated by John Bowden, Fortress Press, 1981.
HILLERS, DELBERT R.,   *Lamentations.* Doubleday, New York, 1972.
Interpretation, Vol. XXXIX 2, April 1985. This issue is devoted to the Book of Daniel.
Interpretation, Vol. XXXIX 4, October 1985. This issue is devoted to Jewish Christian dialogue.
JEFFREY, ARTHUR,   "Introduction" Daniel *The Interpreters Bible,* Vol. 6, Nashville, Abingdon Press, 1956.
KITTO, H.D.F.,   *The Greeks,* Baltimore, Maryland, Penguin Books reprinted with revisions, 1957.
KLEIN, RALPH W.,   "Ezra and Nehemiah in Recent Studies," *The Mighty Acts of God.* Edited by Frank Moore Cross, Werner E. Lemke, and Patrick D. Miller Jr., Doubleday Co. Inc., Garden City, New York, 1976.
KOESTER, HELMUT,   *Introduction to the New Testament.* Vol. 1, History, Culture, and Religion of the Hellenistic Age. Philadelphia, Fortress Press, 1982.
MEYERS, JACOB M.,   *Ezra, Nehemiah.* Doubleday and Company, Inc., Garden City, New York, 1965.

OLMSTEAD, A. T., *History of the Persian Empire.* University of Chicago Press, Chicago, 1978.

PORTEOUS, NORMAN W., *Daniel,* Philadelphia, The Westminster Press, 1965.

ROWLEY, H. H., "The Unity of the Book of Daniel," *The Servant of the Lord,* Oxford, Basil, Blackwell, 1965.

RUSSELL, D. S., *The Method and Message of Jewish Apocalyptic,* Philadelphia, The Westminster Press, 1964.

SAGGS, H.W.F., *The Greatness That Was Babylon.* Hawthorne Books, Inc., New York, 1962.

SMITH, MORTON, *Palestinian Parties and Politics That Shaped the Old Testament.* Columbia University Press, New York, London, 1971.

ZAEHNER, ROBERT CHARLES, *The Teachings of the Magi,* London, Allen and Unwin, 1956.

THE USE OF COMPUTERS IN BIBLICAL STUDIES

The use of computers offers another approach to the study of the scriptures. "In Quest of Computer Literacy" by Robert A. Kraft, *The Council on the Study of Religion Bulletin,* Vol. 15, Number 2, April 1984, p. 42, which is concerned primarily with a project in Septuagint studies, but suggests that within a few years computers will be used very widely in biblical studies. A second article by Kraft "Offline: Computer Research for Religious Studies" appears in the October 1984 *Council Bulletin* which refers to several currently available computer programs.

The obvious problem in applying computers to the study of the Bible is that many of the most interesting and most important issues in biblical study are conceptual rather than factual or quantifiable. However, this is a challenge to the technical and scholarly imagination which even the beginning student may welcome and try to overcome.

INDEX